OXFORD WORLD'S

LIVES OF THE C

GAIUS SUETONIUS TRANQUILLUS is best known for his *Lives of the Caesars*, starting with the dictator Julius Caesar and ending with the emperor Domitian, which was published in the reign of the emperor Hadrian (117–38 CE). Suetonius was probably born around 70 CE either in north Africa or in Italy. His father, a Roman knight, fought in the civil war of 69 CE. Suetonius himself was educated at least partly in Rome and was a friend of the younger Pliny who obtained a number of favours on his behalf. A fragmentary inscription from north Africa makes clear that Suetonius held a succession of posts at court, working perhaps for Trajan and certainly for Hadrian. He thus had privileged access to the imperial archives as well as the emperor himself. A passage from the anonymous *Life of Hadrian* records that Suetonius was dismissed for lack of respect to Hadrian's wife Sabina.

Besides the *Lives of the Caesars*, his writings also include *On Illustrious Men* which survives in fragments (among them short biographies of Virgil, Horace, and Lucan) and numerous other scholarly works now almost entirely lost. Suetonius probably died some time after 130.

CATHARINE EDWARDS is Reader in Classics and Ancient History at the University of Bristol. Her writings include *The Politics of Immorality in Ancient Rome* (Cambridge, 1993) and *Writing Rome: Textual Approaches to the City* (Cambridge, 1996).

OXFORD WORLD'S CLASSICS

For over 100 years Oxford World's Classics have brought readers closer to the world's great literature. Now with over 700 titles—from the 4,000-year-old myths of Mesopotamia to the twentieth century's greatest novels—the series makes available lesser-known as well as celebrated writing.

The pocket-sized hardbacks of the early years contained introductions by Virginia Woolf, T. S. Eliot, Graham Greene, and other literary figures which enriched the experience of reading. Today the series is recognized for its fine scholarship and reliability in texts that span world literature, drama and poetry, religion, philosophy and politics. Each edition includes perceptive commentary and essential background information to meet the changing needs of readers.

OXFORD WORLD'S CLASSICS

SUETONIUS

Lives of the Caesars

Translated with an Introduction and Notes by
CATHARINE EDWARDS

OXFORD
UNIVERSITY PRESS

OXFORD
UNIVERSITY PRESS

Great Clarendon Street, Oxford OX2 6DP

Oxford University Press is a department of the University of Oxford.
It furthers the University's objective of excellence in research, scholarship,
and education by publishing worldwide in

Oxford New York

Athens Auckland Bangkok Bogotá Buenos Aires Calcutta
Cape Town Chennai Dar es Salaam Delhi Florence Hong Kong Istanbul
Karachi Kuala Lumpur Madrid Melbourne Mexico City Mumbai
Nairobi Paris São Paulo Shanghai Singapore Taipei Tokyo Toronto Warsaw

with associated companies in Berlin Ibadan

Oxford is a registered trade mark of Oxford University Press
in the UK and in certain other countries

Published in the United States
by Oxford University Press Inc., New York

Database right Oxford University Press (maker)

First published as an Oxford World's Classics paperback 2000

British Library Cataloguing in Publication Data

Data available

Library of Congress Cataloging in Publication Data

Data available

ISBN 0–19–283271–9

3 5 7 9 10 8 6 4

Typeset in Ehrhardt
by RefineCatch Limited, Bungay, Suffolk
Printed in Great Britain by
Clays Ltd, St Ives plc

CONTENTS

INTRODUCTION

SUETONIUS' *Lives of the Caesars*, starting with Julius Caesar and
ending with the Emperor Domitian, has always had its place as a
source of extraordinary tales of imperial vice—and at times of
imperial virtue. Suetonius presents us with shocking accounts of
Caligula's plan to make his horse consul (*Cal.* 55) and of Nero
singing while Rome burns (*Nero* 38), as well as with edifying
descriptions of Augustus' splendid redevelopment of the city of
Rome (*Aug.* 28–30) and Titus' decision to put the state before his
love for Berenice (a phrase from ch. 7 of Suetonius' *Life* is said to
have inspired Racine's *Bérénice*). Centuries later rulers might aspire
to being hailed as another Augustus or Titus—and dread being
labelled another Caligula or Nero.

More recently, while some readers have continued to enjoy
Suetonius as a fund of fascinating, indeed, sometimes outrageous
anecdotes, many have chosen to treat him as a rather frustrating and
untrustworthy source of 'facts' about Roman emperors, which the
modern scholar needs to correct (as far as possible), supplement, and
rearrange, if a coherent biographical narrative is to be produced.
However, to read Suetonius in this way is perhaps to miss his significance. Suetonius himself certainly offers little in the way of chronological narrative and it would be rash to rely on the factual accuracy
of the stories he tells about the Caesars. But what he has to say about
the eccentricities and achievements of emperors, their virtues and
vices, gives us valuable insights into ancient Roman debates about
imperial power and how it should be exercised.

The kings of Rome had been driven out by the first Brutus,
according to Roman myth, and, under the republic, Romans saw
themselves as fiercely opposed to monarchy. Yet, while Julius Caesar
met a bloody end for his autocratic pretensions, his heir Augustus
was able to establish one-man rule and pass his position on to his
heir. How was it possible for one man to control public affairs yet not
be king? Even that master of public relations Augustus seems sometimes to have misjudged his subjects' expectations, as Suetonius'
account reveals (see e.g. ch. 70). A century after Augustus' death
(when Suetonius was writing), the question of how an emperor

should behave was still a vexed one. This issue is a central concern in
Suetonius' *Lives*.

Suetonius' life

Gaius Suetonius Tranquillus, born around 70 CE, was of an equestrian family (see 'Roman knight' in Glossary), perhaps from Hippo
Regius in North Africa, possibly from Italy itself. His father served
as a military tribune in the Thirteenth Legion during the civil wars
of 69 CE (*Otho* 10). Suetonius was educated partly in Rome, spend-
ing some time in the rhetorical schools, before embarking on a public
career. He secured a posting to Britain as military tribune, around
the year 110 or 111, through the patronage of the younger Pliny, but
did not take it up (Pliny, *Letters* 3. 8). Pliny seems to have acted as his
patron on a number of occasions, also securing for him the legal
advantages of fatherhood—Suetonius and his wife were childless
(*Letters* 10. 94; see *Aug.* 34 and note). It is known, from a fragmentary inscription found at Hippo, that Suetonius held a succession of posts at court, including a period in charge of the imperial
libraries in Rome, as minister *a bibliothecis*, another as minister *a
studiis*, probably in charge of the emperor's own archives, and
another in charge of the emperor's correspondence, as minister *ab
epistulis* (the last office under the emperor Hadrian, earlier ones
probably under Trajan). These official posts should probably be seen
as recognition of Suetonius' literary distinction (literary studies and
a public career were very much intertwined for Suetonius as for
many of his contemporaries). They were highly influential positions
which gave him close access to the emperor.

Suetonius' *Lives of the Caesars* is known to have been dedicated to
the praetorian prefect, Septicius Clarus, who was in post 119 to 122
CE. A passage from the anonymous *Life of Hadrian* (written in the
late third or early fourth century) records that both Suetonius and
Septicius were dismissed for lack of respect toward Hadrian's wife
Sabina (11. 3). There are no further references to his career, though
from a passage in *Titus* (ch. 10), it seems he was probably still writing
after 130. Thus, although it is not clear exactly when Suetonius
began writing or when various sections of the *Lives* may have been
published, they can safely be dated to the reign of Hadrian (117–38
CE). Besides the *Lives of the Caesars*, which have survived almost

complete (only the opening chapters of *Julius Caesar* are missing),
and his earlier biographical work *On Illustrious Men* (of which sections survive relating to the lives of literary figures), he was also the
author of a number of works now lost (in Greek as well as Latin),
including treatises on Roman games and festivals, on Greek games,
on famous courtesans, on kings, on public offices, on Rome and its
customs, on the Roman year, on Cicero's *Republic*, on Greek terms of
abuse, on the correct terms for clothing, on critical marks in texts,
and on bodily defects. This range of interests is often reflected in the
Lives of the Caesars which offer a wealth of detail concerning, particularly, games given by emperors, as well as descriptions of their
physical appearance, which may well owe something to Suetonius'
work on bodily defects.[1] For a Roman author of the early second
century, Suetonius was unusually learned in Greek.

The structure of the Lives

Most of the *Lives* begin with an account of the family and birth of
the subject, sometimes with accompanying omens (these sections are
missing from *Jul.*). Suetonius next gives an account of the subject's
career up to his accession to supreme power (this section is lengthy
in *Jul.*, considerably shorter in most later *Lives* where the subject
comes to power when younger). In *Julius*, this material, together
with an account of Caesar's victory games, takes up around half the
Life. Suetonius then sets out his plan for the remainder (ch. 44):
'As he was contemplating and setting about these projects death cut
him short. But before I give an account of that, it will not be inappropriate to set out in summary form the details of his appearance,
comportment, dress, and conduct, as well as matters relating to his
governmental and military undertakings.' Suetonius then proceeds
to deal with these topics, taking little or no account of chronology,
before describing Caesar's increasingly tyrannical manner as a prel-
ude to the conspiracy against him, his death, the reading of his will,
his funeral, and public reactions to it.

Chronological order is quite explicitly rejected in *Augustus*, where
Suetonius briefly justifies his preference for arrangement by topic:
'Having stated the main themes, as it were, of his life, I shall set out

[1] For a useful discussion of Suetonius' scholarly interest in games, see Andrew
Wallace-Hadrill, *Suetonius: The Scholar and his Caesars* (London, 1983), 46–8.

the individual details, not according to the order of events but by
topic [*per species*] so that they may be more clearly perceived and
assessed' (*Aug.* 9). Suetonius is aiming not to tell a story but to
present his reader with a summation of the life of each ruler. Later
readers have sometimes found this alienating. Writing in the seventeenth century Francis Bacon commented: 'For as when I read in
Tacitus the actions of Nero or Claudius, with circumstances of
times, inducements, and occasions, I find them not so strange: but
when I read them in Suetonius Tranquillus gathered into titles and
bundles, and not in order of time, they seem more monstrous and
incredible; so it is of any philosophy reported entire and dis-
membered by articles.'[2] Other critics, too, have objected to the lack
of chronological structure in a work of biography on the grounds
that it fails to illustrate character development or to explain
inconsistencies of character.[3]

The structure varies considerably between one *Life* and another.
The headings Suetonius chooses are not necessarily treated in a fixed
order. In *Caligula*, for instance, no account is given of his family
(apart from a lengthy portrait of his father); this has already been set
out at the beginning of *Tiberius*. The sections on personal appearance and habits are not always placed in the same position relative to
other topics (sometimes they are given at the beginning of the character section, as in the case of *Jul.*, sometimes after the subject's
death). However, while the arrangement may vary, it is not random.

Suetonius is often criticized for presenting his readers with a
quantity of facts in no particular order. More recently a number of
scholars have sought to revise this judgement and have offered persuasive arguments for seeing Suetonius as the author of a sophisti-
cated work characterized by considerable subtlety.[4] The order in
which material is presented may sometimes have an ironic effect, for
instance; Nero is praised for his filial devotion in an early chapter of
the *Life* (*Nero* 9), yet this apparent virtue will require reassessment
when the reader comes to the allegations of incest between Nero and
his mother which Suetonius discusses later (*Nero* 28). Similarly, in
the case of Domitian, Suetonius includes among his praiseworthy

    [2] In 'The Advancement of Learning', pp. 204–5 in Francis Bacon, *A Critical Edition
of the Major Works*, ed. Brian Vickers (Oxford, 1996).
    [3] Cf. Alan Wardman, *Plutarch's Lives* (London, 1974), 144 ff.
    [4] e.g. Croisille and Barton—see Select Bibliography.

deeds the punishment of a Roman knight for taking back the wife he had divorced on the grounds of adultery (*Dom.* 8). A few chapters earlier, Suetonius tells us that Domitian divorced his wife because of her affair with the actor Paris but then took her back, as he was unable to bear the separation (*Dom.* 3). Suetonius does not explicitly mention the emperor's hypocrisy but allows it to emerge from his portrait.

Perhaps not surprisingly, given his own role in the imperial administration, Suetonius devotes considerable space to each emperor's conduct of imperial business. He has shown, he writes of Augustus, 'how he governed the state throughout the entire world in war and in peace' (*Aug.* 61). Suetonius examines emperors' measures with regard to the city of Rome (including building and games), to Italy, and to the provinces. He looks at treatment of the senate, the Roman knights, and the people. He considers an emperor's activities regarding religion. Emperors in the Roman world were the ultimate point of appeal and were often characterized as founts of justice. The way in which individual emperors dispense justice is given particular attention in the *Lives* (see e.g. *Claud.* 14–15).[5]

Different categories of virtue and vice also play a central role in substantial sections of his *Lives of the Caesars* (an approach not found in the writings of other biographers). Suetonius moves through selected categories of moral behaviour, choosing various examples from his subject's life to illustrate, for instance, his clemency or his avarice. That of Tiberius, for example, moves from consideration of his luxury and lust (chs. 42–5), to his avarice (chs. 46–9), to his cruelty (50–62).[6] In organizing his material in this way, Suetonius adopts a standard device of ancient rhetoric, division of the topic into themes. This can cause the reader some confusion as Suetonius quite often moves from one theme to another without making explicit the change of topic.[7] In ch. 26 of *Nero*, for instance, Suetonius lists five vices and then gives examples of them but without making clear which anecdotes illustrate which particular vices.

[5] For an analysis of these sections, see Wallace-Hadrill, *Suetonius*, ch. 6.
[6] Suetonius' use of these categories is well analysed by Andrew Wallace-Hadrill, *Suetonius*, ch. 7.
[7] As Townend notes; G. B. Townend, 'Suetonius and his Influence', in T. A. Dorey (ed.), *Latin Biography* (London, 1967), 85.

In some *Lives*, vices take centre stage. The *Lives* of *Caligula*, *Nero*, and *Domitian* are organized around apparently simple divisions: the acceptable deeds are listed first and then the crimes. Suetonius comments at *Caligula* 22: 'The story so far has been of Caligula the emperor, the rest must be of Caligula the monster.' Similarly in ch. 19 of *Nero* he observes: 'These deeds, some of them meriting no reproach, others even deserving some praise, I have gathered together to separate them from the shameful deeds and crimes with which I shall henceforth be concerned.' While of Domitian, he writes: 'his disposition towards mercy and integrity did not continue, though his decline into cruelty was more rapid than his decline into greed' (*Dom.* 10). These three *Lives*, in particular, proceed in terms of a pattern of disappointed expectation (a pattern which finds its mirror image in his account of the unexpectedly virtuous emperor Titus; see *Titus* 7).

Many of the virtues and vices Suetonius describes relate clearly to the emperor's public role. But Suetonius is also notorious for the space he devotes to his subjects' sex lives (sexual activity takes up two substantial chapters, 68 and 69, even in the case of that pillar of virtue Augustus). Though the Christian Jerome took the view that Suetonius' freedom in writing of the emperors was equalled by the freedom with which they lived, many later critics have been much quicker to reprove Suetonius for the inclusion of salacious material. J. W. Duff, for instance, commented: 'A great deal of it partakes of the nature of a *chronique scandaleuse* based upon tittle-tattle about the emperors and compiled by a literary man with the muck-rake, too keen upon petty and prurient detail to produce a scientific account of his subjects.'[8] Details of what we might describe as 'private life' often appear in the later sections of the *Lives*. After describing his military and political life, Suetonius notes of Augustus (ch. 61): 'I shall now discuss his personal and domestic life, giving an account of his character and fortune at home and with his family, from his youth until his dying day.' But although Suetonius does conceive of Augustus' personal life as in a sense separate from his public activities, he hardly characterizes it as 'private'. Romans traditionally viewed the personal lives of public figures as a legitimate public concern. Cicero's speeches are filled with detailed accounts of his opponents'

---

[8] J. W. Duff, *Literary History of Rome in the Silver Age* (London, 1927), 508.

sexual and sumptuary vices which have seemed to many modern readers wholly irrelevant to the question at issue; for a Roman audience such details, as well as providing a source of entertainment, had a crucial role to play in determining the personal character of the individuals involved.[9]

The details of emperors' 'private' lives provided by Suetonius should not then be seen as 'simple facts', included to satisfy the idle curiosity of the reader. For Romans, a public figure revealed a huge amount about himself: by the way he chose to decorate his house—Augustus' simple residence makes clear he has no aspirations to tyranny (*Aug.* 72); his style of dress—Julius Caesar's ungirt tunic reflects his unbounded appetite for power (*Jul.* 45); and by his eating habits—Claudius' habit of eating at the wrong time is a telling symptom of a more general failure to grasp what was appropriate behaviour for a ruler (*Claud.* 33). However, while such matters were deemed material to judging leading public figures, they were not considered part of the proper subject matter of history writing. In telling us what Augustus liked to eat, what scenes decorated the walls of Tiberius' bedroom, Suetonius is offering us the kind of glimpses into his subjects' lives that have no equivalent in the work of historians. Here, too, there is an interesting contrast between Suetonius and his fellow biographer, the Greek author Plutarch, whose *Julius Caesar* offers no equivalent to Suetonius' thirty-odd chapters on Caesar's personal details (chs. 45–75).

Biography: Suetonius and Plutarch

Suetonius was some years younger than Plutarch (b. before 50 CE, d. after 120), the other great biographer whose works have survived from antiquity. Besides his *Parallel Lives* (which include a life of Julius Caesar), Plutarch had also written biographies of the Caesars (only those of Galba and Otho survive). Of earlier works of biography very little remains. Though Suetonius and Plutarch are sometimes included by modern scholars among the 'historians' of antiquity, they certainly did not consider themselves as such. Indeed, it is important to consider further the relationship between

[9] See Edwards, *The Politics of Immorality in Ancient Rome* (Cambridge, 1993).

biography and history, for Suetonius' *Lives* are quite self-consciously
'not-history'.

Plutarch, in characterizing his own enterprise, offers the following
articulation of the distinction between biography and history: 'It is
not histories we are writing but Lives. And it is not always the most
famous deeds which reveal a man's good or bad qualities: a clearer
insight into a man's character is often given by a detail, a word, or a
joke, than by conflicts where thousands die, or by the greatest of
pitched battles, or by the siege of cities' (*Alexander the Great* 1. 1–2).[10]
This emphasis on details, on throwaway remarks, is an important
one to which we shall return. A distinction of this kind had already
been articulated centuries earlier by another Greek writer, the historian Polybius (b. *c.*200 BCE, d. after 118 BCE; *Histories* 10. 24). This
distinction was a particular concern for biographers of prominent
political rather than literary figures. No comparable statements
survive from Suetonius but such issues may well have been raised in
the opening chapters of the first *Life*, that of Julius Caesar, which are
now lost.

Suetonius' work is much more emphatically 'not-history' than
that of Plutarch. For Plutarch's mode of organization is essentially
chronological in contrast to Suetonius' thematic approach; Plutarch,
for instance, gives a fairly full narrative of the campaigns of Julius
Caesar, while Suetonius covers ten years of campaigning in Gaul in
just one paragraph, although he elsewhere uses numerous incidents
from Caesar's campaigns to illustrate his personal characteristics.
Suetonius' approach may be seen as more in the antiquarian tradition than that of Plutarch. Plutarch presents the purpose of his
Lives as the moral education of the reader, that they may, by
examples of virtue, become better men themselves (*Pericles* 1–2;
Aemilius Paulus 1). In general, Plutarch is rather more inclined
towards panegyric, although he also sees value in negative moral
examples (*Demetrius* 1. 4–7). Plutarch's writing also reveals an interest in psychological analysis in terms which can be quite readily
understood (or, at least, appropriated) by the modern reader. Nevertheless, individual character, was even for Plutarch, not so important
as we might suppose. As Momigliano points out: 'it gives us some-

---

[10] On Plutarch's approach to biography in general and to the *Lives* of Romans in
particular, see C. B. R. Pelling's introduction to his edition of *Plutarch's Life of Antony*
(Cambridge, 1988).

thing to think about that Hellenistic and Roman biographers often wrote series of biographies of men of the same type—generals, philosophers, demagogues—and therefore seem to have cared for the type rather than for the individual.'[11]

We could perhaps surmise that Suetonius chose to abandon chronology as an organizing principle of his work at least partly in response to Tacitus' *Histories* and *Annals* which, while positioning themselves as history, necessarily focused on the reigns of individual emperors (and covered the period from Tiberius to Domitian). One point we should bear in mind is that the biographer expects some existing knowledge of the historical framework on the part of his readers. Indeed, Suetonius, in recounting anecdotes, frequently leaves out the names of people who were very probably well known (a tendency more noticeable in the later *Lives*).[12] History's proper concerns were war and politics. Biography, as we have seen, could include a much wider range of material, including the relatively mundane.

Character and causation

Suetonius aims to give his readers insights into the characters of individual Caesars through a wide variety of means. Telling details about their personal tastes have an important part to play. Other areas which Suetonius emphasizes include, in some cases, an emperor's literary style. We should not underestimate the significance of literary culture in an emperor's self-presentation—particularly in relation to the senatorial and equestrian élite. A telling symptom of Caligula's madness is that he dislikes those almost universally acknowledged classic authors, Virgil and Livy (*Cal.* 34). Many emperors gave readings of their works to their friends and acquaintances and expected informed praise (see e.g. *Aug.* 85, *Claud.* 41, and *Dom.* 2). Moreover, literary style, as Suetonius himself makes clear, was thought to be an important index of character (see. e.g. *Aug.* 86, and *Dom.* 20). This connection is regularly made by other ancient authors, too. The younger Seneca, for instance, writing in the time of the emperor Nero, observes of Augustus' associate

---

[11] Arnaldo Momigliano, *The Development of Greek Biography* (Cambridge, Mass., 1971), 13.

[12] Cf. Townend, 'Suetonius and his Influence', 83–4, 87.

Maecenas that his style of speaking was as effeminate as the way he walked and that the perverse way he arranged his words declared their author to be equally 'unusual, unsound, and eccentric' (*Letters* 114. 4–6). It matters, then, that Augustus writes elegantly and without artifice (*Aug.* 86) or that Claudius' literary style lacks good taste (*Claud.* 41).

Physical appearance was also thought to reveal character and Suetonius includes a brief description of each of his subjects. On the whole, the emperors favoured by Suetonius are physically attractive (e.g. *Aug.* 79), while those he criticizes are ugly (e.g. *Cal.* 50). The ancient science of physiognomics (with which Suetonius himself seems to have been familiar) offered a complex scheme for interpreting physical characteristics. As Tamsyn Barton has recently shown, Suetonius' description of Nero highlights his mottled body, thereby implying resemblance to a panther, the epitome of evil and effeminate characteristics, while his weak eyes could be read as a sign of cowardice and his spindly legs of lustfulness.[13]

It is often suggested that a person's character was viewed in antiquity as fixed from birth. Suetonius comments, in relation to several of his subjects, that even in their youth they showed signs of the vices they were to display more fully in later life (see in particular *Tib.* 57, *Cal.* 11, *Nero* 26, and *Dom.* 1). One exception is the emperor Otho. Suetonius first presents us with a man devoted to the pleasures of the flesh, an intimate friend of Nero who shares all his vices. Yet this same man dies probably the noblest death of all the twelve Caesars (the importance of the manner of death as a touchstone of an individual's worth is discussed below).

All the same, it is highly significant that Suetonius almost never seems to be concerned with *why* emperors were the way they were (though he does suggest that poverty and fear exacerbated Domitian's character defects, *Dom.* 3). This is one of the most striking ways in which Suetonius' 'biographies' are quite unlike modern works of biography. Following the approach established by Lytton Strachey's *Eminent Victorians* (1918), modern biographers have generally sought to *explain* their subjects' characters. Childhood traumas, for instance, or relations with parents regularly play a crucial part. More often than not the subject's sexuality is presented

---

[13] Barton, 'The *inventio* of Nero: Suetonius', in J. Elsner and J. Masters (eds.), *Reflections of Nero* (London, 1994), 56–8.

as the key to his or her character. Sexual behaviour has an important part to play in Suetonius' *Lives*, of course, as we have seen. For many readers, Tiberius disporting himself in the swimming-pool with little children, or Caligula treating senators' wives as if they were slave-girls, are among the most memorable episodes. But these stories are not presented by Suetonius as having a key explanatory role. Rather, sexuality offers one more sphere in which emperors may be judged and compared.

Deaths

Each Caesar's death and funeral, unsurprisingly, forms the conclusion to his *Life*. We should note, however, the emphasis Suetonius places on the manner in which each Caesar dies and the large amount of space he often devotes to a narrative of the death. In Suetonius, as often in Latin literature, we are presented with death as a moment of truth. The ancient Romans took great pleasure in reading about the deaths of famous men, to judge from a comment Cicero makes, writing in the mid-first century BCE, in a letter to his friend, the historian Lucceius: 'the critical and varied accidents of often excellent men inspire wonder, suspense, joy, disturbance, hope, fear; but if, indeed, they conclude with a memorable death, the mind of the reader is filled with the most delightful pleasure' (*Letters to his Friends* 5. 12.5). Such literature became even more popular under the principate, it seems, and particularly so in the early years of Suetonius' own life. Titinius Capito, minister *ab epistulis* under Domitian and later emperors, wrote deaths of famous men (according to Pliny, *Letters* 8. 12). Gaius Fannius wrote three books on the fate of those killed or sent into exile under Nero (Pliny, *Letters* 5. 5. 3).

Suetonius seems to have been much influenced by this tradition. Imperial deaths are the principal occasions on which Suetonius shifts into a narrative mode.[14] Suetonius' narratives of the deaths of Julius Caesar (*Jul.* 81–2) and of Nero (*Nero* 40–9) are among the most gripping chapters in his writing. The first blows and Caesar's reaction to them are carefully set out. We are left with the final and vivid image of Caesar's corpse being carried away, 'one arm dangling' (ch. 82). Suetonius takes us on Nero's last terrifying journey,

---

[14] Richard Lounsbury, *The Arts of Suetonius: An Introduction* (New York, 1987), ch. 4 has some perspicuous comments on these sections.

recounting each stage in his indecisive struggle to end his own life. His account of the murder of Caligula is also full of telling detail (*Cal.* 58). Though Suetonius' *Life of Domitian* is brief, three long chapters (15–17) are devoted to signs of his impending death and the narrative of the death itself, culminating in Domitian struggling frantically to wrest a dagger from the treacherous steward. The variant traditions on Galba's dying words as he is killed by Roman soldiers sum up the difficulty of judging that emperor (*Galba* 20). Even less eventful deaths are highly significant. Augustus, the model emperor, ends his life neatly, quoting the final lines of a comic play (*Aug.* 99). Is Suetonius (or Augustus?) inviting us to see the emperor's career as a piece of consummate play-acting?

Omens, portents, and dreams

Accounts of omens and portents make up a significant part of Suetonius' *Lives*, as do astrological predictions (though they have received negligible consideration in the work of modern scholars). They are usually associated with births, deaths, and accessions to power. Tiberius' rise to power is signalled by an eagle perching on the roof of his house on the island of Rhodes (*Tib.* 14). The future power of Vespasian is foreshadowed by the development of an abnormally large branch on a tree sacred to Mars (*Vesp.* 5). When a young boy's hair turns white during a sacrifice, this is seen as predicting that a young ruler, Nero, will be succeeded by an old one, Galba (*Galba* 8). When an imperial death is imminent statues or tombs are struck by lightning (e.g. *Aug.* 97; *Claud.* 46; *Dom.* 15) or trees wither (e.g. *Galba* 1; *Dom.* 15). Suetonius does not endorse all the alleged omens he refers to, ascribing, for instance, the story of Nero strangling snakes as a baby to gossip (*Nero* 6). But more often their predictive power is taken for granted, the foolishness of those who ignore them underlined.[15]

Dreams, too, have an important predictive role. Julius Caesar's wife Calpurnia dreams the night before he is assassinated that her husband is murdered in her arms (*Jul.* 81). Nero dreams that the statues of conquered peoples in Pompey's theatre come to life and crowd around him (*Nero* 46). The dream's warning is soon con-

---

[15] See Paul Plass, *Wit and the Writing of History* (Madison, 1988), 77–8.

firmed when the Gauls revolt. Again, in contrast to modern (particularly Freudian) perceptions of the dynamics of personality, sex is not a key element in ancient dream analysis. Indeed, instead of seeing dreams about fast chariots as really about sex, ancient dream interpreters would see dreams about sex as being really about something else.[16] When Julius Caesar dreams that he is having sex with his mother (*Jul.* 7), this is seen as a very good sign: 'for dream-interpreters explained it as a portent that he would rule the world, because his mother, whom he had seen subjected to himself, was none other than the earth, which is held to be the mother of all.' Here, too, then, sections of Suetonius' *Lives* which are often ignored by modern scholars repay serious consideration.

Deciphering the imperial image?

Suetonius chose to write *Lives* of twelve men, not just of one. The *Lives of the Caesars* need to be read against one another if we are to appreciate their nuances. To a significant degree, the stories he tells us about one ruler can only be made sense of in comparison with representations of other rulers. Julius Caesar, assassinated for his tyrannous aspirations, was a problematic example. Augustus, it seems, set the standard for his successors and tends to serve as the point of reference in the *Lives of the Caesars*. Other emperors are, at least implicitly, approved of or criticized in so far as they resemble him—or fail to. This was very probably the case with the judgements of their contemporaries, too. Suetonius tells us how Nero, at the start of his reign, promised to rule according to the example of Augustus (*Nero* 10).

Other models underlie the portraits of emperors who deviate from the Augustan ideal. An influential figure here, with a long literary pedigree, is that of the eastern tyrant whose ruthless and untrammelled autocracy in the political sphere has its counterpart in the unbridled indulgence of licentious appetites in bed, at table, and elsewhere. Similar stories are often told about different rulers; 'bad' emperors seduce well-born women and boys and spend extraordinary sums on recherché pleasures, as well as murdering innocent senators. Accusations of tyranny are clearly part of what is at stake in

[16] On this see S. R. F. Price, 'The Future of Dreams: From Freud to Artemidorus', *Past & Present*, 113 (1986), 3–37.

numerous stories told about Caligula, Nero, and Domitian, in particular. Caligula, for instance, in building his bridge of boats across
the Bay of Naples, is explicitly likened to the Persian Xerxes, a
paradigmatic tyrant (*Cal.* 19). Indeed, we might well expect such
stories to be told even about an emperor who could be unpopular for
quite other reasons. An emperor who failed to be sufficiently defer-
ential to the Roman élite (and it is their views which survive) could
well find himself represented as a monster of excessive lusts. In
reading Suetonius' *Nero*, for instance, we must not forget that it was
based on accounts produced under the Flavian emperors (Vespasian,
Titus, and Domitian) who had a strong interest in discrediting the
last of the Julio-Claudians. As we shall see later, too, imaginative
invention was often characterized in antiquity as a desirable quality
in a writer of invective (p. xxvii). Suetonius' ancient readers would
expect his descriptions of imperial vices to be embroidered.

Scholarly commentators often pass over the more outrageous
vices Suetonius attributes to his subjects. Suetonius relates at *Nero*
29 that a mock marriage was staged in which Nero's freedman
Doryphorus played the groom and Nero the bride—on the wedding
night 'he even imitated the shouts and cries of virgins being raped'.
Modern commentators pause only to dispute the identity of the
freedman. But whether the freedman was actually Doryphorus or
Pythagoras, or, as is quite possible, the event never took place, the
story serves an important function in Suetonius' account as an
emblem of Nero's perversity. The man occupying the position of
greatest power in the world submits himself to an ex-slave. Not only
does he take on a feminine sexual role but he embellishes his part
with horribly realistic sound-effects—another reminder of Nero's
shameful career as an actor specializing in female leads (including
Canace in labour with her incestuous offspring; *Nero* 21).

Both Otho and Vitellius mirror at least some of Nero's vices (*Otho*
2, and 7 where he is hailed as 'Nero'; *Vit.* 4). But then, they would,
wouldn't they? The victorious Flavians no doubt encouraged those
who painted their immediate predecessors as susceptible to the worst
excesses of luxury and lust. It is striking that, according to Suetonius, when Titus was young, people expressed their anxieties about
his future as their ruler by explicitly comparing him to Nero (*Titus*
7). Readers of Suetonius need to be alert to the ways in which a
stereotype such as that of the tyrant may inform the way an emperor

is represented, or the ways in which representation of one emperor may be modelled on that of another.[17]

At first sight, Suetonius' approach can sometimes seem rather like that of imperial panegyric. The younger Pliny's speech in praise of the Emperor Trajan, the only example to have survived from the early principate (it was later taken as a model for such speeches), is articulated in terms of a series of contrasts between the virtues of Trajan and the vices of his predecessors. Yet this similarity is perhaps misleading. Pliny's *Panegyric* presents us with a clear and consistent picture of what an emperor should be like, a great military leader, a fount of justice, liberal but not too liberal in the provision of games, and so on. The picture which emerges from Suetonius is much less clear. How desirable was it, even, for the emperor to be a great general? Suetonius points out that Nero had no interest in expanding the empire (*Nero* 18). This might look like a criticism, but it comes in the first half of Suetonius' biography, that which treats those of Nero's deeds 'meriting no reproach' or even 'deserving some praise' (*Nero* 19). And we might note that Augustus, too, is presented by Suetonius as having no ambition to extend the empire further (*Aug.* 21).

While history in Rome was traditionally written by men who had been involved in public life for readers of similar background, the point of view—and the audience—of Suetonius' work is rather less obvious. That Suetonius should be seen as spokesman for an equestrian 'party' (representatives of a newly emerging bureaucratic élite, alienated from the traditional senatorial aristocracy) was the view put forward by Francesco della Corte and developed by Eugen Cizek.[18] More recently scholars have doubted that 'senatorial' and 'equestrian' viewpoints can be so neatly separated. There is little a senator would object to in the *Lives* (though Suetonius' relative lack of interest in military glory might not be to the taste of some). Indeed, we find Suetonius implicitly disapproving of a plan to replace senators with equestrians and freedmen as commanders of the armies (*Nero* 37).

It has also been suggested that the *Lives of the Caesars* might be

---

[17] Cf. Richard Saller, 'Anecdotes as Historical Evidence for the Principate', *Greece & Rome*, 27 (1980), 69–83.

[18] F. della Corte, *Suetonio Eques Romanus* (2nd edn., Florence, 1967), and Eugen Cizek, *Structures et idéologie dans la 'Vie des douze Césars'* (Paris, 1977).

seen as a manifesto addressed to Hadrian. As Wallace–Hadrill
emphasizes, while one may see Suetonius as sharing with his friend
Pliny a view of how emperors ought to behave, unlike Pliny's
Panegyric of the emperor Trajan, Suetonius' *Lives* do not offer
explicit guidance. 'The ideal is not the conclusion, so much as the
presupposition of the *Caesars*.'[19] But here, too, we face the question:
how far is a monolithic ideal even implicitly present?

Suetonius is eclectic in his use of sources (this is discussed further
below) and his own accounts of the Caesars can often read in
a disconcertingly fragmentary manner. Townend, for instance,
criticizes Suetonius for his lack of 'conscious effort to build up a
coherent character, such as one finds in Plutarch'.[20] Suetonius, he
notes reproachfully, 'never makes up his mind about the true nature
of his subject'.[21] Sometimes Suetonius seems to present a kaleido-
scope of different perspectives on an individual without feeling the
need to reconcile them. Chapter 25 of the life of Claudius, for
instance, recounts at great length a number of measures which are, it
at first appears, initiated by the emperor himself and seem quite
consistent with his interests as Suetonius describes them more
generally (he exempts the people of Ilium from tribute, supporting
his action with reference to an ancient document; he performs elaborate religious rituals of great antiquity to celebrate the concluding
of treaties with foreign kings). Yet this chapter concludes with the
assertion that 'these and his other acts . . . he conducted not so much
according to his own judgement but rather according to that of his
wives and freedmen'. Different accounts of the same event appear to
co–exist in Suetonius' *Lives*; he relates anecdotes referring to two
scarcely compatible versions of the death of Claudius. Agrippina is
presented as solely responsible at *Claudius* 44, while at *Nero* 33 Nero
is portrayed as complicit with her.

The biographer's focus is very much on the emperor; Suetonius
gives short shrift even to the most important events which take place
in the emperor's absence (Corbulo's eastern successes under Nero
are only fleetingly mentioned, *Nero* 39). Some sections of the *Lives*
are given almost from the emperor's point of view (this is particularly the case when Suetonius is narrating an emperor's death). At

[19] Wallace-Hadrill, *Suetonius*, 24.
[20] Townend, 'Suetonius and his Influence', 83.
[21] Ibid. 92.

other times, however, the viewpoint is much less clear. Are we to empathize with the soldiers Galba refuses to bribe (*Galba* 16)? Or with the commoners threatened by Caligula at his games (*Cal.* 30)? In some ways this is Suetonius' strength. Rather than seeing his *Lives* as a missed opportunity to divulge the 'real' Julius Caesar or the 'truth' about Nero, we should rather relish the contradictions, for these may be seen as reflecting not only the inevitably contradictory natures of a group of powerful individuals but also the diverse ways in which they were judged by their contemporaries and by later Romans, too. Suetonius' *Lives* offer us a rich instance of the imperial image as a site where multifarious and incompatible expectations repeatedly clash.

A major determinant of the tensions that can be traced in Suetonius' *Lives* is the different and contradictory models of rulership looked to both by emperors themselves and by those assessing their behaviour. Some later emperors looked back to Augustus, as we have seen—but Augustus' long career could itself be seen as offering contradictory guidance. Should one imitate the unforgiving triumvir (*Aug.* 15) or the lenient princeps (*Aug.* 51)? Suetonius' repeated focus on the quality of *civilitas* implies as an ideal the *civilis princeps*, the emperor who plays down anything that might set him apart from other citizens (see e.g. *Aug.* 52–6; *Tib.* 26–32; *Vesp.* 12).[22] But not all Romans wanted an 'ordinary citizen' emperor in a homespun toga. Emperors who used the vast resources at their disposal to stage astonishingly lavish games could count on huge popularity with some of their subjects (while others might strongly disapprove—particularly if they felt they themselves might have to foot the bill through increased taxes). On the whole, Suetonius himself is very positive about lavish games and critical of emperors who skimp (see e.g. *Aug.* 43, *Tib.* 47).

Emperors in the Roman world were often treated as gods (many were formally deified after their death). For some of their subjects this was the most apt way of making sense of their power. Yet such honours sat very uneasily with notions of the emperor as 'first citizen'. Augustus and Vespasian, in particular, as they are presented by Suetonius, struggle to find ways of dealing with this. Augustus turns down the offer of a temple (*Aug.* 52). Vespasian doubts his own

[22] Cf. Andrew Wallace-Hadrill, '*Civilis princeps*: Between Citizen and King', *Journal of Roman Studies*, 72 (1982), 32–48.

capacity to work miracles yet heals the lame and the blind (*Vesp.* 7). Dying, he jokes about deification (*Vesp.* 23). Caligula, by contrast, loses no opportunity to stress his own godlike status in the most outrageous ways, having the heads of some of the most famous statues of the gods replaced with his own likeness, a temple constructed to his own godhead, and joining his own palace to the Capitol, the centre of Roman religion (*Cal.* 22). Suetonius' own perspective here may appear clearer—the moderation of Augustus and Vespasian is good, the excesses of Caligula are bad. But this is not to say that he is sceptical about the divinity of those emperors who have been officially deified.

Even where Suetonius' point of view seems straightforward, for instance with regard to imperial luxury, his accounts still permit the reader to glimpse an alternative perspective. Augustus, as he emerges from some of Suetonius' stories, can be seen as anxious to distance himself from any hint of eastern tyranny; we might note, for instance, the self-conscious simplicity of his personal living arrangements (*Aug.* 72). Suetonius seems to approve of this attitude. Some later emperors, however, apparently relished such comparisons. Caligula is said to have remarked that 'a man should either be frugal or be Caesar' (*Cal.* 37). For some imperial subjects, too, there may have been something rather impressive about the emperor Nero's declaration that only in his monstrous Golden House could he finally 'live like a human being' (*Nero* 31), even if Suetonius counts this among his crimes. Certainly Suetonius himself seems to revel in giving his readers the full details of Nero's folly.

Several emperors are criticized by Suetonius for their ill-treatment of the senate. However, when Caligula, for instance, humiliated senators in public (*Cal.* 26) his stock may well have risen with their social inferiors. Exploring strategies for expressing their power, such emperors may have looked, whether consciously or unconsciously, to the semi-mythical example of eastern tyrants such as Xerxes; as we saw earlier, according to Suetonius, some people thought Caligula was deliberately taking Xerxes as a model when he constructed a bridge over the Bay of Naples (*Cal.* 19). Perhaps he hoped to intimidate his subjects by laying claim to tyrant status. Part of the effectiveness of such a strategy would have lain in the high profile of such behaviour in the literary tradition on tyrants. Emperors themselves were not simply passive victims of stereotyping but played an active role in manipulating and developing the symbolic vocabulary through which their power was projected and made sense of.

The 'worst' of Suetonius' Caesars are the ones who are most outspoken in characterizing their own power. The remarks attributed to Caligula and Nero may have been jokes, if chilling ones, but they had a point. Nero observes that 'not one of his predecessors had known what he might do' (*Nero* 37). Caligula comments to his own grandmother: 'Remember, I can do anything I please and to anybody' (*Cal.* 29).[23] As Paul Plass has emphasized, emperors' jokes often serve to problematize the point of view of Suetonius' account. 'Fact on the one side, fiction on the other and frequently mediated by a miragelike, witty intermediate region that offers multiple, unresolved perception of political reality.'[24] When Caligula said (*Cal.* 55) that he wanted to make his horse consul (if he said that), did he mean it? Was it another symptom of mental derangement? Or was he perhaps poking fun at Roman senators who still valued the consulship even when it brought no real power? Does Suetonius allow for that possibility or does he think Caligula meant what he said? Certainly the inclusion of such excesses serves to make Suetonius' *Lives* far more entertaining—not an insignificant factor.

Suetonius does not offer his reader a final verdict on any of the Caesars (though he perhaps comes close to this in observing of Vespasian that his only vice was his love of money, *Vesp.* 16). Instead, we are offered a variety of ways of seeing each of them. We might see this as an acknowledgement of the impossibility of knowing what any emperor was 'really like', either for us or even for that emperor's contemporaries.

Suetonius' style

Suetonius' style has tended to receive little attention from modern scholars. Where his style is discussed, it is often in disparaging terms. He inevitably suffers by comparison with his contemporary Tacitus, that master of dazzling ironies. Some modern scholars have dismissed Suetonius as shifting between styles under the influence

[23] The significance of such comments is well explored in Plass, *Wit and the Writing of History*, 153.
[24] Ibid. 11.

of whatever source he was using at the time: Suetonius' style is to have no style.

Among ancient writers we can, however, find at least some admirers of his style.[25] The collection of biographies of later emperors known as the Augustan History describes Suetonius as 'a most correct and truthful author, whose characteristic it is to love brevity' (*Firmus, Saturninus, Proculus, and Bonosus* 1. 1–2). We might compare, too, the characteristics of the 'Plain style', principally clarity and brevity, which Quintilian praises in his treatise on the education of an orator (*Institutes of Oratory* 12.10.58 ff.). Suetonius was not, of course, attempting to write in the grand manner which was thought appropriate to history. Nevertheless, as we have already seen, his writing is hardly 'artless'—and even where it seems so, this may be deliberate.

Suetonius' writing offers no philosophical or moral generalization. He provides only the occasional explicit comment on the actions or traits he describes, disapproving, for instance, of Tiberius' harshness towards his exiled wife (*Tib.* 50) and Vitellius' brutal behaviour on visiting the battlefield at Betriacum (*Vit.* 10). For many scholars, this lack of comment has made Suetonius seem much more reliable as a source. He has no particular agenda, it is supposed. For Townend, the frustratingly fragmentary and inconsistent nature of the pictures of emperors given by Suetonius ultimately offers comfort: 'There is something solidly authentic about Suetonius' emperors, even if individual stories remain suspect. He allows us to construct our own figures from his materials, and we feel that the results are real.'[26] One could, though, make a case for arguing that this is deliberate strategy on Suetonius' part. He is himself, as his comments on Julius Caesar's prose style reveal (*Jul.* 56), a far from unsophisticated reader.

The profusion of detail in Suetonius' writing has already been noted. Plutarch, as we saw, stressed the importance of detail in revealing the nature of a biography's subject. But the wealth of detail in Suetonius could be seen as serving other functions, too. Ancient rhetoricians were very sensitive to the emotional impact and persuasive force of apparently casual details. Suetonius does not attempt to enter into the thoughts of his subjects but the inclusion of such

---

[25] As Lounsbury emphasises in his recent study, *Arts of Suetonius*. See esp. ch. 5.
[26] Townend, 'Suetonius and his Influence', 93.

details does serve to arouse an empathetic response on the part of the reader. We might think, for instance, of Otho, as he hurries to meet his fellow conspirators, being held up by his untied sandal (*Otho* 6), or Julius Caesar casually yet fatefully thrusting a note warning him of the conspiracy into a bundle of papers to read later (*Jul.* 81). Lounsbury characterizes this as a 'sensational' treatment—as opposed to the more 'intuitive' treatment offered in Tacitus' work which focuses rather on the 'psychological essence' of a scene.[27] For many readers it is this level of detail which gives Suetonius' writing its plausibility. Townend characterizes the *Lives of the Caesars* as 'full of vital characters and utterly convincing detail'.[28] For ancient rhetoricians one function of 'enargeia' ('vivid description') was that it made a story come to life for the listeners. In particular, the inclusion of telling details could give persuasive force to a scene entirely invented by the orator. Such inventions were thought quite legitimate and served to parade an orator's persuasive skills. Quintilian comments in his treatise on the education of an orator: 'It reinforces the case greatly if one adds to the actual facts a credible picture of events, so that the listeners feel that they themselves witnessed the scene' (4. 2. 123). For this reason, too, we should hesitate before assuming Suetonius is giving us the unvarnished truth.[29]

Use of sources

There is not space here to give a detailed account of the range of sources both narrative and documentary, which Suetonius is thought to have used in compiling his *Lives*. A number of earlier historians are named, for instance the elder Pliny, though usually only when they provide first-hand evidence.[30] It is clear that he was often reliant on the same narrative sources as the historian Tacitus (e.g. the work of Cluvius Rufus). Suetonius seems to be quite familiar with the writings of the emperors themselves (Tiberius' autobiography, *Tib.* 61, or Nero's poems, *Nero* 52). Suetonius also makes extensive use of less obvious sources, such as the writings of grammarians.[31]

---

[27] Lounsbury, *Arts of Suetonius*, 76.
[28] Townend, 'Suetonius and his Influence', 93
[29] See Barton, 'The *inventio* of Nero'.
[30] Cf. Wallace-Hadrill, *Suetonius*, 64.
[31] As Wallace-Hadrill makes clear; *Suetonius*, ch. 3.

Unlike historians, Suetonius did not need to aim for seamless grandeur. Suetonius has no stylistic anxieties about quoting in Greek or using technical vocabulary. He could include verbatim quotations from emperors—and others; Suetonius offers his readers scraps of graffiti and obscene verses chanted at triumphs. While a historian such as Tacitus would compose an idealized speech, designed to suggest the character of the speaker, Suetonius quotes the actual words of his subjects, cataloguing, for instance, the idio-syncrasies of Augustus' Latin. Here, too, he is much closer to Roman traditions of antiquarian and technical literature than to history writing (there are reasons for supposing he was the first reputable author of formal prose to do this). In particular, he makes extensive use of the letters of the emperor Augustus to which he must have had access while working at the palace. It is, however, striking that he makes no direct quotations from the letters of any later emperor (apart from at *Nero* 23, where he does not claim to have seen an original). The only later private document he refers to is the text of Nero's poems (*Nero* 52). Scholars have generally taken this to suggest that he was dismissed from office when only the first two of his *Lives* were completed.

On two occasions when Suetonius makes use of documentary sources to refute earlier writers he seems to be addressing errors in Tacitus' account of the Julio-Claudians: at *Tiberius* 21 where he discusses Augustus' attitude to Tiberius and at *Caligula* 8, where he quotes the public records in support of the view, disputed by Tacitus, that Caligula was born at Antium.[32]

Suetonius' influence

Suetonius had some influence on the authors of the later Augustan History (as well as on Marius Maximus whose work, now lost, aimed to continue Suetonius' series of Caesars). Their *Lives* are generally organized chronologically but express explicit approval of Suetonius' writing, as we have seen.[33] In the ninth century the *Lives of the Caesars* was followed more closely as a model by Einhard for his life of Charlemagne, which is organized by topic.[34] In the fourteenth

---

[32] Townend, 'Suetonius and his Influence', 88–9.
[33] Ibid. 96–7.
[34] Ibid. 97–106.

century Petrarch made extensive use of Suetonius as a source in composing his *Lives of the Illustrious Romans*, though his mode of organization is his own.

More than two hundred editions of Suetonius were published between 1470 and 1829.[35] He appears to have enjoyed consistent popularity at least until the nineteenth century. Before 1700 editions of Suetonius were as numerous as those of Tacitus and more so than those of Plutarch (Latin was, of course, more widely read than Greek but vernacular translations of Plutarch do not seem to have outnumbered those of Suetonius).[36] The salacious nature of some of Suetonius' material meant, however, that he was rarely recommended reading in schools.

Suetonius' style was much admired in his numerous influential treatises by the Spanish Humanist scholar Juan Luis Vives (1492–1540), a friend of Erasmus. Erasmus himself chose to produce an edition of Suetonius, with the purpose, he states in his preface, of encouraging princes 'to order their lives and habits as if in a mirror' (1517)—while in a number of other works he draws on Suetonius constantly for examples of how rulers ought and ought not to behave. Politian, another prominent Humanist, who was professor of Greek and Latin at the Florentine Academy, delivered a course of lectures on historiography which presented Suetonius as its foremost exemplar (Politian was not unusual at this time in seeing no sharp distinction between biography and history). The scholar Isaac Casaubon (1559–1614) published an edition of Suetonius (1595, revised 1610) with full commentary (in print until 1736), praising him for his accuracy of both manner and matter. Suetonius was generally popular in the sixteenth and seventeenth centuries, as a fund of evocative details as well as an important source of information about Roman emperors. Among British authors, Ben Jonson based much of his *Sejanus* (performed 1603) on material in Suetonius, while Philemon Holland's 1606 translation was used extensively by Philip Massinger for his play based on events under the emperor Domitian, *The Roman Actor*, first performed in 1626. The royalist writer Sir Robert Filmer, whose *Patriarcha, or the natural powers of kings* was written around 1639, exploited Suetonius' work in defending the position of Charles I against

---

[35] Lounsbury, *Arts of Suetonius*, 26.
[36] Ibid. 32–3, 146 n. 5.

parliamentarian critics (their preferred classical author, by contrast, was that defender of the republic, Cicero).

By the later nineteenth century Suetonius had fallen out of favour as a 'literary' author.[37] His works were dismissed in one footnote by the influential critic Eduard Norden in *Die antike Kunstprosa* ('Ancient literary prose') of 1898,[38] while J. W. Mackail, in his 1895 *Latin Literature*, another highly influential work, describes Suetonius' style as 'the beginning of barbarism; and Suetonius measures more than half the distance from the fine, familiar prose of the Golden Age to the base jargon of the authors of the Augustan History'.[39] Latin prose authors are no longer selected for study purely on the basis of their suitability as models for Latin prose composition and Suetonius will continue to be read as a source of information about imperial Rome. In recent years he could be said to have entertained millions through the medium of the television drama series *I, Claudius* based on Robert Graves's historical novels, which drew very extensively on Suetonius' *Lives of the Caesars*. Robert Graves's own translation of the *Lives* is itself a classic, whose literary elegance reflects little of Suetonius' own style—and whose substance often departs considerably from Suetonius' Latin. Suetonius' greatest value lies in the perspective he offers on how emperors were seen and judged by their fellow Romans.

[37] As Richard Lounsbury emphasizes, in his survey of responses to Suetonius through the centuries, *Arts of Suetonius*, ch. 2.

[38] i. 387 n. 1.

[39] p. 231.

NOTE ON THE TEXT AND TRANSLATION

IN translating Suetonius, I have attempted to keep as close to the Latin as is consistent with readable English, while also capturing something of the flavour of Suetonius' varied style. I have largely followed Ihm's magisterial Teubner text of 1908.

It is not possible in a volume of this scale to offer more than the briefest of notes (the Glossary explains some Roman technical terms). For this reason I have made no attempt to be comprehensive in indicating, for instance, where Suetonius' account is at variance with those available in other sources, or where modern scholars generally believe Suetonius to be mistaken. Instead, I have made it a priority to contextualize comments which would otherwise be puzzling, point up connections and parallels within and between Suetonius' *Lives*, and in general make it easier for readers to grasp the nature of Suetonius' enterprise. Those who seek guidance as to how far they should trust the accuracy of particular pieces of information offered by Suetonius will often be better served by consulting modern biographies of Roman emperors, or, in the case of the year of the four emperors, Kenneth Wellesley's useful study *The Long Year 69 AD* (London, 1975)—though these works are sometimes over-optimistic in their faith in his veracity. As a general rule, one should avoid relying on any of Suetonius' statements relating to numbers (e.g. dates, ages, prices).

Ancient Roman place-names have generally been retained, with a few exceptions.

I am most grateful for the comments made by Judith Luna of Oxford University Press and for the careful scrutiny undertaken by Elizabeth Stratford, the copy-editor, which did much to improve my original text. Thanks also go to Alessandro Schiesaro for reading the introduction and suggesting a number of useful changes and to Neville Morley for help with the maps.

SELECT BIBLIOGRAPHY

Editions, Translations, and Commentaries

Suetonius De vita Caesarum libri viii, ed. M. Ihm (Teubner; Leipzig 1908).

The Historie of the twelve Caesars, Emperors of Rome, trans. Philemon Holland (London, 1606).

Suetonius with an English translation by J. C. Rolfe, Latin and English, 2 vols. (Loeb Classical Library; Cambridge, Mass., 1914).

The Twelve Caesars, trans. Robert Graves; revised with introduction by Michael Grant (Penguin, 1979).

Divus Julius, ed. with commentary by H. E. Butler and M. Cary (Oxford, 1927).

Augustus, ed. with commentary by E. S. Shuckburgh (Cambridge 1896).

Augustus, ed. with commentary by John Carter (Bristol, 1982).

Caligula, ed. with commentary by Hugh Lindsay (London, 1993).

Claudius, ed. with commentary by J. Mottershead (Bristol, 1986).

Nero, ed. with commentary by Brian Warmington (Bristol, 1977).

Nero, ed. with commentary by K. R. Bradley (Brussels, 1978).

De vita Caesarum libri VII–VIII, ed. with translation and commentary by G. W. Mooney (London, 1930).

Lives of Galba, Otho and Vitellius, ed. with commentary by Charles Murison (Bristol, 1992).

Lives of Galba, Otho and Vitellius, ed. with translation and commentary by D. Shotter (Warminster, 1993).

Domitian, ed. with commentary by Brian W. Jones (London, 1996).

Critical Works

Barry Baldwin, *Suetonius* (Amsterdam, 1983).

Tamsyn Barton, 'The *inventio* of Nero: Suetonius', in J. Elsner and J. Masters (eds.), *Reflections of Nero*.

Eugen Cizek, *Structures et idéologie dans la 'Vie des douze Césars'* (Paris, 1977).

Catherine Connors, 'Famous Last Words', in J. Elsner and J. Masters (eds.), *Reflections of Nero*.

J.-M. Croisille, 'L'Art de la composition chez Suétone, d'après les vies de Claudius et de Néron', *Annali dell'istituto italiano per gli studi storici*, 2 (1969/70), 73–87.

Catharine Edwards, *The Politics of Immorality in Ancient Rome* (Cambridge, 1993).

J. Elsner and J. Masters (eds.), *Reflections of Nero* (London, 1994).

Richard Lounsbury, *The Arts of Suetonius: An Introduction* (New York, 1987).

F. G. B. Millar, *The Emperor in the Roman World* (London, 1977).

Arnaldo Momigliano, *The Development of Greek Biography* (Cambridge Mass., 1971)

Paul Plass, *Wit and the Writing of History* (Madison, 1988).

S. R. F. Price, 'The Future of Dreams: From Freud to Artemidorus', *Past & Present*, 113 (1986), 3–37.

Richard Saller, 'Anecdotes as Historical Evidence for the Principate', *Greece & Rome*, 27 (1980), 69–83.

W. Steidle, *Sueton und die antike Biographie* (Munich, 1951).

G. B. Townend 'The Hippo Inscription and the Career of Suetonius', *Historia*, 10 (1961), 99–109.

—— 'Suetonius and his Influence', in T. A. Dorey (ed.), *Latin Biography* (London, 1967), 79–111.

Andrew Wallace-Hadrill, *Suetonius: The Scholar and his Caesars* (London, 1983).

—— '*Civilis princeps*: Between Citizen and King', *Journal of Roman Studies*, 72 (1982), 32–48.

Alan Wardman, *Plutarch's Lives* (London, 1974).

A. J. Woodman, 'History, Biography or Panegyric?', in his edition *Velleius Paterculus: The Tiberian Narrative* (Cambridge, 1977).

Further Reading in Oxford World's Classics

Julius Caesar, *The Civil War*, trans. and ed. J. R. Carter.

—— *The Gallic War*, trans. and ed. Carolyn Hammond.

Juvenal, *The Satires*, trans. Niall Rudd, ed. William Barr.

Lucan, *Civil War*, trans. and ed. Susan H. Braund.

Plutarch, *Greek Lives: A Selection of Nine Lives*, trans. Robin Waterfield, ed. Philip A. Stadter.

—— *Roman Lives: A Selection of Eight Lives*, trans. Robin Waterfield, ed. Philip A. Stadter.

Tacitus, *Agricola and Germany*, trans. and ed. Anthony R. Birley.

—— *The Histories*, ed. David Levene; revision of the translation of W. H. Fyfe.

Virgil, *The Aeneid*, trans. C. Day Lewis, ed. Jasper Griffin.

CHRONOLOGY

BCE:

100   Birth of Julius Caesar (?).

82–80 Sulla dictator. Proscriptions.

63   Consulship of Cicero. Catiline's rebellion quashed. (23 Sept.) Birth of Octavian/Augustus. Julius Caesar made Pontifex Maximus.

61   Trial of Clodius for sacrilege.

61–60 Caesar's campaigns in Spain.

60   So-called 'first triumvirate' of Pompey, Caesar, and Crassus.

59   Consulship of Caesar and Marcus Calpurnius Bibulus. Caesar given Gallic command.

55   Caesar's command extended; campaigns in Britain.

54   Caesar in Britain and Germany.

53   Defeat and death of Crassus fighting the Parthians at Carrhae.

51   Debate about supersession of Caesar.

49   Outbreak of civil war between Julius Caesar and Pompey. Caesar briefly dictator.

48   Caesar defeats Pompey at Pharsalus. Escape and death of Pompey. Caesar dictator.

46   Caesar, back in Rome, embarks on extensive reforms. Triumphs for Gaul, Egypt, Pontus, and Africa.

45   Defeat of Pompey's sons at Munda. Caesar has triumph for Spain.

44   (15 March) Assassination of Caesar. Octavian (Augustus) returns to Italy and opposes Mark Antony. Antony given five years' command in Cisalpine and Transalpine Gaul.

43   Consuls Hirtius and Pansa killed at Mutina. Octavian declared consul. Triumvirate of Antony, Octavian, and Lepidus.

42   Julius Caesar officially deified. Battle of Philippi. Defeated, Cassius and M. Brutus commit suicide. Birth of Tiberius.

41   Antony in the east, meets Cleopatra. Civil war in Italy between Octavian and Lucius Antonius.

41–40 Parthians invade Syria and Asia Minor.

40   Lucius Antonius surrenders Perusia to Octavian. Pact of Brundisium between Antony and Augustus.

39   Pact of Misenum between triumvirs and Sextus Pompeius. Octavian divorces Scribonia.

38   Octavian marries Livia and comes into conflict with Sextus Pompeius.

37   Triumvirate renewed at Tarentum. Antony joins Cleopatra.

36   Octavian and Agrippa defeat Sextus Pompeius at Naulochus. Lepidus sidelined.

35–34   Octavian's successful campaigns in Illyria.

32   Consuls and many senators join Antony. Preparation for war.

31   Battle of Actium. Antony and Cleopatra defeated.

30   Fall of Alexandria. Antony and Cleopatra commit suicide.

29   Octavian returns to Italy and celebrates triple triumph.

28   Constitutional reorganization. Census. Purge of senate.

27   Octavian receives governorship of Spain, Gaul, Syria, Cyprus, and Egypt for ten years, while remaining consul. Given the title Augustus. On campaign in Spain and Gaul 27–24.

25   Marriage of Julia and Marcellus.

23   Augustus resigns the consulship but retains tribunician power and supreme military command. Death of Marcellus.

21   Marriage of Julia and Agrippa.

20   Parthians return captured Roman standards.

19   Augustus' imperium made valid in Rome.

18   Senate purged.

18–17   Legislation on marriage and adultery.

17   Secular Games. Augustus adopts his grandsons Gaius and Lucius.

12   Death of Agrippa. Tiberius in command in Pannonia. Augustus Pontifex Maximus.

11   Marriage of Julia and Tiberius.

10   Birth of Claudius.

7   Tiberius celebrates triumph after campaign on the Rhine. Augustus divides Rome into fourteen administrative regions.

6   Tiberius given tribunician power for five years. He retires to Rhodes.

5   Gaius Caesar introduced to public life and designated consul for 1 CE.

3   Birth of Galba.

2   Lucius Caesar introduced to public life and designated consul for 4 CE. Dedication of temple of Mars the Avenger and Forum of Augustus. Augustus receives title 'Father of the Fatherland'. Julia banished for adultery.

CE:

2   Tiberius back in Italy. Death of Lucius Caesar.

3   Augustus' powers of supreme military command renewed.

4   Death of Gaius Caesar. Augustus adopts Agrippa Postumus and Tiberius. Senate purged.

4–6   Tiberius campaigns in Germany.

7/8   Banishment of Agrippa Postumus and younger Julia.

9   Three legions under Quintilius Varus destroyed by Germans. Birth of Vespasian.

12   Tiberius' second triumph. Birth of Caligula.

14   Death of Augustus; accession of Tiberius.

15   Birth of Vitellius.

15–16 Germanicus on campaign in Germany.

16   Trial and suicide of Libo Drusus.

19   Death of Germanicus at Antioch.

20   Trial and suicide of Gnaeus Piso.

23   Death of Drusus.

26   Tiberius leaves Rome for Capri.

29   Death of Livia. Exile of elder Agrippina.

31   Consulship and execution of Sejanus.

32   Birth of Otho.

33   Death of elder Agrippina.

37   Death of Tiberius; accession of Caligula. Suicide of Tiberius Gemellus. Birth of Nero.

38   Death and deification of Drusilla. Caligula marries Lollia Paulina.

39   Execution of Gaetulicus. Exile of younger Agrippina. Birth of Titus. Caligula divorces Lollia Paulina and marries Milonia Caesonia. Leaves Rome to visit Rhineland.

41   Assassination of Caligula; accession of Claudius. Birth of Britannicus.

43   Invasion of Britain.

44   Claudius' triumph.

48	Claudius censor. Marriage and execution of Silius and Messalina.
49	Marriage of Claudius and younger Agrippina.
50	Nero adopted by Claudius.
51	Birth of Domitian.
53	Nero marries Octavia.
54	Death of Claudius (subsequently deified); accession of Nero. War in Armenia.
55	Murder of Britannicus.
59	Murder of younger Agrippina.
60	Armenia subjugated by Corbulo. Revolt of Boudicca in Britain.
62	Death of Burrus. Retirement of Seneca. Execution of Octavia. Nero marries Poppaea.
64	Fire of Rome.
65	Conspiracy of Piso. Death of Poppaea.
66	Nero marries Statilia Messalina. Visit of Tiridates to Rome. Nero's tour of Greece.
67	Vespasian given command of Judaea.
68	Revolt of Vindex and Galba. Suicide of Nero; accession of Galba.
69	Otho declared emperor; Galba murdered. First battle of Betriacum. Otho, defeated, commits suicide. Vitellius recognized as emperor. Vespasian proclaimed in the east. Second battle of Betriacum. Vitellian forces defeated. Vespasian's forces take Rome. Vitellius killed; accession of Vespasian.
70	Vespasian arrives in Rome. Titus captures Jerusalem.
71	Triumph of Vespasian and Titus. Titus receives tribunician power.
79	Death of Vespasian (subsequently deified); accession of Titus.
81	Death of Titus (subsequently deified); accession of Domitian.
82–3	Campaign against the Chatti. Domitian's first triumph.
89	Victory in Pannonia. Domitian's second triumph.
95	Execution of Flavius Clemens.
96	Assassination of Domitian; accession of Nerva.
98	Death of Nerva; accession of Trajan.
117	Death of Trajan; accession of Hadrian.
138	Death of Hadrian; accession of Antoninus Pius.

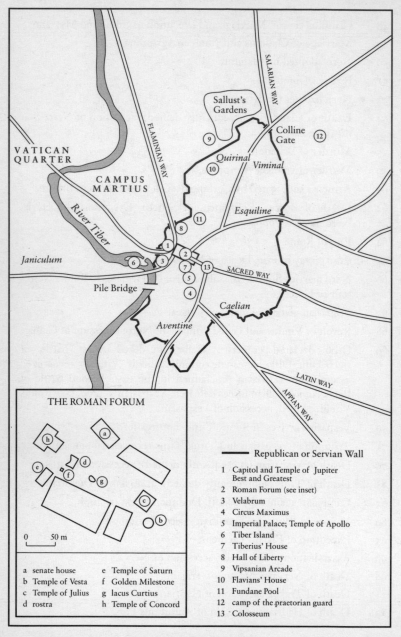

THE ROMAN FORUM

0   50 m

a   senate house   e   Temple of Saturn
b   Temple of Vesta   f   Golden Milestone
c   Temple of Julius   g   lacus Curtius
d   rostra   h   Temple of Concord

——— Republican or Servian Wall

1   Capitol and Temple of Jupiter
    Best and Greatest
2   Roman Forum (see inset)
3   Velabrum
4   Circus Maximus
5   Imperial Palace; Temple of Apollo
6   Tiber Island
7   Tiberius' House
8   Hall of Liberty
9   Vipsanian Arcade
10   Flavians' House
11   Fundane Pool
12   camp of the praetorian guard
13   Colosseum

MAP 1. Plan of Rome

MAP 2. Italy

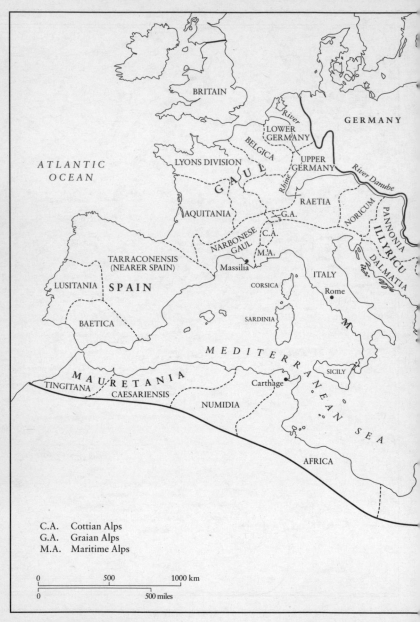

ATLANTIC
OCEAN

BRITAIN

GERMANY

River

LOWER
GERMANY

BELGICA

LYONS DIVISION

UPPER
GERMANY

GAUL

River Danube

Rhine

RAETIA

AQUITANIA

G.A.

NORICUM

PANNONIA

ILLYRICU

NARBONESE
GAUL

C.A.

M.A.

DALMATIA

TARRACONENSIS
(NEARER SPAIN)

Massilia

ITALY

Rome

LUSITANIA

SPAIN

CORSICA

BAETICA

SARDINIA

M E D I T E R R A

N E A N

MAURETANIA

SICILY

TINGITANA

CAESARIENSIS

Carthage

S E A

NUMIDIA

AFRICA

C.A.   Cottian Alps
G.A.   Graian Alps
M.A.   Maritime Alps

0   500   1000 km

0   500 miles

MAP 3. The Roman Empire in 96 CE

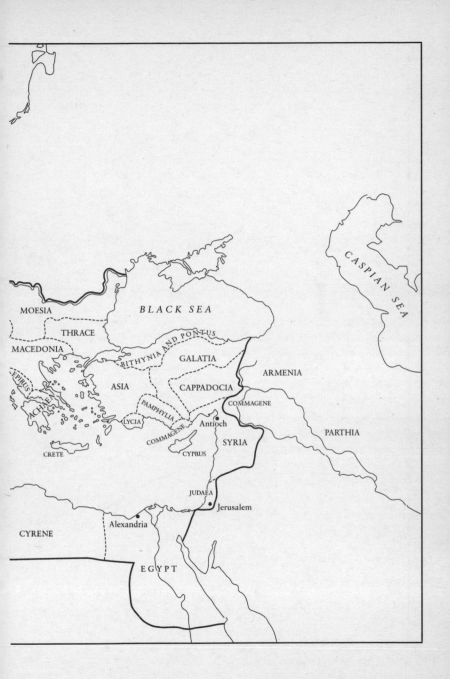

LIVES OF THE CAESARS

THE DEIFIED JULIUS CAESAR

[1] In the course of his sixteenth year, he lost his father.* In the following consulate, when he was Flamen Dialis elect, he divorced Cossutia,* whose family was of equestrian rank but very wealthy, and to whom he had been betrothed before assuming the toga of manhood. He then married Cornelia, whose father Cinna was four times consul. By her he soon had a daughter, Julia, and he could not be induced to divorce her despite all the efforts of the dictator Sulla. Thus, having been stripped of his priesthood, his wife's dowry, and his family estates, he was even treated as an adherent of the opposing faction, so that he was forced to withdraw from public life and to change his hiding-place each night, though suffering from an increasingly severe case of quartan fever, as well as having to buy off his pursuers, until finally he secured forgiveness, through the intervention of the Vestal Virgins and his relatives, Mamercus Aemilius and Aurelius Cotta. It is well known that Sulla, though he had long held out against the entreaties of his most distinguished close advisers, finally gave in to their persistence, declaring (divinely inspired or through shrewd foresight): 'Have your way—and have your man—but be aware that the man you so desired to save, believing him to be attached to the aristocratic cause for which you have fought alongside me, will be its downfall. For in Caesar there are many Mariuses.'*

[2] For his first military service he was stationed in Asia, among the companions of the governor Marcus Thermus. When Thermus sent him on a mission to Bithynia to summon the fleet he lingered at the court of Nicomedes—and there was a rumour that he had submitted himself to the king's pleasure, a rumour which strengthened when he returned to Bithynia a few days later to obtain money that was allegedly owed to a freedman, one of his clients. He fulfilled the rest of his service with better repute—Thermus awarded him a civic crown for his role in the capture of Mytilene. [3] He also served under Servilius Isauricus in Cilicia but only for a short time. For when news came of Sulla's death, he hurried back to Rome, hoping to take advantage of the unrest caused by Marcus Lepidus' measures.* Yet he declined to attach himself to Lepidus, though major

inducements were offered, distrusting both the man himself and the circumstances, which were less promising than he had hoped.

[4] However, once the civil unrest was quelled, he brought a charge of extortion against Cornelius Dolabella,* an ex-consul who had celebrated a triumph. When Dolabella was acquitted Caesar decided to withdraw to Rhodes, so that the ill-feeling against him might die down and that he might rest and have the leisure to study under Apollonius Molon, the leading teacher of oratory.* As he was crossing over to Rhodes, during the winter season, he was captured near the island of Pharmacussa by pirates, who held him captive for forty days in a state of extreme indignation, with just one doctor and two personal attendants for company; he had immediately dispatched his companions and his other slaves to raise money with which he might be ransomed. Once he was set ashore, having paid out fifty talents, he raised a fleet on the spot without delay and set off in pursuit of the departing pirates. Having got them in his power, he inflicted on them the punishment with which he had often jokingly threatened them.*

Mithridates was laying waste some neighbouring regions, so, lest he should seem to be idle when allies were in danger, he crossed over from Rhodes (which he had finally reached) to Asia. Having secured some auxiliaries and driven the king's prefect from the province, he confirmed alliances with those states which were wavering and undecided.

[5] When he was serving as military tribune, the first office to which he was elected on his return to Rome, he made great efforts to support those who sought to restore the powers of the tribunes of the plebs, which had been weakened by Sulla. Through legislation proposed by Plotius, he also brought about the recall of Lucius Cinna, his wife's brother, and those who, along with him, had supported Lepidus in the civil unrest and had fled to Sertorius, after the consul's death.* He himself gave a speech in favour of the measure.

[6] When he was quaestor, following the deaths of his aunt Julia* and his wife Cornelia, he delivered the customary eulogies of them from the rostra. In the course of the eulogy of his aunt, he made the following comments concerning the origins on both sides of his aunt's and father's family: 'On her mother's side, my aunt Julia was descended from kings, on her father's she was related to gods. For the Marcius Rex family—that was her mother's name—goes back to

Ancus Marcius,* while the Julii, to which our family belongs, go back
to Venus. Her family is therefore distinguished by the sanctity of
kings, who are mighty amongst men, and by the majesty of the gods,
to whom kings themselves are subject.'

In place of Cornelia, he took as wife Pompeia, the daughter of
Quintus Pompeius, and granddaughter of Lucius Sulla. Later on he
divorced her, on the grounds that she had committed adultery with
Publius Clodius, for the rumour that Clodius had approached her,
disguised as a woman, in the course of a public religious festival was
so persistent that the senate set up an inquiry into the profaning of
rituals.*

[7] The province of Further Spain was allotted him as quaestor;
making his rounds of the local courts, dispensing justice, in accordance with his praetor's mandate, he came to Gades and, noticing a
statue of Alexander the Great at the temple of Hercules, he let out a
groan, as though exasperated at his own lack of achievement, for he
himself had done nothing memorable at the age when Alexander had
already conquered the world.* He at once sought to be released from
his duties, in order to seize as soon as possible the greater opportunities on offer in Rome. He was also troubled by a dream on the
following night. For he dreamed that he was committing incest with
his mother. Even this spurred him on to greater hopes, for dream-
interpreters explained it as a portent that he would rule the world,
because his mother, whom he had seen subjected to himself, was
none other than the earth, which is held to be the mother of all.

[8] Thus having left his province early, he approached some Latin
colonies which were agitating to secure full citizenship,* and he
might have spurred them to dare action, if the consuls had not kept
some legions, raised for Cilicia, there for a while to guard against
this. [9] Not long afterwards, he was embarking on more ambitious
projects in Rome. Indeed, just a few days before he took up the
aedileship, he fell under suspicion of having conspired with the
ex-consul Marcus Crassus, as well as Publius Sulla* and Lucius
Autronius (who had been convicted of bribery after winning the
consular elections*), their plan being to attack the senate on New
Year's Day and, after the slaughter of their chosen victims, for
Crassus to usurp the dictatorship, while Caesar would be made his
Master of Horse; then, when they had organized the state according
to their wishes, the consulship would be restored to Sulla and

Autronius. Tanusius Geminus mentions the plot in his history, as does Marcus Bibulus in his edicts and Gaius Curio the elder in his speeches. Cicero, too, seems to be referring to this in a letter to Axius in which he says that in his consulship Caesar brought about the tyranny he had contemplated when he was aedile. Tanusius adds that Crassus, either repenting or fearful, did not appear on the day fixed for the massacre and for this reason Caesar did not give the signal which it had been agreed he was to give. Curio says the arrangement was that he would let his toga slip from his shoulder. Curio is also the source, along with Marcus Actorius Naso, for the story that Caesar had also conspired with the youth Gnaeus Piso, who was given the province of Spain, though it was not his turn and he had not asked for it, because he was suspected of involvement in intrigue at Rome; also, that they had agreed that the two of them would stir up revolution, Piso abroad and Caesar in Rome, by means of the Ambrani and the Transpadanes* but that Piso's death brought their plans to nothing.

[10] When he was aedile, besides the Comitium, Forum, and basilicas, he also decorated the Capitol with arcades built for the occasion, in which part of the equipment for his shows was displayed in great profusion.* He provided wild beast fights and games, both in collaboration with his colleague and on his own account, with the result that what had been paid for jointly was also attributed to him alone. Thus, his colleague Marcus Bibulus did not conceal the fact that he had suffered the same fate as Pollux, for just as the temple in the Forum that was sacred to the twin brothers was simply known as the temple of Castor, so the munificence of himself and Caesar was spoken of simply as Caesar's. In addition to this, Caesar provided a set of gladiatorial games, though with fewer pairs of fighters than he had planned, for the great number of gladiators he had assembled struck such terror into his opponents that a bill was passed limiting the number of gladiators which any individual might keep in the city.

[11] Having won the favour of the people, he made an attempt, through the agency of the tribunes, to have Egypt awarded him as a province by plebiscite, seizing the opportunity to ask for this extraordinary post when the Alexandrians had expelled their king, who had been termed ally and friend by the senate,* and the expulsion was widely condemned. But he was not successful, due to the opposition of the aristocratic faction. Therefore he sought to diminish their authority by every means possible and to this end he restored the

trophies of Gaius Marius (commemorating his victories over Jugurtha and over the Cimbri and Teutones) which had been torn down by Sulla. And, in conducting prosecutions for murder,* he included among the murderers those who, through the proscriptions,* had received money from the treasury for the heads of Roman citizens, although such cases had been exempted by the Cornelian laws. [12] He also bribed someone to bring a charge of treason against Gaius Rabirius* who had been of particular service to the senate some years previously when it was seeking to bring under control the troublesome tribune, Lucius Saturninus. And when he had been selected by lot to pass sentence on the defendant, he condemned him with such eagerness that nothing helped Rabirius in his appeal to the people so much as the harshness of his judge.*

[13] Having put aside his hope of securing a province,* he sought appointment as Pontifex Maximus—not without a considerable amount of bribery. Contemplating the magnitude of his debts, he is said to have announced to his mother, when she kissed him as he was leaving for the assembly on the morning of the election, that he would not come home unless he was Pontifex. And he so decisively beat two formidable rival candidates, in age and rank far his superiors, that he won more votes in their own tribes than either of them secured overall.*

[14] When, after the conspiracy of Catiline had been discovered, the entire senate supported the death penalty for those involved in the crime, as praetor elect he was the only one to advocate separating them to be imprisoned in different towns and confiscating their property. Nevertheless, he inspired such fear in those proposing the harsher penalty, emphasizing how unpopular they would later be with the Roman people, that Decimus Silanus, the consul designate, was not ashamed to suggest a milder interpretation of his own proposal (it would have been a disgrace to change it), alleging that it had been understood as harsher than he had intended.* Thus, Caesar would have prevailed, having persuaded many, including Cicero (the brother of the consul),* to adopt his view, if Marcus Cato's speech had not confirmed the resolution of the wavering senate. Yet even then Caesar continued his attempts to impede the proceedings, until the armed troop of Roman knights, which was standing guard around the place, threatened to kill him as he carried on unabashed, even brandishing their drawn swords at him in such a way that those

closest to him moved away from where he was sitting and it was with difficulty that a few were able to shield him with their arms and their togas. At that point, quite terrified, he desisted and even kept away from the senate for the rest of the year.

[15] On the first day of his praetorship,* he summoned Quintus Catulus to a people's inquiry concerning the restoration of the Capitoline,* proposing a bill to transfer the responsibility to someone else.* But he was no match for the united actions of the aristocrats and abandoned the proposal when he perceived that they had at once left off their attendance on the new consuls and had hurried together in groups determined to offer resistance to his measures.* [16] However, he showed himself the most stalwart backer and defender of Caecilius Metellus, tribune of the plebs, who was attempting to introduce highly disruptive measures in spite of his colleagues' veto, until eventually both of them were suspended from the exercise of public office by a decree of the senate.* Nevertheless, Caesar had the audacity to continue to exercise his office and to dispense justice. Then, learning that there were those who were prepared to contain him through armed force, he sent away his lictors, threw aside his magistrate's toga, and hid himself away at home, planning to keep a low profile, given the current circumstances. And on the following day a rather unruly mob flocked to him spontaneously and of their own accord, offering him their help in reasserting his position; when he restrained them, quite contrary to expectations, the senate (which had been hastily summoned to deal with the same crowd) made him a vote of thanks through its leading men, and then, having summoned him to the senate house, praised him in the highest terms and restored him to his former position, cancelling the earlier decree.

[17] However, he encountered further trouble when he was named as one of the associates of Catiline, both by the informer Lucius Vettius, at a hearing conducted by the quaestor Novius Nigrus, and in the senate house by Quintus Curius, to whom a sum of money had been publicly voted, since he was the first to unveil the plans of the conspirators. Curius maintained he had his information from Catiline, while Vettius even promised a document in Caesar's handwriting that had been given to Catiline. Caesar, however, could in no way tolerate this and, having demonstrated, invoking Cicero as witness, that he himself had of his own accord reported information

about the conspiracy to Cicero, he ensured that Curius did not receive his reward. As for Vettius, his bond was declared forfeit, his goods were seized, and he was severely fined and almost torn apart in a public assembly before the rostra. Caesar then committed him to prison, inflicting the same treatment on the quaestor Novius, because he had allowed a magistrate with powers superior to his own to be summoned to his court.

[18] Having been allotted Further Spain as his province, following his praetorship, Caesar disposed of his creditors, who sought to prevent him leaving, by means of guarantees and set off before the provinces had been officially provided for—though this was contrary to precedent and to law. It is unclear whether he was afraid of a suit which was being prepared to be brought against him once he was out of office,* or whether he wanted to bring help to the allies who were begging for aid as soon as possible. Once his province was brought to order, not waiting for his successor, he left for Rome with equal rapidity, to procure both a triumph and the consulship. However, since the elections had already been announced and no account could be taken of his candidacy unless he entered the city as a private citizen, and since his intrigues to secure exemption from the laws were provoking widespread criticism, he was obliged to give up the triumph, to avoid being excluded from the consulship.* [19] Of the two rival candidates for the consulship, Lucius Lucceius and Marcus Bibulus, he allied himself with Lucceius, having made an agreement with him that, since Lucceius was less popular but had greater financial resources, he should promise the electors money from his own funds in both their names. When the aristocrats discovered this, they were seized with fear that Caesar as consul would stop at nothing, if he had a colleague who went along with him and shared his views, so they authorized Bibulus to promise the same amount, many of them contributing money. Even Cato could not deny that such gifts were for the good of the state.*

Thus it was with Bibulus that he was elected consul. And with the same motive, the aristocrats went to some trouble to ensure that the provinces stipulated for the consuls elect were those of the least moment, that is, woodland and pastures.* Severely goaded by this insult, he sought with all manner of services to attach himself to Gnaeus Pompey, who was in dispute with the senate because it had been slow to ratify the arrangements he had made after his victory

over King Mithridates. Caesar reconciled Pompey with Marcus
Crassus, who had been his enemy since they had been constantly at
odds with one another as consuls. Caesar entered into an agreement
with each of them, that no action should be taken in public which
was contrary to the wishes of any one of the three.

[20] His very first act once consul was to ensure that the proceedings, both of the senate and of the people, should be compiled and
published on a daily basis. He even reinstated the ancient practice by
which, in the months when he did not hold the fasces, he would be
preceded by an orderly, while the lictors would follow behind him.*
However, after the promulgation of the agrarian law, he had his
colleague forcibly expelled from the Forum, when the latter
announced adverse omens.* On the following day Bibulus complained
in the senate, but no one could be found who dared to give an
opinion or offer any censure in response to this piece of arrogance—
though such decrees were frequent in much less serious cases. Bibulus was thus reduced to such despair that he hid himself away at
home until his time as consul came to an end, and did nothing but
issue proclamations announcing adverse omens.* From that time on
Caesar alone administered all public business and dispensed all justice, so that some city-dwellers, putting their seals as witnesses to a
document, jokingly put as the date, not the consulship of Caesar and
Bibulus but the consulship of Julius and Caesar (thus referring twice
to the same man, once with his name, once with his *cognomen*). Soon
the following lines were in common circulation:

> It happened when Caesar was consul—not Bibulus,
>   For nothing happened, as I recall, when Bibulus was consul.

The plain of Stellas, which had been consecrated by our ancestors,
and the Campanian territory, which had been left as a source of revenue for the state, he divided up into plots for twenty thousand
citizens, chosen without a ballot, each of whom had at least three
children. In response to a request from the tax-collectors he agreed
that they should be allowed to reduce their payment to the state by a
third but gave them a public warning against making reckless bids
for future tax-collecting contracts.* His other grants, however generous, no one dared oppose—or if they did, they were frightened off.
When Marcus Cato tried to use his veto,* Caesar gave orders that he
should be dragged out of the senate house by a lictor and taken off to

prison. When Lucius Lucullus stood up to him too openly, Caesar
filled him with such fear lest false charges be brought against him
that, of his own accord, Lucullus fell on his knees before him. And
when Cicero, during the course of a court case, lamented the current
state of affairs, Caesar at once arranged for Cicero's enemy, Publius
Clodius, to be transferred at the ninth hour of the same day* from the
patricians to the plebeians, something Clodius had long been striving
for in vain. Finally, in a move to counter all his opponents at once, he
bribed an informer to confess (according to an agreed plan) that he
had been incited to murder Pompey by certain individuals and, when
brought before the rostra, to name the culprits. However, after the informer named one or two to no effect and had aroused suspicions that
he was a fraud, Caesar abandoned hope that this hastily arranged plan
would come off, and is thought to have had the informer poisoned.

[21] At around the same time he took as his wife Calpurnia,
daughter of Lucius Piso who was to succeed him as consul, while his
own daughter Julia he gave away in marriage to Gnaeus Pompey,
after she had broken her engagement to Servilius Caepio (even
though Caepio had only recently been of great service to Caesar in
his conflict with Bibulus). Once this new link was forged, he began
always to ask Pompey his opinion first, although it had been his
practice to begin with Crassus—and it was customary for the consul
to observe throughout the year the same order which he had established on the first of January.

[22] Thus with the support of his father-in-law and of his son-in-
law, he chose Gaul over all the other provinces, since it offered both
profits and the potential for winning triumphs. Initially, indeed, he
received only Cisalpine Gaul with the addition of Illyria, in accordance with the Vatinian law, but was soon granted 'long-haired' Gaul
also,* as the senators feared that if they refused him this the people
would give it to him. Elated by the pleasure of this success, he had no
qualms, a few days later, in boasting to a packed meeting of the
senate that he had got what he wanted in spite of the opposition and
laments of his enemies, and that from that time forth, he would be
mounting on their heads.* And when someone insultingly observed
that such an action would be difficult for any woman, he replied,
taking up the joke, that Semiramis had reigned in Assyria and the
Amazons had controlled a large part of Asia.*

[23] When his consulship had come to an end and the praetors

Gaius Memmius and Lucius Domitius embarked on an inquiry into his actions during the preceding year, he referred the matter to the senate. And when they did not take it up and three days had been spent in fruitless argument, he left for his province. One of his quaestors was at once arraigned on a number of charges, as a preliminary to proceedings against Caesar himself. Soon, he, too, was summoned to court by Lucius Antistius, tribune of the plebs. However, by appealing to the college of tribunes as a whole, he managed to ensure that he did not stand trial, on the grounds that he was absent on state business. Thus, in order to guarantee his security for the future he took great pains always to put the annual magistrates in his debt, and he would not help any candidates or allow them to be elected unless they undertook to defend him when he was away. Against this purpose he had no hesitation in demanding oaths and even bonds from some people. [24] However, when Lucius Domitius, who was a candidate for the consulship,* openly threatened to do as consul what he had been unable to do as praetor and take control of Caesar's armies, Caesar obliged Crassus and Pompey to come to Luca, a town in his province, where he induced them to stand for the consulship again in order to keep Domitius out. He also contrived through their influence to have his own provincial command extended by five years. Emboldened by this he added to the legions which had been granted him by the state other legions paid for from his own resources. One of these was actually raised in Transalpine Gaul and had a Gallic name—it was known as the Alauda.* This he trained with Roman discipline and decked out with Roman equipment. Later on he gave the entire legion Roman citizenship. After that he did not pass up any opportunity for waging war, no matter how unjustified or how perilous, attacking without provocation allies, as well as enemies and barbarous peoples,* so that at one point the senate sent legates to report on the state of the Gallic provinces and several took the view that Caesar ought to be handed over to the enemy.* But when matters turned out well, he requested and received days of supplication* more frequently and in greater numbers than anyone had ever done before.

[25] His actions during the nine years* for which he held the command were essentially as follows. All of that part of Gaul which is bounded by the pastures of the Pyrenees, the Alps, and Mount Cebenna,* and by the rivers Rhine and Rhône, and whose circum-

ference is around three thousand two hundred miles, he made a
province of the empire (with the exception of some allied states
which had been of service), imposing on this territory a tribute of
forty million sesterces per year. He was the first of the Romans to
construct a bridge and attack the Germans who live beyond the
Rhine, inflicting devastating defeats on them. He also attacked the
Britons, a people previously unfamiliar, and after defeating them
demanded tribute and hostages. Amongst all these successes, he
experienced setbacks on only three occasions. During the British
campaign, his fleet was virtually destroyed due to a violent storm. In
Gaul, a legion was routed at Gergovia, and Titurius and Aurunculus,
his legates, were killed in an ambush on the borders of Germany.

[26] During the same period he lost first his mother, then his
daughter, and not much later his grandchild also. Also during this
time, when the state was in chaos following the murder of Publius
Clodius,* the senate had voted that there should be a single consul
only, naming Gnaeus Pompey. Though the tribunes of the plebs
wanted to make Caesar Pompey's colleague, he persuaded them
rather to propose to the people that he should be permitted to stand
for a second consulship when his provincial command was drawing
to an end, while absent from Rome, so that he would not be obliged
for that purpose to leave the province too soon, before the campaign
was rounded off.* Once he had secured this, he developed more ambitious plans, and, full of expectation, let slip no opportunity to offer
anyone any kind of largesse or assistance, publicly or privately. With
his war spoils, he embarked on the construction of a forum, the land
for which cost more than a hundred million sesterces.* He offered the
people gladiatorial games and a public banquet in memory of his
daughter—something which no one had ever done before.* In order
to arouse people's expectations to the highest degree, he had some of
the preparations for the banquet carried out in his own house—
although he had given a contract to the markets, too. He gave orders
that, whenever famous gladiators fought and were unpopular with
the people, they should be forcibly removed and kept for him.* The
new recruits he had trained not in the gladiatorial school or by professional trainers but by Roman knights in their own homes and even
by senators experienced in warfare, exhorting them with entreaties,
as is shown by his letters, to take the greatest care in the training of
individuals and to direct their exercises in person. He doubled the

legions' pay in perpetuity.* Since corn was plentiful, he had it doled out without limit or measure and on occasion gave each man a slave from among the captives.

[27] In order to retain his connection with Pompey, however, and Pompey's good will, he offered him as wife Octavia, his sister's granddaughter,* although she was married to Gaius Marcellus, and himself asked to marry Pompey's daughter, though she was engaged to Faustus Sulla. When he had put all Pompey's associates and a large part of the senate under obligation to himself through loans made with low interest or none at all, he wooed with the most lavish generosity both those whom he selected from all the remaining orders and those who made requests to him of their own accord, even including freedmen and slaves who were particularly favoured by their patrons or masters. Indeed, he was the only recourse—and a most willing one—for those who were accused of crimes, those who were in debt and spendthrift young people, making exceptions only in the case of those who were so weighed down by accusations or poverty or who were so much in thrall to luxury that even he could not rescue them. To these he would say clearly and openly that what they needed was a civil war.

[28] He took no less trouble to win over kings and provinces throughout the world, offering thousands of prisoners as a gift to some, and to others auxiliary troops, beyond what was authorized by the senate and people, whenever and wherever they required them. Besides this he enhanced the foremost cities of Italy, of the Gallic provinces and the Iberian, as well as those of Asia and Greece, with the most splendid public works. By this time everyone was astonished by his actions and wondered what their object might be. The consul Marcus Claudius Marcellus proclaimed in an edict his intention to take action on a matter of greatest importance to the state and proposed to the senate that Caesar's command should be concluded early, since the campaign was completed, peace prevailed, and the victorious army ought to be disbanded. Nor should his candidacy in the elections be admitted, if he remained absent from Rome, since Pompey, despite his subsequent action, had not annulled the plebiscite. For it had happened that when Pompey drew up the law concerning the rules governing magistracies, he had forgotten to make an exception of Caesar's case in the section which debarred those absent from Rome from standing for election, and it was only

when the law was already inscribed on bronze and lodged in the treasury that he corrected the error. Nor was Marcellus satisfied with snatching from Caesar his provinces and his exceptional privilege, but he even proposed that the colonists, whom Caesar had settled in Novum Comum according to the bill of Vatinius, should be deprived of their citizenship, on the grounds that it had been given them to serve Caesar's own plans and was not authorized by law. [29] Caesar, disturbed by these events and thinking (as they say he was often heard to observe) that it was more difficult to force him down now, when he was leader of the state, from first into second place, than it would be to force him from second place to last, resisted with all his resources, working partly through the vetoes of the tribunes and partly through Servius Sulpicius, the other consul. In the following year, when Gaius Marcellus (who had succeeded his first cousin Marcus as consul) continued the same tactics, Caesar engaged as his defenders by means of extensive bribery Gaius' consular colleague, Aemilius Paulus, and Gaius Curio, the most turbulent of the tribunes. However, when he saw that nothing was going his way and that even the consuls elect were opposed to him, he sent letters begging the senate not to deprive him of the privilege the people had granted him, or else to make the other generals give up their armies also. For he was confident, it is thought, that he would more easily be able to summon his veterans together when he wanted them than Pompey would his new recruits. Besides this he proposed to his opponents that, while giving up eight legions as well as Transalpine Gaul, he should be allowed to retain two legions and the province of Cisalpine Gaul or at least one legion and Illyricum, until he should enter his consulship.

[30] However, when the senate would not intervene and his opponents asserted they would make no bargains concerning the welfare of the state, he crossed into Nearer Gaul and, after completing all the local court hearings, stopped at Ravenna, intending to assert his claim through war, if the senate took any oppressive action in response to intervention on his behalf by the tribunes of the plebs.* And this was Caesar's excuse for civil war. However, people think that there were other reasons too. Gnaeus Pompey used to say that because, with the resources of a private citizen, Caesar could not complete the enterprises he had begun, and could not satisfy the expectations he had aroused among the people regarding his return

to Rome, he wanted to turn everything upside down and bring chaos. Others say that he was afraid of being forced to give an account of the actions he had undertaken in contravention of auspices, laws, and tribunician vetoes during his first consulship.* For Marcus Cato repeatedly declared, even swearing it on oath, that he would impeach Caesar as soon as he had disbanded his army. And it was commonly predicted that, if he returned as a private citizen, he would answer the charges surrounded by armed men, on the precedent of Milo.* Asinius Pollio's account* makes this seem more likely, for he records that when, on the field of Pharsalus, Caesar looked out over his slaughtered and scattered enemies, he uttered the following words: 'It was they who wanted this; for I, Gaius Caesar, would have been found guilty, despite all my achievements, if I had not turned to my army for aid.' There are some who think that he had come to love the habit of command, that, having weighed up the relative strengths of his own and his opponents' resources, he grasped the opportunity to seize the power which he had coveted from his earliest youth. Indeed, it seems that this was the view of Cicero who writes in the third book of his 'On Duties',* that Caesar was always quoting some lines of Euripides, which Cicero himself translates:

> If the law is to be broken, let it be broken
>   That power may be gained; otherwise, respect it.

[31] And so when the news came that the tribunician veto had been overridden and that the tribunes themselves had left Rome, Caesar quickly sent ahead his cohorts under cover. Meanwhile, so that suspicion would not be aroused, he concealed his intentions by himself attending some public spectacles, inspecting plans for the school for gladiators he was planning to build, and later, as was his usual way, throwing himself into the entertainment of numerous guests. Then, after the sun had set, he had mules from the neighbouring bakery harnessed to a carriage and embarked on his journey in the greatest secrecy with a small number of companions. His lights went out and he lost his way, wandering for some time until, at dawn, he located a guide and found the route on foot, following narrow paths. He caught up with his cohorts at the River Rubicon, which was the boundary of his province, where he paused for a while, thinking over the magnitude of what he was planning, then, turning to his closest companions, he said: 'Even now we can still turn back. But once we

have crossed that little bridge, everything must be decided by arms.' [32] As he paused, the following portent occurred. A being of splendid size and beauty suddenly appeared, sitting close by, and playing music on a reed. A large number of shepherds hurried to listen to him and even some of the soldiers left their posts to come, trumpeters among them. From one of these, the apparition seized a trumpet, leapt down to the river, and with a huge blast sounded the call to arms and crossed over to the other bank. Then said Caesar: 'Let us go where the gods have shown us the way and the injustice of our enemies calls us. The die is cast.' [33] And so the army crossed over and welcomed the tribunes of the plebs who had come over to them, having been expelled from Rome. Caesar addressed the soldiers, appealing to their loyalty, with tears, and ripping the garments from his breast. It was even thought that he promised equestrian status to each of them but this view is unfounded. For during the course of his speech as he urged them on, he would often point to the finger of his left hand, emphasizing that to give satisfaction to all those who were going to help him defend his dignity, he would happily tear the ring from his own finger. Those on the edge of the assembly could see better than they could hear and conjectured the meaning of his speech on the basis of his gestures. Thus the rumour spread that he had made a promise of the equestrian ring and four hundred thousand sesterces.*

[34] His subsequent actions may be summed up in order as follows. He occupied Picenum, Umbria, and Etruria and, having defeated Lucius Domitius (who had been nominated his successor now that Italy was at war and was in control of Corfinium* with a garrison) then let him go free, he set off along the Adriatic coast for Brundisium.* It was there that the consuls and Pompey had taken refuge, hoping to make the crossing as soon as possible. Having attempted in vain to impede their escape with all manner of strategems, he returned to Rome, where, having summoned a meeting of the senate to discuss public business, he started out against Pompey's strongest forces, which were in Spain under the command of three of his legates, Marcus Petreius, Lucius Afranius, and Marcus Varro, declaring to his associates beforehand that he would go to the general-less army and then turn to the army-less general. And despite having to lay siege to Massilia, a city along his route which closed its doors to him, and delays caused by a severe

shortage of corn rations, he rapidly brought everything under his control.

[35] From here he returned to Rome, then crossed over to Macedonia where he blockaded Pompey for almost four months behind vast ramparts, before finally defeating him at the battle of Pharsalus* and pursuing him, when he fled to Alexandria. Learning that Pompey had been killed, he waged war against King Ptolemy (for he perceived that the king meant to take him, too, unawares). This was under the most difficult circumstances, as both terrain and timing were against him, for it was the winter season and he was fighting within the city walls of an enemy who was both numerous and very shrewd, while he himself lacked all resources and was quite unprepared. When he won nevertheless, he handed over the kingdom of Egypt to Cleopatra and her younger brother, for he feared to make it into a province lest it should at some point offer a power-hungry governor the means to stir up revolution. From Alexandria he crossed over to Syria and then to Pontus, spurred on by the news that Pharnaces, the son of Mithridates the Great, was taking advantage of the troubled times to make war and was now most formidable after numerous victories. Within five days of his arrival and within four hours of laying eyes on the king, Caesar scattered his forces in a single encounter, often noting the good fortune of Pompey who had secured his greatest military reputation through defeating such a feeble enemy. After that he defeated Scipio and Juba who were stirring up what remained of their adherents in Africa, and the sons of Pompey* in Spain.

[36] During the entire course of the civil wars, Caesar suffered no major setbacks, except through his legates. Of these, Gaius Curio died in Africa, while in Illyricum Gaius Antonius* was taken prisoner by the enemy. Publius Dolabella lost his fleet, also off Illyricum, and Gnaeus Domitius Calvinus lost his army in Pontus. Caesar himself always had the greatest good fortune and his victories always seemed assured, except on two occasions, once at Dyrrhachium, when Pompey repulsed him but did not follow up his advantage—Caesar remarked that Pompey did not know how to conquer him—and again in the final battle in the Spanish campaign, when things looked so bad he even contemplated taking his own life.

[37] When the campaigns were finished, he held triumphs on five occasions, four times in the same month,* after the defeat of Scipio

(though not on succeeding days), and one further time, after the
defeat of the sons of Pompey.* His first and most splendid triumph
was celebrated over Gaul, the next over Alexandria, then Pontus,
after that Africa, and finally Spain, on each occasion with different
equipment and displays. On the day of the triumph over Gaul, when
he was travelling through the Velabrum, he was almost thrown from
his chariot when the axle broke. He climbed the Capitol by torchlight, with forty elephants bearing lamps to the right and to the left.
In his triumph over Pontus, one of the the carts in the processions
had on the front of it a placard with the words 'I came, I saw, I
conquered', not detailing the events of the campaign, as was the case
with the others, but emphasizing the speed with which it was
completed.*

[38] To every one of the foot soldiers of his veteran legionaries he
gave as booty (besides the two thousand which he had paid each at
the beginning of the civil conflict) twenty-four thousand sesterces.
He also gave them plots of land, though not all together, so as to
avoid displacing any property holders. To each man of the people he
gave, besides two modii of wheat and two pounds of oil, the three
hundred sesterces he had once promised, along with an extra hundred to make up for the delay. He also remitted a year's rent to those
in Rome who paid up to two thousand sesterces and in Italy up to
five hundred. He added a banquet and a distribution of meat and,
after the Spanish victory, two dinners. For when he decided that the
first had been rather mean and not served with his customary liberality, five days later he provided another one which was most lavish.

[39] He sponsored spectacles of various kinds: a gladiatorial contest, plays in all regions of the city, and performed by actors in every
language, as well as circus performances, athletic contests, and a sea-
battle. In a gladiatorial fight in the Forum, Furius Leptinius, a man
of praetorian family, and Quintus Calpenus, who had once been a
senator and legal advocate, fought to the finish.* The children of the
princes of Asia and Bithynia performed a Pyrrhic dance.* During the
plays, the Roman knight Decimus Laberius performed in a mime he
himself had written and, when he was given five hundred thousand
sesterces and a golden ring,* he left the stage and crossed the
orchestra to take his seat in the fourteen rows.* For the circus races,
the area of the circus itself was extended at either end, with a broad
canal surrounding the circuit. Here the most noble young men made

displays with four-horse and two-horse chariots and by jumping
between pairs of horses. Two squadrons, one of older and one of
younger boys, performed the Troy game.* Five days of animal fights
were provided. For the final one, two battle lines were drawn up,
with five hundred foot soldiers, twenty elephants, and three hundred
knights assigned to each side. And so that there would be more space
for the encounter, the central barriers were removed and in their
place two camps were set up, one facing the other. In a temporary
stadium contructed in an area of the Campus Martius, athletes competed for three days. In the sea-battle, which took place on a lake
excavated in the lesser Codeta,* ships with two, three, and four banks
of oars from the Tyrian and Egyptian fleets engaged, manned by a
huge number of fighters. Drawn by all these spectacles, a vast number of people flooded into Rome from every region, so that many of
the visitors had to lodge in tents put up in the streets or along the
roads. And the crowds were so great on a number of occasions that
many people were crushed to death, even including two senators.

[40] After this Caesar turned to the reorganization of the state,
reforming the calendar which had been so disrupted through the
negligence of the *pontifices* and their arbitrary use of intercalation
over a long period of time* that the harvest festivals no longer fell in
the summer and those celebrating the vintage no longer fell in the
autumn. Caesar adjusted the calendar to the course of the sun, so
that there were three hundred and sixty-five days and, abolishing
the intercalary month, he instituted an extra day to be added to
every fourth year. However, in order to make the arrangement work
from the following first of January, he added two extra months
between November and December. Thus that year, since it also had
an intercalary month according to the old practice, lasted fifteen
months.

[41] He increased the membership of the senate* and made new
appointments to the ranks of the patricians,* as well as adding to the
number of praetors, aediles, quaestors, and also minor magistrates.*
He restored to the senate those who had been expelled as a result of a
decision of the censors* or had been condemned by the court for
electoral corruption.* He shared the choice of higher magistrates
with the popular assemblies so that, except in the case of candidates
for the consulship, half the posts were filled by those chosen by the
people, the rest by those whom he himself selected. He would also

circulate brief written statements to the voting tribes: 'The dictator Caesar to this tribe. I commend to you this man and that man, so that they may hold their positions with the support of your votes.' He also allowed the sons of the proscribed to compete for office.* He reduced the number of categories of judges to two, the equestrian and the senatorial, abolishing that of the paymasters which had been the third.*

He held a census of the people, not in the traditional manner or place, but proceeding street by street, getting information through the landlords of housing blocks. He reduced the number receiving the public corn-dole from 300,000 to 150,000. And, to avoid the convening of further assemblies for enrolment purposes, he arranged that the places of those who died should be filled each year by the praetors from among those not on the list, chosen by ballot.

[42] Having sent out eighty thousand citizens to settle in colonies overseas, he prescribed—in order to maintain the population of the now depleted city—that no citizen older than twenty and younger than forty,* unless he was on military service, should be absent from Italy for more than three years at a time, that no senator's son should travel abroad unless serving as an officer or accompanying a magistrate, and also that cattle farmers should have youths of free birth as no less than a third of their herdsmen. He conferred citizenship on all who practised medicine or taught liberal arts in Rome, so that they would more willingly continue to live in the city and that others, too, might join them. In order to dispel the hope that debts might be abolished—for which there was frequent pressure—he finally decreed concerning money lent at interest that debtors should satisfy their creditors by means of property handed over in accordance with its purchase value before the civil war, deducting from the principal whatever interest had been paid or pledged. This measure reduced the amount of debt by around a quarter. He dissolved all guilds, apart from those of ancient foundation.* He increased the penalties for crimes and, since the wealthy were more ready to become involved in crime because they were merely exiled without loss of property, he prescribed, according to Cicero,* that those guilty of murdering a close relative should forfeit all their possessions, while those guilty of other crimes should forfeit half.

[43] He administered justice most conscientiously and strictly. He even expelled from the senate those condemned of extortion. He

dissolved the marriage of a man of praetorian rank on the grounds that he married his wife just two days after her previous husband had divorced her, although there was no suspicion of adultery. He imposed customs duties on imported merchandise. He banned the use of litters, and the wearing of purple-dyed garments and of pearls, except in the case of those of a particular position and age and on set days. He particularly enforced sumptuary legislation, stationing inspectors all around the meat-market who were to confiscate and bring to him any forbidden delicacies which were put out for sale, and sometimes he sent out lictors and soldiers who were even to remove dishes from dining-tables which had escaped the scrutiny of the inspectors.

[44] Day by day he developed more numerous and more ambitious plans both for the enhancement and improved organization of the city and for the security and expansion of the empire. First, he planned to construct a temple to Mars of unprecedented size, having filled in and made level the lake where he had staged the sea-battle, and also a theatre of enormous magnitude, to be located just by the Tarpeian rock.* He also intended to reduce the body of civil law and reorganize the best and most useful elements of that vast and amorphous collection into the smallest possible number of books. He planned to open libraries of works in Greek and Latin to the most extensive possible public, putting Marcus Varro* in charge of equipping and managing them; also to drain the Pontine marshes, to empty the Fucine lake, to make a road from the Adriatic sea, along the ridge of the Apennines, as far as the Tiber, to cut a canal through the Isthmus, to contain the Dacians who were overrunning Pontus and Thrace; and then to make war on the Parthians, through lesser Armenia, engaging in battle with them, however, only if he had first tested their forces.*

As he was contemplating and setting about these projects death cut him short. But before I give an account of that, it will not be inappropriate to set out in summary form the details of his appearance, comportment, dress and conduct, as well as matters relating to his governmental and military undertakings.

[45] It is said that he was of lofty stature and fair complexion, with well-formed limbs, rather a full face, and keen, dark eyes. His health was good, although towards the end of his life he used to faint all of a sudden and even had nightmares. On two occasions, also, he suffered

an epileptic fit while engaged in public business. He was most particular in the care of his person—not only did he have his hair cut and face shaved scrupulously but he also had his body hair plucked out—as some have alleged with disapproval.* He regretted most bitterly the loss of his looks through baldness and was often the butt of jokes on the subject from his detractors. For this reason he was in the habit of combing his thinning hair upwards from his crown and, out of all the honours decreed to him by the senate and people, he accepted and took advantage of none so willingly as the right to wear his laurel wreath in perpetuity.

Even the manner of his dress was out of the ordinary. For he would wear a broad-striped tunic with fringed sleeves down to his wrists,* and always belted on the outside—though he wore his belt rather loosely.* Indeed, this is what provoked the warning Sulla is supposed to have given the aristocrats on numerous occasions: 'Beware of the boy with the loose belt.'

[46] He first lived in a modest house in the Subura.* Later, however, when he was Pontifex Maximus, he lived on the Sacred Way in the official residence. Many record his great passion for luxuries and refinements: that he had razed to the ground a villa on Lake Nemi, which he had completed from its foundations at vast expense, because he was not completely satisfied with it (even though he was at that time short of funds and in debt); that when he was on campaign, he would take around with him materials for the construction of mosaic and cut-marble floors; [47] that his invasion of Britain was motivated by the hope he would find pearls there and that in estimating their size he would sometimes feel their weight in his own hand; he was a most avid collector of jewels, embossed metalwork, statues, and paintings from earlier times; his fine-looking and well-educated household slaves were purchased at great expense, something of which even he himself was ashamed, so that he would not let the sums be entered in his accounts; [48] he regularly hosted parties throughout the provinces, using two dining-rooms, soldiers and foreigners reclining in one, and respectable Roman civilians with distinguished provincials in the other. He was so strict in the regulation of his household, regarding matters both great and small, that he had his baker put in fetters for serving bread to the guests different from that which was served to himself,* and imposed capital punishment on one of his favourite freedmen because he had

committed adultery with the wife of a Roman knight (even though no complaint was made against him).

[49] There were no stains on his reputation for manliness, apart from his stay with King Nicomedes, which was a constant source of criticism and was mentioned in taunts from every quarter. I shall not discuss* the notorious lines of Licinius Calvus: 'Whatever Bithynia ever owned and Caesar's buggerer'—not to mention the speeches made against him by Dolabella and the elder Curio, in which Curio called Caesar the queen's concubine and the inner partner of the royal litter, while Curio spoke of the whorehouse of Nicomedes and the Bithynian brothel. I am also passing over the edicts of Bibulus in which he decries his colleague as the queen of Bithynia, alleging that the man who was once in love with a king was now in love with a king's power. It was at that time, Marcus Brutus reports, that a certain Octavius, who, being not quite right in the head, was rather outspoken, at a large gathering called Pompey king and greeted Caesar as queen. Gaius Memmius, however, even accuses him of acting as cup-bearer to Nicomedes with the rest of his catamites at a large party, attended by, among others, some Roman traders, whose names Memmius lists. Cicero, however, was not content with having written in certain letters that Caesar had been led by courtiers into the king's chamber where he reclined on a golden bed with purple coverlet, and that the virginity of the man descended from Venus was lost in Bithynia; he once remarked, when Caesar was speaking in the senate in defence of Nysa, the daughter of Nicomedes, and recalling the king's kindness to himself: 'Make no mention of that, I beg you, for it is well known what he gave you and what you gave him.' Finally, in his triumph over Gaul, his men chanted, among the other songs soldiers usually come out with as they march behind the chariot,* the following most notorious lines:

> Caesar had his way with Gaul;
> Nicomedes had his way with Caesar:
> Behold now Caesar, conqueror of Gaul, in triumph,
> Not so, Nicomedes, conqueror of Caesar.

[50] Everyone agrees that he was inclined to be unrestrained and extravagant in love-affairs and that he damaged the reputations of a great many women of rank, including Postumia, wife of Servius Sulpicius, Lollia, wife of Aulus Gabinius, Tertulla, wife of Marcus

Crassus, and even Mucia, the wife of Gnaeus Pompey. Certainly
Pompey was criticized by the elder and the younger Curios and by
many others when, having divorced a wife who had borne him three
children because of the man he used to lament as an Aegisthus,* he
later took the same man's daughter in marriage* because of his own
lust for power. But above all Caesar loved Servilia, the mother of
Marcus Brutus, for whom, during his last consulship, he bought a
pearl worth six million sesterces and, in the course of the civil war, in
addition to other gifts, knocked down to her some extensive estates
which were on sale at auction at a very modest price. Indeed many
were astonished at the low price and Cicero wittily remarked: 'The
price was higher for a third was knocked off.' For it was believed that
Servilia was prostituting her daughter, Tertia,* to him. [51] Nor did
he refrain from affairs in the provinces, as emerges particularly from
this couplet, also declaimed by the soldiers in the Gallic triumph:

Men of Rome, look out for your wives; we're bringing the bald adulterer
  home.
In Gaul you fucked your way through a fortune, which you borrowed here
  in Rome.

[52] He also had love-affairs with queens, among them Eunoe of
Mauretania, the wife of Bogud,* to whom and to whose husband
Caesar gave many, great gifts, as Naso* records. But most particularly
he loved Cleopatra, with whom he often prolonged parties until
dawn, and with her, too, he journeyed by royal barge deep into
Egypt, and would have reached Ethiopia but his army refused to
follow him. Moreover, he welcomed her to Rome* and only let her go
home when he had showered her with the greatest honours and gifts.
The child born to her he allowed to be called by his name. Indeed,
several Greek writers record that he was like Caesar in both appearance and bearing. Mark Antony confirmed to the senate that Caesar
had actually acknowledged the child and that Gaius Matius, Gaius
Oppius, and others of Caesar's friends were aware of this.* However,
Gaius Oppius published a book, as though the matter needed some
excuse and defence, alleging that the boy was not, as Cleopatra
claimed, the child of Caesar. Helvius Cinna, tribune of the plebs,*
confessed to several people that he had had ready the text of a
law, which Caesar had instructed should be passed during his
own absence, to the effect that he should be permitted to marry

whichever and however many women he pleased for the purpose of having children. And lest there should be any doubt as to his shocking reputation for submitting himself to men and for adultery, the elder Curio, in one of his speeches, termed Caesar 'a man to every woman and a woman to every man'.

[53] Not even his enemies denied that he was very sparing in his consumption of wine. It was Marcus Cato who said: 'Caesar's the only man to have tried to overturn the state when sober.' Indeed, Gaius Oppius records that he was so indifferent to what he consumed that, on one occasion, when his host had served stale oil instead of fresh, and no one else would touch the food, Caesar ate heartily, so that he should not seem to be reproaching his host either for carelessness or for lack of manners.

[54] However, he showed no restraint as a magistrate or general. For as some have borne witness in their memoirs, as governor in Spain* he took money from allies on false pretences in order to pay off his debts, and made hostile raids on some towns of the Lusitani, though they had obeyed his orders and opened their gates when he approached. In Gaul, he despoiled shrines and temples to the gods of their offerings and destroyed cities more often in the hope of booty than because they had committed some offence. It was for this reason that he had so much gold and sold it throughout Italy and the provinces for three thousand sesterces a pound.* During his first consulship, he stole three thousand pounds of gold from the Capitol, replacing it with the same quantity of gilded bronze.* He exchanged alliances and kingdoms at a price, extorting from Ptolemy alone nearly six thousand talents, in his own name and that of Pompey. Later, indeed, he covered the burdensome costs of his civil wars, his triumphs and his public munificence through the most outrageous pillage and sacrilege.

[55] As regards both eloquence and military skills he either equalled or excelled in glory the very best. He was certainly counted among the leading advocates, after his speech against Dolabella.* Indeed, when Cicero, in his 'Brutus', goes through the orators, he says he cannot see to whom Caesar would take second place, describing him as maintaining a style of speech which is elegant, impressive, too, and even splendid and ample.* And to Cornelius Nepos he writes thus on the same subject: 'What then? Who, of all those whose only business is oratory, would you place above him as an orator? Whose

witticisms are sharper or more numerous? Who is more vivid or more elegant in his choice of words?' In his youth he seems to have modelled his style on that of Caesar Strabo,* even using for a proposed speech of his own some phrases from the speech Strabo wrote on behalf of the Sardinians. He is said to have had a high voice when speaking in public, with impassioned movements and gestures, and considerable charm. He left a number of speeches, among them some attributed to him on poor grounds. With some justification, Augustus was of the view that the text of Caesar's 'On Behalf of Metellus' was a version taken down by stenographers who failed to follow accurately what he said, rather than written by himself. For in some texts I find that the title is recorded not as 'On Behalf of Metellus' but rather 'A Speech Written for Metellus', although the words seem to be spoken by Caesar, in defence of Metellus and himself, refuting accusations brought against them both by common opponents.* The authenticity of another speech, 'To the Soldiers in Spain', is also doubted by Augustus, although it survives in two sections, one apparently delivered at the first battle, the other at the second (at which Asinius Pollio says he had no time to give an address, as he suddenly came under attack from the enemy).

[56] He also left 'Commentaries' on his actions in the Gallic war and the civil war against Pompey, though the authorship of the works on the Alexandrian war, the African war, and the Spanish war is uncertain. Some think it was Oppius, others Hirtius. Certainly it was the latter who completed the final and unfinished book of the Gallic war.* Cicero has the following comments on Caesar's 'Commentaries', again in the 'Brutus': 'The "Commentaries" he wrote are most worthy of praise. They are plain, direct, and elegant, almost naked in their lack of all ornament. Yet though it was his aim that they should serve others as a ready basis on which those who wished might write proper histories, he perhaps encouraged the foolish who want to crimp and curl their material but he deterred sensible men from putting pen to paper.'* On the same 'Commentaries', Hirtius makes the following pronouncement: 'They are so much approved of in the judgement of all, that they seem to have removed rather than provided an opportunity for writers. Yet the admiration I feel is even greater than that felt by others. For while they know how well and purely they are written, I know how easily and quickly he did it.'* Asinius Pollio thought they were written carelessly and inaccurately,

for often Caesar was too ready to credit other people's accounts of their actions and gave a rather faulty version of his own, perhaps on purpose, perhaps even misremembering. It was his plan to rewrite and correct them. He also left a work in two books 'On Analogy'* and the same number of speeches in criticism of Cato,* as well as a poem entitled 'The Journey'. The first of these works he composed during his crossing of the Alps, when he was on his way back from Cisalpine Gaul to join his army after dispensing justice in the local courts, the speeches against Cato during the time after the battle of Munda, and the poem during a journey of twenty-four days from Rome to the further part of Spain. There are also some letters which he wrote to the senate. He seems to have been the first to send these written in columns to form a short book of record, for previously consuls and generals had always written straight across the scroll.* There are also letters to Cicero* and to close friends concerning private matters, in which, if he wanted to communicate something secretly, he would write in code, changing the order of the letters of the alphabet, so that not a word could be made out. To decipher this and read it, one must substitute for each letter the one which comes four places later, thus 'D' for 'A' and so on. There are also some works which he is said to have written in his boyhood and adolescence, including 'The Praises of Hercules' and a tragedy 'Oedipus', as well as a collection of sayings. However, Augustus prohibited the publication of any of these works,* in a short and direct letter which he sent to Pompeius Macrus, who had been given the task of organizing the libraries.

[57] He was most talented in the use of arms and in horse-riding and had astonishing powers of endurance. On the march, he would sometimes precede his men on horseback, more often on foot, his head uncovered, rain or shine. He completed the most lengthy journeys at incredible speed, covering a hundred miles a day, when travelling light in a hired carriage. If rivers were going to cause delay, he would cross them either by swimming or else using inflated skins as floats, so that he often arrived in advance of the messengers sent to announce him.

[58] In the conduct of his expeditions, it is hard to say whether he was more cautious or more daring. He would never take his troops on a route where they might be vulnerable to ambush unless he had first made an inspection of the country, nor did he transport them to

Britain until he had personally organized an investigation of the harbours, the route and points of access to the island. Moreover, when he heard news that his camp was under siege in Germany, he made his way there through the enemy posts, disguised as a Gaul. He crossed from Brundisium to Dyrrhachium in winter, passing among the ships of the enemy and, when his troops hesitated, after he had ordered them to follow, and would not respond when he repeatedly summoned them, finally he himself, with his head covered, secretly embarked on his own into a little boat by night, not revealing his identity nor allowing the captain to yield to the hostile weather, until he was almost capsized by the waves.

[59] He was never induced to abandon or postpone any enterprise through regard for omens.* He did not put off his expedition against Scipio and Juba,* when the victim escaped as he was trying to make a sacrifice.* Even when he fell to the ground on disembarking from his ship he interpreted this as a positive omen: 'I've got you, Africa,' he said. And in order to get around the prophecies which proclaimed that the name of Scipio was fated to be fortunate and invincible in that province, he included in his entourage a very degraded member of the Cornelian family, who was known as Salvito, due to the disreputable life he led.* [60] He would commence battle not just when he had planned to do so but also if opportunities arose, often straight after a march, and sometimes in the most dreadful weather conditions, when his action would be least expected. It was only towards the very end that he was more reluctant to join battle, considering that, the more victories he had won, the less he ought to tempt fate and that a victory could never bring him as much as a defeat could take away. He never routed his enemies without also driving them out of their camp, not letting up even when they were terrified. When the outcome of a battle was uncertain, he would send away the horses, his own among the first, in order to force his men to stay by removing their means of flight. [61] Indeed, his horse was an extraordinary creature, whose feet were almost human, for its hooves were divided so that they looked like toes. When this horse was born on his estate, seers interpreted it as an omen that Caesar would become lord of all the world. He raised it with great care and was himself the first to ride it—it would tolerate no other rider. Later on he even dedicated a statue of it before the temple of Venus Genetrix.

[62] When his army was losing ground, he would often rally his

men single-handed, standing in the way of those who were fleeing, laying hold of each soldier, even grabbing them by the throat and turning them round to face the enemy. Some of them were indeed so terrified that one standard-bearer even threatened Caesar with the point of his standard when Caesar tried to hold him up, while another left him holding the standard, when Caesar stood in his way. [63] His determination was just as great, and even more clearly demonstrated. After the battle of Pharsalus, when he had sent his forces on ahead into Asia and was crossing the straits of the Hellespont by ferry, Lucius Cassius, who was on the enemy side, obstructed his way with ten battleships. But Caesar did not retreat and, as he drew near, encouraged Cassius to give himself up, then took him on board as a suppliant. [64] Engaged in attacking a bridge near Alexandria, he was forced by a sudden enemy onslaught to take to a boat, which many others also rushed to join. He then jumped into the sea and swam two hundred yards to the nearest ship, all the while holding up his left hand so that the papers he was holding would not get wet, and dragging his military cloak* gripped between his teeth so that it would not be taken by the enemy as a trophy.

[65] The value he placed on his soldiers was determined not by their character or station in life but by their prowess alone. He would treat them with strictness and indulgence in equal measure. For he would not impose restraints on them at all times and in all places but only when the enemy was at hand. Then, however, he would impose the very strictest discipline, never announcing beforehand when a march or battle would take place but keeping his men ready and alert at all times, so that he might suddenly lead them forth wherever he wished. On many occasions he would do this even when he had no cause, particularly during rainstorms or on feast days. Issuing frequent warnings that they should watch him closely, he would often slip away by day or by night and go on a longer march in order to tire out those who were lagging behind. [66] When his men were stricken with fear by rumours concerning the enemy's numbers, rather than seeking to play them down or deny them he would instead reinforce them with exaggeration and embellishment. Thus when there was great alarm at the imminent arrival of Juba, he summoned his soldiers to an assembly and declared: 'You should know that in a very few days the king will arrive with ten legions, thirty thousand cavalry, a hundred thousand light infantry and three

hundred elephants. So let people leave off asking any more questions or speculating, and believe what I say, for my information is reliable. Otherwise I shall give orders that they be put in a worn-out boat to be carried away to whatever lands the wind takes them.'

[67] Some offences he would overlook or not punish in accordance with regular discipline. Rather, while he was extremely strict in investigating and punishing desertion or mutiny, he would take little notice of other things. Sometimes, when they had fought a great battle and been victorious, he would let his men off their duties and allow everyone to indulge themselves as they pleased. And he used to boast that his soldiers could fight well even when they were dripping with perfume.* In assemblies he would address them not as 'soldiers' but by the more flattering term 'comrades'* and he so looked after their appearance that he had their weapons polished and decorated with gold and silver, both for show—and so that the men would keep hold of them more determinedly in battle, fearing the cost of replacement. He had such affection for his men that when news came of the Titurian disaster,* he let his hair and beard grow and would not cut them until he had secured vengeance.

[68] By these means he made his men utterly loyal to him and supremely brave as well. When he embarked on civil war, every centurion of every legion offered to supply a horseman from his own funds and all his soldiers offered their service without pay and without rations—for the wealthier ones took care of the needs of those of limited resources. Nor throughout that long period did anyone whatsoever desert his cause. Indeed, many of them, when as captives they were offered their lives on condition that they take up arms against Caesar, refused. So great was their ability to tolerate hunger and other deprivations, not only when they were besieged but even when they themselves laid siege to others, that when Pompey saw among the defence works at Dyrrhachium* some of the bread made from grasses with which they were sustaining themselves, he remarked that he was at war with wild beasts, and gave orders that the bread should be taken away and concealed from everyone, lest knowledge of the enemy's endurance and tenacity should break the spirits of his men.

How bravely they fought is shown by the fact that on the one occasion, at Dyrrhachium, when the fighting went against them and they asked of their own accord for punishment, their leader felt obliged to console rather than punish them. In other battles, though they were fewer in number, they readily overcame countless enemy troops. Indeed, one cohort of the sixth legion, left in charge of a stronghold, kept four of Pompey's legions at bay for a number of hours, though nearly all of them had been wounded by the enemy's arrows, of which a hundred and thirty thousand* were later found within the palisade. And no wonder if one considers individual cases, such as that of the centurion Cassius Scaeva or the regular soldier Gaius Acilius, not to mention many others. Scaeva had lost an eye and was hit in the thigh and the shoulder, while his shield had received a hundred and twenty strikes, yet he still kept control of the gate into the fortress. During the naval battle at Massilia Acilius had his right hand chopped off when he laid hold of an enemy prow but, imitating the famous example set by the Greek Cynegirus,* leapt into the ship, driving back his assailants with the boss of his shield. [69] During the ten years of the Gallic war, they did not once mutiny. There were a few occasions during the civil wars but they speedily returned to their duties, in response to their general's authority rather than any leniency on his part. For he would never give ground to trouble-makers but always went forth to meet them. Indeed, at Placentia,* though Pompey's forces were still at large, he declared the entire ninth legion dishonourably dismissed, only agreeing to reinstate them after many abject entreaties and when those responsible had been punished. [70] When the men of the tenth legion demanded retirement and bonuses at Rome, threatening serious harm against the city, at a time when the war was raging in Africa, he did not hesitate to go to them, though his friends advised against it, and disband them. But with one word—addressing them as citizens rather than soldiers—he won them over and brought them round, for they at once replied that they were his soldiers and, although he asked them not to, they followed him to Africa of their own accord. Even then he imposed on the most troublesome a fine of a third of the booty and the land which they had been due to receive.*

[71] Even when he was a young man he was unfailing in his care for and loyalty toward his supporters. He defended the young aristocrat Masintha* so stalwartly against King Hiempsal that in the quarrel he pulled the beard of King Juba's son.* When Masintha was declared tributary to the king, Caesar at once snatched him away from those who were trying to arrest him and hid him at his own

house for some time. Soon afterwards, setting out for Spain after his praetorship,* he carried him off concealed in his own litter, which was surrounded by friends paying their respects, as well as the lictors with their fasces.*

[72] He always treated his friends with such consideration and kindness that once, when Gaius Oppius was accompanying him on a journey through woodland and was suddenly taken ill, Caesar let him have the only shelter available, himself sleeping on the ground in the open air. Once he had taken control of the state, however, he promoted to the most elevated positions some who were of very humble origins and, when he was criticized for this, he declared openly that if he had made use of the help of brigands and cut-throats in defending his honour, he would reward even such men with equal favour. [73] On the other hand, he never maintained such serious grudges that he would not readily relinquish them, if the occasion arose. Despite Gaius Memmius' ferocious speeches against him, to which he had replied with equal sharpness, Caesar even gave him his backing when he sought the consulship.* When Gaius Calvus, after writing defamatory epigrams, sent friends to request a reconciliation, Caesar anticipated him, unprompted, with a letter of his own.* As for Valerius Catullus, whose verses about Mamurra had done lasting damage to his reputation* as Caesar did not deny, when he apologized, Caesar invited him to dinner that very day and continued to exchange hospitality with his father, as he was accustomed to do.

[74] Even in taking his revenge he was naturally inclined toward leniency. When he had at his mercy the pirates who had captured him, he had them crucified, since he had earlier sworn that he would do so, but he gave orders that they should be strangled first.* He could never bring himself to harm Cornelius Phagites, who lay in wait for him at night during the time when he was sick and in hiding, so that it was only by handing over a large sum of money that he was able to escape being delivered to Sulla.* When Philemon, his slave-secretary, had promised Caesar's enemies that he would bring about his death through poison, Caesar merely put him to death without further punishment.* When he was summoned as a witness in the case against Publius Clodius, who was accused of adultery with Caesar's wife Pompeia and at the same time of polluting religious rites, he denied that he knew anything of the matter, though his

mother Aurelia and his sister Julia had faithfully told the whole story before the same judges. And when he was asked why, if he knew nothing, he had nevertheless divorced his wife, he replied: 'In my view, my family needs to be as much free of suspicion as free of crime.'*

[75] He certainly showed astonishing moderation and mercy both during the period of his rule and after his victory in the civil war. When Pompey proclaimed that anyone who did not fight for the republic would be deemed an enemy, Caesar declared that he would count among his allies those who were undecided or belonged to neither party. To all those whom he had promoted to the rank of centurion on Pompey's recommendation, he gave permission to go over to Pompey's side. When conditions of surrender were under discussion at Ilerda and, during the frequent comings and goings between the two sides, Afranius and Petreius, suddenly changing their minds, seized some Caesarian agents, who were in their camp and killed them, Caesar could not bring himself to duplicate the act of treachery that had been committed against him.* In the course of the battle of Pharsalus, he proclaimed that citizens were to be spared, and later he allowed each of his men to save any man he chose of the opposite party. And it will be found that, apart from those who died in battle, none of the Pompeians lost their lives, with the exception of Afranius, Faustus, and the young Lucius Caesar.* And even these, it is thought, were not killed through any wish of Caesar's. The first two had rebelled after seeking and obtaining forgiveness, while Lucius Caesar had cruelly put to death Julius' slaves and freedmen with fire and the sword and had also slaughtered the animals which Julius had bought for a public entertainment. Finally, at the conclusion of the war, he gave permission to all those whom he had not already forgiven to return to Italy and to hold magistracies and army commands. He had even restored to their position the statues of Lucius Sulla and of Pompey which had been broken up by the common people.* And thereafter, if anyone planned or said anything threatening against him, he preferred to restrain rather than punish them. He thus took no further action against conspiracies and night-time meetings other than to make clear through edicts that he was aware of them. When people spoke of him critically, he was content to urge in public that they should desist. He bore with good grace the harm to his reputation caused by the most defamatory

book written by Aulus and Caecina and the highly abusive poems of Pitholaus.*

[76] However, other things he did and said outweighed these, so that it is thought he abused his power and was justly killed. Not only did he accept excessive honours—one consulship after another,* the dictatorship in perpetuity, responsibility for morals,* as well as the forename 'Imperator' and the title 'Father of his Fatherland', a statue displayed with those of the kings,* and a raised seat at the theatre—he even allowed privileges to be bestowed on him which were greater than is right for mortals: a golden seat in the senate house and in front of the speaker's platform, a chariot and litter in the procession for the circus games,* temples, altars, statues placed beside those of the gods, a couch,* a priest,* an extra college of Luperci,* and a month of the year named after him.* Indeed, there were no honours which he did not either confer or receive as he willed. His third and fourth consulships he held in name only, contenting himself with the powers of the dictatorship, which had been conferred on him at the same time as the consulships. And in each of these two years, he appointed two consuls in his place for the final three months, in the mean time holding no elections apart from those for tribunes of the plebs and the plebeian aediles. He also appointed prefects, rather than praetors, who were to take care of affairs in the city during his absence.* When one of the consuls suddenly died the day before the Kalends of January, he gave the office to a man who requested it for the few hours it was vacant. And with equal disregard for law and traditional practice, he allocated magistracies for several years in advance, conferred the emblems of consular rank on ten ex-praetors, and admitted to the Senate men who had been given citizenship, some of whom were half-barbarous Gauls. Moreover, he put his own slaves in charge of the mint and the collection of public revenues and delegated the care and command of three legions, which he had left at Alexandria, to Rufio,* the son of his freedman and one of his pretty boys.

[77] His public sayings, as recorded by Titus Ampius,* were characterized by equal arrogance: 'The republic is nothing—just a name, without substance or form,' 'Sulla was a fool when he gave up the dictatorship,' 'Men should now have more consideration in speaking with me and regard what I say as law.' Such was the level of insolence he reached that, when a seer pronounced of a sacrifice

that the entrails were ominous and the heart was missing, Caesar declared that future sacrifices would be better, since such was his wish, nor should it be thought a sign of ill omen, if an animal had no heart.*

[78] However, the extreme and fatal envy he inspired was particularly provoked by the following: when the entire senate came to him, bringing many decrees conferring the highest honours, he received them in front of the temple of Venus Genetrix, without getting up. Some think that he was held back when he tried to rise by Cornelius Balbus. Others believe that he made no attempt to get up and that when Gaius Trebatius actually advised him to rise, he gave him a very hostile look. This action of his seemed the more intolerable, because, when during his triumph he rode past the tribunes' benches, he himself had been so indignant at Pontius Aquila,* one of the tribunes, who had remained seated, that he declared: 'So tribune Aquila, take the republic from me!' And for days afterwards he would make no promises to anyone, except with the condition, 'So long as Pontius Aquila permits.' [79] He added to this insult, showing his contempt for the senate, another deed of even greater insolence. For when, at the time of the Latin festival* he was returning to the city, amid the other excessive and unprecedented demonstrations by the people, one member of the crowd had placed a laurel crown, bound with a white ribbon,* on his statue and the tribunes of the plebs, Epidius Marullus and Caesetius Flavus had given orders that the ribbon should be removed from the crown and that the man should be thrown into chains. Caesar, regretting, perhaps, that the reference to kingship had met with such a poor reception, or else, as he claimed, that he had been robbed of the glory to be had from refusing the honour, took the tribunes severely to task and deprived them of their authority. And after that time he was never able to shake off the rumour that his ambition was to take the title of king, even though, when the common people greeted him as king, he replied that he was not King but Caesar* and when, during the Lupercalia,* the consul Antony several times brought a diadem toward his head as he stood before the rostra, he pushed it away and had it sent to the Capitol to Jupiter Best and Greatest.* Indeed, various rumours were in circulation—that he was planning to move to Alexandria or to Troy, taking with him the riches of the empire, since Italy was now depleted by levies, and leaving the city of Rome

to be looked after by his associates; and that at the next meeting of the senate Lucius Cotta would announce the proposal of the Board of Fifteen* that, since the oracular books stated that the Parthians could not be beaten except by a king, Caesar should be given the title 'king'.*

[80] It was for this reason that the conspirators decided to speed up their planned action, in order to avoid having to give their assent to such a proposal. And so they all brought together the various plans which they had previously pondered separately in groups of two or three. For the people were unhappy at the present state of affairs, making covert—and even public—criticisms of Caesar's tyranny and demanding champions. When foreigners were admitted to the senate, the following placard was set up: 'Well done, those who refuse to show a new senator where the senate house is!' And the following verse was heard everywhere:

> Caesar led Gauls in his triumph—and into the senate house;
> The Gauls put aside their trousers and put on the broad stripe.*

When Quintus Maximus, who had been made suffect consul for three months, entered the theatre and the lictor gave the usual sign to take note of his arrival, there was a unanimous shout, 'He is no consul!' At the elections, after the tribunes Caesetius and Marullus had been removed from their posts, a number of votes were found proposing them as consuls. Some people wrote on the statue of Lucius Brutus:* 'If only you were living!' and on that of Caesar himself:

> Brutus was made first consul, since he threw out the kings,
> He, since he's thrown out the consuls, eventually gets to be king.

More than sixty people were involved in the conspiracy against him; the leaders were Gaius Cassius and Marcus and Decimus Brutus. At first they were in doubt as to whether, during the elections in the Campus Martius when he was calling the tribes to vote, they should divide into groups and throw him from the bridge,* then hold him and kill him, or else if they should attack him on the Sacred Way* or at the entrance to the theatre. When it was announced that the senate meeting on the Ides of March would take place in Pompey's Senate Chamber,* they readily chose this time and place instead.

[81] Caesar's murder was, however, foretold by clear portents. A

few months beforehand, some colonists, sent in accordance with the Julian law to the colony of Capua,* were tearing down some ancient tombs, in order to construct villas, and were working all the harder since, looking carefully, they were discovering a number of vessels of ancient workmanship, when they found a bronze tablet, fixed on a tomb, which was said to be that of Capys,* founder of Capua, and bearing a message in Greek words and characters to this effect: 'When the bones of Capys are moved, it shall come to pass that one of his descendants shall be slain at the hands of a kinsman, and soon afterwards avenged—a great disaster for Italy.' The source for this— lest anyone should think it a fiction or fantasy—is Cornelius Balbus, a very close friend of Caesar. And just a few days before, the news came that some herds of horses which Caesar had dedicated to the River Rubicon when he crossed it, letting them wander free without a keeper, were obstinately refusing food and weeping copiously. When Caesar was making a sacrifice the seer Spurinna warned him to look out for danger which would come no later than the Ides of March. The day before the same Ides, when a king's bird* was flying toward Pompey's Senate Chamber, with a laurel sprig in its mouth, other birds of various kinds from a nearby grove attacked it and tore it to pieces in the same Chamber. And that very night which ushered in the fatal day, Caesar himself had a dream, in which he was some- times flying above the clouds and sometimes joining his right hand with that of Jupiter,* while his wife Calpurnia had a vision in which the pediment* of the house fell in and her husband was run through in her arms. Then suddenly the doors of the bedchamber flew open of their own accord.

Because of these things—and because his health was poor— Caesar long debated whether to stay in and postpone the business he had meant to undertake in the senate. In the end, when Decimus Brutus pressed him not to disappoint the packed meeting which had now been waiting for some time, he made up his mind and set out, when it was almost the fifth hour.* He thrust in amongst the papers he held in his left hand, intending to read them later, the message which someone he met on the way held out to him, giving him warning of the conspiracy. Then, though he could not get favourable omens, despite sacrificing a number of victims, he entered the Senate Chamber, dismissing religious scruple and mocking Spurinna for making false predictions, since the Ides of March had come and brought him no harm. Spurinna, however, replied that though they had come, they had not yet gone. [82] When he was seated, the conspirators gathered around him, as if to show their respect, and immediately Tillius Cimber, who had taken on the task of initiating the action, came up close to Caesar, as though about to make a request. When Caesar shook his head and waved him away, putting off his business for another time, Cimber grabbed his toga at the shoulders. Caesar then cried out 'But this is force!' and one of the Casca brothers stabbed him from behind, just below the throat. Caesar grabbed Casca's arm and ran him through with a writing implement but, as he tried to leap forward, he was held back by another wound. When he realized that he was being attacked on all sides with drawn daggers, he wrapped his toga around his head, at the same time using his left hand to pull it down over his thighs, so that, with the lower part of his body also covered, his fall would be more decent. And so it was that he was stabbed twenty-three times, saying nothing and letting out merely a single groan, at the first blow—though some people relate that when Marcus Brutus came at him, he said in Greek: 'You, too, my son?' He lay lifeless for some time, after everyone had run off, until three young slaves put him on a litter and carried him home, one arm dangling. Among all those wounds, according to Antistius the doctor, none was fatal with the exception of the second he received, in his breast.

It was the conspirators' intention to drag the dead man's body into the Tiber,* seize his goods and rescind his legislation, but they abandoned this plan through fear of the consul Mark Antony and the Master of Horse, Lepidus. [83] In response to the request of his father-in-law, Lucius Piso, Caesar's will was opened and read out in Antony's house (he had written it on the Ides of September of the previous year* in his villa near Lavicum and given it for safe-keeping to the chief Vestal Virgin). Quintus Tubero records that, from the time of Pompey's first consulship right up to the start of the civil war, he was in the habit of designating Gnaeus Pompey as his heir and this was announced to a gathering of soldiers. But in his final will, he designated as his three heirs his sisters' grandsons, Gaius Octavius to receive three-quarters of the estate, and then Lucius Pinarius and Quintus Pedius to share the rest.* At the end of the document, he even adopted Gaius Octavius into his family and gave him his name. Quite a few of his assailants were nominated as tutors to his son, in case he should have one, while Decimus Brutus was even among the heirs in the second rank.* To the Roman people he left his gardens on the banks of the Tiber for public use and to each man three hundred sesterces.

[84] When the funeral was announced, a pyre was built on the Campus Martius next to the tomb of Julia* and on the rostra was placed a golden shrine, modelled on the temple of Venus Genetrix.* Within was an ivory couch with gold and purple coverings and at its head stood a pillar hung with the clothes he was wearing when he was killed. Since it seemed there would not be enough time in the day for those making offerings, instructions were given that there should be no procession but that they should make their way by any city streets they chose and bring their gifts to the Campus Martius. As part of the funeral games, some songs were sung which were adapted from Pacuvius' 'Judgement of Arms' to express grief and anger at Caesar's killing:

> Did I save these that they should murder me?

as well as comments to similar effect from Atilius' 'Electra'.* In place of the funeral oration, the consul Mark Antony had a herald read out the senate's decisions to vote Caesar all honours both human and divine and also the oath by which they all had bound themselves to ensure his safety. To these statements he added a few brief words of his own. Magistrates and ex-magistrates carried the bier from the rostra down into the forum. While some were urging that he be cremated within the temple of Jupiter Capitolinus and others in Pompey's Senate Chamber, all of a sudden two figures appeared, girt with swords and each brandishing two javelins. With blazing torches they set fire to the bier and immediately the crowd of bystanders loaded on dry branches, the judgement seats, and the benches, as well as anything else that could serve as an offering. Then the flute-players and the actors* tore off the clothes which they had taken from among the triumphal finery to wear for the occasion, ripped them up and threw them into the flames, while veteran legionary soldiers threw on the weapons with which they had decked them-selves out for the funeral. A considerable number of matrons, too, threw on the jewellery they were wearing, as well as the amulets and togas of their children. At the height of public grief, a crowd of foreigners gathered in groups and lamented Caesar, each in their

own way, in particular the Jews,* who flocked to the funeral pyre
night after night. [85] Straight after the funeral the common people
made for the houses of Brutus and Cassius armed with torches and
were only just held back. Encountering Helvius Cinna* and confus-
ing his name with that of Cornelius Cinna for whom they were
searching because the previous day he had spoken out in strong
terms against Caesar, they killed him and carried round his head
impaled on a spear. Later on they set up a solid pillar of Numidian
marble almost twenty feet high in the Forum and inscribed it with
the words 'To the Father of the Fatherland'. And for long afterwards
they continued to make sacrifices there, undertake vows, and to sort
out certain disputes by an oath made in Caesar's name.

[86] Caesar left some of those close to him with the suspicion that
he had no wish to live much longer and had taken no precautions,
since his health was deteriorating, and that it was for this reason that
he took little notice either of portents or of the advice of his friends.
There are those who think that he had such faith in the most recent
decree of the senate and their oath that he dismissed the armed
guard of Spanish troops who had previously attended him. Others
take a different view, holding that he preferred to fall victim just
once to the plots that threatened him from all sides, rather than be
perpetually on guard against them. Some say that he was even in the
habit of remarking that his safety was more a matter of concern for
the republic than it was for him. After all, he had long ago achieved
outstanding powers and honours. However, if anything happened
to him, the republic would not remain at peace but, its condition
quickly deteriorating, it would soon suffer civil war.

[87] Nearly all authorities agree that his death was of just the kind
of which he approved. For once, when he read in Xenophon* that
during his last illness Cyrus had sent some instructions concerning
his funeral, he expressed contempt for this slow mode of death,
preferring a sudden and rapid end. The day before he died, a discussion had arisen over dinner at Marcus Lepidus' house as to what was
the best way to finish one's life, in which Caesar voiced his preference for a death which was quick and unexpected.

[88] He died in the fifty-sixth year of his life* and was included in
the ranks of the gods, not only by formal decree but also by the
conviction of the common people. Indeed, at the first games which
were given after his deification by his heir Augustus, a comet shone,

appearing around the eleventh hour* for seven days in succession and
it was believed to be the soul of Caesar who had been received into
heaven. For this reason, a star is placed on top of the head of his
statue.

It was decided that the Senate Chamber, in which he was killed,
should be closed off and that senate meetings were never to take
place on the Ides of March which should be renamed the Day of
Parricide. [89] Of the murderers, virtually none survived more than
three years or met a natural end. All were condemned, each meeting
a different fate, some by shipwreck, others in battle. A few even took
their own lives with the same dagger they had used to make their
impious attack on Caesar.

THE DEIFIED AUGUSTUS

[1] That the Octavii were in ancient times the leading family in Velitrae* is affirmed by many indications. An area in the busiest part of town long ago had the name 'Octavian' and an altar was to be seen dedicated by an Octavius. This man, when serving as leader in a war with a neighbouring people, happened to be in the middle of making an offering to Mars when he heard the news that the enemy had suddenly attacked. Snatching the victim's entrails from the fire, he presented them half raw before commencing the battle from which he returned victorious. There was also a decree of the people on record, prescribing that in future, too, the entrails should be offered to Mars in the same way and that the remaining parts of the sacrificial victims should be given to the Octavii.

[2] The family had been enrolled in the senate among the minor families* by King Tarquinius Priscus. Then, soon afterwards, they were included among the patricians by King Servius Tullius. In the course of time they transferred themselves to the plebeians, then, after a long interval, they returned, through the agency of the Deified Julius, to the patriciate.* The first of the family to be elected to a magistracy by the vote of the people was Gaius Rufus. As an ex-quaestor, he fathered two sons, Gnaeus and Gaius, who in turn produced the two branches of the Octavian family. These two branches were very different in their fortunes: Gnaeus and his descendants all held the highest magistracies, while Gaius and his progeny, whether by chance or through their own wishes, remained in the equestrian order down to the time of Augustus' father.

An ancestor of Augustus served as a military tribune in Sicily under the command of Aemilius Papus during the Second Punic War.* Augustus' grandfather, a man of considerable wealth, lived in great tranquillity to a ripe old age, having satisfied his ambitions with service as a municipal magistrate. That story is, however, told by others; Augustus himself writes no more than that he was born into an old-established and prosperous equestrian family, his father being the first in the family to attain senatorial rank. Mark Antony taunts Augustus with having as his great-grandfather an ex-slave who had earned his living as a rope-maker in the neighbourhood of Thurii, while his grandfather was a financial agent. I have not been able to find out anything more about Augustus' ancestors on his father's side.

[3] His father, Gaius Octavius, was from his earliest years a man of great wealth and reputation, so I at least am surprised that some claim that he too was a financial agent and even that he was employed to distribute bribes and perform other services relating to elections in the Campus Martius.* For he grew up sustained by an ample fortune and had no trouble in securing offices which he fulfilled with distinction. After his praetorship he acquired by lot the province of Macedonia. On his way to the province he carried out an extraordinary commission from the senate, wiping out the gang of runaway slaves (remnants of the armies of Spartacus and Catiline) who were occupying the countryside around Thurii.* In governing his province he displayed justice and bravery in equal measures. Not only did he defeat the Bessi* and the Thracians in a great battle but his treatment of our allies was such that Cicero, in letters which are in existence, urged and advised his brother Quintus (at that time serving as proconsul of Asia with too little success) that he should imitate his neighbour Octavius in securing the favour of our allies.* [4] Returning from Macedonia, he met a sudden death before he could declare himself a candidate for the consulship. Three children survived him: the elder Octavia, whose mother was Ancharia, and the two he had by Atia, the younger Octavia and Augustus.

Atia was the daughter of Marcus Atius Balbus and Julia, who was the sister of Julius Caesar. Balbus' father's family came from Aricia and displayed many senatorial portraits,* while on his mother's side he was very closely related to Pompey the Great. He himself served as praetor before going on to take part in the twenty-man commission responsible for dividing the Campanian territory among the Roman people, as prescribed by the Julian law.* Here again Mark Antony has disparaged Augustus' ancestry, casting aspersions on his mother's family also. He alleges that Augustus' maternal great-grandfather came of African stock and earned his living first by keeping an oil-shop and later a bakery in Aricia. Cassius of Parma, for his part, taunts Augustus in a letter with being the grandson not only of a baker but also of a money-changer, alleging: 'Your mother's dough came from the crudest bakery in Aricia; a money-changer from Nerulum shaped the loaf with his filthy hands.'

[5] Augustus was born a little before sunrise eight days before the Kalends of October* in the consulship of Marcus Tullius Cicero and Gaius Antonius, at the Ox Heads in the Palatine district, on the spot where he now has a shrine, established shortly after he died. For, according to senate records, one Gaius Laetorius, a young man of patrician family, in an attempt to mitigate a penalty for adultery, which he claimed was too severe for one of his age and family, also drew to the attention of the senators the fact that he was the possessor and, as it were, guardian of the spot which the Deified Augustus first touched at his birth, and sought pardon for the sake of what he termed his own particular god. It was then decreed that this part of the house should be consecrated. [6] To this day his nursery is displayed in what was his grandfather's country home near Velitrae. The room is very modest, like a pantry. People in those parts believe he was actually born here. No one goes into this room unless it is essential and even then they undergo ritual purification first, for there is a long-established belief that those who enter incautiously are seized with trembling and fear. Indeed, this was later confirmed. The new owner of the villa, either by chance or because he wanted to test the story, went to sleep in that room and it happened that before the night was far advanced he was suddenly thrust out by an unknown force and they found him lying with his bed-clothes outside the door, in a semiconscious state.

[7] When he was a baby Augustus was given the name Thurinus, either to commemorate the place of his ancestors' origin, or because it was in the area around Thurii that his father Octavius, soon after his birth, had successfully waged war on the runaway slaves. That he was surnamed Thurinus I can relate on reliable authority for I myself obtained a little bust of him when he was a child, an old one of bronze with this name inscribed on it in letters of iron, now almost worn away. I made a present of this bust to the emperor,* who worships it among the Lares of his private apartment. But Mark Antony in his letters regularly calls Augustus Thurinus by way of an insult. Augustus responded to this merely with an expression of surprise that his old name should be thrown at him as if it were a term of abuse. Later on he took the surnames of Gaius Caesar and then of Augustus, the first in accordance with the will of his great-uncle, the second on the proposal of Munatius Plancus. Responding to the suggestion of others that Augustus ought to be called Romulus

on the grounds he too was, as it were, a founder of the city, Munatius argued successfully that he should rather take the name Augustus, a name not only new but also grander. For holy places, also, and places where something has been consecrated by augural rites are termed 'august' [*augusta*], either from the term for an increase in dignity [*auctus*] or from the phrase denoting the movements or feeding of birds [*avium gestus gustusve*], as Ennius* too tells us when he writes:

> After renowned Rome was founded with august augury . . .

[8] He lost his father when he was four years old. In his twelfth year, he gave a funeral oration in honour of his grandmother Julia in front of an assembly of the people. Four years after he had taken on the toga of manhood he received military gifts in Caesar's African triumph, although he had taken no part in the war on account of his age. Soon afterwards, when his great-uncle had set out for Spain to make war on the sons of Pompey, Octavian went out after him, although he had only just recovered from a serious illness.* Moreover, despite suffering a shipwreck and travelling with only a handful of companions along roads beset by the enemy, he won the good opinion of Caesar who soon came to appreciate not only his endeavour in making the journey but also the strength of his character.

After he had retaken the Iberian provinces Caesar was planning an expedition against the Dacians and then the Parthians; Octavian, who had been sent on ahead to Apollonia, devoted himself in the mean time to study. When he first learned that Caesar had been killed and that he himself was his heir, he hesitated for some time as to whether he should call on the neighbouring legions for assistance, eventually dismissing the idea as premature and hasty. Instead, he returned to Rome to claim his inheritance, despite his mother's unease and the insistent attempts of his stepfather, the ex-consul Marcius Philippus, to dissuade him. Then he levied armies and held control of the state, first with Mark Antony and Marcus Lepidus, then just with Antony for nearly twelve years, and lastly for forty-four years on his own.

[9] Having stated the main themes, as it were, of his life, I shall set out the individual details, not according to the order of events but by topic so that they may be more clearly perceived and assessed.

He was five times involved in civil war, with campaigns at Mutina, Philippi, Perusia, in Sicily, and at Actium. In the first and last, he fought against Mark Antony, the second against Brutus and Cassius, the third against Lucius Antonius, brother of the triumvir, and the fourth against Sextus Pompeius, son of Gnaeus Pompey. [10] In all cases his reason and motive for embarking on civil war was the following: he held that his foremost duty was to avenge the death of his great-uncle and protect his achievements. As soon as he returned from Apollonia, he decided to attack Brutus and Cassius first by force, hoping to catch them unawares, then, when they foresaw the danger and escaped, through the courts where they were declared guilty of murder in their absence. Moreover, he himself provided games to celebrate Caesar's victories, since those who had been given responsiblity for this had not dared to do it. And, in order that he might have more authority in carrying out this and other plans, when one of the tribunes of the plebs happened to die, he offered himself as a candidate, even though he came from a patrician family and was not a senator.* However, the consul Mark Antony, whom he had counted on as his prime supporter, opposed all his undertakings, demanding a heavy bribe without which he refused even common and ordinary justice in any matter. So he transferred his support to the optimates, though he knew they regarded him with hostility, particularly because he was fighting a campaign to expel Decimus Brutus (who was at that time besieged in Mutina) from the province conferred on him by Caesar and ratified by the senate. With the encouragement of some, Octavian contracted hired assassins against him. Then, when the plot was discovered and he feared retaliation, he engaged the services of veterans to protect himself and the republic, offering them as large a reward as he was able. Placed in command of the army he had raised, with the rank of pro-praetor, he was instructed to give support to Hirtius and Pansa (who had become consuls) in the war against Decimus Brutus. Within three months he had brought to an end in two battles the war which had been entrusted to him. In the first, Mark Antony writes that he had run away, finally reappearing two days later with neither military dress nor horse. In the second it was commonly agreed that he had fulfilled his role not only as leader but even as a soldier in the midst of the fighting, taking the standards on his own shoulders, when the standard bearer of his legion was seriously wounded, and carrying them for some time.

[11] Since, in the course of this war, Hirtius died in the line of

battle and Pansa not long afterwards from a wound, a rumour developed that both had been killed through his agency so that, with Antony routed and the state bereft of both consuls, he would be left with sole command over the victorious forces. Indeed, the death of Pansa aroused such suspicion that the doctor Glyco was imprisoned on the grounds that he had applied poison to the wound. Aquilius Niger adds to this that Octavian himself actually killed one of the consuls, Hirtius, in the heat of the battle. [12] However, when he learned that Antony, having fled from Rome, was welcomed by Marcus Lepidus and that other leaders and armies were seeking to come to terms in support of their party, he renounced the optimates' cause without delay, alleging as the pretext for his change of side the words and acts of certain men, some of whom called him a boy, while others pronounced that he should be honoured then disposed of,* so that neither he nor the veterans would need to receive their due. And, to display more clearly how much he regretted his former association, he imposed an enormous fine on the citizens of Nursia and, when they could not pay it, banished them from their city, because they had at public expense erected a monument to those of their fellow citizens who had fallen at Mutina, inscribing on it that they had given their lives for liberty.

[13] Having embarked on an alliance with Antony and Lepidus, although he was weak and unwell, he brought the war at Philippi to a close also, in two battles, in the first of which he was driven from his camp and scarcely managed to escape to Antony's wing.* He was not restrained in victory but sent the head of Brutus to Rome to be thrown at the foot of Caesar's statue, and was savage in his treatment of the most prominent of the captives, not even sparing them insulting language. When one begged him piteously for burial he is said to have replied that the birds would decide. When two others, a father and son, begged for their lives, they say he ordered them to draw lots or play mora,* to determine which of them should have his own life spared, and watched them both die, for, when the father, who had offered to be the one to die, was killed, he then made the son take his own life too. For this reason the others, amongst whom was Marcus Favonius (that emulator of Cato), when they were led past in chains, respectfully acknowledged Antony as victorious general but openly reviled Octavian with the most insulting abuse.

After victory, responsibilities were divided between them, with

Antony taking control of the east and Octavian assuming the task of returning the veterans to Italy and securing land for them in the municipalities. However, he could satisfy neither the veterans nor the landowners, for the latter complained that they were being pushed off their land and the former that they were not being given the treatment their good service had deserved.

[14] At that time he forced Lucius Antonius (who, trusting in the consulship, which he held at the time, and in his brother's power, was plotting to seize control) to take refuge in Perusia* and starved him into surrender, not without enduring great risks himself both before the war and during it.* For, when, during some games, he gave orders that the official should remove a common soldier who was sitting in the fourteen rows reserved for the orders,* a rumour was spread by his detractors that he had later had this same man tortured and killed, and he only just escaped death himself, as an angry crowd of soldiers gathered. What saved him was the sudden appearance of the missing man, safe and sound. Then, when he was offering a sacrifice near the walls of Perusia, he almost fell into the hands of a group of gladiators who had burst out of the town.

[15] After the capture of Perusia,* he inflicted punishment on a large number of people, responding to all those who begged for mercy or sought pardon with the same words: 'You must die.' Some people record that three hundred senators and equestrians were selected from those who had surrendered to be slaughtered like sacrificial victims on the Ides of March at the altar dedicated to the Divine Julius. There are some who relate that he engineered the war with the specific purpose that those who were secretly opposed to him and supported him through fear rather than choice would be tempted to follow Lucius Antonius' lead, and that when he had defeated them and confiscated their property he would be able to give the veterans the rewards they had been promised.

[16] The Sicilian war* he began early on but it was long drawn out with frequent interruptions, sometimes for the ships to be repaired which he had lost as a result of two wrecks caused by storms, even though it was summer, and sometimes when peace was made in response to the demands of the people (for supplies were cut off and there was a famine of increasing severity). Eventually, once the ships were repaired and twenty thousand slaves were given their freedom so that they could serve as oarsmen, he created the Julian harbour at

Baiae by letting the sea into lakes Lucrinus and Avernus. And, having trained his forces here the whole winter long, he defeated Sextus
Pompeius between Mylae and Naulochus, though on the brink of
battle he had been so deeply asleep all of a sudden that his friends
had to wake him so that he could give the signal. This was, I should
think, the source of Mark Antony's criticisms: that he could not even
give his line of battle a proper inspection but lay on his back in a
stupor, his gaze heavenward, and did not get up and appear before
his men until Marcus Agrippa had already routed the enemy ships.
Others criticize his words and actions, claiming that when the ships
were lost in the storm he had cried out that he would conquer even
against the will of Neptune and that the next time the circus games
were held, he had Neptune's image removed from the festival procession.* And scarcely did he endure any more or greater dangers in
any of his other wars. When his army had crossed over to Sicily and
he had returned to the mainland to collect the remaining part of his
forces, he was ambushed by Sextus Pompeius' commanders, Demochares and Apollophanes, and in the end only just managed to escape
with one boat. Again, when he was going on foot via Locri to
Regium, he caught sight of some of Pompeius' biremes coasting
along the shore and, thinking they were his, went down to the water,
where he was almost captured. Morever, as he was escaping along
remote footpaths, a slave of his one-time friend Aemilius Paulus, still
grieving at the proscription of Paulus' father* for which Augustus
had been responsible, saw this as an opportunity for revenge and
tried to kill him. After the flight of Pompeius, his other colleague
Marcus Lepidus, whom he had summoned from Africa to his aid,
ambitious and confident with his twenty legions, laid claim to sole
power with dire threats. Augustus wrested his army from him and,
allowing him his life in response to his entreaties, banished him to
Circeii* for the rest of his life.

[17] He finally broke off his alliance with Antony, which had
always been shaky and unreliable, though patched up at various
times with reconciliations, and, in order to demonstrate more clearly
how Antony had abandoned the ways of a Roman citizen, he made
sure that the will (which Antony had left in Rome) naming even his
children by Cleopatra among his heirs, was opened and read out
before an assembly of the people. Once Antony was declared an
enemy, however, he did send out to him all his relatives and friends,

including Gaius Sosius and Gnaeus* Domitius, who were still at that time consuls. He publicly gave leave, also, to the people of Bononia* not to join all of the rest of Italy in swearing to uphold his own cause, on the grounds that they had been among the clients of Antony's family from days of old. Not long afterwards he was victorious in the naval battle at Actium,* though the battle continued until such a late hour that even the victor was obliged to spend the night on board ship. Leaving Actium, he moved on to winter quarters on Samos, where he received the disturbing news that the troops whom, after the victory, he had selected from all the army divisions and sent on ahead to Brundisium, were mutinying, demanding booty and their discharge. Octavian set out for Italy, his crossing twice disrupted by storms, first as he passed between the headlands of the Peloponnese and Aetolia and then again off the Ceraunian mountains.* He lost a number of his galleys on each occasion, while the one he was travelling in had its rigging torn away and its rudder broken. After remaining in Brundisium a mere twenty-seven days, during which time he satisfied all the demands of his soldiers, he travelled around via Asia and Syria to Egypt. He laid siege to Alexandria, where Antony and Cleopatra had taken refuge, and soon gained possession of the city. Antony, indeed, who made a belated attempt to come to terms, he forced to kill himself (Octavian viewed his dead body). Cleopatra he greatly desired to lead as a captive in his triumphal procession and even had Psylli* brought to her who were to suck out the venomous liquid—it was believed that her death was caused by the bite of an asp. He honoured them both with a joint burial, giving orders that the tomb which they themselves had started to build should be completed. The younger Antony (the elder of his two sons by Fulvia) Octavian dragged away from a statue of the Deified Julius where he had taken refuge when his repeated entreaties were having no effect, and killed. Caesarion too, whom Cleopatra claimed was fathered by Julius Caesar, he had captured as he tried to flee, tortured, and put to death. The other children of Antony and Cleopatra he spared and, afterwards, as if they were bound to him by family ties, he provided for them and looked after them in a manner appropriate to their rank.

[18] At that time also he paid homage to the sarcophagus containing the remains of Alexander the Great, laying a golden crown on it and scattering it with flowers when it was brought out from its inner

chamber for him to see.* When he was asked if he would also like to view the tomb of the Ptolemies, he replied that he wanted to see a king, not dead bodies. He reduced Egypt to the status of a province and, so as to make it a readier and more fruitful source for Rome's grain supply, he made use of his soldiers to clear out all the channels into which the Nile overflows, as they had silted up over the years. So that the victory at Actium would be even more celebrated in the memory of future generations, he founded the city of Nicopolis nearby and established games there to take place every five years. He enlarged the ancient temple of Apollo and, having adorned the place where his camp had been with spoils from the enemy ships, he dedicated it to Neptune and Mars.

[19] After this there were quite a few disturbances, plans for rebellion, and conspiracies, which he took action against, having got wind of them on a number of different occasions before they came to fruition. They included that of the young Lepidus,* later that of Varro Murena and Fannius Caepio, shortly afterwards that of Marcus Egnatius, then Plautius Rufus and Lucius Paulus, husband of the emperor's granddaughter.* Besides these, there was Lucius Audasius, who had been charged with forgery and was both aged and infirm, and Asinius Epicadus, a half-breed of Parthian blood, and finally Telephus, a woman's slave and usher. For among those who conspired against him and endangered his life were numbered even men of the lowest sort. Audasius and Epicadus planned to bring his daughter Julia and grandson Agrippa from the islands where they were confined, to the armies, while Telephus planned to attack both the emperor and the senate, in the belief that he himself was destined by fate to rule. Indeed, on one occasion a servant attached to the Illyrian army was arrested one night just by his sleeping quarters, armed with a hunting knife, having slipped past the door-keepers. It was unclear whether he had lost his mind or was feigning insanity, for he could not be made to say anything even under torture.

[20] He himself conducted a total of two foreign wars, that against Dalmatia when he was still a young man and that against the Cantabrians, after the defeat of Antony.* He was even wounded in the course of the Dalmatian war, when in one battle his right knee was hit by a stone, and on another occasion he suffered wounds to a leg and both arms when a bridge collapsed. His other wars were conducted through legates, though he did intervene or come near to it during

the campaigns against the Pannonians and Germans, advancing from Rome as far as Ravenna, Milan, and Aquileia. [21] Nevertheless, he conquered Cantabria, Aquitaine, Pannonia, Dalmatia together with the whole of Illyria, also Raetia and the Vindelicii and Salassi, peoples of the Alpine regions, in some cases leading the troops himself, in some with others acting under his auspices. He also put a stop to the incursions of the Dacian forces, slaughtering three of their leaders as well as a large number of men. He forced the Germans back beyond the River Albis,* with the exception of the Suebi and the Sigambri who submitted to him. These he transported to Gaul where they were settled in a region on the banks of the Rhine. Other peoples who gave trouble he also reduced to submission. Nor did he make war on any people without just and pressing cause. So far was he from being motivated by the desire for additions to his territories or to his martial glory that he forced certain German chieftains to take an oath in the Temple of Mars the Avenger that they would faithfully observe the peace that they themselves requested, and from some, indeed, he tried to exact hostages of a new kind— women—because he felt they did not care enough about men who were left as pledges. Yet he allowed everyone the opportunity to take back their hostages whenever they wished. Nor, in the case of those engaging in more protracted or perfidious rebellion, did he ever exact any more severe penalty than the sale into slavery, in accordance with the law, of captives who were not to be employed in a nearby region nor to be set free within a thirty-year period. Through his reputation for virtue and moderation, he induced even the Indians and Scythians, peoples known to us only by report, to send agents, unprompted, in order to obtain the friendship of himself and the Roman people. The Parthians, too, readily conceded to him, even when he laid claim to Armenia, and, offering hostages as well, returned the military standards, when he asked for them, which they had taken from Marcus Crassus and Mark Antony.* Morever, when a number of men were competing to be their king, they would not approve a candidate until one was chosen by Augustus.

[22] Since the foundation of the city, Janus Quirinus had been closed before Augustus' time on only two occasions.* Having obtained peace by land and by sea, he closed it on three occasions in the space of a much briefer period. Twice he entered the city celebrating an ovation, after the battle of Philippi and, again, after the

Sicilian war. He held three regular triumphs, for Dalmatia, Actium, and Alexandria, all in the same continuous three-day period.

[23] He suffered only two humiliating disasters, both, indeed, in Germany, that of Lollius and that of Varus.* The Lollian disaster was more a matter of loss of face than of real damage, but in the Varian he sustained the almost catastrophic loss of three legions, slaughtered together with their commander, their legates, and all their auxiliary forces. When it was first reported he set up watches throughout Rome in case there should be any disturbance and he extended the periods of office for the provincial governors so that the allies would be kept in check by men of experience who were known to them. He vowed major games to Jupiter Best and Greatest, in the hope that the state might return to a better condition (which had come about in the course of the war against the Cimbri and the Marsi). Indeed, it is said that he was so disturbed that for months at a time he let his beard and hair grow and would hit his head against the door, shouting: 'Quintilius Varus, give me back my legions!' And for years he marked the anniversary of the disaster as a day of mourning and sadness.

[24] In military matters he brought changes and innovations in many areas and also reinstated some practices from the old days. He enforced discipline most strictly, not allowing even his legates to visit their wives, except most grudgingly and in the wintertime. A Roman knight, who had cut off the thumbs of his young sons so that they might be unfit for military service, he had sold at auction, together with his property. However, when he saw that some tax-gatherers were about to buy him, he made him over to a freedman of his own so that he would be allowed to live as a free man, though kept away from the city. When the tenth legion were insolent in obeying orders he gave them all a dishonourable discharge and, when other legions insistently demanded release, he let them go but without the rewards they were due for their length of service. If any of his cohorts yielded ground in battle, he had every tenth man killed and fed the rest on barley.* If any centurion left his post he punished him with death, as he did the ordinary soldiers. In the case of other offences, he applied various humiliating penalties; for instance, men might be ordered to stand for the whole day in front of the commander's quarters, sometimes wearing unbelted tunics or else carrying ten-foot measuring poles or even a lump of turf.*

[25] After the civil wars neither in the assembly nor in his edicts did he address any soldiers as his 'comrades' but as 'soldiers', nor did he allow his sons* or stepsons, when they held military commands, to use any other term of address, for he thought the term 'comrades' too ingratiating to be consistent with military order, or the current state of peace, or the dignity of his own family.* Except in the case of fire in Rome or if disturbance was feared when there were difficulties with the corn supply, he used freedmen as soldiers on only two occasions, once to protect those colonies adjoining Illyria and once to safeguard the bank of the River Rhine. These men he levied from men and women of some wealth and immediately set them free, placing them under the same standard so that they were not mixed with the men of free birth, nor equipped with the same arms. As military prizes he was more ready to confer trappings or collars (prized for their gold and silver) rather than he was crowns for scaling ramparts or walls, which brought greater honour. The latter he distributed very sparingly but without favour and often even to private soldiers. He presented Marcus Agrippa with a blue banner in Sicily after his naval victory.* It was only those who had celebrated triumphs, although they had accompanied him on military expeditions and taken part in his victories, that he did not consider should share in such honours, on the grounds that they themselves also had the right to award them to whomever they chose. His view was that nothing so little became a great leader as haste and rashness. Often he would proclaim the following: 'Make haste slowly!'; 'A safe commander's better than a bold one',* and 'Whatever is done well is done with speed enough.' He said that one should never embark on a battle or a war unless the hope of profit was shown to be greater than the fear of loss. For he used to compare those who sought a minimal gain at no small risk to someone going fishing with a golden hook, when no catch could bring a profit equal to the loss if the hook were gone.

[26] He received magistracies and honours before the prescribed age, some of which were newly devised and in perpetuity. The consulship he appropriated in his twentieth year, having positioned his legions near the city ready to attack and sent men to demand it for him in the name of the army.* However, when the senate hesitated, the centurion Cornelius, who led the delegation, threw back his cloak, pointed to the hilt of his sword and did not shrink from

saying in the senate house: 'This will do it if you don't.' His second consulship he held nine years later and the third after a further year; after that he was consul for successive years until he held the office for the eleventh time.* Subsequently he turned it down on the many occasions it was offered, until after a great interval of seventeen years, he accepted it for the twelfth time and then two years later he sought it of his own accord for the thirteenth time,* so that it was as holder of the highest magistracy that he led each of his two sons, Gaius and Lucius, into the Forum to embark upon their public careers. The five consulships from the sixth to the tenth he held for the full year, the others for nine, or for six, or four, or three months, though the second he held just for a few hours. For, on the morning of the first day of January, after he had sat for a short time in his curule seat in front of the temple of Capitoline Jupiter, he gave up the honour and appointed another to his place as substitute. He did not begin them all in Rome,* though, taking up his fourth in Asia, his fifth on the island of Samos, and his eighth and ninth in Tarraco.

[27] For ten years he ruled as part of the triumvirate for reconstituting the state. Although he resisted somewhat longer than his colleagues the option of proscriptions, once they were embarked upon he was more severe than either of the others. For while they were swayed in many cases by personal considerations and entreaties in favour of particular individuals, he alone argued strongly that no one should be spared. He proscribed even Gaius Toranius, his own guardian, who had been his father Octavius' colleague as aedile. Julius Saturninus records this, too, that when the proscriptions were finished and Marcus Lepidus, speaking in the senate, defended what had happened but offered hope of clemency for the future, on the grounds that sufficient punishment had been exacted, Octavian by contrast declared that he had only consented to the proscriptions on condition that all possibilities would remain open to him in future. However, as a sign that he regretted this intransigence, he later raised Titus Vinius Philopoemen to the status of knight because he was said to have concealed his patron when the latter was proscribed.* As triumvir, too, he provoked unpopularity in many ways. For once, when he was addressing the soldiers and a crowd of civilians had been allowed to listen, he noticed that Pinarius, a Roman knight, was writing something down and, thinking that he was an informer and a

spy, gave orders that he be run through on the spot. As for the consul designate, Tedius Afer, who had been complaining spitefully about some deed of his, he terrified him with such dire threats that he hurled himself to his death. And when the praetor Quintus Gallius came to pay his respects with some folded tablets covered by his cloak, Octavian, suspecting him of concealing a sword, did not dare to have him searched at once, in case it should turn out to be something else, but soon afterwards had him seized from the tribunal by centurions and their men and subjected to torture as if he were a slave. And, when he admitted nothing, he gave orders that he should be killed, first gouging out the man's eyes with his own hand. He wrote, however, that the man had asked for an audience then treacherously attacked him and that, after he had been thrown into custody and then sent into exile, he had met his end in a shipwreck or an attack by thieves.

He accepted tribunician power in perpetuity and on one occasion and then another chose a colleague,* each for periods of five years. He also accepted the supervision of morals and of laws in perpetuity and it was through this authority, even though he was not censor, that he three times conducted a census of the people, the first and third times with a colleague,* the second on his own.

[28] On two occasions he considered yielding up the state, first just after the fall of Antony, mindful that Antony had often criticized him for standing in the way of its restoration, and then as a result of exhaustion after a long illness, even going so far as to summon the magistrates and senate to his house and giving them an account of the state of the empire. However, taking the view that he himself would be in some danger as a private citizen and that it was rash to entrust the state to the judgement of the many, he continued to hold power. It is hard to say whether his intentions were outdone by his achievements. These intentions he would emphasize from time to time, even committing himself to them in an edict with the following words: 'May I maintain the state safe and sound, in its rightful condition and may I reap the fruits of this result which I seek so that I am spoken of as the man responsible for this best of regimes and that when I die I shall carry with me the hope that the foundations which I have laid for the state will remain in place.' And he brought about his own wish, doing his utmost to ensure that no one regretted the new form of government. As for the city itself, which was not

decked out in a manner fitting such a great empire and which was also subject to fires and floods, he so improved it that it was with justification that he boasted he had found it a city of brick and left it a city of marble.

[29] He undertook much public building. Foremost among his projects were: his Forum with the Temple of Mars the Avenger; the Temple of Apollo on the Palatine; the Temple of Jupiter the Thunderer on the Capitol. His reason for constructing the new Forum was the large number of people and the amount of judicial activity which seemed to render the existing two forums insufficient, thus requiring a third in addition. So, even before the Temple of Mars was completed, the Forum was quickly put into public use and it was provided that public trials, separate from other trials, as well as the selection by lot of jurors, would take place there. He had vowed the Temple of Mars when he undertook the war at Philippi to avenge his father. Accordingly he decreed that it was here that the senate would conduct its debates as to whether wars should be waged or triumphs awarded, from here that those about to undertake provincial commands should set out, to here that victorious leaders should bring the insignia of their triumph on their return. The Temple to Apollo he had erected on the site of that part of his Palatine residence which the *haruspices* had announced was desired by the god when it was struck by lightning. To this he added a portico with Latin and Greek libraries. And it was here that, in his later years, he would often conduct meetings of the senate and revise the lists of jurors. The Temple of Jupiter the Thunderer he consecrated after he had an escape from danger. For once when he was travelling by night on campaign in Spain, a flash of lightning struck his litter and killed the slave who was lighting the way. Some works, also, he undertook in the name of others, that is, his grandsons, his nephew, his wife, and his sister, such as the Portico and Basilica of Gaius and Lucius, similarly the Porticos of Livia and of Octavia and the Theatre of Marcellus. As for other prominent men, he often exhorted them, so far as the resources of each permitted, to beautify the city with monuments, whether new or restored and improved. At that time, many men undertook many projects; for instance, Marcius Philippus the Temple of Hercules of the Muses, Lucius Cornificius the Temple of Diana, Asinius Pollio the Atrium of Liberty, Munatius Plancus the Temple of Saturn, Cornelius Balbus a theatre, and

Statilius Taurus an amphitheatre, while Marcus Agrippa undertook many outstanding enterprises.

[30] The area of the city he divided into regions and districts and made provisions so that the former were watched over by magistrates, selected by lot each year, and the latter by 'masters' who were chosen from the common people of each district. To protect against fires, he instituted night-watches and guards. In order to prevent floods, he widened and cleared the channel of the Tiber, which had become congested with rubble and projecting buildings. So that the city was more easily accessible from all quarters, he himself took responsibility for repairing the Flaminian Way as far as Ariminum,* and assigned the rest to men who had celebrated triumphs, who were to use their spoils to pave them. He rebuilt temples which had collapsed from old age or been destroyed in fires, and these and others he decked out with the most spendid gifts, depositing as a single gift in the chamber of the Temple of Capitoline Jupiter sixteen thousand pounds of gold, as well as pearls and other precious stones valued at fifty million sesterces.

[31] When, after the death of Marcus Lepidus, he at last accepted the office of Pontifex Maximus* (which he had never ventured to take from him while he was still living), he had collected from all over and burned whatever works in Greek or Latin were popularly supposed, on the basis of no or unreliable authority, to be prophetic (there were more than two thousand of them). He kept only the Sibylline books, even from these making a selection, and deposited them in two golden cases under the pedestal of the Palatine Apollo. Since the calendar which had been brought to order by the Divine Julius* was subsequently confused and muddled through neglect, he restored it to its previous order. In the course of this process, he gave his own name to the sixth month rather than September, the month of his birth,* on the grounds that both his first consulship and also his most splendid victories had fallen in the former. He increased not only the number and dignity of the priesthoods but also their privileges, especially in the case of the Vestal Virgins. And when the death of one required that another be chosen to fill her place and many people engaged in intrigue to prevent their daughters being included among those in the lottery, Augustus swore that if any of his granddaughters had been of the right age he would have put her name forward. He reinstituted many ancient rituals, too, which had gradually fallen

into disuse, such as the augury of Safety,* the office of the Flamen Dialis, the Lupercalia, the Secular Games, and the Compitalician Games. He forbade beardless young men to participate in the Lupercalia and also with regard to the Secular Games banned young people of either sex from being present at any spectacle which took place by night, unless they were accompanied by an older relative. He laid down that the *lares Compitales* should be decked with flowers twice a year, in spring and summer.

After the immortal gods he honoured the memory of leaders who had found the empire of the Roman people small and left it great. For this reason he restored the public works each had undertaken, leaving the inscriptions in place, and dedicated statues of all of them with their triumphal ornaments in the two colonnades of his Forum, also proclaiming too in an edict that he had done this so that he himself, while he lived, and the rulers of later ages would be required by the Roman people to take the lives of these men as their model. The statue of Pompey he moved from the meeting-hall in which Gaius Caesar was killed and installed on a marble arch opposite the main entrance of Pompey's Theatre.

[32] Many reprehensible practices had remained from the lawlessness customary in times of civil war or had even arisen in peacetime to the detriment of public order. For a large number of robbers went about openly, armed with swords, ostensibly for their own protection. In the countryside, travellers were seized and committed to the slave prisons of landowners, with no distinction drawn between slave and free. Numerous gangs were formed, on the pretext of being new work associations, but with exclusively criminal intentions. Augustus therefore brought the robberies under control by stationing watchmen in suitable locations, inspected the slave-prisons, and abolished any work associations which were not established and legitimate. He had burned the records of old debts to the treasury, which were the most frequent excuse for false accusations. Property in the city to which the state had a disputed claim he judged to belong to the current holders. The names of those who had been under accusation for a long time or those against whom the accusation served no other purpose than to give pleasure to their enemies he removed from the lists, stipulating that if anyone wished to renew the case, he would risk incurring himself the penalty prescribed for the crime.* However, lest a crime should slip away unpunished or a business suit

collapse from delay, he appointed an additional thirty days, on which honorary games had been taking place, for the prosecution of legal business. To the three divisions of jurors he added a fourth, composed of men of a lower census class, to be called the *ducenarii** and to give judgement in cases involving lesser amounts. He enrolled as jurors men aged at least twenty-five* (that is five years younger than was previously the rule). However, when many men sought to evade court duties, he grudgingly conceded that each division should take it in turns to have a year's exemption and that the usual practice of holding court business during the months of November and December should be abandoned.

[33] He himself pronounced judgement with great thoroughness and often up to nightfall, with his litter positioned near the tribunal if his body was ailing, or even from his bed at home. However, he administered justice not only with great diligence but also with particular mercy and if anyone were plainly guilty of parricide, he is said to have posed his questions thus: 'Surely you did not kill your father?' so that the accused would avoid the punishment of being sewn into the sack,* which is only imposed if he confesses. And when the case concerned the forgery of a will and all the witnesses were liable under the Cornelian law,* he would pass to those who considered the case with him, not only the two tablets, indicating guilt or acquittal, but also a third which could excuse those who were shown to have been induced to sign by trickery or misunderstanding. Every year he referred appeals in cases involving litigants at Rome to the urban praetor, and those involving inhabitants of the provinces to men of consular rank, placing one of them in charge of the business for each province.

[34] He revised the laws and in some cases enacted new ones such as those relating to excessive expenditure, to adultery, to chastity, to electoral improprieties, and to the regulation of marriages. With this last he was introducing measures rather more severe than with the others and was prevented by the clamour of protesters from making them law until he had omitted or modified some of the penalties, allowing an exception of three years* and increasing the rewards.* And when, during the public shows, a knight insistently called for the law's abolition, Augustus drew attention to the children of Germanicus whom he had summoned and seated, some beside him and some in their father's lap, indicating with his gestures and

expression that they should not balk at following the young man's example.* When he learned, too, that the force of the law was being evaded through betrothals to young girls and through frequent remarriages, he shortened the duration of betrothals and imposed a limit on divorces.

[35] Since the number of senators was swelled by a disorderly and undignifed rabble—for there were more than a thousand of them, some most unworthy men who had been admitted after Caesar's death through favour or bribery (these were commonly referred to as Orcini*)—Augustus returned it to its former size and glory by means of two reviews, the first conducted by the senators themselves in which each man chose one other, the second by himself and Agrippa. It was on this occasion that he is believed to have presided protected by a cuirass under his tunic and wearing a sword at his side, with ten strong men, friends from the senatorial order, standing around his seat. Cremutius Cordus writes that no member of the senate was allowed to approach him unless on his own and once his toga had been searched. Some senators he induced to resign through shame, though even to these he allowed the right to wear senatorial garb, sit in the front rows at the games, and take part in public banquets. And so that those who were selected and approved should fulfil their duties with greater seriousness and also less inconvenience, he prescribed that, before taking his seat, each man should make an offering of incense and wine at the altar of the deity in whose temple the meeting took place; that regular senate meetings should take place no more than twice in each month on the Kalends and the Ides, and that in the months of September and October the only members required to attend were those chosen by lot whose number would be sufficient for the enactment of legislation. He also established a council, whose membership was renewed by lot every six months and with whom he would discuss matters of business before referring them to a full meeting of the senate. When it came to issues of moment he would ask for senators' opinions, not in the traditional order, but in any order he pleased so that everyone was on the alert in case he had to give an opinion rather than merely agreeing with what had already been said.

[36] He also initiated many other developments including the following: that the proceedings of the senate should not be published; that magistrates should not take up posts in the provinces immedi-

ately on leaving office; that a fixed sum should be allowed the provincial governors for the mules and tents which were usually contracted for at public expense; that responsibility for the treasury
should pass from the urban quaestors to the ex-praetors or praetors;
that the centumviral court* which by custom had been convoked by
ex-quaestors, should be convoked by the Board of Ten.* [37] So that
more men could participate in state administration, he devised some
new official posts: for the supervision of public works, of roads, of
aqueducts, of the Tiber channel, of the distribution of grain to the
people, as well as for the prefecture of the city, the Board of Three
for selecting senators, and another for reviewing the companies of
knights, whenever necessary. He appointed censors—an office which
had long been left vacant. He increased the number of praetors.* He
even demanded that whenever he himself accepted the consulship he
should have two colleagues rather than one, but did not get his way,
for everyone insisted that his honour was already sufficiently limited
as he did not hold office alone but with a colleague.

[38] He was no less generous in honouring military achievements,*
ensuring that more than thirty generals were awarded proper triumphs, while a greater number were awarded triumphal ornaments.
So that the sons of senators would more readily become accustomed
to public life, he gave permission for them to wear the broad stripe
from the time when they assumed the toga of manhood and to attend
the senate house, and, when they served in the army for the first
time, he gave them as posts not only the tribunate in a legion but also
the command of a cavalry division. And so that no one should lack
military service, he often put two holders of the broad stripe in
charge of a single cavalry division.

He frequently reviewed the companies of knights, reintroducing
the custom of the parade after a long interval. However, he did not
allow anyone to be forced to dismount by an accuser in the course of
the parade, which often used to happen, and he gave permission to
the elderly or anyone with a conspicuous bodily defect to send their
horse forward for review and themselves come on foot, if they should
be summoned. Later on he allowed those who were over thirty-five
and did not wish to retain it to give up their horse. [39] With the help
of the ten men he had been granted, on his request, by the senate, he
required each knight to give an account of himself, imposing punishments on some of the reprobates and demotions on others and

warnings of various kinds on many more. The mildest form of warning was to hand over to them in public some tablets which they were
to read silently on the spot. Others were taken to task because they
had borrowed money at a low rate of interest and then invested it at a
higher rate.

[40] If there were insufficient candidates of senatorial rank standing for election as tribunes, he appointed some from among the
Roman knights, with the provision that when they finished their
term of office they might be members of whichever of the two orders
they chose. However, when a large number of knights who had lost
much of their ancestral fortunes during the civil wars did not dare to
sit in the first fourteen rows at the theatre, through fear of incurring
the penalties of the Theatre Law, Augustus announced that none
were liable if they themselves or their parents had ever possessed the
equestrian census.* He held a census of the people district by district
and, so that the commoners should not be called away from their
work too frequently for the purpose of collecting their corn rations,
he decided to distribute tickets for four months' supply three times
per year; but at their request he allowed a return to the previous
system whereby each person collected his own ration on a monthly
basis. He also restored the older arrangements for elections,* bringing
corruption under control through a variety of penalties, and distributing to his fellow members of the Fabian and Scaptian tribes a
thousand sesterces each of his own money on the day of the election,
to stop them from looking for any money from the candidates. He
thought it a matter of great importance to preserve the people pure
and untainted by any admixture of foreign or servile blood, giving
grants of Roman citizenship most rarely and placing a limit on
manumissions. When Tiberius wrote to him on behalf of a Greek
client, he replied that he would only make the grant if the man came
to him and explained why he deserved to have it. And when Livia
sought citizenship for a Gaul from a tributary province, he refused
it, offering instead immunity from taxation with the comment that
he would rather endure some loss of revenue than that the honour of
Roman citizenship be made commonplace. Not only did he put
many obstacles in the way of slaves seeking freedom, and still more
in the way of those seeking freedom with citizenship, by making
careful provision for the number, situation, and status of those who
were set free, but he also stipulated that no one who had ever been

bound or tortured should ever receive citizenship, no matter what their degree of freedom.* He sought, too, to revive the ancient manner of dress and once, when he saw at a public meeting a crowd of people dressed in dark clothes, he grew angry and cried out:

Behold the Romans, lords of the world, the toga'd race!*

and he made it the business of the aediles to prevent anyone being seen again in or near the Forum unless wearing a toga and without a cloak.

[41] He often showed generosity to all classes when the opportunity arose. For when the regal treasures were brought to the city in the Alexandrian triumph he made ready money so plentiful that interest rates fell and land values greatly increased, and afterwards, whenever there was a surplus from the property of those who had been condemned, he loaned it without interest for fixed periods to those who could give security for double the sum. He increased the property qualification for senators, requiring one million, two hundred thousand sesterces rather than eight hundred thousand, making up the amount in the case of those who did not have it. He often gave presents of money to the people, of differing sums, sometimes four hundred, sometimes three hundred, occasionally two hundred or five hundred sesterces per man. Nor indeed did he overlook the young boys, although it was not customary for them to be included before their eleventh year. When the corn-supply was under threat, he often gave out grain to each man at a very low price, sometimes for nothing, and he doubled the money tokens.*

[42] However, so that he would be recognized as a ruler who sought the public good rather than popularity, when the people complained at the scarcity and high price of wine he reproved them most severely: his son-in-law Agrippa had made sure through the provision of numerous aqueducts that no one should go thirsty. And again, when the people demanded gifts of money which had been promised, he replied that he was a man of his word. However, when they called for something which had not been promised, he criticized their shamelessness and impudence in an edict and made it clear that he would not give anything, although he had been planning to. With no less seriousness and firmness, when he discovered that many slaves had been freed and added to the list of citizens, he proclaimed that nothing would be given to those to whom nothing had been

promised,* while to the rest he gave less than he had promised, so that the sum set aside was enough to go round. At one time, when there was a serious food shortage and measures to relieve it were fraught with difficulty, he expelled from the city slaves who were for sale, as well as the schools of gladiators and all foreigners, with the exception of doctors, teachers, and some household slaves. Then, when the corn supply was restored, he wrote that he was moved to abolish the distribution of grain permanently, since people's reliance on it had led to the neglect of agriculture. However, he would not carry out his plan, he wrote, since it was bound to be restored at some point as a measure to secure popular favour. And subsequently he regulated the business to take as much account of the farmers and merchants as of the people.

[43] In the frequency, variety, and magnificence of the games he provided he outdid all who had gone before. He says that on four occasions he gave games in his own name and on twenty-three in the name of other magistrates who were either away from Rome or lacked sufficient resources. Sometimes he even provided games in the individual districts of the city on many stages with actors speaking all sorts of languages. He provided gladiatorial games not only in the Forum and amphitheatre but also in the Circus and the voting enclosures, though these were sometimes nothing more than wild beast fights. He provided a show of athletes in the Campus Martius, for which wooden seating was constructed, and also a naval battle, having excavated ground near the Tiber in the area which is now the Caesars' grove. On the days when games took place, he stationed watchmen around the city so that it would not be at the mercy of thieves when there were so few people who stayed at home. In the Circus he gave entertainments consisting of chariots, runners, and animal fighters, some of them young people of the highest families. In addition to this he gave very frequent performances of the game of Troy with older and younger boys, taking the view that it was a noble and ancient custom for the pick of the nobility to acquire fame in this manner. When Nonius Asprenas was disabled through falling during the game Augustus honoured him with a golden collar and permitted him and his descendants to call themselves 'Torquati'.* Soon afterwards, however, he called an end to these games when the orator Asinius Pollio complained earnestly and bitterly in the senate about the fall sustained by his grandson Aeserninus, who had also

broken his leg. Sometimes Augustus would even employ Roman knights in his plays and gladiatorial shows, until a senatorial decree forbade the practice.* After that he put on show no one of decent family other than a young man, Lycius, and only then as a sight, for he was less than two feet tall, and weighed only seventeen pounds but had a booming voice. On one day during the gladiatorial games he exhibited in the arena the first Parthian hostages ever brought to Rome and then seated them in the second row above his box. He was also in the habit of providing additional sights, if there was something available which was unusual and worth seeing. These displays would take place on days when there were no games, in whatever location was suitable. Thus, a rhinoceros was shown in the voting enclosures, a tiger in the theatre, and a serpent of fifty cubits in front of the Comitium. When he was giving votive games in the Circus he happened to fall ill and led the procession of sacred chariots reclining in his litter. On another occasion, at the inauguration of the games with which he dedicated the Theatre of Marcellus, he chanced to fall flat on his back as the joints of his curule chair had come loose. And at the games given for his grandsons, when the populace were afraid the seating was going to collapse and could not by any means be calmed or reassured, he went over from his own place and sat in the area which had given most cause for concern.

[44] The most disorderly and unruly behaviour of audiences at the games he regulated and brought under control, prompted by the insulting treatment of a senator who, when he went to some well-attended games at Puteoli, was not offered a seat by anyone. Thus, a decree of the senate was passed prescribing that whenever any kind of public spectacles were given anywhere, the first row of seats was to be reserved for senators; and Augustus banned the ambassadors of free and allied peoples from sitting in the orchestra in games at Rome, since he had discovered that sometimes even freedman came on embassies. He separated the soldiers from the civilians. To married men of the common people he assigned their own rows, while youths had a special section next to that of their tutors, and he decreed that no one dressed in dark clothing should sit in the central rows.* Nor did he allow women to watch gladiatorial fights except from the highest seats (though it had been the custom for men and women to watch such shows together).* To the Vestal Virgins alone he gave a separate place in the theatre, opposite the praetor's

tribunal.* As for shows involving athletes, he was so strict in exclud-
ing women from them that, when a boxing match was arranged for
the games given in honour of his appointment as Pontifex Maximus,*
he put it off until the morning of the following day and proclaimed
that he did not wish to see women in the theatre before the fifth hour.

[45] He himself was in the habit of watching the circus games
from the upper-storey apartments* of his friends and freedmen, but
sometimes he would sit in the imperial box and in the company of his
wife and children. He would stay away from the games sometimes
for several hours or occasionally whole days, but he excused himself
and sent others who were to take his place presiding. However,
whenever he was present, he would not occupy himself with any
other business. This was either to avoid the criticisms which he was
aware had been made by the people of his father Julius Caesar, since
the latter used to spend time at the games reading and replying to
letters and reports, or else because of his own enthusiasm for and
pleasure in watching the games, which he made no attempt to cover
up but often frankly admitted. For this reason, even at other people's
games and gladiatorial fights he would offer from his own funds
rewards and prizes, numerous and splendid, and whenever he was
present at a contest of the Greek kind* he rewarded all the participants according to their merits. He was keenest on watching boxers,
particularly those of Latin birth, and not only the recognized and
regular performers, whom he would even pit against Greeks, but also
the urban rabble who, though untrained, would fight boldly in the
narrow streets. Indeed, he honoured with his concern all the different sorts of people involved in providing different varieties of games
for the public. He maintained and reinforced the privileges of the
athletes. He forbade people from providing gladiatorial games without allowing contestants to appeal for their lives if conquered. He
limited the right of magistrates, sanctioned by an old law, to punish
actors at any time and in any place, restricting this to the duration of
the games and within the theatre. Nevertheless, it was always with
great severity that he regulated the wrestling matches and gladiatorial contests. And the misbehaviour of the actors he curtailed to
such a degree that when he found out that Stephanio, an actor in
Roman plays, was attended by a Roman matron with her hair
cropped to look like a boy, he gave orders that the actor should
be whipped with rods in the three theatres.* As for Hylas, the

pantomime actor,* when the praetor made a complaint, Augustus
had him scourged in the atrium of his own house, with everyone
watching; while Pylades was banned from Rome and from Italy
because, when a member of the audience hissed him, he gestured
with his finger* to make an exhibition of him.

[46] Once the city and its affairs were thus put in order, he added
to Italy's population by himself establishing twenty-eight colonies*
and endowed many places with public works and sources of revenue.
In some respects and to some degree he even gave Italy the same
status and dignity as Rome, devising a new manner of election in
which the colony decurions cast votes in each of the colonies for the
city magistracies, then sent them under seal to Rome in time for the
election day.* To sustain the supply of men of good family and keep
up numbers among the common people, he appointed to equestrian
military positions even those who were recommended by one of
the towns, while to those common people who, when he visited the
regions of Italy, could prove that they had sons or daughters, he
would give out a thousand sesterces for each child.

[47] The more important provinces, and those which could not
easily or safely be ruled by magistrates with an annual term of command, he himself took charge of, while the others he left to the
proconsuls to be distributed by lot. However, he changed the
arrangements for a number of provinces over the years and frequently made visits to many provinces in both categories. Some of
the allied cities* whose ungoverned behaviour threatened disaster he
deprived of their freedom, while to others he offered relief from
their burden of debt and rebuilt others which had been destroyed in
earthquakes. Some he rewarded for the services they had rendered
the Roman people with a grant of Latin or Roman citizenship.*
Indeed, it is my belief that there was not a province which he did not
visit, with the exception of Africa and Sardinia; when he meant to
cross over to these from Sicily, in pursuit of the defeated Sextus
Pompeius, he was held back by continuous and severe storms and
never thereafter had the opportunity or reason to make the journey.

[48] Those kingdoms which he had gained control of through
conquest with a few exceptions he either restored to those from
whom he had taken them or else joined them to other foreign
nations. The kings to whom he was allied he also joined to one
another with mutual ties and was always very quick to promote and

encourage marriages and friendships among them. He would always treat all of them with consideration as integral parts of the empire and when a ruler was too young or was failing in his powers he would appoint a regent until he had grown up or recovered his strength. Many of their children he brought up and educated together with his own.

[49] From his military forces, he stationed legions and auxiliaries in the different provinces. He posted one fleet to Misenum and the other to Ravenna to protect the upper and lower seas. The remaining forces he assigned to protect either the city or his own person, having dismissed the band of Calagurritani* whom he had kept about him as part of his bodyguard until the defeat of Antony, and then the band of Germans whom he kept until the defeat of Varus. However, he never allowed more than three cohorts in the city and these were not to have a permanent base. The others he would station in winter and summer quarters in the surrounding towns. For all soldiers, wherever they were he applied a fixed system of salaries and bonuses, stipulated in accordance with each man's rank, the length of his military service, and the rewards he would receive on his retirement, so they would not be tempted to revolt afterwards in protest over their age or lack of means. So that he would always have ready funds available to maintain them and give them their benefits, he established a military treasury to be supplied by new taxes. And so that events in all the provinces could be more speedily and promptly reported and known, he first stationed young men and later vehicles at short intervals along the military roads. The latter arrangement seems more convenient as it means that the men who have brought the letters from a particular place can themselves be questioned, if this is necessary.

[50] In sealing official documents, reports and letters, he first used a sphinx, then an image of Alexander the Great* and finally one of himself, sculpted by the hand of Dioscurides, which later emperors also continued to use as a seal, following his example. To all his letters he would add the exact time, not only of day but also of night, to indicate when they had been sent.

[51] There are many great instances of his clemency* and his lack of pretention. I shall refrain from recording each and every example of those of the opposite faction to whom he gave immunity and even allowed to hold office in the state. He was content to punish two men

of the common people, Junius Novatus and Cassius Patavinus, one with a fine and the other with a mild form of exile, although the former had publicly circulated the most bitter letter concerning Augustus under the name of the young Agrippa,* while the latter had proclaimed at a large dinner party that he lacked neither the strong desire to run the emperor through nor the spirit to do it. And at a trial, when chief among the charges made against Aemilius Aelianus of Corduba was that he was in the habit of expressing his bad opinion of Caesar, the emperor turned to the accuser and, feigning anger, said: 'I wish you would give me proof of that; I shall give Aelius reason to know that I, too, have a tongue and I shall have more to say about him.' And he took the inquiry no further either at that time or later. Moreover, when Tiberius complained rather forcefully about the same thing in a letter, he replied: 'My Tiberius, do not give way to your youthful impulses or get too angry at anyone who speaks ill of me. We should be satisfied if we have the means to prevent anyone from doing us ill.'

[52] Although he knew it was the custom to dedicate temples even to proconsuls, he would not allow them to be dedicated to himself in any province unless they were dedicated to Rome also. Within the city of Rome itself, indeed, he most obstinately refused this honour. Even the silver statues which had earlier been set up to honour him he had melted down, every one, and, with the money raised, he dedicated golden tripods to Palatine Apollo. When the people strongly pressed him to accept the dictatorship,* he went down on one knee, threw back his toga, and bared his breast, beseeching them to refrain.

[53] He always shrank from the title 'Master'* as an insult and a reproach. On one occasion at the games when he was watching a farce, the line was spoken: 'O good and just master!' and the whole audience indicated their enthusiastic agreement, as if the words were addressed to the emperor. He immediately called a halt to their unbecoming adulation with his gesture and expression and, on the next day, reproached them most severely in an edict. Thereafter he would not even allow his children and grandchildren to call him 'master', whether jokingly or in earnest, and forbade them to use such obsequious titles even among themselves. Almost always his arrival at or departure from Rome or any other town was in the evening or at night so that people would not be troubled by the need

to pay him respect.* When consul, he went about in public places on foot and at other times in a sedan chair. All and sundry were permitted to attend his receptions, including the common people,* and he acknowledged the wishes of his petitioners with such good humour that once he teased a man that he was as nervous of handing over his petition as if he were giving a present to an elephant. On days when the senate met, he always greeted the senators in the senate house,* addressing each by name with no one prompting him, while they remained in their seats. Even as he left, he would pay his respects in the same manner, while they stayed seated. In the case of many, he discharged the mutual obligations of friendship, and did not fail to attend all their feast days until he was advanced in years and had once been made uncomfortable by the crowd at a betrothal ceremony. When the senator Gallus Cerrinius had suddenly lost his sight and decided to end his life by starvation, Augustus went in person to console him, though he was not a close friend, and persuaded him to live.

[54] When he spoke in the senate, someone might say to him: 'I do not understand' or another: 'I would argue against you, if I had the chance.' From time to time when he stormed out of the senate in anger at the unbridled exchanges between the speakers, people would remind him that senators should be allowed to speak their minds on matters of state. When, during a senate review, each man was selecting his own candidate,* Antistius Labeo chose Marcus Lepidus who had been the emperor's enemy and was now in exile. Asked if there were not other men more worthy, Labeo replied that each man made his own judgement. Yet no one suffered for his outspokenness or rudeness.

[55] Even when pamphlets insulting him were circulating in the senate, he was not alarmed but took great care to refute them. Without enquiring about the authors, he merely prescribed that in future anyone who under a false name produced pamphlets or poems defaming someone should be brought to trial. [56] When he was attacked by people's spiteful or malicious jokes, he protested in an edict. However, he vetoed attempts to legislate against freedom of speech in wills.* Whenever he took part in elections for public office, he went the round of the tribes with the candidates he was recommending and entreated their support in the traditional manner. He himself would cast his own vote with his tribe, just like one of the

people. When he was a witness in court proceedings he allowed himself to be questioned and contradicted with an even temper. His Forum he made rather narrow, not daring to expropriate the owners of the adjacent houses. He never recommended his sons to the people for election without adding the words: 'If they deserve it.' When they were still boys and everyone stood to greet them in the theatre and remained standing to applaud them, he complained in the strongest terms. He wished his friends to be prominent and influential in the state, yet to have the same legal status as other men and to be governed just the same by the laws and the courts. When his close friend Nonius Asprenas was brought to trial, accused of poisoning by Cassius Severus, Augustus asked the senate to advise him where his duty lay, for he was unsure whether, if he stood by him, he might be thought to be protecting a guilty man from justice, while if he kept away, he might be thought to be betraying his friend and condemning him in advance of the verdict. And with their general agreement he sat in the court for some hours, but in silence and without even speaking to praise the defendant's character. He did appear on behalf of his clients, for instance, one Scutarius, one of his former special officers, who was accused of slander. In the case of only one man from among all those brought to trial did he bring about an acquittal and even then only after he was begged to, making a successful appeal to the accuser in the presence of the jury. The defendant was Castricius who had brought the conspiracy of Murena* to his attention.

[57] One may easily imagine how much he was loved for these virtues. The decrees of the senate I pass over as they could seem motivated by necessity or reverence. The Roman knights on their own initiative and by common consent celebrated his birthday over two days every year. People of every rank, fulfilling a vow made for his good health, would throw a coin into the lacus Curtius* every year and on the Kalends of January, too, on the Capitoline they would give a new year's gift, even when he was away from Rome. With these funds he purchased the most precious images of the gods which he dedicated in each district of the city, such as an Apollo in the Street of the Sandal Makers, a Jupiter in the Street of the Tragedian and so on. When his house on the Palatine was destroyed by fire,* veterans, guilds,* the tribes, and even individuals from other walks of life with great willingness brought funds for its rebuilding, each in

accordance with his own means, though the emperor would take only a little from each of the heaps, keeping no more than a penny from anyone. And when he returned from a provincial command, they attended him not only with congratulations but also with songs. It was the custom, too, that whenever he entered the city no one suffered punishment.

[58] All joined together with alacrity and unanimity in conferring upon him the title 'Father of the Fatherland'.* First of all the common people made the attempt, sending messengers to him at Antium. When he would not accept it they greeted him in throngs, crowned with laurel, as he arrived at the games in Rome. Soon afterwards the senators made the attempt in the senate house, issuing no decree or proclamation, but making the offer through Valerius Messala. Expressing the views of all, he said: 'May good fortune attend you and your house, Caesar Augustus! For with these words, in our view, we are praying for the perpetual happiness of the state and the felicity of this city. With one voice, the senate, together with the people of Rome, salutes you as Father of the Fatherland.' Moved to tears, Augustus replied to him with these words (which I quote directly as I did those of Messala): 'My highest hopes realized, O senators, what else can I ask of the gods, but that they permit me to retain your general good will to the very end of my days?' [59] In honour of the doctor Antonius Musa, through whose skill the emperor recovered from a dangerous illness,* they raised money to set up a statue, next to the image of Aesculapius.* Some heads of families stipulated in their wills that sacrificial victims should be driven to the Capitoline by their heirs and that a thank-offering should be made on their behalf, because Augustus had survived them, and that they should carry before them a placard to proclaim their purpose. A number of Italian cities made the anniversary of his first visit to them the first day of their year. And many of the provinces, besides setting up temples and altars, established five-yearly games in nearly all their towns.

[60] The friendly and allied kings, each in his own kingdom, founded cities named Caesarea and they resolved jointly, with all of them contributing to the cost, to complete the Temple of Olympian Zeus at Athens, on which work had begun long ago,* and to dedicate it to his Genius. And often they would leave their kingdoms and pay their respects to him, as clients, dressed in togas and without their

regal insignia,* not only when he was in Rome but even when he travelled in the provinces.

[61] Since I have now described him as a commander and magistrate and shown how he governed the state throughout the entire world in war and in peace, I shall now discuss his personal and domestic life, giving an account of his character and fortune at home and with his family, from his youth until his dying day.

His mother he lost during his first consulship and his sister Octavia* in his fifty-fourth year.* To both he paid particular respect when they lived and the greatest honours when they died. [62] When he was a young man he had been betrothed to the daughter of Publius Servilius Isauricus but when, after their first dispute, he was reconciled to Antony and both their armies entreated them to cement the alliance with a family tie, Augustus married Antony's stepdaughter Claudia, who was Fulvia's daughter from her marriage to Publius Clodius and only just of marriageable age. However, when relations soured with his mother-in-law, Fulvia, he divorced her before he had consummated the marriage. Soon afterwards he took as wife Scribonia, who had previously been married to two men of consular rank and had already produced children for one of them. He divorced her, too, 'unable to tolerate her bad character any longer', as he wrote and at once broke up Livia Drusilla's marriage to Tiberius Nero, although she was pregnant at the time. Her he loved dearly, favouring her all his life beyond all others.

[63] From Scribonia he had a daughter, Julia, but from Livia no children, despite his dearest wish. Though a child was conceived, it was born prematurely. He married Julia first to Marcellus, son of his sister Octavia, although he had only just reached adulthood; then, when he died, to Marcus Agrippa, having persuaded his sister to give up her son-in-law to him (for at that time Agrippa was married to one of the two Marcellas and had children by her). When he too had died, Augustus considered possible matches, even with members of the equestrian order, over a long period of time, before chosing his own stepson Tiberius, forcing him to divorce his pregnant wife by whom he was already a father. Mark Antony writes that Augustus first betrothed Julia to his own son Antony, and later to Cotiso, king of the Getae, at the same time requesting in turn the hand of the king's daughter for himself.*

[64] From Agrippa and Julia he had three grandsons, Gaius,

Lucius, and Agrippa, and two granddaughters, Julia and Agrippina. The younger Julia he married to the son of Lucius Paulus the censor and Agrippina to Germanicus, his sister's grandson. Gaius and Lucius he adopted into his own household, having made a ritual purchase of them with penny and scales* from their father Agrippa, and, from a tender age, brought them up to serve the state, having them designated consuls* and sending them off to tour the provinces and armies. He so educated his daughter and granddaughters that they even acquired the habit of working wool,* and forbade them to say or do anything underhand or which might not be reported in the daily chronicles.* So strictly did he prohibit them from associating with anyone outside the family that he wrote to Lucius Vinicius, a distinguished and honourable young man, to reprove him for his immodest action in once coming to pay his respects to his daughter at Baiae. He himself taught his grandsons to read, to take notes, and many other skills,* particularly insisting that they take his handwriting as their model. Whenever he dined with them he would always sit them with him on the lowest couch,* and whenever he made a journey they would always precede his carriage or ride beside him on horseback.

[65] But his happiness and confidence in the offspring of his house and their upbringing were destroyed by Fortune. The Julias, his daughter and granddaughter, he sent into exile, for they were tainted with every form of vice. He lost both Gaius and Lucius within the space of eighteen months, Gaius dying in Lycia and Lucius in Massilia. He adopted his third grandson Agrippa and, at the same time, his stepson Tiberius, by a law passed by the assembly of the curiae in the Forum.* But he disinherited Agrippa soon afterwards because of his low and violent character and sent him away to Surrentum.* Yet he bore the deaths of his dear ones more readily than their disgrace. For he was not so very cast down by the loss of Gaius and Lucius, but in the case of his daughter he sent a complaint to the senate to be reported by a quaestor, while he himself stayed away, and, for a long time, overcome with shame, he avoided people's company and even contemplated having her killed. Certainly, when at around that time one of the freedwomen, Phoebe, who had been party to her activities, hanged herself, he observed that he would rather have been the father of Phoebe. In her place of exile he banned Julia from drinking wine or enjoying any other relative

luxury and would allow no man, whether slave or free, to go near her
without his express permission, insisting that he should be informed
in such cases of the individual's age, stature, colouring, and even
whether he had any distinguishing features or scars. After five years
he at last had her transferred from her island* to the mainland and a
somewhat milder regime. He could by no means be persuaded that
she should be recalled altogether, and when the Roman people
repeatedly entreated him and pressed him insistently he called out
before a public meeting that they should have such daughters and
such wives. When his granddaughter Julia produced a child after her
fall from grace, he insisted that it should be neither acknowledged
nor brought up. When Agrippa became no more tractable but rather
more unbalanced daily, he had him taken to an island* and posted a
detachment of soldiers to guard him there. He even prescribed
through a senatorial decree that he should be held in perpetuity in
that particular place. And whenever anyone referred either to him or
to one of the Julias he used to groan and even exclaim:

> Oh, that I had never married and died without children!*

The only terms he used for them were his three sores or his three
cancers.

[66] While he did not readily make new friends, he cherished his
existing ones most constantly, not only acknowledging fittingly the
virtues and merits of each of them but even putting up with their
vices and faults, provided they were not excessive. From among all
his friends, scarcely any can be found who fell into disgrace, aside
from Salvidienus Rufus and Cornelius Gallus. The former he had
raised to the rank of consul and the latter to the prefecture of Egypt,
in both cases from humble beginnings. Salvidienus he handed over
to the senate for punishment when he plotted revolution, while
Gallus he banned from his home and from his provinces because of
his ungrateful and malicious temper. But when he, too, as a result of
the condemnations and senatorial decrees of his accusers, was forced
to die, Augustus praised the loyalty of those who were so indignant
on his behalf, yet also shed tears and bemoaned his lot, that he alone
had not the power to decide how far he wished to take his anger
toward his friends. His other friends, despite occasional disagree-
ments, flourished till the end of their days, in power and wealth the
leading men of their respective orders. He sometimes found Marcus

Agrippa too impatient and Maecenas too talkative, to mention no others; for the former, when he had some slight reason to suspect Augustus' feelings had cooled and that Marcellus was preferred to himself, left everyone behind and went off to Mytilene, while the latter gave away to his wife Terentia the secret that Murena's conspiracy had been discovered.*

He required from his friends their good will in return, as much from the dead as from the living. For, although he was far from seeking to be made people's heir and would never accept anything left to him in the will of someone he did not know, the final judgements of his friends he scrutinized with the greatest of care, nor was his regret feigned if his treatment was too mean or unaccompanied by compliments, nor his joy, if he was acknowledged with gratitude and affection.* It was his custom when he received legacies or inheritances* from anyone who was a parent either to pass it on at once to their children, or, if they were not yet of age, to give it back to them with interest on the day they received their toga of manhood or married.

[67] As patron and master he was no less exacting than he was kind and forgiving. Many of his freedmen he honoured greatly and was very close to them, such as Licinus and Celadus and others. When his slave Cosmus spoke very ill of him he merely put him in irons. When, as he was walking together with his steward Diomedes, they were suddenly attacked by a wild boar and Diomedes in fear got behind him, he chose to see this as evidence of cowardice rather than of intent to harm, and, because there had been no plot, turned a situation involving serious danger into a joke. But when he discovered that Polus, who was among the dearest of his freedmen, was having affairs with married women of rank, he forced him to kill himself. And, because his secretary Thallus had revealed the contents of a letter for five hundred denarii, he had his legs broken. As for the tutor and attendants of his son Gaius, because they had taken advantage of his ill-health and death to indulge their pride and greed in his province, he had them thrown into the river with heavy weights loaded onto their necks.

[68] In his early youth he was accused of many kinds of vice. Sextus Pompeius attacked him for being effeminate.* Mark Antony alleged he had bought his adoption by his uncle with sexual favours, while Antony's brother Lucius asserted that after his chastity had been assailed by Caesar he had even submitted himself to Aulus

Hirtius in Spain for the sum of three hundred thousand sesterces and that he was in the habit of applying hot nutshells to singe his legs,* so that the hairs would grow softer. On one occasion, however, on a day when games were being held, the entire people interpreted as an insult directed at him and with great accord showed their approval of a line proclaimed on stage by a special priest of the Mother of the Gods,* as he beat his drum:

> See how an effeminate rules the globe with his finger!*

[69] Not even his friends deny that he committed adultery, suggesting by way of excuse that his motive was not lust but policy, as he sought to find out the plans of his opponents more easily through each man's wife. Mark Antony objected not only that he had contracted his marriage to Livia in excessive haste but that he had in front of her husband led the wife of a man of consular rank from the dining-room off into his bedroom, later returning her to the party with burning ears and dishevelled hair,* also, that he divorced his wife Scribonia because she showed too openly her resentment at the influence of his mistress, and that he got his friends to procure women for him, stripping naked respectable married ladies and grown girls not yet married to inspect them, as if they were the wares of Toranius the slave-dealer. Antony even wrote to him in the following words, without any note of coolness or hostility: 'What's troubling you? That I'm having a go at the queen? Is she my wife? Have I just started this or has it been going on for nine years? So do you only have a go at your Drusilla? As you are a man in good health, I'm sure when you read this you'll have been going at Tertulla or Terentilla or Rufilla* or Salvia Titisenia or all of them. Does it matter where and with whom you get your thrills?'

[70] There were also stories about a rather secret dinner he arranged, which was commonly referred to as the dinner of the Twelve Gods.* For this the guests reclined in the dress of one or other of the gods or goddesses, with Augustus himself attired as Apollo.* Not only do Antony's letters take him to task for this most acerbically, naming each of the guests, but there are also some notorious verses whose author is unknown:

> As soon as that company of villains had hired their costumes,
> Mallia saw six gods and six goddesses,

> While Caesar impiously dared to play at being Apollo
> And represented new adulteries of the gods at his banquet.
> At this time all deities removed themselves from earth
> And Jupiter himself abandoned his golden throne.*

Stories about the banquet were fuelled by the fact that the city was at that time suffering from hunger and food shortages and on the following day there was a protest that all the food had been eaten by the gods and that Caesar was indeed Apollo but Apollo the Tormenter (the god is worshipped under this title in one part of the city). He was also notorious for his passion for precious tableware and Corinthian bronze and for his love of gambling. Indeed, in the time of the proscriptions, the following words appeared on his statue: 'My father dealt in silver, I deal in Corinthian,'* for it was thought that the names of some men had been included among those proscribed because of their Corinthian vases. Then, during the Sicilian war, the following epigram was current:

> After he was twice defeated at sea and lost his ships,
> Hoping to win at something, he gambled constantly.

[71] Of all these accusations and slanders, the allegations that he had submitted himself to men he refuted with the greatest of ease through the purity of his life both at the time and later, similarly his alleged greed for riches, since on the capture of Alexandria he took nothing for himself from the royal treasure apart from one murrine* goblet and soon afterwards he had melted down all the golden vessels, which had been in everyday use.* As regards the affairs with women, the allegations held. Indeed, later on he had a keen taste for deflowering virgins, who would even be procured for him from all over the place by his wife. He was not concerned at all at his own reputation for gambling, playing unpretentiously and openly for his own amusement, even when he was an old man, not only in the month of December* but also on other holidays and even on working days. There is no doubt about this; a letter exists in his own hand in which he says:

I dined, my dear Tiberius, with the same men. Vinicius and the elder Silius joined the party. During the meal we gambled like old men, both yesterday and today. When the dice were thrown, whoever had got a 'dog' or a six put in a denarius for each of the dice. Then whoever threw a Venus scooped the lot.*

And again in another letter he wrote:

My dear Tiberius, we enjoyed a very pleasant Quinquatria.* For we played games all day long and made the gaming board hot. Your brother made a great fuss, though in the end he didn't lose much at all, for little by little against his expectations he won back most of the large sums he had initially lost. For my part, I lost twenty thousand sesterces, since I was playing extravagantly with an open hand, as I generally do. For if I had asked everyone to return for the stakes I had let go, or had kept for myself what I gave away to others, I would have been fifty thousand up. But I prefer it like this, for my generosity will bring me celestial glory.

He wrote to his daughter: 'I have sent you two hundred and fifty denarii, the same amount I gave to each of my guests, in case they wanted to play dice or odds and evens during dinner.'

[72] It is generally agreed that in other aspects of his life he was very restrained, attracting no suspicion of any other faults. He lived at first near the Roman Forum, at the top of the Ringmakers' steps, in a house which had belonged to the orator Calvus. Later he lived on the Palatine but in the no less modest house which had belonged to Hortensius. It was notable neither for its size nor for its decor, having within it small colonnades of Alban stone* and no marble decoration at all nor any suites with lavish flooring. And for more than forty years, he slept in the same bedroom winter and summer, and even though he found the city detrimental to his health in winter, he still continued to spend his winters in town. If ever he had some business he wanted to conduct in secret or without interruption, he had a particular room on a higher level which he used to call his Syracuse or his little workshop and this is where he would go, or else to the suburban villa of one of his freedmen. When he was ill he would sleep in the house of Maecenas. For relaxation he would generally repair to the coast and the islands off Campania, or else to the towns closest to Rome, Lanuvium, Praeneste, and Tibur, too, where he would frequently pronounce judgement from the portico of the Temple of Hercules. He was angered by extensive and luxurious places in the country and when his granddaughter Julia had had a rather lavish place built he had it razed to the ground. His own country places, modest as they were, he furnished not with statues or painted panels but rather with terraces and plantations and objects notable for their great age and rarity, such as the enormous bones of

huge monsters and beasts from Capri, which were said to be the bones of giants, and the weaponry of heroes.

[73] The plainness of his household utensils and furniture is evident even now from the remaining couches and tables, many of which are scarcely smart enough for an ordinary citizen. They say that he would always sleep on a bed which was low and equipped with simple coverings. He rarely wore clothes which were not produced in his own household by his sister, his wife, his daughter, or his granddaughters.* His togas were neither close-fitting nor voluminous, his purple stripe neither broad nor narrow.* His shoes were a little raised to make him seem taller than he was. At all times he would keep clothes for public wear and shoes in his bed-chamber, ready for any sudden and unexpected occasions.

[74] He gave dinner parties with great frequency, though they were always formal, having great care for the rank and personal qualities of his guests. Valerius Messala relates that he never invited anyone who was a freedman to dinner with the exception of Menas, and even then only after he had been deemed of free birth, as a result of the defeat of Sextus Pompeius' fleet.* Augustus himself writes that he once invited a man in whose villa he used to stay* and who had earlier acted as his scout. Often he would arrive at the dinner party rather late and leave rather early, so that the guests would begin their meal before he had taken his place and would stay on after he had left. He would serve a dinner of three courses or, when he was being particularly generous, six; while avoiding extravagance he was always hospitable. He would draw into the general conversation those who were silent or whispering and he would provide entertainers and actors and even street performers from the circus, and frequently story-tellers also.

[75] Holidays and religious festivals he would observe lavishly on the whole, but sometimes just with amusements. On the Saturnalia,* and at other times if the fancy took him, he would sometimes distribute gifts of clothing, gold and silver, and sometimes coins of every denomination, including old ones issued by kings and other nations, and occasionally nothing but hair-cloth, sponges, pokers, tongs, and other things of that kind with mysterious and punning labels. At dinner parties he would auction lots of widely differing value or else pictures with only their reverse sides on view, thus through the dictates of chance frustrating or fulfilling the hopes of

the purchasers. He would insist that every couch* should make bids and have a share in either the loss or the gain.

[76] As for food (for I do not omit even this), he ate sparingly and generally only simple food. He had a particular taste for coarse bread, small fish, moist cheese moulded by hand, and green figs from the second crop. He would even take food before dinner, the time and place dictated by his stomach. These are his own words from his letters: 'I had some bread and some little figs in my carriage.' And another time: 'When I was on my way home from the Regia in my litter, I ate an ounce of bread and a few grapes from a hard-skinned cluster.' And again: 'No Jew, my dear Tiberius, observes his Sabbath fast* so scrupulously as I have kept fast today, for it was only in the baths after the first hour of the night that I ate two mouthfuls of bread before I was rubbed with oil.' Because of his carelessness in this respect, he would often eat on his own either before the beginning or after the end of a dinner party, while during the party itself he would not touch a thing.*

[77] He was naturally inclined to be very sparing in his consumption of wine also.* Cornelius Nepos records that when he was with his troops at Mutina he would not usually have more than three glasses at dinner. Later on, even when he was indulging himself most freely, he never had more than a pint; if he had more than this, he would throw it up. His favourite wine was Raetican but he rarely drank before dinner. Instead of a drink he would have some bread soaked in cold water or a piece of cucumber, a tender lettuce-heart or an apple, fresh or dried, with a tart flavour.

[78] After lunch, he would take a short rest, just as he was, with his clothes and shoes on and no blanket for his feet, putting his hand over his eyes. After dinner he withdrew to his couch where he would work by lamplight. There he would remain until late into the night when he had completed what remained of the day's business or most of it. He went thence to bed where he would sleep no more than seven hours and even then not continuously for he would wake up three or four times in the course of those hours.* If, as happens, he could not get back to sleep, he would summon readers or story-tellers and when sleep had returned to him he would often not wake until after first light. When he was awake after dark, he would always have someone sitting with him. He hated having to get up early and, if he had to rise earlier than usual for reasons of business or for some

religious purpose, to minimize the inconvenience he would stay as close by as possible in the room of one of his friends. Still, he was often short of sleep and would drop off as he was being carried around the streets or when there was some delay and his litter was set down.

[79] His appearance was striking and he remained exceedingly graceful all through his life, though he cared nothing for adorning himself. He was so little concerned about arranging his hair that he would employ several hairdressers simultaneously for speed and sometimes he would have his hair clipped and his beard shaved at the same time, while he himself meanwhile was reading something or even doing some writing. The expression of his face, whether he was speaking or silent, was so calm and serene that one of the leading men of Gaul confessed to his fellows that he was so impressed and won over that he abandoned his plan to throw the emperor over the cliff, when he was admitted to his presence as he was crossing the Alps. His eyes were clear and bright; he liked it to be thought that they revealed a godlike power and was pleased if someone who regarded him closely then lowered their gaze, as though from the sun's force.* In old age, however, the sight of his left eye diminished. His few teeth were weak and decayed. His hair curled slightly and was yellowish. His eyebrows met. His ears were of medium size. His nose protruded above then curved in below. His complexion was between dark and pale. He was short of stature (although his freedman and record-keeper Julius Marathus relates that he was five feet nine inches tall*) but did not appear so because his limbs were well made and well proportioned so that one only noticed his height by comparison when someone taller was standing next to him.

[80] It is said that his body was mottled with birthmarks spread out over his chest and stomach which in their shape, number, and arrangement resembled the constellation of the bear, but that he also had numerous callouses, resembling ringworm, which were caused by itching on his body and harsh and frequent use of the strigil.* He was rather weak in his left hip, thigh, and leg so that sometimes he even limped but he got his strength back through treatment with sand and reeds.* In the index finger of his right hand, too, he sometimes felt such a weakness that when it was bent up and contracted in the cold he was hardly able to write even with a fingerstall made of

horn. He also complained about his bladder, though the pain was relieved when he finally passed some stones in his urine.

[81] In the course of his life he experienced a number of severe and dangerous illnesses, particularly after the conquest of Spain, when, desperately ill as a result of abscesses in his liver, he was obliged to undergo an unusual and dangerous remedy; since hot fomentations were unsuccessful the doctor, Antonius Musa,* made him submit to cold ones. Some maladies recurred every year and at a particular time. Around the time of his birthday* he was frequently unwell. In early spring he suffered from an enlargement of the midriff, while when the winds were southerly it was catarrh. His constitution was disturbed as a result, so that he could not easily tolerate either cold or heat.

[82] In winter he wrapped himself up in four tunics and a thick toga, as well as an undershirt, a woollen vest, and coverings for his thighs and shins. In the summer he would have the doors of his bedroom open and often he would sleep in an open court beside a fountain, with someone fanning him, too. He could not bear the sun even in winter and he would wear a broad-brimmed hat when he went for a walk in the open at home also. Journeys by litter he would make by night and in short and easy stages so that it would take him two days to reach Praeneste or Tibur.* And if a place could be reached by sea, he always preferred to take a boat. Such was the state of his health that he took great care of himself, above all bathing only rarely. More often he would be rubbed with oil or work up a sweat by a fire, after which he had poured over him water, either cool or lukewarm from the heat of the sun. Whenever he needed to use hot salt water or sulphur baths for his muscles, he made do with sitting in a wooden tub, which he himself referred to by the Spanish term *dureta*, and immersing his hands and feet in turn.

[83] Immediately after the civil wars he stopped taking part in exercises with horse or arms in the Campus, at first turning to passball and balloon-ball,* but not long afterwards confining himself to riding or going for walks, at the end of which he would do some running and jumping, wrapped in a cloak or blanket. For relaxation he would sometimes go fishing with a rod, and sometimes play at dice, or marbles or nuts with little boys. Boys whose looks and manners were endearing he would seek out from all over the place, but

particularly Moors and Syrians. For he loathed dwarves and cripples and anything like that as ill-omened and freaks of nature.

[84] From his earliest youth he pursued eloquence and the liberal arts with the utmost diligence. During the war at Mutina, despite the mass of things he had to attend to, he is said to have spent some time each day reading, writing, and declaiming. Indeed, thereafter he never once addressed the senate, or people, or army without first preparing and organizing his speech, although he was quite capable of speaking off the cuff without preparation. And so that he would not risk forgetting, or waste time in memorizing, his practice was to read everything out from a written text. Remarks also to individuals and even to his wife Livia, if they were about something serious, he would always write out and read from his notes, in case in speaking off the cuff he should say less or more than he meant to. His manner of speaking was attractive and quite particular; he practised regularly with an elocution teacher. But sometimes when his throat troubled him he addressed the people by means of a herald.

[85] He composed numerous works of various kinds in prose, some of which he would read to a family gathering or as if to an auditorium, for instance his 'Reply to Brutus concerning Cato'.* He read these volumes through almost to the end, but handed them over to Tiberius to finish when he was tired, being then advanced in years. He also wrote, 'Exhortations to Philosophy' and something 'On his own Life',* which he described in thirteen books up to the Cantabrian war and no further. His ventures into poetry were brief. One book, written by him in hexameter verse, survives which has as its subject and title 'Sicily'. There is another, similarly brief, 'Epigrams' which he mainly composed when taking his bath. However, the tragedy which he began with great enthusiasm he later destroyed when the writing did not go well. And when his friends asked what was happening to Ajax he replied that Ajax had fallen on his sponge.*

[86] He cultivated an elegant and restrained manner of speaking which avoided the vanity of an artificial style of arrangement, as well as the 'rank odour', as he termed it, 'of far-fetched vocabulary'; his principal concern was to express his meaning as clearly as possible. The better to achieve this end, and so that nowhere would a reader or a listener be confused or slow to understand, he had no hesitation in putting prepositions before the names of cities nor in repeating rather frequently conjunctions whose omission leads to some obscur-

ity, even if it is more stylish. Affected writers and those fond of archiac forms, as erring in opposite directions, he despised equally and sometimes took them to task, particularly his friend Maecenas whose 'scented curls', as he called them, he attacked relentlessly, making fun of him through parody. But he did not spare Tiberius either, watching out for his sometimes effete and far-fetched expressions. Mark Antony, however, he laid into as a madman on the grounds that he aimed to produce writings which would be admired rather than understood. Then, making a joke of his perversity and inconsistency in choosing a style of speaking, he added this comment: 'Are you so uncertain, too, whether you should take as a model Annius Cimber* or Veranius Flaccus that you even make use of terms which Sallustius Crispus took from Cato's "Origines"?* Or do you think the high flown style of Asiatic orators with their empty phrases should be adopted into our own language?'* Once, when in a letter he was praising the intelligence of his granddaughter Agrippina, he commented: 'But you really must take care that you do not write or speak with affectation.'

[87] Some characteristic expressions he used rather frequently in everyday speech can be seen in letters in his own hand, in which he sometimes writes, when he wants to say that certain men will never pay: 'they'll pay on the Greek Kalends.'* And when he wants to encourage his addressee to put up with present circumstances whatever they are, he says: 'Let us be satisfied with the Cato we have.' To convey the speed of something fast, he says, 'Quicker than asparagus cooks.' He would often say *baceolus* ['idiotic'] instead of *stultus* ['stupid'], *pulleiacus* ['darkish'] for *pullus* ['dark'], *vacerrosus* ['crack-brained'] for *cerritus* ['insane'] and talked of feeling *vapide* ['flat'] rather than *male* ['ill'], as well as using *betizare* ['go like a beet'] instead of *languere* ['feel weak'] or, as common people say, *lachanizare* ['flop']. He would also say *simus* for *sumus* ['we are'] and used *domos* for the genitive singular form [of *domus* 'house'] instead of *domuos*. His usage of these two forms was invariable, in case anyone should mistake for errors what was his usual practice. In an examination of his handwriting the following characteristics stand out: he does not divide up his words and when there is not space for all the letters in a line, instead of running them on into the next line, he writes them underneath and draws a line around them.

[88] He did not particularly observe orthography, that is the

practice and rule of spelling as taught by the grammarians, and seems rather to have followed the guidance of those who advise writing words as they are spoken. As for his changing or leaving out not just letters but even syllables, that is a mistake people often make. I would not myself have pointed it out except that, to my surprise, others have reported that he appointed a replacement for a provincial governor who was an ex-consul on the grounds that he was an uncouth and ignorant fellow, for he had noticed that the man wrote *ixi* for *ipsi* ['themselves']. If he wanted to write in code, he would put 'b' for 'a', 'c' for 'b' and so on for the rest of the alphabet but putting a double 'a' for 'x'.

[89] Nor was his interest in the teachings of the Greeks any less keen. His teacher of declamation was Apollodorus of Pergamon whom, despite the man's great age, he took with him from Rome when, still in his youth, he made a journey to Apollonia.* Later he took his fill of various kinds of learning in the company of Areus, the philosopher, and his sons Dionysius and Nicanor. He did not, however, reach the stage of being able to speak Greek fluently or compose anything in it. If it was required, he would put something together in Latin and have others translate it. Yet he was not altogether unfamiliar with their poetry and even took pleasure in old comedies, often having them put on in public shows. When reading authors in Greek or Latin, he looked out most particularly for precepts and examples which would be of benefit in public or private life. These he would often copy out word for word and send to members of his household, or to those in charge of armies or provinces or to the city magistrates, whenever any of them was in need of advice. Sometimes he would even read out texts in their entirety to the senate and would have them included in edicts to the people, for instance Quintus Metellus' 'On Increasing the Population' and Rutilius' 'On Limiting Building', so as to show people in both cases that he was not the first to raise such matters but that they had been a cause of concern in earlier days.* He gave every encouragement to the men of talent of his day. When they gave recitations of their work he was a well-disposed and patient listener, not only in the case of poetry and history, but also speeches and treatises. He took great offence, however, if anything was written about him which was not weighty and by the best of authors, often instructing the praetors that his name should not be made commonplace in speaking competitions.

[90] In matters to do with the divine, we are told that his attitudes were as follows: he showed some weakness in being so afraid of thunder and lightning that he always took with him a sealskin for protection* and at any sign of a big storm he would take refuge in a room which was underground and vaulted. As I said earlier,* he once had a close brush with lightning when making a journey by night.

[91] He paid regard both to his own dreams and dreams others had about him. Though he had made a decision because of ill health not to leave his tent at the battle of Philippi, he did leave it nevertheless because of the warning in a friend's dream. This was fortunate, as it turned out, for the camp was captured and his litter was run through and pulled apart in the enemy attack, as it was thought he was still lying there. Always during the spring he himself would have frequent and alarming dreams which were without substance and came to nothing. At other times they were less frequent but more likely to have significance. As he used to make constant visits to the Temple of Jupiter the Thunderer which he had dedicated on the Capitoline, he dreamed that Jupiter Capitolinus complained to him that he had taken away his worshippers and that he himself replied that he had placed Jupiter the Thunderer there beside him as a doorkeeper. Soon after, in consequence, he had bells put on the apex of the Thunderer's roof, since these usually hang from doors. It was also because of a dream that on a particular day every year he would beg from the people, holding out his empty hand for them to put pennies in.*

[92] He would respect some auspices and omens as the most reliable of indicators. If his shoes were put on in the morning the wrong way, the left instead of the right, it was a bad omen. If, when he was embarking on a long journey by land or by sea, there happened to be drizzling rain, it was good omen indicating that he would return soon and with success. However, he was particularly influenced by prodigies. When a palm tree* sprang up between the joints in the paving in front of his house he moved it to the inner court of his household gods and took great care to ensure its flourishing. When a most ancient oak tree on the island of Capri, whose branches had withered and drooped to the ground, recovered at his arrival, he was so delighted that he handed over Aenaria to the city of Naples in exchange for the island.* He also had regard for particular days, never setting out on a journey the day after market-day,* or embarking on

any important business on the Nones; though in this case, as he writes to Tiberius, all he feared was the unlucky sound of the name.*

[93] As for the religious customs of foreigners, some he regarded with reverence as ancient and traditional, while the rest he held in disdain. For he was initiated into the mysteries at Athens* and when later at Rome he was sitting in judgement in a case concerning the privileges of priests of Athenian Ceres and some rather secret matters were being discussed, he sent away the court and the crowd of bystanders and heard the disputants alone. On the other hand, not only did he omit to make a small detour to see Apis,* when travelling through, but he even praised his grandson Gaius because on a journey through Judaea he did not pay his respects in Jerusalem.*

[94] And now that we are on this subject, it would not be irrelevant to add an account of the events before his birth, on the very day he was born, and subsequently, from which could be drawn the hope and expectation of his greatness and enduring good fortune. When, in ancient times, part of the wall of Velitrae had been touched by lightning, this was seen as a sign that a citizen of the town would one day be ruler; bolstered by this, the people of Velitrae immediately waged war with the Roman people, and on many subsequent occasions too, almost to their own destruction. Finally, however, it became clear that this event had been a sign portending the power of Augustus. Julius Marathus records that a few months before Augustus was born a prodigy was generally observed at Rome, which announced that nature was bringing forth a king for the Roman people. The senate, he continues, was most alarmed and agreed that no child born in that year should be raised. However, those whose wives were pregnant ensured that the decree was not registered in the treasury,* since each hoped that the prodigy referred to his own child. I read in the books of Asclepiades of Mendes, entitled 'Theologoumena', that Atia, attending the sacred rites of Apollo in the middle of the night, had her litter positioned in the temple and fell asleep, while the other matrons were also sleeping. All of a sudden, a serpent slid up to her, then quickly went away. On waking, she purified herself, as she would after sleeping with her husband. And at once there appeared on her body a mark in the image of a snake and she was never able to get rid of it, so that ever afterwards she avoided going to the public baths. Augustus was born ten months later and for this reason is believed to be the son of Apollo. It was

Atia, too, who before she gave birth, dreamed that her insides were carried to the stars and spread over all the earth and the skies. Octavius, the father, dreamed that the sun rose from Atia's womb.

On the day Augustus was born, when the conspiracy of Catiline was being discussed in the senate house and Octavius stayed away until late because his wife was in labour, Publius Nigidius, hearing why he was delayed, when informed of the hour of the birth, asserted (as is generally known) that the master of the world was born. When Octavius, who was leading an army through remote regions of Thrace, sought guidance concerning his son at some barbarian rituals in the grove of Father Liber,* the same prediction was made by the priests, for so great a flame had leapt up when they poured wine on the altar, that it passed beyond the peak of the temple roof and right up to the sky, a portent which had only previously occurred when Alexander the Great* offered sacrifice at that altar. And on the very next night thereafter, he dreamed he saw his son of greater than mortal size with a thunderbolt and sceptre and emblems of Jupiter Best and Greatest and a radiate crown, on a chariot decorated with laurel drawn by twelve horses of astonishing whiteness.

When Augustus was still a baby, as is recorded in the writings of Gaius Drusus, he was placed one evening by his nurse in his cot on level ground but the next morning he had disappeared. He was only found, after a long search, in a tower of great height where he lay facing the rising sun. When he first began to speak, he ordered some frogs to be silent who happened to be croaking in his grandfather's villa and they say that from that time no frog croaked there. When he was having a snack in a grove by the fourth milestone along the road to Campania, suddenly an eagle snatched the bread from his hand and, after flying up high into the air, unexpectedly came back and, dropping down gently, returned it to him. After the dedication of the Capitoline temple, Quintus Catulus* had dreams for two nights in succession: first that Jupiter Best and Greatest, when a number of youths were playing around his altar, took one of them aside and placed in the fold of his toga the image of the republic, which he carried in his hand; and, on the next night, that he noticed the same boy in the lap of Capitoline Jupiter and when he gave orders that the boy be brought down, this was forbidden by a warning from the god, as the boy was being reared for the salvation of the state. And on the next day Catulus encountered Augustus, who was otherwise unknown to him, and looking upon him with wonder, remarked on his great similarity to the boy in his dream. Others give a different account of Catulus' first dream, namely that when a number of well-born youths asked Jupiter for a guardian, he pointed out one of their number, on whom they were to depend for all their wishes and, having touched the boy's mouth with his fingers then brought them to his own lips. Marcus Cicero, when following Julius Caesar up to the Capitol, happened to tell his friends of his own dream of the previous night: a boy of noble appearance was let down from the sky on a golden chain. He came to rest before the doors of the Capitoline temple and was presented with a whip by Jupiter. Immediately afterwards Cicero saw Augustus, who was then relatively unknown and had been summoned to the ceremony by his great-uncle Caesar, and declared that he was the one whose image had appeared to him in his dream.

When Augustus took on the toga of manhood, his broad-striped tunic was ripped in two and fell at his feet. Some interpreted this as meaning no less than that the order whose emblem this was would some time become subject to him. The Deified Julius, in the course of taking over a place for his camp at Munda, when a palm tree was discovered in the wood which was being cut down, gave orders that it be preserved as an omen of victory. From this a shoot at once sprang forth which within a few days had so matured that it not only equalled its parent in size but even overshadowed it and it was filled with the nests of doves, even though that breed of bird has a particular aversion to hard and spiky leaves. They say that Caesar was particularly influenced by that sign in wishing for no other successor than his sister's grandson. Having withdrawn to Apollonia, Augustus went with Agrippa to the studio of the astrologer Theogenes. When a great and almost incredible future was predicted for Agrippa, who was the first to put his questions, Augustus concealed the details of his own birth and kept refusing to reveal them, through fear or shame that he himself would turn out to be of lesser importance. However, when, after much persuasion, he slowly and unwillingly disclosed them, Theogenes jumped up and venerated him. Soon Augustus had acquired such faith in fate that he made public his horoscope and had a silver coin struck with the image of the star sign Capricorn, under which he was born.

[95] When he returned from Apollonia, after the death of Caesar, and entered the city, all at once, although the sky was clear and calm, a circle appeared around the sun, like a rainbow, and suddenly the monument to Caesar's daughter Julia was struck by lightning. In Augustus' first consulship, when he was taking the auspices, twelve vultures appeared, as they had to Romulus,* and, when he slaughtered the victims, all their livers were found to be doubled inwards underneath; all the experts agreed in interpreting this as an omen portending a good and great future.

[96] He even sensed in advance what would be the outcome of all his wars. When the troops of the triumvirs had withdrawn to Bononia an eagle, which came to rest on the top of his tent, set upon two ravens who were attacking it from each side, bringing them to the ground. From this the entire army drew the conclusion that such a dispute would arise between the colleagues as indeed happened, and predicted what the outcome would be. When Augustus was travelling to Philippi a Thessalian declared that his victory was assured on the authority of the Deified Julius, whose image had appeared to him when he was travelling along a byway. When a sacrifice that was being offered near Perusia did not go well and he gave orders that more victims should be offered, the enemy suddenly burst in and seized all the ritual equipment. The *haruspices* agreed that the dangers and setbacks which were predicted for the sacrificer would all befall those who had taken the entrails, and this was exactly what happened. The day before he and his fleet engaged in the Sicilian war, he was walking along the shore when a fish jumped out of the water and landed at his feet. When at Actium he was going to join the fray, he met an ass with his driver. The man's name was Eutychus, while the animal was called Nicon.* After his victory he placed bronze images of them both in the temple which he had made of the place where his camp had been.

[97] His death also, which I shall recount later, and his divinization thereafter were both foretold through the clearest signs. When he was performing the rites* to mark the end of the lustrum in the Campus Martius with a great crowd of the people in attendance, an eagle flew around him a number of times, then went over to a nearby temple where it landed on the first letter of the word 'Agrippa'. Noticing this, he instructed his colleague Tiberius to pronounce the vows which it is customary to undertake for the next lustrum. For he

himself, although the tablets were written out and ready, was not willing to embark upon what he would not bring to a conclusion. At around the same time, the first letter of his name was struck from the inscription on his statue by a bolt of lightning. This was understood to mean that he would only live for a further hundred days, for that was the significance of the letter 'C', and that it would come to pass that he would be included among the gods, for 'aesar', the remaining part of the name 'Caesar', means 'god' in the language of the Etruscans.

Then, when he was about to send Tiberius to Illyria and planning to accompany him as far as Beneventum,* he was held up by litigants requiring his judgement in one case after another and declared that, whatever tried to delay him, he would stay in Rome no longer, and this was soon seen as another omen. For, having embarked on his journey, he got as far as Astura, and thence, contrary to his usual practice, put to sea before daybreak, as the wind was favourable; thus he succumbed to an illness, which began with diarrhoea. [98] Then, having travelled along the Campanian coast and around the neighbouring islands, he rested for four days in an inlet by Capri, feeling particularly inclined to enjoy leisure and the company of his friends. As he happened to be sailing past the bay of Puteoli, the passengers and sailors of an Alexandrian ship, which had just arrived, dressed in white, wearing crowns, and offering incense, heaped upon him great praise, saying that it was thanks to him that they lived, travelled, and enjoyed liberty and good fortune. Greatly pleased by this event, he divided four hundred gold coins amongst his companions, extracting an undertaking on oath from each of them that they would only spend the money on Alexandrian merchandise. And for the rest of the days which followed, he gave out, amongst other presents, togas and Greek cloaks, proposing a rule that Romans should adopt Greek dress and language, and Greeks Roman dress and language. He was an enthusiastic observer of the exercises of the ephebes, of whom there was still a significant number on Capri, according to the traditional practice.* He even provided a feast for them which he himself attended, allowing them, even demanding of them, licence to joke and fight over tokens for apples and sweets and all kinds of things. Indeed, he indulged in every kind of fun.

The neighbouring part of the island of Capri he termed the City of Do-nothings, on account of the idleness of those of his companions who had retreated there. But one man, of whom he was very fond, Masgaba by name, he used to call 'Ktistes',* as though he were the island's founder. This Masgaba had died the previous year and Augustus, noticing, as he looked out from the dining-room, that his tomb was surrounded by a crowd of people and many lights,* composed a line of poetry off the cuff, which he declaimed out loud:

> The founder's tomb I see in flames.

And, turning to Tiberius' friend, Thrasyllus, who was reclining opposite him and knew nothing of the matter, he asked him which of the poets he thought was the author. When Thrasyllus hesitated, he added another line:

> Seest thou Masgaba honoured with lights?

and asked his opinion on this one also. When the other replied simply that, whoever wrote them, they were very good, he burst out laughing and made many jokes. Shortly thereafter he crossed over to Naples, even though his digestive system was already weakened through intermittent illness. Nevertheless he sat through the whole of the five-yearly gymnastic contest which had been established in his honour, then set out with Tiberius for their destination. But, his condition worsening on the way back, he finally took to his bed at Nola and held a long meeting in secret with Tiberius, whom he had recalled from his expedition. After this, he was unable to give his mind to any further matter of importance.

[99] On his last day, he kept asking whether there was any disturbance in the streets because of him. Asking for a mirror, he gave instructions that his hair should be combed and his drooping features rearranged. Then, when the friends he had summoned were present, he inquired of them whether they thought he had played his role well in the comedy of life, adding the concluding lines:

> Since the play has been so good, clap your hands
> And all of you dismiss us with applause.*

Then he sent everyone away and suddenly, in the middle of questioning some people who had come from Rome about the illness of Drusus' daughter, he slipped away, as he was kissing Livia, with these words: 'Live mindful of our marriage, Livia, and farewell.' Thus did he have the good fortune to die easily and as he had always

wished. For whenever he heard that anyone had died quickly and
without suffering, he would pray that he himself and his dear ones
would have a similar 'euthanasia'* —that was even the term he used.
Before he died he gave only one indication that his mind was disturbed, when he suddenly took fright and complained that he was
being taken away by forty young men. And this too was really a
premonition rather than a symptom of mental failing, for that was
the number of the praetorian soldiers who carried him forth for the
funeral. [100] He died in the same bedroom as his father Octavius,
when two Sextuses, Pompeius and Appuleius, were consuls, on the
fourteenth day before the Kalends of September,* at the ninth hour,
when he was thirty-five days short of seventy-six years.

Councillors from the towns and colonies carried his body from
Nola as far as Bovillae,* by night, because of the season of the year,
and in the intervals it was placed in the basilica or the largest temple
in one of the towns. From Bovillae, it was taken by the equestrian
order who carried it to Rome where it was placed in the vestibule of
his house. The senators so competed to show devotion in the elabor-
ation of the funeral and in honouring his memory that amongst
many other proposals some were of the view that the funeral procession should come through the triumphal gate, that the Victory from
the senate house should head the procession, and that the dirge
should be sung by boys and girls who were the children of the
leading citizens. Others recommended that on the day of the funeral
people should take off their gold rings and replace them with iron
ones, and some that his bones should be collected up by priests of
the senior colleges.* There was even one who advocated that the name
of the month of August should be transferred to September, since he
had been born in the latter and died in the former. Another man
proposed that the entire period from the day he was born to the day
he died should be termed the Augustan age and should appear as
such in the records. However, though a limit was placed upon the
honours, his eulogy was delivered twice, once by Tiberius in front of
the Temple of the Deified Julius and once in front of the old rostra
by Drusus, Tiberius' son. Then he was carried on the shoulders
of senators to the Campus Martius, where he was cremated. There
was even an ex-praetor who swore that after the cremation he saw
Augustus' image ascending into the sky. The remains were gathered
by leading men of the equestrian order, dressed in unbelted tunics,

their feet bare, before being enclosed in the Mausoleum. This monument he had had built between the Flaminian Way and the Tiber bank in his sixth consulship and had planted around it trees and walkways which he had then made available for public use.

[101] In the consulship of Lucius Plancius and Gaius Silius, three days before the Nones of April,* one year and four months before his death, he had made a will, in two books, partly in his hand and partly in those of his freedmen Polybius and Hilarion, and deposited it with the Vestal Virgins. This they now brought forth, together with three rolls, sealed in the same manner. All of these were opened in the senate and read out. He designated as primary heirs Tiberius, who was to receive one half and one sixth of his property, and Livia, who was to receive a third. They were also ordered to take his name. His secondary heirs* were Drusus, the son of Tiberius, who was to receive one third, while the remainder went to Germanicus and his three male children. In third place were many relatives and friends. To the Roman people he left forty million sesterces, to the tribes* three million five hundred thousand, to the praetorian guard a thousand each, to the city cohorts five hundred, and to the legionaries three hundred. This sum, he ordered, was to be paid at once for he always had it to hand and ready. He gave various legacies to other people, some amounting to twenty thousand sesterces. These were to be paid out on a day in a year's time, with the excuse that the size of his holdings was limited and even his heirs would get no more than a hundred and fifty million. For, although he had in recent years received fourteen hundred million through the wills of his friends, almost all of this, together with the estates of his two fathers* and his other inheritances he had spent for the benefit of the state. He gave orders that if anything happened to the Julias, his daughter and granddaughter, they were not to be buried in his tomb. As for the three rolls, in one he set out the instructions for his funeral, in the second a list of his achievements, which he wished to have inscribed in bronze and set up in front of his Mausoleum,* while in the third he gave an account of the entire empire, how many soldiers there were serving in each place and how much money there was in the treasury, in the provincial accounts, and in outstanding taxes. He added the names of his freedmen and slaves from whom details could be obtained.

TIBERIUS

[1] The patrician branch of the Claudii—for there was also a plebeian one, no less distinguished in influence or standing—had its origins at Regilli,* a town of the Sabines. From there, accompanied by a large band of clients, the family moved to Rome, not long after the city's foundation, at the instigation of Titus Tatius, Romulus' partner in power—or, as is more generally held, that of Atta Claudius, the head of the family—about six years after the expulsion of the kings.* Co-opted into the ranks of the patricians, they received from the state land for their clients beyond the River Anio and a plot to serve for their own burial at the foot of the Capitoline hill. In succeeding years, they obtained twenty-eight consulships, five dictatorships, seven censorships, six triumphs, and two ovations. Though the family was identified by a variety of forenames and *cognomina*, they agreed to renounce the forename of Lucius, after one who carried the name was convicted of robbery and another of murder. However, to the *cognomina* they added that of Nero, which, in the language of the Sabines, means brave and strong.

[2] Many of the Claudii are known to have rendered numerous outstanding services to the state—and also disservices. To mention only the most important: Appius Caecus* argued successfully against entering into alliance with King Pyrrhus, pointing out the harm it would bring. Claudius Caudex* was the first to lead the fleet across the straits and drive the Carthaginians from Sicily. Tiberius Nero, when Hasdrubal came from Spain with a great army, checked him before he could join his brother Hannibal.* Against these must be weighed Claudius Regillianus, who, when he was a member of the council of ten for drafting laws, attempted to ascribe servile status to a freeborn girl so that he could gratify his lust.* This was the cause of another secession of the plebs from the patricians. Claudius Russus* set up a statue of himself crowned with a diadem at the Forum of Appius* and sought to get all Italy in his power through patronage. Claudius Pulcher,* when he was taking the auspices in Sicily and the chickens would not eat, defied the omen, throwing the chickens into the sea with orders that, if they would not eat, then they must drink, and began his sea-battle. When he was defeated and received

instructions from the senate to appoint a dictator, he named his messenger Glycias, making further mockery of the state's perilous situation.*

Among the women, too, there are similar examples of good and evil, since the family may claim both the Claudia who, when the ship carrying the sacred objects of the Idaean mother of the gods* ran aground in the Tiber, pulled it from the shallows, having prayed out loud that the ship would follow her only if her chastity were irreproachable; and that other Claudia* who was brought before the people on a kind of treason charge unprecedented for a woman, because, when her carriage was making slow progress due to the density of the crowd, she openly proclaimed her wish that her brother Pulcher were alive again, so that he might lose another fleet and reduce Rome's crowds. Indeed, it is notorious that, with the exception of Publius Clodius who, with the aim of sending Cicero into exile had himself adopted by a man who was not only plebeian but also younger than himself,* the Claudii were always conservatives to a man and resolute defenders of the influence and standing of the patricians. Indeed their arrogance and contempt for the plebs was such that even when on a capital charge before the people they would not wear mourning or plead for mercy. Several of them in the course of an argument or a brawl struck tribunes of the plebs. Indeed one of them, who was a Vestal Virgin, as her brother celebrated a triumph without the people's authorization, climbed into his chariot and rode with him all the way to the Capitol, so that none of the tribunes could lawfully veto his action or prevent him.*

[3] Tiberius Caesar was born from this stock—and indeed on both sides, for his father's family was descended from Tiberius Nero and his mother's from Appius Pulcher, both of whom were sons of Appius Caecus. He was also a member of the Livii, for his maternal grandfather had been adopted into that family. Although the latter were plebeians, yet their distinction was such that they had been honoured with eight consulships, two censorships, three triumphs, and even a dictatorship and the post of Master of Horse. Though the family boasted many noble men, Salinator and the Drusi stood out. Salinator, as censor, gave to all the tribes a mark of dishonour on the grounds of inconsistency, because, although after his first consulship they had charged him with and convicted him of many offences, they had gone on to elect him consul a second time and censor.* Drusus

aquired the *cognomen* borne by himself and his descendants when he killed Drausus, the enemy's general, in single combat. It is even said that it was he who, when he was propraetor, brought back from the province of Gaul the gold which had long ago been given to the Senones to ransom the Capitol—despite the story that it was seized from them by Camillus. His grandson, because of his brilliant manœuvres against the Gracchi, was given the title 'Patron of the Senate'. This man's son was murdered through the trickery of his opponents, as he pursued numerous different strategies in the course of a similar dispute.

[4] Nero, the father of Tiberius, served as quaestor under Julius Caesar, and contributed much to the victory when he was put in charge of the fleet during the Alexandrian war. For this reason he was made a pontifex, taking the place of Publius Scipio, and sent to establish colonies in Gaul, including those at Narbo and Arelate.* However, when Caesar was murdered, and everyone else, fearing the anger of the mob, voted for an amnesty, he supported a move to reward the tyrannicides. Later, when his praetorship was about to expire and a dispute arose among the triumvirs at the end of the year, he held on to the insignia of his office after the proper term and followed the consul Lucius Antonius, brother of the triumvir, to Perusia. He alone maintained his allegiance, fleeing when all the others on his side had surrendered, first to Praeneste, then to Naples, finally, having vainly tried to enlist slaves by promising them their freedom, escaping to Sicily. However, resentful that he had not at once been given access to Sextus Pompeius and that he was not permitted to use the fasces, he went over to Mark Antony in Achaia. With him he shortly returned to Rome, once peace had been negotiated between all parties. There he surrendered his wife Livia Drusilla in response to the suit of Augustus, even though she was at that time pregnant and had already borne him a son. Not long after that day he died. Two children survived him, Tiberius Nero and Drusus Nero.

[5] Some believe Tiberius was born at Fundi, on the feeble grounds that his maternal grandmother came from there and that, shortly after the time of his birth, an image of Good Fortune was set up in the town by order of the senate. However, as many more reliable sources claim, he was born at Rome, on the Palatine hill, on the sixteenth day before the Kalends of December,* when the consuls

were Marcus Aemilius Lepidus (for the second time) and Lucius
Munatius Plancus, in the course of the war at Philippi. For that is
how it appears in the gazette and the public records. Yet there are
still some who write that he was born in the previous year, the
consulship of Hirtius and Pansa, and others, that it was the year
after, that of Servilius Isauricus and Lucius Antonius.

[6] His infancy and boyhood were unhappy and disturbed, as he
accompanied his parents in their flight here, there, and everywhere.
On one occasion, in Naples, when, with an enemy attack imminent,
they attempted to make their way secretly to a ship, he twice nearly
gave them away with his wailing, once when he was taken from his
nurse's breast, and again when he was taken all of a sudden from
his mother's arms by people who were trying to help the poor
women in their plight. He was taken all around Sicily, too, and
Greece and was given over publicly to the protection of the
Spartans, because they were clients of the Claudii. Travelling on
from there by night, he nearly lost his life when a fire suddenly
flared up in the woods, completely surrounding the party, so that
Livia's hair and clothes were singed. The gifts which he received
in Sicily from Pompeia, the sister of Sextus Pompeius, a robe, a
brooch, and a golden amulet, may still be seen even now at Baiae.
Once back in Rome, he was adopted as heir in the will of the senator
Marcus Gallius. Accepting the inheritance, he soon renounced the
name, on the grounds that Gallius had been among the enemies of
Augustus.

When he was nine years old he gave a speech on the rostra in
praise of his deceased father. Later, as an adolescent, he accompanied
Augustus' chariot in the triumph after Actium, riding the left trace-
horse, the right one being ridden by Marcellus, the son of Octavia.
He presided at the city festival and took part, during the circus
games, in the game of Troy as leader of the band of older boys.

[7] The chief events of his adolescence, once he had assumed the
toga of manhood, and of that part of his life preceding the start of his
reign were as follows. He provided a set of gladiatorial fights in
memory of his father and another in memory of his grandfather
Drusus at different times and in different places, first in the Forum
and then in the amphitheatre, even recalling some gladiators who
had earned their retirement with a payment of a hundred thousand
sesterces each. He also gave other games, though without attending

them himself.* All was done magnificently, thanks to the funds of his mother and stepfather.

He took as his wife Agrippina, the daughter of Marcus Agrippa and niece of Caecilius Atticus,* to whom Cicero wrote his letters. From her he acknowledged a son, Drusus, but although she suited him well and was indeed pregnant again, he was forced to set her aside and then straight afterwards to marry Julia, the daughter of Augustus. This caused him great anguish for he loved Agrippina dearly and disapproved of Julia's mode of life, having sensed that she desired him even when her former husband was living—as indeed was generally recognized. After the divorce he regretted having sent Agrippina away and once, when by chance he caught sight of her, he went after her, his eyes so full of tears and sadness that measures were taken to ensure she should never come into his sight again. At first he lived with Julia harmoniously and with affection, but soon they fell out and so severely that he lived apart from her thereafter, once the child, which was the bond of their union, was gone (born at Aquileia, it died in infancy). He lost his brother Drusus in Germany and accompanied his body all the way back to Rome, walking before it the entire distance.

[8] Embarking on his civil career, he acted as advocate for King Archelaus, as well as for the people of Tralles and the Thessalians, each being prosecuted on a different charge before Augustus as judge. He made a speech to the senate on behalf of the people of Laodicea, Thyatira, and Chios who had suffered a terrible earthquake and were begging for assistance. Fannius Caepio, who had conspired with Varro Murena against Augustus, he summoned before the judges on a charge of treason and secured his condemnation. At the same time, he was responsible for two public offices, one being that of the corn supply which was at that time limited, the other an investigation into slave-prisons throughout Italy. Their governors had a bad reputation since they were alleged to detain travellers, as well as those who tried to hide themselves there in fear of military service.

[9] His first military post was as tribune, serving in the Cantabrian campaign. Then, having led an army into the east, he restored the kingdom of Armenia to Tigranes, crowning him with a diadem on the tribunal. He also took back the standards which the Parthians had taken from Marcus Crassus.* After this he had charge of Gallia

Comata* for about a year, at a time when it was troubled by barbarian incursions and disputes amongst its nobles. Then he made war on the Raeti and Vindelici,* then the Pannonians, then the Germans. In the war against the Raeti and Vindelici, he conquered the Alpine tribes, in the Pannonian war the Breuci* and Dalmatians, and in the German war he took forty thousand prisoners whom he drove into Gaul, assigning them territory on the banks of the Rhine. Because of these achievements he received an ovation and entered the city in a chariot,* having earlier, as some people believe, been granted triumphal ornaments—a new kind of honour which no one had been given before. He secured his magistracies before the usual age, holding almost in succession the quaestorship, the praetorship, and the consulship. In the interval between his first and second consulships, he even received a five-year grant of tribunician power.

[10] In the midst of such fortunate circumstances, relatively young and in good health, he suddenly decided to retire, withdrawing himself as far as possible from public life. It is uncertain whether this was because he hated his wife—for, while he did not dare to accuse her of anything or to divorce her, neither could he bear to continue living with her—or because he could thus ensure that people did not tire of his presence, for absence would safeguard his prestige, perhaps even adding to it, if the state should have need of his services. Some think that, as Augustus' children* were by then grown up, he was ceding to them of his own accord the role of second in command which he had long occupied as if it were his, following the example of Marcus Agrippa, who went away to Mytilene when Marcus Marcellus took public office, so that he should not seem either to stand in his way or to overshadow him through his presence. This was the reason he himself adduced—though later on. At the time, he sought leave of absence, claiming he had had enough of public life and needed a rest from his labours. He did not relent even in the face of his mother's urgent prayers and his stepfather's complaints to the senate that he was being deserted. Indeed, when they persisted in their attempts to restrain him, he refused to eat for four days. When he eventually received permission to go, he left his wife and son in Rome and went at once to Ostia, offering not a word to any of those who came after him and kissing goodbye only a few at the moment of departure.

[11] From Ostia he sailed along the shore of Campania, pausing

only briefly when news came that Augustus was ill. But when a rumour circulated that he was lingering in the hope of fulfilling his highest ambition, he made his way to Rhodes, though the weather was all but against him, for he had been won over by the island's beauty and healthy atmosphere when he stopped off there on the way back from Armenia. Here he contented himself with a modest town house and a country villa not much more spacious, and adopted a private mode of life. From time to time, attended by neither lictor nor messenger, he would take a walk in the gymnasium exchanging greetings with the ordinary Greeks in the manner of an equal. One morning, when he happened to be making plans for the day, he announced that he would like to make a visit to whoever in the town was sick. His attendants misinterpreted this wish and gave orders that all the sick were to be brought into the public portico and there laid out in groups according to the manner of their affliction. Distressed by this unexpected occurrence, he long debated what to do, eventually going around to each individual, apologizing for what had happened even to the humblest and most insignificant.

Only one single occasion was noted on which he manifestly made use of his tribunician power: he was a regular attender of the schools and lecture halls of the professors and once, when a rather fierce quarrel had arisen among the opponents of the Sophists, one man was bold enough to abuse him because he took sides and expressed his support for the opposition. And so he quietly withdrew to his house and at once reappeared with his attendants. The man who had abused him was summoned by the herald to appear before the tribunal where Tiberius ordered that he be taken to prison.

Subsequently he learnt that Julia his wife had been convicted of licentiousness and adultery and that, on Augustus' authority, a divorce notice had been issued in his name. And, although he was pleased by the news, yet he did his duty as far as he could, writing frequent letters to the father on behalf of the daughter, urging that, whatever her merits, she be allowed to keep whatever gifts he had ever given her.* When the period of his tribunician power had elapsed, he finally admitted that what he had hoped to avoid through his withdrawal was nothing other than the suspicion that he was a rival to Gaius and Lucius. Since he was now safe from such accusations, as they were established and evidently occupied the second position, he sought permission to see his relatives again, for he missed them very much. However, his request was not granted and he was even told that he should give up all care for his relatives whom he had abandoned so willingly.

[12] Thus he stayed on at Rhodes against his will, only with his mother's help securing the position of legate of Augustus, as a pretext for his humiliating position. From that time then, his life was not just private but fraught with fear and danger and he concealed himself in the country inland in an attempt to avoid the attentions of those stopping off on sea journeys who persistently sought him out. Indeed, no general or magistrate, whatever their destination, failed to put in at Rhodes. And greater causes for concern were added to these. For, when he went to Samos to visit his stepson Gaius, who had a command in the east, he perceived him to have grown hostile as a result of accusations made by Marcus Lollius, his companion and instructor. Tiberius had also fallen under suspicion of having some centurions to whom he was patron, when they returned to their camp from leave, send ambiguous messages to a number of men which seemed to suggest he was testing whether these individuals might be persuaded to join a rebellion. When he was informed of this by Augustus, he insistently demanded that someone, of no matter what rank, be appointed to act as scrutineer of his actions and words.

[13] He dropped his usual equestrian and military exercises and put aside the national dress, wearing instead a Greek cloak and slippers. In this manner he passed nearly two years, accruing more contempt and hatred daily, so that the people of Nemausus* tore down his images and statues and when, at a private party, his name came up in conversation, there was one man who promised Gaius that, if the order were given, he would at once sail to Rhodes and return with the head of the exile—for so was he termed. Thus he was forced, not at this point by fear but by a crisis, to demand, through his own most insistent prayers and those of his mother, that he be allowed to return. And his demands were successful, though partly indeed by chance. For Augustus had determined that he would make no decision regarding this matter unless his elder son Gaius was in agreement. It happened at that time that Gaius had fallen out with Marcus Lollius and was thus ready to listen to his stepfather's requests. And so with Gaius' permission Tiberius was recalled, but on condition that he should acquire no public role or office.

[14] He returned in the eighth year after his withdrawal with great and firm hopes for the future, hopes which he had entertained since his early youth as a result of omens and predictions. When Livia was pregnant with him she sought out various omens to discover whether or not she would produce a male child. An egg was taken out from under a hen and warmed in turn with her own hands and those of her attendants and from this a chick hatched out crowned with a magnificent crest. And the astrologer Scribonius promised great things for the child, even that he would one day hold power, though without regal insignia (for at that time, the rule of the Caesars was still unknown). Then, when he embarked on his first military campaign and was leading his troops through Macedonia into Syria, it happened that altars at Philippi consecrated in earlier times by victorious legions all of a sudden blazed with fire of their own accord. And soon after, passing near Patavium on his way to Illyricum, he made a visit to the oracle of Geryon where he drew a lot which gave instructions that, if he wished for guidance, he was to throw golden dice into the fountain of Aponus.* It turned out that the dice he threw displayed the highest score. Even today you can see these dice under the water. A few days before he was recalled, an eagle—which had never before been seen on Rhodes—perched on the roof of his house. And the day before he was informed about his recall, as he was changing his tunic, his clothes seemed to burst into flames. It was at this time too that he had particular experience of the powers of the astrologer Thrasyllus, when, as he sighted a ship, he declared that good tidings were on their way. And this happened as they were taking a stroll together, at the very moment when Tiberius had determined that Thrasyllus should be thrown into the sea, for, since events were turning out for the worse against his predictions, he had judged Thrasyllus to be a traitor whom he had rashly taken into his confidence.

[15] On his return to Rome, he immediately introduced his son Drusus to public life but transferred his own household from the old house of Pompey in Carinae to the Gardens of Maecenas on the Esquiline* and devoted himself completely to a life of retirement, attending only to his personal business and taking no part in public duties. But when, within the space of three years, Gaius and Lucius had died, he was adopted together with their brother Marcus Agrippa* by Augustus, though he himself first had to adopt Germanicus, his own brother's son. And after this he performed

none of the actions of a family head and retained no aspect of the powers he had given up. For he could neither make gifts nor free slaves and was unable to receive any inheritances or legacies, except as additions to his personal fund.* And from that time no measure was omitted which might add to his status, the more so when, after Agrippa was excluded and banished, it was clear that hope of the succession lay with him alone.

[16] He received a second grant of tribunican power for five years and was given the task of pacifying Germany. The envoys of the Parthians, when they brought their instructions to Augustus in Rome, were given orders to attend Tiberius in his province also. However, when news came of a revolt in Illyricum, he went over to take charge of the new campaign, which was the most serious military enterprise against an external enemy since the Punic wars. This he conducted over a three-year period with fifteen legions and the same number of auxiliary forces, in the face of great difficulties in all quarters and a terrible shortage of resources. And although several times recalled, he nevertheless persevered, fearing that, if they gave ground voluntarily, the enemy, being close by and most formidable, might press forward. His perseverence brought great rewards, for he conquered and brought under control all of Illyricum which lies between Italy, the kingdom of Noricum, Thrace, and Macedonia, between the River Danube and the Adriatic sea.

[17] His glory was increased still further by circumstances. For around this time, Quintilius Varus with his three legions perished in Germany and it was universally believed that the victorious Germans would have joined forces with the Pannonians, if Illyricum had not first been defeated. Because of this he was awarded a triumph and many other great honours. And some people even took the view that he should be given the *cognomen* 'Pannonicus', others opting for 'Unconquered', and quite a few for 'Pious'. However, Augustus intervened concerning the matter of the *cognomen*, repeating his promise that Tiberius would be happy with the name he would receive on the death of his father. Tiberius himself deferred the triumph while the state was in mourning for the Varian disaster. Nevertheless, he entered in the city clad in his bordered toga and crowned with a laurel wreath and mounted a tribunal which had been set up in the Saepta, where he took his seat beside Augustus, flanked by the two consuls, while the senate stood in attendance.

From there, having addressed his greeting to the people he was taken on a circuit of the temples.

[18] The next year he returned to Germany and, realizing that the Varian disaster had come about as a result of the general's foolhardiness and negligence, he took no actions without the backing of his council; though in all other situations he had been content to rely on the judgement of himself alone, now, against his habit, he consulted with numerous men as to how the war should be conducted. He also paid greater attention to detail than he had previously. When he was about to cross the Rhine he subjected all the baggage to a fixed limit and would not embark on the crossing until, standing on the bank, he had made an examination of the loads carried by the waggons, to make sure that nothing was being transported which was not permitted and necessary. Once on the further side of the Rhine, he ordered his manner of living as follows: he took his food seated directly on the ground and often spent the night without a tent for shelter;* he would give orders for the next day, along with notice of any last-minute tasks, in writing, adding the warning that if anyone was uncertain of anything he was to apply to him personally and no other, no matter what hour of the night.

[19] His disciplinary regime was extremely harsh, with punishments and humiliations drawn from the examples of antiquity, so that even a legionary legate who had sent a few soldiers across the river with one of his freedmen to do some hunting received a mark of shame. Although he left almost nothing to fortune and chance, he embarked on battles with rather greater heart whenever it happened that he was working by night and the lamp, suddenly and for no reason, flickered and went out; for he had faith, as he used to say, in an omen tried and tested in all his own military campaigns and those of his ancestors. However, just as the campaign was brought to a successful conclusion, he came very close to being assassinated by one of the Bructeri* who had infiltrated his attendants but betrayed himself through his nervousness. A confession of his planned crime was extracted from him through torture.

[20] After two years' absence he returned from Germany to Rome where he celebrated the triumph* which he had earlier postponed, accompanied by his legates who had been awarded triumphal ornaments at his request. But before he took the route towards the Capitoline, he alighted from his chariot and went down on his knees

to honour his father who was presiding. Bato, the general of the
Pannonians, he enriched with great gifts and installed in Ravenna,*
thus expressing his gratitude that when he and his army were
trapped in a difficult place, Bato had allowed them to escape. Then
he provided a banquet of a thousand tables for the people of Rome
and each man received a gift of three hundred sesterces. With the
profits of his campaigns, he dedicated the Temple of Concordia as
well as the Temple of Castor and Pollux in his own name and that of
his brother.

[21] Not long after this, a law was passed, on the motion of the
consuls, making him jointly responsible with Augustus for the
administration of the provinces and appointing them both to the
censorship. After the census was completed, Tiberius was on his way
to Illyricum, when he was suddenly called back to find Augustus
stricken, though still living, and they spent an entire day closeted
together. I know the tale is commonly told that when Tiberius had
just left after their secret conference, the voice of Augustus was
heard by his attendants to utter the words: 'Alas for the wretched
Roman people who will be at the mercy of such slow-grinding jaws!'
Nor am I unaware of the story told by some that Augustus clearly
and with no concealment disapproved of Tiberius' fearsome disposition so that sometimes when engaged in lighthearted and
relaxed conversation he would break off when Tiberius appeared.
Nevertheless, so the story goes, he was won over by his wife's
entreaties and agreed to the adoption, perhaps moved by the hope
that, with such a successor, he himself would one day be the more
regretted. And yet I cannot be made to believe that the most circum-
spect and sagacious emperor would have acted in any way rashly
concerning a matter of such importance. Rather, having weighed up
the vices and the virtues of Tiberius, he judged the virtues to be
dominant, particularly since he had sworn before a public assembly
that he was adopting him for the good of the Roman state and had
described him in letters as a superlative military man and the sole
defence of the Roman people. By way of example, I include some
excerpts from these below:

Farewell, most sweet Tiberius, and good luck in your enterprise. You lead
your men for me and for the Muses. Most sweet man, and—if this isn't
so, may I never be happy myself—most brave, most dutiful general.
Farewell.

Truly do I praise the conduct of your summer campaigns, my Tiberius. In my view no one else could have done as well as you did in the face of so many difficulties—and such apathy on the part of your men. Those who were with you all agree that the famous line can be applied to you:

'One man alone through his care has saved our state.'*

If anything arises which requires more careful thought, or if I am annoyed about something, how much indeed, by Jupiter, do I long for my Tiberius and those lines of Homer come to mind:

'If only he should follow, we too might return home both,
Though from the raging flames, for he is very wise.'*

When I hear and read that you are worn out by your ceaseless labours, the gods forsake me if my body does not shiver in sympathy. I beg you to spare yourself, lest news of your failing should finish off your mother and me and expose the Roman people to danger concerning the future of their empire.

If you are not to be well, it makes no difference to me whether I myself am well or ill.

I beseech the gods to spare you for us and keep you healthy now and in the future, if they are not wholly hostile to the people of Rome.

[22] Tiberius did not make public the news of Augustus' death until young Agrippa had met his end. The tribune who had been appointed as his guard killed him after receiving letters ordering him to do so. As for these letters, there was some doubt whether Augustus had left them when he died, to remove a source of dissension in the aftermath; or whether Livia had dictated them in Augustus' name—with or without the knowledge of Tiberius. When the tribune reported that his orders had been carried out, Tiberius replied that he had given no such orders and that the tribune should render an account of himself to the senate—perhaps by this means he sought for the present to avoid unpopularity. Soon, through his silence, the matter was quite forgotten.

[23] However, after he had convened the senate by means of his tribunician power and had begun his address, suddenly, as if unable to sustain his grief, he let out a groan and, wishing that his life as well as his voice would fail him, handed over the text of his speech to be continued by his son Drusus. Then he had Augustus' will brought in and read out by a freedman. Only those witnesses drawn from the senatorial order were allowed to be present; the others identified

their seals outside the senate house. The will began as follows: 'Since harsh fortune has robbed me of my sons Gaius and Lucius, Tiberius Caesar shall be heir to two-thirds of my estate.' This too increased the suspicions of those debating the matter that he had chosen Tiberius as successor through necessity rather than preference, since he had not refrained from prefacing his will in this way.

[24] Although he did not hesitate to take on and to exercise imperial power and had an escort of soldiers (thus possessing both the reality of rule and its appearance), for a long time he refused the actual title. When his friends urged him to take it, with impudent hypocrisy he reproved them, saying they did not know what a monster the empire was, and when the senate begged him, going down on their knees, he put them off with ambiguous answers and crafty delaying tactics, so that the patience of some was strained to breaking-point and one exclaimed, amid the shouting, 'Either do it or have done with it!' And another openly complained that, while others were slow to do what they promised, he was slow to promise what he was already doing. At last, acting as if under compulsion and lamenting that he was shackling himself to a wretched and onerous burden, he accepted the principate, but only in such a way as to create the hope that he would one day lay it down. These were his words: 'Until I reach the point when you can deem it right to give me some rest in my old age.'

[25] The reason for his delay was the fear of disasters which were impending on all sides—so that he often used to say he was holding a wolf by its ears. For Agrippa's slave, whose name was Clemens, had gathered a considerable force of men to revenge his master, Lucius Scribonius Libo, a man of noble birth, was secretly devising a revolution and a double mutiny had arisen in the armies of Illyricum and Germany. Both armies made many demands for extra privileges, most particularly, that they should receive pay equal to that of the Praetorian guard. Moreover, the troops in Germany disdained an emperor not of their own making and urged Germanicus, who was at that time their commander, to seize the supreme power—though he firmly resisted their demands. Fearing this possibility most particularly, Tiberius asked the senate to appoint him to any public office it pleased, for no man on his own could manage the whole empire, unless with a colleague—or many colleagues. He also made out that he was ill so that Germanicus would be reassured that he would soon

succeed or at least become partner in the empire. Once the mutinies were quelled, he also managed to capture Clemens by means of a trick. Unwilling to undertake harsh measures too soon into his reign, he waited until his second year in office to expose Libo before the senate, content in the mean time to be merely on his guard. When they were offering sacrifice together among the *pontifices*, Tiberius took care that a knife of lead was substituted for the usual sacrificial one and when Libo requested a private audience he would not grant it except in the presence of his son Drusus, and throughout the interview he held on to Libo's right arm, pretending to lean on it for support, as they walked together.

[26] However, once his fears had subsided he behaved in a very unassuming manner, at least at first, and gave himself fewer airs than an ordinary citizen.* Many spendid honours were offered to him but he accepted only a few modest ones. He grudgingly permitted his birthday, which fell during the Plebeian circus games, to be marked by the addition of one extra two-horse chariot. He refused to allow temples or priests to be decreed to him, not would he even permit statues or images of himself unless with his prior consent. And these were only allowed on condition that they would be placed not among the statues of the gods but among the other temple ornaments. He intervened to prevent an oath being taken to ratify his acts* and also to stop the month of September being called Tiberius and that of October Livius.* He refused to take 'Imperator' as a forename, or to take the *cognomen* 'Father of the Fatherland' and he also turned down the proposal to adorn his entrance hall with the civic crown.* And although he had a right to it as Augustus' heir, he did not use the name 'Augustus' in writing letters to anyone except kings and princes. He held only three consulships after succeeding to power, one for a few days, another for three months, and a third, while he was away from Rome, until the Ides of May.*

[27] He was so opposed to flattery that he would permit no senator to approach his litter to pay his respects or to broach some matter of business, and indeed once, in his attempts to avoid a man of consular rank who went down on his knees to beg his pardon, he fell flat on his back. And if, in the course of a conversation or a formal speech, some too flattering remark was made about him, he did not hesitate to interrupt at once, chastise the speaker, and correct him. When a certain fellow called him 'Master' he told him not to

address him again in this insulting way.* When another man spoke
of his 'sacred tasks' and yet another reported that he had come to
the senate on the emperor's authority, he obliged them to correct
themselves and speak of 'persuasion' rather than 'authority' and
'laborious' rather than 'sacred'.

[28] However, when it came to insults, hostile rumours, and lam-
poons concerning himself and his family he was calm and patient
and would often proclaim that in a free state minds and tongues
should be free.* When once the senate demanded that such crimes
and such offenders should be prosecuted, he observed, 'We do not
have so much leisure that we ought to concern ourselves in more
business. Once you go down this road, you won't be able to undertake anything else. Under this pretext, everyone's quarrels will fall to
you to deal with.' We also have a most unassuming comment which
he made to the senate: 'If someone speaks against me, I shall take
care to give an account of my words and actions; if he does so again,
we shall be mutual enemies.'* [29] And this was more remarkable
because he himself almost exceeded politeness in addressing and
paying his respects to individual senators and the senate as a whole.
Falling out with Quintus Haterius in the senate, he said: 'I ask you to
forgive me, if I have, as a senator, spoken too freely against you.' And
then, addressing himself to all, he remarked:

O senators, I have said on this and on many previous occasions, that a
good and beneficent emperor to whom you have entrusted so much power
and so freely, should be the servant of the senate, often of the citizens as
a whole, and frequently even of particular individuals. I do not regret
having said this; as my masters you have been and are still good, just,
and kind.

[30] Maintaining the traditional dignity and power of both senate
and magistrates, he even introduced some appearance of a free state.
For there was no public or private issue no matter how small or how
great which was not referred to the senate: taxes and monopolies; the
construction and repair of public works; even the recruitment and
disbanding of soldiers and the stationing of legions and auxiliary
forces; finally, questions such as whose commands they would like
extended, who should be put in charge of other military campaigns,
and what replies, and in what form, should be sent to the letters of
kings. He forced the commander of a cavalry troop who was accused

of violence and looting to plead his case before the senate. He was always unaccompanied when he entered the senate. Once when he was ill he was brought in a litter but he sent his attendants away.

[31] When some measures were passed contrary to the opinion he had expressed he did not even make a complaint. Though he was of the view that magistrates elect ought to remain in Rome so they might accustom themselves to their duties, one of the praetors elect was granted permission to travel abroad with ambassadorial status.* On another occasion, though he took the view that some money which had been left to the Trebiani for the purposes of building a new theatre should be used instead for the construction of a road, he was not able to prevent the wishes of the testator from being confirmed. Once when there happened to be a division of opinion over a senatorial motion and he joined the side whose numbers were fewer, no one followed his lead. Other matters, too, were always conducted through the magistrates and in accordance with the regular law, and so great was the authority of the consuls that some African ambassadors complained to them that the time they spent with Caesar (to whom they had been sent) was wasted. And this was no surprise when all could see that he himself, too, stood to greet the consuls and made way for them in the street.

[32] He reproved men of consular status who had command of armies, on the grounds that they had not made reports to the senate of their activities and that they had referred to him the award of some military honours, as if they themselves did not have authority for such awards. He praised a praetor most warmly because, when embarking on his term of office, he revived the ancient custom of commemorating his ancestors in his public address. He attended the funeral processions of some illustrious persons even as far as the pyre. He showed the same restraint in dealing with humble persons and matters of lesser import. When he summoned the magistrates of Rhodes because they had addressed public documents to him without the proper concluding formula,* without even upbraiding them he sent them back with orders merely to rewrite the documents. The grammarian Diogenes used to offer a lecture in Rhodes every seventh day and when Tiberius came to hear him on a different day, Diogenes did not receive him but sent a message through a slave boy that he should come back on the right day. When Diogenes came to Rome to greet him and stood at his door, his only reproof was to tell

him to come back in seven years' time. When governors tried to persuade him to increase the burden of taxes on the provinces, he replied that it was the job of a good shepherd to shear his flock, not to skin it.

[33] He showed only gradually what kind of emperor he was, for a long time presenting himself as merely unpredictable, though more generally inclined to benevolence and disposed to favour the public good. And at first he would only intervene to prevent errors. Thus, he rescinded certain regulations made by the senate and frequently offered himself as adviser to magistrates presiding in court, taking his seat either next to them or opposite them at the end of the platform. And if there was any suggestion that the accused had been acquitted through personal influence, he would at once approach the judges, either from the floor or from the quaestor's tribunal and remind them of the laws, of their oath, and of the nature of the offence on which they sat in judgement. He also undertook to provide remedies if idleness or bad habits caused a lapse in public morality.

[34] He cut back expenditure on games and gladiatorial shows, limiting the wages of actors and restricting the number of pairs of gladiators. He complained bitterly that the price of Corinthian vases had soared to great heights and that thirty thousand sesterces had been paid for three mullets,* imposing limits on the price of tableware and specifying that the senate should carry out annual checks on market prices. To the aediles he entrusted the task of regulating inns and cook-shops* to such an extent that not even pastry might be put on sale. And, in order to encourage public parsimony through his own example, he himself would often have served at formal dinners half-eaten dishes from the previous day or one half of a boar, insisting that it was just as good as a whole one.* He issued an edict against kissing on everyday occasions and prohibiting the exchange of New Year's gifts after the Kalends of January. He had been in the habit of returning gifts in person, of four times the value of those he received, but stopped doing this since he was annoyed at being interrupted throughout the month by those who had not been able to gain access to him on the holiday itself.

[35] In the case of women of good family who had prostituted their chastity, where there was no member of the public to act as accuser, he passed a law that they would be judged by a council of their relatives in the traditional manner. He excused from his oath a

Roman knight who divorced his wife, though he had previously
sworn he would never separate from her, when he found her committing adultery with their son-in-law. Women of ill-repute had
started registering themselves as prostitutes, in order to lose the
status and dignity of matrons and thus to escape the penalties specified by the law,* and the most profligate young persons of both the
senatorial and equestrian orders were voluntarily assuming the status
of the legally infamous, in order to free themselves from the restrictions which senatorial legislation had placed on their appearances in
the theatre and arena.* All such persons were made liable to exile so
that no one should be able to evade the law by means of such subter-
fuge. He stripped a man of his senatorial status on learning that he
had retired to his villa before the beginning of July, so that he could
rent a house in the city more cheaply after that date.* Another he
deposed from the quaestorship because he married a woman on the
day before the distribution of posts and divorced her the day
afterwards.*

[36] He suppressed foreign cults and the religions of the Egyptians and the Jews, obliging those who practised such rituals to burn
their religious garments and all their paraphernalia. The young men
of the Jewish people he had sent to regions where the climate was
severe, ostensibly on military service. The rest of that people, and
others of similar beliefs, he banished from the city, with the penalty
of slavery for life if they did not obey. He also banished astrologers,
though he excused those who asked forgiveness and promised they
would give up their art.

[37] He gave particular attention to securing relief from bandits
and robbers, as well as from lawless rebellions. Throughout Italy he
stationed armed forces in greater numbers than was customary. At
Rome, he established barracks where the praetorian guard, who had
previously been billeted in lodgings in different places, would be
concentrated. He took great care to contain public unrest most
severely, if it arose, and to prevent it arising in the first place. When a
fight in the theatre ended in violent death, he had sent into exile both
the heads of the gangs and the actors about whom the dispute had
arisen and no popular protests ever succeeded in making him recall
them. When, at the funeral of a chief centurion, the populace of
Pollentia* would not allow the procession to leave the forum until
they had extorted from the heirs money to pay for gladiatorial

games, he dispatched one cohort from Rome and another from the kingdom of Cottius,* concealing the purpose of their journey, and had them suddenly reveal their arms and sound their trumpets, then rush into the town where they put most of the populace and the local magistrates in prison for life. He abolished the practice of asylum,* whether established by law or by custom, wherever it was observed. When the people of Cyzicus* dared to commit violence of a serious kind against Roman citizens, he took away from them the freedom which they had been granted for their part in the war against Mithridates.

He embarked on no military campaigns himself after becoming emperor but contained enemy attacks through the agency of his generals and even then with some delay and only when necessary. Hostile kings he controlled more through threats and complaints than force. Some he lured to Rome with flattery and promises and would not allow them to return home, such as Marobodus the German, Rhascuporis from Thrace, Archelaus from Cappadocia, in the last case reducing his kingdom to a province of the empire.

[38] For two entire years after becoming emperor he did not set foot outside the city gates. Subsequently he left only to visit nearby towns, never venturing further than Antium,* and even then only very rarely and for a few days. Yet he often pronounced that he meant to review the provinces and the armies and made preparations for such an expedition nearly every year, with transport arranged and provisions organized throughout the towns and colonies. Finally, he permitted vows to be undertaken for the outward and homeward journey, so that the people jokingly called him 'Callipides'—famous in the Greek proverb for running without making the slightest progress.

[39] However, after the loss of both his sons—Germanicus had died in Syria, Drusus in Rome—he sought retirement in Campania, so that almost everyone firmly believed and observed that he would never return and indeed that he would shortly die. Both views were justified—almost—for he never again returned to Rome and, a few days after his departure, when he was dining at a villa called Spelunca near Tarracina,* a mass of huge rocks suddenly fell from above, crushing many of the guests and attendants; he himself was lucky to escape. [40] He travelled through Campania, and once he had dedicated the Capitol at Capua and the Temple of Augustus at

Nola—the alleged reason for his journey—he took himself to Capri, an island of which he was especially fond since it was accessible only by means of a single small beach and was otherwise surrounded by a rocky cliffs of great height and deep seas. He was immediately recalled, however, by the insistent entreaties of the populace, because of the disaster which had occurred at Fidenae* where, during some gladiatorial games, more than twenty thousand people had met their deaths through the collapse of the amphitheatre. He travelled over to the mainland and made himself available to all, which was the more striking given that, on leaving the city, he had given an order that no one should disturb him and, throughout his trip, he had rejected any who tried to approach him.

[41] On returning to the island, however, he threw off all concern for public affairs, to such a degree that he never thereafter filled vacancies in the equestrian jury divisions, nor did he change any appointments among the military tribunes, nor the prefects, nor the provincial governors. For several years he ruled Spain and Syria without consular governors. He allowed Armenia to be taken over by the Parthians, and Moesia to be laid waste by the Dacians and Sarmatians and the provinces of Gaul by the Germans. Great was the disgrace to the empire and no less great the danger.

[42] Nevertheless, having obtained the licence afforded by seclusion, far from the eyes of the city, he finally gave in simultaneously to all the vices he had so long struggled to conceal.* I shall give a detailed account of each from its inception. Even when he was a new recruit in the army camp they used to call him 'Biberius' instead of Tiberius, 'Caldius' for Claudius, and 'Mero' for Nero because of his excessive liking for wine.* Later, when he was emperor and actually engaged in the correction of public morals, he spent a day and a night and the following day in continuous feasting and drinking with Pomponius Flaccus and Lucius Piso, immediately thereafter appointing one governor of Syria and the other urban prefect—even in the letters of appointment he declared them to be his dearest friends at any hour of the day or night. When he was invited to dinner by Cestius Gallus, a lecherous and profligate old man, who had once been given a mark of dishonour by Augustus and whom he himself had criticized in the senate a few days earlier, he accepted with the condition that Cestius change or omit nothing of his usual arrangements and that the attendants should be naked girls. He pre-

ferred a little-known candidate for the quaestorship above some men
of noble family because at a dinner the man had drained an amphora
in response to his challenge. He made a payment of two hundred
sesterces to Asellius Sabinus for a dialogue in which he had set up a
competition between a mushroom, a fig-pecker, an oyster, and a
thrush.* He created a new post with responsibility for pleasures, to
which he appointed the Roman knight Titus Caesonius Priscus.

[43] Then, on retiring to Capri, he even established a suite which
was to be the location for his secret pleasures. Here groups of girls
and adult pathics selected from all over and the most inventive of
sexual deviants whom he used to call 'tight-bums',* would take it in
turns to engage in filthy threesomes in his presence, so that the sight
would arouse his flagging libido. The bedrooms were variously
decked out with paintings and sculptures showing the most provoca-
tive images and figures, while the library was equipped with the
works of Elephantis,* so that an illustration of the required position
would always be available if anyone needed guidance in completing
their performance. In the woods, too, and groves all over the island,
he set out his 'haunts of Venus' where boys and girls dressed up as
Pan and the nymphs solicited outside caves and grottoes. People used
quite openly and commonly to talk of 'the old goat's den', making a
play on the name of the island.*

[44] He became notorious for still greater and more extreme
depravity so that it is almost a crime to describe, to hear, let alone to
believe it, the story being that he trained some boys of tender age,
whom he called his little fishes, to slip between his thighs when he
was swimming and provoke him playfully with their licking and
biting. And he even had well-grown infants, not yet weaned, suck on
his male member, as if it were a breast—for his age and nature
inclined him particularly to this kind of pleasure. Thus when a picture by the artist Parrasius was bequeathed to him with the condition that if he were offended by the subject matter (it represented
Atalanta* pleasuring Meleager with her mouth), he should instead
have a million sesterces, he not only preferred to keep the picture but
set it up in his bed-chamber.* It is even said that once, when he was
conducting a sacrifice, he was smitten with the face of the attendant
carrying the incense box and could not contain himself but as soon as
the holy act was completed he at once led him aside and took his
fill of foul pleasure both from the boy himself and also his brother,

who was the flute-player. Then, as they both complained at the humiliation, he had their legs broken.

[45] The degree to which he used to abuse women even of the most distinguished kind is shown most clearly by the death of a woman called Mallonia. When she was brought to him but persistently refused to comply any further, he turned her over to the informers and, even when she stood trial, he would not desist from asking her if she was sorry, so that in the end she left the court, rushed home, and stabbed herself, publicly condemning the hairy, stinking old man and his obscenely filthy mouth. Hence a line from an Atellan play during the next games was taken up with great enthusiasm and much repeated: 'the old goat is licking the does' behinds.'

[46] When it came to money, he was mean and grasping, never providing a salary for those who accompanied him on his travels and military expeditions but only offering their board and lodging. Only on one occasion did he treat them generously and that was with his stepfather's resources. Drawing the men up into three groups according to their rank he gave the first six hundred thousand sesterces, the second four hundred and the third—whom he called his Greeks* rather than his friends—two hundred.

[47] As emperor he completed no public works of any splendour and the few things which he made a start on, the Temple of Augustus and the restoration of Pompey's Theatre, were still unfinished many years later.* He gave no games at all himself and attended those given by others only very rarely lest any demands should be made of him, particularly after he was forced to buy the freedom of the comic actor Actius.* Having provided assistance for a few impoverished senators, he avoided helping any more by declaring he would assist no one else, unless they could give the senate proof that their circumstances were no fault of their own. In this manner many were frightened off through modesty and shame, amongst these Hortalus, grandson of the orator Quintus Hortensius, who, persuaded by Augustus, had brought up a family of four, despite his limited resources.

[48] On two occasions in total he showed generosity to the people. Once when he offered three-year loans to the value of a hundred thousand sesterces without interest and again when he gave compensation to some owners of apartment blocks on the Caelian hill which

had burnt down. The first offer he was forced into by the people's demands for help during a financial crisis, after he had already issued a decree through the senate that money lenders should invest two-thirds of their funds in property and that debtors should at once discharge their debts in the same proportion but these measures had failed to solve the problem. On the second occasion, too, he was relieving extreme misfortune. However, he rated this act of generosity so highly that he demanded the name of the Caelian hill should be changed, thenceforth becoming the hill of Augustus. To the soldiers, once he had paid out at double rate what had been stipulated in Augustus' will, he made no further grants, apart from one of a thousand denarii each to the praetorian guard to reward them for not falling in with the plans of Sejanus,* and some rewards for the Syrian legions, because they alone had included no image of Sejanus among their standards. Only very rarely would he discharge veterans, hoping they might die of old age and thus save him their retirement money. He gave no financial aid to the provinces, with the exception of Asia, after some cities were destroyed through an earthquake.

[49] Soon, as time went by, he even turned toward confiscations. It is generally agreed that Gnaeus Lentulus Augur, who was a very wealthy man, was driven through fear and mental torment to take his own life—and to make the emperor himself his sole heir. Lepida, too, a woman of most noble birth, was condemned through the influence of the ex-consul Quirinus, a childless man of immense wealth, who had divorced her, then, after twenty years, accused her of once having procured poison to use against him. Besides this, the foremost men of the provinces of Gaul, Spain, Syria, and Greece were deprived of their property on the most trivial and outrageous charges, some being accused merely of having part of their property in ready money.* In the case of a great many states and private individuals, ancient immunities, as well the the rights to exploit mines and collect taxes, were taken away. Moreover, Vonones the King of the Parthians who, after being expelled by his countrymen, had come to Antioch with a quantity of treasure, entrusting himself to the good faith of the Roman people, was perfidiously robbed and killed.

[50] The loathing he felt for his family was first revealed in the case of his brother Drusus, when he brought forth a letter in which Drusus had debated with him the possibility of forcing Augustus to restore liberty,* and later with regard to the rest of them. So far was

he from showing his wife Julia, when she was in exile, a measure of respect and kindness—the least one might expect—that, when her father's orders confined her to a single town, he further forbade her to leave the house or to have any contact with other people. Moreover, he also cheated her of the allowance made her by her father and of her yearly income, alleging that this was a matter of law, since Augustus had made no arrangements for these in his will.* He was angered by his mother Livia on the grounds that she claimed an equal share in his power. He avoided meeting her too frequently or having private conversations with her of any length in order not to give the impression that he was following her advice—though, actually, he sometimes needed it and would make use of it. He was very much offended, too, by a senatorial decree proposing that his titles should include 'son of Livia' as well as 'son of Augustus'. For this reason he would not permit that she be called 'Mother of the Fatherland' nor that she should receive any signal public honour. Moreover, he often warned her that she should abstain from involvement in more serious matters which were not suitable for a woman, especially after he heard that, when a fire had broken out near the Temple of Vesta, she had become involved, urging on the people and soldiers to make still greater efforts, just as she used to do in the time of her husband.

[51] Afterwards, his hostility became patent, for the following reason, so people say. In response to her frequent demands that he appoint to the jurors a certain man who had been given citizenship, he replied that he would only do this on condition that the records plainly stated that his mother had forced him into it. Incensed by this, she brought forth from a hiding place and read out some old notes Augustus had sent her concerning Tiberius' morose and inflexible character. He was so angered that she had kept these for so long and used them against him with such malice that some people think that this was one of his reasons for withdrawing, if not the principal reason. For the whole of the three years when he was away and his mother was still living, he only saw her on one occasion and that was for a few hours on a single day. Soon after, when she was ill, he did not trouble to come to her, then, when she was dead, the impression he gave that he might attend the funeral led to a delay of many days, so that her body was putrid and rotten by the time she was buried. He would not permit her to be deified, although she had requested

it. Her will he ignored as void and within a short time he brought
ruin on all her friends and the members of her household, even those
to whom, on her deathbed, she had entrusted her funeral arrangements. One of these, though he was a member of the equestrian
order, was actually condemned to the treadmill.

[52] As for his sons, he loved neither his natural child Drusus, nor
his adoptive son Germanicus with a father's tenderness. He resented
the former for his vices—Drusus was somewhat wild and careless in
his manner of living. Thus, he was not even much affected by his
death but, with only the briefest pause, returned almost at once from
the funeral to his usual matters of business, forbidding a longer
period of mourning. Indeed, when some ambassadors from Ilium
were offering him their condolences a little late, he laughed at them
and replied that he should offer them his in return, for the loss of
their eminent citizen Hector.* He so disparaged Germanicus that he
made light of his most illustrious deeds as insubstantial and criticized his most glorious victories as crippling to the state. Indeed,
when Germanicus without permission travelled to Alexandria
because of the severe famine which had suddenly afflicted the city,
Tiberius complained about him in the senate. It is even believed that
he was the cause of his death through the agency of Gnaeus Piso, the
legate of Syria. Some people think that Piso, when he was accused of
the crime soon afterwards, would have revealed his instructions, had
Tiberius not made sure that they were taken from him, as he tried to
show them to someone in secret, and that he himself was murdered.
Because of this the words 'Give us back Germanicus!' were written
up in many places and at night frequently called out. He himself
confirmed suspicions when, afterwards, he inflicted cruel treatment
on Germanicus' wife and children, too.

[53] When Agrippina, his daughter-in-law, after her husband's
death complained a little too freely, he seized her with his hand and
said in Greek, 'Do you think you are hard done by, my daughter, if
you do not rule?' After that he did not deign to converse with her
again. Indeed, after she would not risk eating an apple he offered her
at his table, he no longer invited her to dine, pretending that she had
accused him of poisoning her, when the affair had been deliberately
set up so that he would offer her the fruit to make trial of her, and
she would fear it as certain death. On top of all this, having alleged
falsely that she was seeking refuge now at Augustus' statue, now

from the armies, he sent her into exile to Pandateria and, when she complained about him, he had a centurion beat her until she lost an eye. Moreover, when she was determined to starve herself to death he gave orders that her mouth be forced open and food stuffed into it. Then, after she persevered and thus died, he attacked her with the most appalling accusations and, when he was persuading the senate to include her birthday among the days of ill omen, he even made a merit of the fact that he had not had her strangled with a noose and thrown onto the Gemonian steps.* In recognition of such clemency, he permitted a decree to be passed thanking him and consecrating a golden offering for Capitoline Jupiter.

[54] Since he had four grandsons, three—Nero, Drusus, and Gaius—from Germanicus, and one—Tiberius—from Drusus, when he lost his own sons he commended the two oldest sons of Germanicus (Nero and Drusus) to the senate, and celebrated the day when each assumed the toga of manhood with gifts to the common people. But when he discovered that the prayers which were publicly made at the start of the year included prayers for their health too, he addressed the senate to the effect that such honours should not be offered except to those who were experienced and mature of age. And from that time, he made clear his true feelings towards them, loading them with all manner of accusations and implicating them in offences through a variety of deceptions, so that they were incited to make complaints about him and were then betrayed. He sent letters making the most bitter and numerous accusations against them and, once they had been declared public enemies, he had them starved to death, Nero on the island of Pontia and Drusus in the innermost depths of the Palatine. It is thought that Nero was forced into taking his own life, when an executioner, sent as if on the authority of the senate, showed him the noose and the hooks.* Drusus, however, was so deprived of food that he had even tried to eat the stuffing from his mattress. The remains of both were so dispersed that it was almost impossible to collect them up.

[55] Besides his old friends and the members of his household, he demanded twenty men from among the leading citizens who were to be his counsellors in public affairs. Of all these, he allowed only two or three to survive, striking down the rest, one for one reason, another for another. Among these Aelius Sejanus brought many others with him in his downfall. This man he had advanced to a

position of the highest power not through benevolence but so that, by means of his plans and trickery, the children of Germanicus might be disposed of and thus his natural grandson, offspring of his son Drusus, might be confirmed as his heir.

[56] He was no more well disposed towards the insignificant Greeks who were his table companions and provided him with much entertainment. When he interrogated a man called Xeno, whose manner of speaking was somewhat affected, as to what his horrible dialect was, and the man replied that it was Doric, he banished him to Cinaria, believing that he was being reproached with his old place of exile, since the Rhodians spoke the Doric dialect. Being in the habit of posing questions taken from his daily reading at the dinner table, when he learnt that the scholar Seleucus was asking his servants about what books he was reading at the time so that he could come prepared, he first banned him from his table and later even compelled him to take his own life.

[57] Even when he was a boy his savage and tenacious nature was not completely hidden.* Theodorus of Gadara, his teacher of rhetoric, it seems, first observed this, most perceptively, and described it in most accurate terms, for when he castigated him he would call him *pleon haimati pephuramenon*, that is 'mud steeped in blood'. But it emerged somewhat more clearly when he was emperor, even in the early stages when he was still winning people's favour through his pretence of moderation. When a buffoon called out loud to the corpse, as a funeral went by, that he should tell Augustus that the people had not yet received the legacies he had bequeathed them, Tiberius ordered that he be brought in and be given what was coming to him; when he was executed, he would tell Augustus the truth. Soon afterwards in the senate, when a certain Roman knight called Pompeius stoutly maintained his opposition on some issue, Tiberius threatened him with imprisonment, asserting that from being Pompeius he would become a Pompeian, thus exulting over him with a nasty play on the man's name and the eventual fate of the party.

[58] At around the same time, when he was asked by a praetor whether he should have the courts assemble to consider cases of treason, he replied that the laws were to be applied, and he did apply them with the greatest cruelty. A certain man had removed the head from a statue of Augustus so that he might replace it with the head of someone else. This matter was brought before the senate and,

because there was some uncertainty, the witnesses were examined under torture. The defendant was found guilty and in time malicious accusations of the following kind resulted in capital trials: beating a slave near a statue of Augustus, or changing one's clothes there; carrying a coin or a ring bearing his image into a lavatory or a brothel; criticizing any of his words or deeds. Indeed, a man lost his life because he permitted honours to be offered him in his colony on the same day that they had once been offered to Augustus.

[59] He committed many other cruel and savage acts besides these, ostensibly motivated by a concern for dignity and the wish to improve morals* but really because his nature was so inclined, so that quite a few persons complained in verse of the evils he had already committed and anticipated those to come.

> O bitter and cruel one, shall I sum you up in a few words?
> I'm damned if even your mother can love you.

> You are no knight and why is that? You haven't got the hundred
>   thousands.
> If the whole truth be sought, your fortune was exile on Rhodes.*

> You have transformed the golden age of Saturn, Caesar;
> While you live, the age will be always iron.*

> He's tired of wine, since now he thirsts for blood.
> That he drinks as greedily now as he used to drink wine without
>   water.*

> O Romulus, behold Sulla, fortunate for himself not for you.*
> Behold, too, if you will, Marius, returned to Rome,

> Behold the hands of an Antony,* bringing civil war
> And dripping with gore from more than one slaughter,

> And say: Rome is falling! Whoever comes to rule from exile,
> Rules with much bloodshed.

At first, he insisted that such things should be seen as made up by people who could not tolerate the treatment they deserved and were prompted by malice and ill-temper rather than expressing true feelings. He used to say repeatedly: 'Let them hate me provided they respect me.'* Later he himself gave clear proof of their accuracy and firm foundation.

[60] Within a few days of his arrival on Capri, as he was engaged in some secret business, a fisherman appeared without warning and offered him a gift of a large mullet. Filled with alarm that the fisher-

man had clambered up to him through the rugged and wild area in
the furthermost part of the island, he gave orders that the man's face
should be scrubbed with the fish he had brought. Indeed, when the
man gave thanks, in the course of his punishment, that he had not
brought the emperor the enormous lobster which was also in his
catch, Tiberius gave orders that his face should also be mangled with
the lobster. He inflicted capital punishment on a soldier of the praetorian guard because he had stolen a peacock from the emperor's
pleasure-garden. Once, when he was on a journey and the litter in
which he was travelling was held up by briars, he had the man
responsible for finding the way, a centurion of the first cohorts,
stretched out on the ground and beaten almost to death.

[61] Soon he broke out into all manner of cruelty, with no shortage of victims, since he persecuted first the friends and even
acquaintances of his mother, then those of his grandchildren and
daughter-in-law, then those of Sejanus. After the latter's death, he
became even more savage. From this above all it was clear that,
rather than Sejanus urging him on, the man had merely given
Tiberius the opportunities the latter wanted—though in the brief
account in which he summed up his life, Tiberius dared to record
that he had punished Sejanus when he learned of his hostility to the
children of his son Germanicus, those boys whom he himself had
had killed, one when Sejanus was already in disgrace and the other
when he had finally been overthrown.

To go through his cruel deeds one by one would take a long time.
It will suffice to recount, by way of example, the different types of
savagery in which he engaged. No day, however holy or sacred, was
free from human punishment; some he put to death on New Year's
Day. Many were accused and condemned with their children—and
some by their own children. Relatives were forbidden to grieve for
those condemned to death. Splendid rewards were decreed for
accusers and sometimes even for witnesses. Never was the word of an
informer doubted. Every crime was treated as a capital offence, even
when it was just a matter of a few simple words. A poet was prosecuted for including criticisms of Agamemnon* in a tragedy, a historian for describing Brutus and Cassius as the last of the Romans.
Authors were attacked and books banned,* even though some years
previously they had been well received by audiences which had
included the emperor Augustus. Some were thrown into prison and

forbidden not only to read but even to talk and converse together. Summoned to plead their case, some opened their veins at home, certain that they would be condemned and desiring to avoid torment and shame; others drank poison in the middle of the senate house. Yet these men were still dragged to prison, half-dead and trembling, with their wounds bound up. None of those punished was spared being dragged with the hook and thrown onto the Gemonian steps; on one day twenty people were dragged and thrown down, including women and children. Since by tradition it was forbidden that virgins should be strangled, young girls were strangled after first being violated by the executioner. Those who wanted to kill themselves were forced to live. For he believed death to be such a light punishment that when he heard that one of the condemned, Carnulus by name, had anticipated his execution, he cried out: 'Carnulus has escaped me!' When he was looking over prisons and a man called out for a speedy end, he replied: 'I am not yet ready to favour you.' A man of consular status recorded in his annals that he was once present at a large party also attended by the emperor and when the latter was suddenly and loudly asked by a dwarf, who was standing among the clowns near the table, why Paconius lived so long when he was guilty of treason, Tiberius at once reprimanded his insolence, yet a few days later he wrote to the senate, instructing them to decide on Paconius' punishment as soon as possible.

[62] His savagery grew and intensified, when he learned to his great anger how his son Drusus had died. Having earlier attributed his death to disease and a life of self-indulgence, he at last discovered that his son had been poisoned, tricked by his wife Livilla and Sejanus. Then he spared no one torture or execution, so devoting his whole attention for days at a time to this one investigation that, when the arrival was announced of a guest from Rhodes, whom he had summoned to Rome by a friendly letter, he had the man subjected to torture without delay, supposing someone had arrived who was an important witness for the case, then, when his mistake came to light, put to death, so that he would not publicize his mistreatment.

In Capri they still point out the place he used for his executions. From here, according to Tiberius' orders, after long and excruciating torment, the condemned would, while he looked on, be thrown into the sea, where a team of men from the navy would round up the corpses and beat them with poles and oars, in case any breath of life should remain to them. He had even, among various forms of torture, devised one whereby the victims were tricked into drinking a large measure of wine, then suddenly had their private parts bound with cords so that they swelled up, tormented at once by the cords and by the urge to urinate. Thus, if death had not intervened—and Thrasyllus deliberately, so people say, gave him hope of a longer life, thus persuading him to keep some projects for the future—people believe Tiberius would soon have killed more victims and would indeed have spared none of his remaining grandsons, since he was already suspicious of Gaius and spurned Tiberius on the grounds that he was the offspring of his mother's adultery. Nor is this unlikely, for he used frequently to call Priam* fortunate, on the grounds that he had survived all his descendants.

[63] There is much to indicate how, in the midst of all this, he was not only an object of hatred and loathing but was also himself dogged by great fear and was even the victim of insult.* He gave orders that no one was to consult the *haruspices* in secret or without witnesses. He even attempted to disband those oracles which were situated near the city of Rome but gave up, terrified by the power of the Praenestine lots, for although he had them sealed in a casket and brought to Rome he could not find them in it until the casket was taken back to the temple.* Having assigned provinces to one or two ex-consuls, he could not bring himself to let them go but detained them for so long that, after several years, he granted them successors without their having left the city. In the mean time, they retained their official titles and he even went on giving them many instructions, which they were supposed to have executed through their legates and assistants.

[64] After their condemnation, he would never permit his daughter-in-law and grandsons to be transported anywhere unless they were chained and enclosed in a litter, while soldiers prevented travellers or anyone they encountered on the way from ever looking in on them or even stopping.

[65] Sejanus' plans to usurp his power—though Tiberius was already aware of the public celebrations of his birthday and the golden images of him which were everywhere honoured—he only just managed to overturn; and even then rather through cunning and deceit than through his authority as emperor. For first of all, in order to get him away while appearing to honour him, he made him his

colleague in his own fifth consulship, which he took on after a long interval and in absence for precisely this purpose. Then, having given him the false hope that he might marry into the imperial family and receive tribunician powers, he made accusations against him, when he least expected it, with a shameful and wretched speech in which, among other things, he begged the senators to send one of the consuls to bring him, a lonely old man, into their presence, along with a military escort for protection. Then, too, distrustful and fearing a riot, he gave orders that his grandson Drusus, who at that point was still being held in chains at Rome, should, if the occasion required, be released and given command of the armies. He even had ships made ready, as he contemplated taking refuge with some or other of the legions, and from the highest peak kept watching out for the signals which he had instructed should be raised from afar, as each stage in the plan was reached, in case the messengers were delayed. However, even when Sejanus' conspiracy was suppressed, he felt no more secure nor at ease, for the next nine months not stirring from his villa, which is called the villa of Jupiter.

[66] His troubled mind was further tormented by varied taunts from all quarters, for every single one of the condemned heaped all kinds of abuse on him either in his presence or through placards set up in the front row of the theatre. He reacted to these in very different ways, sometimes, through shame, wanting to keep them all unknown and hidden, sometimes making light of the same accusations and himself repeating and publicizing them. Indeed, he was even attacked in a letter from Artabanes, the king of the Parthians, who accused him of parricide, murder, cowardice, and luxury and advised him to end his own life as soon as possible to appease the most intense and well-justified hatred felt by his citizens.

[67] In the end, he came to feel thorough disgust at himself and, in the following words which begin one of his letters, he confessed all but the worst of his faults: 'Gentlemen of the senate, what am I to write to you? How shall I write to you? What in the end shall I leave unwritten at this time? If I know, may the gods and goddesses condemn me to a worse fate than that I feel is mine today.' It is believed, however, that he was aware of what would happen long before, through knowledge of the future, and he perceived what bitterness and notoriety would be his lot. So that when he began his reign, he refused most obstinately the title of 'Father of the Fatherland' and

would not permit an oath to be sworn in support of his acts, lest he should soon to his shame be found unworthy of such great honours.* One may gather this from the speech which he made concerning both offers, when, for instance, he said that, so long as he was of sound mind, he would always be himself and would never change his character but that one should avoid establishing the precedent, whereby the senate bound itself to approve anyone's acts when he might, by some chance, undergo some change. And he also said:

If at some time, however, you come to doubt my character and my devotion to you—and before that happens, I would rather my own death should preserve me from the loss of your good opinion—the title 'Father of the Fatherland' would bring me no additional honour but would rather be a reproach to you either for your rashness in conferring the title upon me or for your inconsistency in changing your opinion of me.

[68] He was big and strong in body, his height being above average and his chest and shoulders broad, with the rest of his body right down to his toes being well in proportion. His left hand was the more agile and powerful and his joints were so strong that he could push one through a fresh and sound apple and with the tap of a finger he could injure the head of a boy or even a youth. His complexion was pale and his hair at the back of his head grew far down, so that it covered his neck, which seems to have been a family trait. His face was noble though affected by sudden and violent flashes of emotion, with very large eyes, which, astonishingly, could see even at night and in darkness (though only briefly when he had just woken up; then they would lose their sharpness). When he walked, he held his neck stiffly drawn back, with rather a severe expression on his face. For the most part he was silent, only speaking very rarely, even with those closest to him and then with no alacrity. When he spoke, he would always gesticulate rather affectedly with his fingers. All these characteristics, which were unpleasant and suggested arrogance, Augustus had observed and he often tried to make excuses for them to the senate and people, claiming that these faults were ones he was born with and not a reflection of his character. Tiberius enjoyed extremely good health, suffering from virtually no illness throughout the period of his rule, even though from the time he was thirty he had relied on his own judgement and taken no advice or help from doctors.

[69] He had little regard for the gods or anything to do with religion, since he was a devotee of astrology, convinced that fate rules all. However, he was unusually alarmed by thunder and, when the heavens were unsettled, he would always wear a laurel wreath on his head, on the grounds that laurel leaves are never struck by lightning.

[70] He was extremely keen on literary pursuits in both Latin and Greek. In Latin oratory, he took as his model Corvinus Messala, whom he had in his youth observed when Corvinus was an old man. However, affectation and an excess of pedantry made his style obscure, so that he was sometimes judged to perform better when speaking off the cuff than when he had prepared. He also composed a lyric poem, with the title 'Lament for the Death of Lucius Caesar'. He also wrote poetry in Greek in the manner of Euphorion, Rhianus, and Parthenius.* These poets he particularly admired, placing copies of all their works in the public libraries, and setting up their images among those of the most ancient and distinguished authors. For this reason, numerous learned men competed to produce many editions of their works, dedicated to the emperor. However, his greatest passion was for mythology, to the extent that he made himself seem foolish and absurd; for he used to make trial of scholars, a class of men on whom, as was noted above, he was especially keen: 'Who was Hecuba's mother? What was Achilles' name when he was among the virgins? What songs used the Sirens to sing?' And on the first day after Augustus' death when he entered the senate, as if to show his respect and piety, he offered a sacrifice with incense and wine, but without music, following the practice of Minos, who had done this on the death of his son.* [71] However, although he spoke Greek fluently and easily, he would not use the language on all occasions and particularly avoided doing so in the senate,* to the extent that he would first ask pardon for using a foreign term before pronouncing the word 'monopolium'.* And when the word 'emblema'* came up in some senatorial decree, he expressed the opinion that the term should be changed and a Roman word be found in place of the foreign one, or, if none could be found, that the notion should be expressed in a more roundabout way. When a soldier was asked in Greek to give evidence, Tiberius forbade him to reply unless it was in Latin.

[72] On two occasions only during the period of his retirement did he attempt to return to Rome. Once, travelling by trireme, he came

as far as the gardens just by the artificial lake for sea-battles and stationed a guard on the banks of the Tiber to turn away those who came to meet him. The second time he travelled on the Appian Way as far as the seventh milestone from Rome. However, he turned back, having seen the walls of the city but come no closer. With regard to the first occasion, his reasons are unclear. On the second, he was alarmed by a portent. He kept a snake as a pet and when he went to feed it from his own hand, as he usually did, and discovered that it had been consumed by ants, he took this as a warning to beware the power of the many. Then, having made a rapid return to Campania, he was overcome by weakness at Astura, but recovering a little, went on to Circeii. So that no one should suspect that he was ill, he not only attended the games in the army camp but even, when a boar was let into the arena, aimed javelins at it from above. At once a pain gripped his side, his condition worsening when, covered in sweat, he was exposed to a draught. However, he held out, continuing his journey a little further and even when he reached Misenum he was still adhering to his daily routine, still including parties and other pleasures, partly because he could not resist them and partly to conceal his condition. For when the doctor Charicles, who was going off on leave and consequently, as he left the party, took his hand to kiss it, Tiberius, suspecting him of trying to feel his pulse, gave orders that he should come back to the table and resume his place, then prolonged the dinner till late. Not even at that time did he give up his habit of standing in the middle of the dining-room, with a lictor by his side, and addressing each guest by name as they said goodbye.

[73] In the mean time, when he read in the senate records that some accused persons, concerning whom he had written briefly to the effect that they had been named by an informer, had been discharged without even a hearing, he roared that he was being held in contempt and determined to return to Capri by whatever means he could, for he dared undertake no measures except from a place of safety. But he was detained by bad weather and by the increasing severity of his illness and he died not long afterwards at the villa of Lucullus, in the seventy-eighth year of his life and the twenty-third of his reign, on the seventeenth day before the Kalends of April, in the consulship of Gnaeus Acerronius Proculus and Gaius Pontius Nigrinus.* Some people believe that he was the victim of a slow and

debilitating poison given him by Gaius, others that in recovery from a chance fever he asked for food but was denied it. Some say that a pillow was forced onto him, when he asked for a ring which had been removed from him when he passed out. Seneca writes that when he realized he was dying he removed the ring as if to give it to someone but held onto it for a little while then put it back again on his finger, tightening his left hand into a fist and keeping it this way for some time. Then all at once he called for his servants and, when no one came, rose to his feet and, his strength failing, fell down not far from his bed.

[74] On his final birthday, he dreamt that the Apollo Temenites,* a statue of great size and wonderful workmanship which he had brought to Syracuse to place in the library of the new temple, made a sign to him that it could not be dedicated by him. And, a few days before he died, the lighthouse at Capri collapsed as the result of an earthquake. At Misenum, when the hot ashes and embers which had been brought in to warm his dining-room had subsided and long been cold, they suddenly blazed up again in the early evening and continued to give light until late into the night.

[75] The people were so delighted at his death that when they first heard the news some ran about shouting 'Into the Tiber with Tiberius!' while others prayed to Mother Earth and the shades that he should be given no place in the underworld except among the wicked, while others threatened his corpse with the hook and Gemonian steps,* their resentment at the memory of his earlier cruelty exacerbated by a more recent atrocity. For, in accordance with a decree of the senate, there was always a space of ten days before the condemned actually received their punishment and it happened that some were due to be killed on the day Tiberius' death was announced. These men begged people for protection but, since Gaius was still away and there was no one who might be approached and appealed to, the guards strangled them and threw them onto the Gemonian steps, fearing to do anything contrary to the rules. On account of this people's resentment increased still further, for the tyrant's savagery seemed even to have survived his death. When they sought to move the body from Misenum, many cried out that they should move it instead to Atella* where it should be half-burned in the amphitheatre,* but it was taken to Rome by some soldiers and cremated in a public funeral.

[76] Two years before he had made two copies of his will, one in his own hand and the other in that of a freedman but to the same effect, and had had them witnessed with the seals of some very lowly persons. According to this will, he made his grandsons Gaius, son of Germanicus, and Tiberius, son of Drusus, his heirs in equal part, each to be sole heir if the other died. He left legacies for many people including the Vestal Virgins, as well as to every soldier in the army and each member of the Roman commons, and also to the individual magistrates of the city districts.

CALIGULA

[1] Gaius Caesar's* father Germanicus, the son of Drusus and the younger Antonia, was adopted by his paternal uncle Tiberius.* He held the quaestorship five years in advance of the time laid down by law and went straight on to the consulship.* He had been sent out to take command of the army in Germany when news came of the death of Augustus. The legions most obstinately refused to acknowledge Tiberius as emperor and sought instead to offer supreme control of the empire to Germanicus. He, however—with greater loyalty or courage it is hard to say—held them back and not long afterwards defeated the enemy, securing a triumph. Made consul for the second time, he was sent away, before he could take office, to bring order to the East. After he had defeated the King of Armenia and made Cappadocia a province, he died at Antioch, in his thirty-fourth year, of a long-drawn-out illness—indeed there was some suspicion of poison. For dark patches appeared all over his body and he foamed at the mouth, and besides this, when he was cremated, his heart was found intact amongst his bones; it is thought that the heart, when infected with poison, cannot be destroyed by fire. [2] The plot to kill him, people thought, was initiated by Tiberius, through the agency and offices of Gnaeus Piso, who at that time was governor of Syria. He made no secret of the fact that he had to make an enemy either of the father or of the son, as if there were no other option, and even when Germanicus was ill, he set upon him, offering the most bitter insults in word and deed without the least restraint. For this reason, when he returned to Rome, he was almost torn to pieces by the people, while the senate condemned him to death.*

[3] That Germanicus had all the virtues of body and spirit to a degree achieved by no other man is generally agreed. His person was striking, his valour conspicuous, his talent for eloquence and learning, both Greek and Roman, was outstanding. He was noted for his kindliness of disposition and was remarkably successful in his endeavours to secure people's goodwill and to merit their affection. One aspect of his appearance out of proportion with the rest was the thinness of his legs but even this he gradually managed to improve through assiduous riding after meals. He often struck down an

enemy fighting at close quarters. He took on court cases even after
he had celebrated his triumph. Among the many testimonies he left
to his learning were comedies in Greek. He sought to act as an
ordinary citizen both at home and abroad, entering free and allied
cities without an escort of lictors. Wherever he came across the
funeral monuments of famous men, he used to make offerings to
their spirits. Intending to bring together in one grave the remains of
those who had fallen years previously in the Varian disaster,* he
himself began the task of gathering them, picking them up with his
own hands. Towards his detractors, whoever they were and whatever their motives, he remained gentle and without malice, so that
even when Piso was countermanding his orders and vexing his
clients, he was reluctant to grow angry with him until he was convinced that he was the victim of poison and curses. Even then he
only went so far as to renounce his friendship, in the manner of
our ancestors, and to invoke revenge from his household should
anything happen to him.

[4] Endowed with this rich crop of virtues, Germanicus was so
esteemed and loved by his family that Augustus (to say nothing of
the rest of his relatives), after debating long as to whether to designate him his successor, had him adopted by Tiberius. He was so
much loved by the common people, as many writers report, that
whenever he arrived anywhere or left anywhere vast crowds came to
meet him or see him off, sometimes even endangering his life.
Indeed, when he was returning from Germany after the suppression
of the mutiny, all the praetorian cohorts came to meet him, although
it had been announced that only two were to undertake this duty,
while all the people, whatever their age, sex, or status, flooded out of
Rome as far as the twentieth milestone.

[5] However, by far the most important and surest verdicts on him
date from after his death.* On the day he died temples were attacked
with stones, the altars of the gods were overturned, the household
gods of some families were cast out into the street, and others
exposed their wives' new babies. Indeed, they say that even the barbarians, some of whom were engaged in a civil war while others were
at war with us, agreed to a truce, as if they themselves had suffered a
common loss. They say, too, that some princes shaved off their
beards and had their wives' hair cropped as a sign of the greatest
grief, while even the king of kings* is said to have abstained from

hunting expeditions and from banqueting with his magnates, which among the Parthians is the sign of public mourning.

[6] Back in Rome, the citizens, shocked and grieving at news of his ill health, had been waiting for further information, when towards evening a report spread, its source unclear, to the effect that he was recovering. At once crowds flocked to the Capitol with torches and sacrificial victims. They almost tore off the temple doors such was their impatience at any delay to their offerings. Tiberius was roused from sleep by their voices as they rejoiced on all sides, chanting:

> Rome is safe, our fatherland safe, for Germanicus is safe.

And when at last his death became known, no consolation, no orders could contain the public mourning, which lasted even through the feast days of the month of December.* The dreadfulness of later events increased the reputation of the dead man and regret for his loss. All believed and with good reason that only respect for Germanicus and fear of him had held in check the cruelty to which Tiberius soon gave rein.*

[7] Germanicus was married to Agrippina, daughter of Marcus Agrippa and Julia, and through her fathered nine children. Two of these were lost as infants, while a third died on the verge of boyhood, a child noted for his sweetness of disposition, whose portrait, showing him as Cupid, Livia dedicated in the temple of Capitoline Venus, while Augustus had another placed in his bedroom which he used to kiss every time he entered the room. The other children survived their father: three were girls, Agrippina, Drusilla, and Livilla, born within the space of three years, and there were the same number of boys, Nero, Drusus, and Gaius Caesar. Nero and Drusus were condemned as enemies of the state by the senate. Tiberius was their accuser.*

[8] Gaius Caesar was born the day before the Kalends of September, in the year when his father and Gaius Fonteius Capito were consuls.* Differing accounts make it impossible to be sure where he was born. Gnaeus Lentulus Gaetulicus* writes that he was born at Tibur, Pliny* that he was born in the region occupied by the Treviri, in a place called Ambitarvius, where the rivers* meet. The latter adds in support of his version that altars are displayed there, with the inscription: 'For Agrippina's delivery'. Verses which were circulating soon after he became emperor suggest that he was conceived in the legions' winter quarters.

> Born in a camp, brought up with his father's troops,
> Clearly he was destined to be our emperor.

I find, from official records, that he was born at Antium. Pliny refutes Gaetulicus, arguing that his falsehood was motivated by a desire to flatter the young and arrogant prince, adding to his glory by locating his birth in the town sacred to Hercules. He could with more confidence twist the story, for about a year before another of Germanicus' sons had indeed been born at Tibur, also bearing the name Gaius Caesar (his delightful character and early death were mentioned earlier*). Pliny's own argument is refuted by chronology. For those who record the doings of Augustus agree that when Germanicus, after the end of his consulship, was sent to Gaul, Gaius was already born. Nor do any of these altar inscriptions help Pliny's case, for Agrippina gave birth to two daughters while in that region and the term used for 'delivery', *puerperium*, is the same whether the child born is male or female, for in the old days girls were known as *puerae*, while boys might be known as *puelli*.* Besides this, a letter survives written by Augustus to his granddaughter Agrippina a few months before he died which mentions this Gaius in the following terms (for no other child called Gaius was living at that time):

I arranged yesterday with Talarius and Asillius that they shall escort the child Gaius, if the gods are willing, on the fifteenth day before the Kalends of June.* I am also sending with him a doctor, one of my slaves, whom I have told Germanicus to keep if he wishes. Farewell, my Agrippina, and take care that you reach your Germanicus safely.

In my opinion it is quite evident that Gaius could not have been born in a place to which he was first taken from Rome when he was two years old. These facts call into question the verses, which are in any case anonymous. We should believe the only possibility which remains (and which is supported by the authority of official documents), particularly when Gaius himself preferred Antium to all other resorts, loving it as people love the place where they were born. They even say that he was sick of Rome and sought to transfer to Antium the seat and capital of empire.*

[9] His nickname 'Caligula'* he took from a joke current in the camp, for he was carried around among the troops in the dress of an ordinary soldier. The love and favour he enjoyed among them, as a result of being brought up in their midst, is strikingly shown by the

fact that, when the soldiers were in uproar and on the point of frenzy after the death of Augustus, just the sight of him was undoubtedly enough to change their minds. For they only left off when it was reported that Caligula was to be removed because of the danger posed by the mutiny and transferred to the next town. Only then were they overcome with remorse and sought to stop and hold back the carriage, begging to be spared from the threatened shame.

[10] He also accompanied his father on the journey to Syria. On his return from there he lived first with his mother, then, when she was sent into exile, with his great-grandmother, Livia Augusta. When she died, despite his youth he delivered a eulogy for her on the rostra. Next he lived in the house of his grandmother, Antonia. Then, in his nineteenth year he was summoned by Tiberius to Capri, where on the very same day he took on the dress of a grown man and made a dedication of his first beard, though without any of the ceremony which had attended his brothers' coming of age. In this place he was beset by every kind of trap, as people sought to trick him or force him into making complaints, but he never gave them satisfaction. He behaved as though he had forgotten the fate of his family, as if nothing had happened to any of them, while the things he himself had suffered he passed over with a capacity for dissimulation which defied belief. So obsequious was he to his grandfather and the latter's courtiers that it has fairly been observed of him that there was never a better slave—nor a worse master.

[11] Yet even at that time he was not able to control his savage and reprehensible nature.* Indeed, he showed the keenest interest in witnessing the sufferings and torments of those condemned to be tortured, while at night he was in the habit of going out, disguised in a wig and long cloak,* to indulge in gluttony and adultery, and he sought out performances of dancing and singing with the greatest appetite. Tiberius suffered this behaviour lightly, hoping these activities might serve to calm his vicious character. That character was so perceptively assessed by the old man, shrewd as he was, that he used every so often to remark that Caligula alive would bring death for himself and all others, that he was rearing a viper for the Roman people—and a Phaethon* for the world.

[12] It was not long after this that Caligula took in marriage Junia Claudilla, daughter of that most noble man Marcus Silanus. At that time it was intended that he should become augur in place of his

brother Drusus but before he had taken on the office of augur he was promoted to the pontificate—supported by strong endorsements of his piety and distinction. And as the royal house was stripped bare of its other hopes and Sejanus was soon afterwards suspected of treachery and disposed of, he came gradually to hope that he himself might succeed.* To increase his chances, after Junia Claudilla had died in childbirth, he lured Ennia Naevia, wife of Macro, who at that time commanded the praetorian guard, to commit adultery, even promising her marriage if he managed to secure the empire—and he guaranteed this with an oath and a written bond. Having through her wormed his way into Macro's favour, he administered poison to Tiberius, as some believe, and, while he still breathed, ordered first that his ring be pulled off, then, since Tiberius seemed to be resisting, that a pillow be put over his mouth, and he himself with his own hands strangled him.* A freedman, who exclaimed at the dreadfulness of the crime, was immediately sent to be crucified. This seems quite plausible, for some authors report that he himself confessed, if not to the deed itself of parricide, then certainly to planning it, for he often used to boast as a sign of his family loyalty that, in order to avenge the deaths of his mother and his brothers, he had entered the bedroom armed with a dagger while Tiberius slept, then, overcome with pity for the man, had thrown away the weapon and withdrawn. Nor had Tiberius, though aware of what had happened, dared to interrogate him or follow the matter up.

[13] Having thus secured the empire, he was the answer to the prayer of the Roman people, or should I say, all humankind—the ruler most highly favoured by the greater part of provincials and soldiers, many of whom had known him as a child, and by all the people of Rome who remembered his father Germanicus and pitied the sufferings of his family. Thus it was that, as he came from Miscnum, though wearing mourning and accompanying the funeral train of Tiberius, among the altars, sacrificial victims, and blazing torches he encountered thronging crowds of people rejoicing greatly who greeted him with auspicious names: 'star', 'chick', 'child', and 'little chap'.

[14] When he entered the city, with the full consent of the senate—and of the crowd that was bursting into the senate chamber—he overrode the wishes of Tiberius, who had in his will named his other grandson, still a child, as co-heir.* And absolute

power over all matters was conceded to him with such public rejoicing that within the next three months, or even less, more than 160,000 victims are said to have been sacrificed. When, a few days later, he crossed over to the islands nearest to the Campanian coast, vows were made to secure his safe return lest the slightest occasion be omitted for displaying care and concern for his well-being. And indeed, when he was in ill health, everyone around the Palatine watched through the night, and there were even some who vowed to fight as gladiators to secure the sick man's recovery, while others posted public notices in which they promised their own lives.* Besides the great affection of the citizens he also enjoyed notable favour from foreigners. For Artabanus, king of the Parthians, who had always shown hatred and contempt for Tiberius, of his own accord sought the friendship of Caligula, attended a meeting with a consular legate, and crossed the Euphrates to offer his respects to the eagles and standards of Rome and to the portraits of the Caesars.

[15] Caligula himself sought to stimulate people's devotion by courting popularity in all sorts of ways. Having praised Tiberius with much weeping before the people and given him a splendid funeral, he at once hurried off to Pandateria and the Pontian islands to collect the ashes of his mother and brothers, his family feeling made all the more conspicuous by a terrible storm. Approaching with reverence, he himself placed the ashes in the urn. No less display attended the journey to Ostia—a standard flying on the stern of the ship—then on up the Tiber to Rome, where he had them carried on two biers into the Mausoleum of Augustus by the most eminent men in the equestrian order, at midday when crowds filled the streets. He also prescribed funeral offerings to be made for them every year on a day of public remembrance, and, more grandly still, circus games in honour of his mother and a carriage in which her image might be transported in the procession. But in memory of his father he gave the month of September the name 'Germanicus'.* After this, by senatorial decree he heaped upon his grandmother Antonia whatever honours had been bestowed on Livia Augusta. His paternal uncle, Claudius, who was at that time only a Roman knight, he made his colleague in the consulship. He adopted his stepbrother, Tiberius Gemellus, on the day he attained his toga of manhood, and gave him the title Prince of Youth.* As for his sisters, he ensured that the following words were added to all oaths: 'Nor shall I hold myself

nor my children dearer than I hold Gaius and his sisters,' while proposals of the consuls* were to include the words: 'That all may be well and fortunate with Gaius Caesar and his sisters.' As a further bid to secure popularity he freed those who had been condemned or exiled and declared an amnesty regarding any criminal accusations outstanding from the previous reign. So that no informer or witness would afterwards remain in fear, he ordered that the records relating to the cases against his mother and his brothers be carried to the Forum and burnt, having first called out loud upon the gods as witnesses that he had not read or touched any of them.* When someone offered him a document concerning his own security he refused to accept it, insisting that he had done nothing which would make anyone hate him, and he claimed he had no ears for informers.

[16] He banished from the city those monsters of lust, the 'tight-bums'*—only with great difficulty was he dissuaded from having them drowned. He made it legal to obtain, to possess, and to read the writings of Titus Labienus, Cremutius Cordus, and Cassius Severus, which had been banned by senatorial decree,* on the grounds that it was much in his interest that their contents be transmitted to future generations. He made available details of the imperial economy, which Augustus had been in the habit of publishing but which Tiberius had kept back. He allowed magistrates freedom in dispensing justice, without having to appeal to him. He inspected the Roman knights strictly and carefully but with moderation, making a public display of withdrawing the horse from those who were guilty of some evil or shame but in the case of those guilty only of a minor misdemeanour, merely omitting their names from the list as it was read out. To lighten the workload of jurors he added a fifth division to the existing four.* He attempted to restore the practice of elections, thereby giving the vote back to the people. Although Tiberius' will had been annulled, he straight away fulfilled its legacies faithfully and without argument, as well as those set out in the will of Julia Augusta,* which Tiberius had set aside. He relieved Italy of the one two-hundredth auction tax. He gave compensation to those who had suffered losses through fire. And in cases where he restored a ruler's authority, he also returned all the money which had in the mean time been collected as customs duty or revenue—Antiochus of Commagene received a hundred million sesterces which had been collected by the treasury. To make clear how he encouraged good

deeds, he gave eight hundred thousand sesterces to a freedwoman because she had kept silent about her patron's crime though suffering terrible tortures when under interrogation. In recognition of these actions, he was voted in addition to his other honours a golden shield which every year on the appointed day the colleges of priests would carry to the Capitol, accompanied by the senate and a chorus of boys and girls of noble birth who would sing an ode in praise of his virtues. It was also decreed that the Parilia* should be transferred to the day on which he acceded to power, as it marked a new beginning for the city.

[17] He held the consulship four times, the first from the Kalends of July for two months, the second from the Kalends of January for thirty days, the third lasted until the Ides of January and the fourth until the seventh day before the Ides of the same month.* Of all these only the last two were held continuously. He embarked upon the third on his own at Lugdunum.* This was not, as some thought, because of pride or carelessness but because, since he was away, the news could not be conveyed to him that the other consul had died just before the Kalends. He twice gave to the people a gift of three hundred sesterces and twice also hosted a most plentiful banquet for the senatorial and equestrian orders, even including their wives and children. At the second feast he gave out formal attire to the men, and to the women and boys ribbons of red and purple. And, in order to increase public enjoyment in perpetuity, he added an extra day, which he termed 'Iuvenalis', to the Saturnalia.

[18] He gave several gladiatorial games, some held in the amphitheatre of Statilius Taurus and some in the Saepta. Among the fighters he included bands of African and Campanian boxers, the very best of both regions. He did not always preside over the games himself but sometimes entrusted the task to magistrates or friends. He provided theatre shows all the time of many kinds and full of variety. Some of them were even staged by night and the whole city was lit up. He also threw gifts of various kinds and distributed a basket of savouries to each man. While people were eating he sent over his own portion to a Roman knight who was sitting across from him and consuming his meal with relish and delight, while to a senator, who behaved similarly, he sent a note announcing that he would make him a praetor out of the regular order. He also gave a great many circus shows which lasted from morning till night, the

interval consisting sometimes of the baiting of panthers, sometimes of military exercises from the Troy game.* In some special games, the arena was scattered with red and green and all the chariots were driven by men of the senatorial order. Some games he gave on the spur of the moment, when, as he was inspecting the Circus equipment from the Gelotian house some people in the nearby houses begged him for them.

[19] Besides this he also thought up a new and previously unheard-of variety of spectacle. For he made a bridge across the middle of the bay of Baiae to the promontory of Puteoli—a space of about three thousand six hundred paces*—by bringing together cargo ships from all around, anchoring them together in two lines and then heaping on top of them earth, to resemble the Appian Way. Across the bridge he travelled back and forth for two days in succession. On the first day his horse was decked out with trappings and he himself was distinguished by his oak wreath, his Spanish shield, his sword, and his golden cloak. On the second day he wore the dress of a charioteer and drove a chariot pulled by a pair of famous horses, carrying with him a boy called Dareus, one of the Parthian hostages, and escorted by the entire praetorian guard and a posse of friends travelling in war chariots. I know that many people believe Caligula thought up the idea of a bridge to outdo Xerxes, who excited much admiration when he threw a bridge over the rather more narrow Hellespont.* Others are of the opinion that he wanted the fame of his great achievement to inspire terror among the Germans and Britons whom at that time he planned to take on. But I remember my grandfather saying, when I was a boy, that the reason for the project had been given away by courtiers who reported that the astrologer Thrasyllus had reassured Tiberius, when he was anxious about who might succeed him and favoured his real grandson, that Gaius was no more likely to rule the empire than he was to ride with horses across the bay of Baiae.

[20] He also gave shows away from home: in Sicily he gave city games at Syracuse and in Gaul he gave mixed games at Lugdunum. Here he also held a competition for eloquence in Greek and Latin and they say that in this competition the losers were obliged to give prizes to the winners and to make speeches praising them, while those who found least favour were ordered to erase what they had written either with a sponge or with their tongues, unless they

preferred the option of being beaten with rods or being thrown into the nearest river.

[21] He completed some public works, such as the Temple of Augustus and Pompey's Theatre, left half-finished by Tiberius.* He began work on an aqueduct near Tibur and an amphitheatre next to the Saepta. Of these works his successor Claudius completed the former* and abandoned the latter. In Syracuse the city walls and the temples to the gods which had collapsed through old age were repaired. He had intended also to rebuild Polycrates' palace on Samos, to complete the temple to Apollo of Didyma at Miletus, to found a city on an Alpine ridge, and above all to dig a canal through the Isthmus of Greece*—he had already sent out a chief centurion to survey the project.

[22] The story so far has been of Caligula the emperor, the rest must be of Caligula the monster.

He took on many titles—the 'Pious', 'Son of the Camp', 'Father of the Forces', and 'Caesar Best and Greatest'*. On one occasion at dinner at his house, when he heard some kings who had come to Rome to pay him their respects arguing among themselves as to which of them came of the noblest line, he declaimed:

Let there be one Lord, one King!*

He came very close to assuming a diadem on the spot and turning what looked like a principate into the appearance of a monarchy. But when he was reminded that his own position had risen above that of princes or even of kings, he began from that time to lay claim to the majesty of a god. He gave orders that statues of gods noted for their religious and artistic importance, including the statue of Zeus from Olympia,* were to be brought from Greece in order that their heads might be removed and replaced with copies of his own. He extended a part of the palace right into the Forum, taking over the temple of Castor and Pollux as his own vestibule. Often he would stand between the divine brothers displaying himself for worship by those visiting the temple. Indeed, some hailed him as Jupiter Latiaris.* He also set up a temple to himself as god with priests and the most exotic sacrificial victims. In the temple there was a golden statue exactly resembling him which was dressed every day in clothes identical to those he himself was wearing. All the richest men used their influence or offered bribes to become priests of his cult. The sacrificial victims included flamingos, peacocks, black grouse, different breeds of guinea-hens, and pheasants, which were offered up, a different kind each day. While by night he would repeatedly invite the full and shining moon to share his bed and his embraces, in the daytime he used to talk privately with Capitoline Jupiter, sometimes whispering to him, then offering his own ear in turn for a reply, at other times speaking quite loudly and even cursing. For his voice was heard threatening:

Raise me up or you I'll . . .*

Finally, however, he was won over by the god, he claimed, and persuaded to share his home. He had a bridge built right over the temple of the Deified Augustus, joining the Palatine to the Capitol. Soon, in order that he might be still closer, he had foundations laid for a new house in the Capitoline temple precinct.

[23] Because of Agrippa's humble origins, he did not like to be thought of or referred to as his grandson. He would become angry if anyone in a speech or poem included Agrippa among the family of the Caesars. Instead, he used to claim that his mother was born of an incestuous relationship between Augustus and his daughter Julia. Not content with this insult to Augustus, he forbade ritual celebrations commemorating his victories at Actium and off the coast of Sicily, on the grounds that they had been terrible and disastrous for the Roman people. He frequently called his great-grandmother Livia Augusta 'Ulysses dressed as a Roman matron'. He even had the gall to accuse her of low birth, asserting in a letter to the senate that her maternal grandfather was a town-councillor of Fundi, when it was clear from public monuments that Aufidius Lurco had held high office in Rome. When his grandmother, Antonia, came seeking a private audience, he would only see her in the presence of the prefect Macro. It was because of this kind of humiliation and annoyance that she died—though some are of the opinion that she had been given poison, too. He offered her no honours after her death and observed her burning funeral pyre from his dining-room. His brother Tiberius* he caught off guard, sending a military tribune on the spur of the moment to put him to death, while his father-in-law Silanus he compelled to commit suicide by slitting his throat with a razor. He alleged that Silanus, when he himself had put to sea under turbulent conditions, had stayed behind in the hope of gaining control of the

city if anything should happen to the emperor. As for Tiberius, he claimed that he smelt of an antidote of the kind people take when they are afraid of poison. Silanus indeed was prone to seasickness and wanted to avoid the discomfort of a voyage, while Tiberius had taken medicine to cure his persistent and increasingly severe cough. His uncle Claudius Caligula preserved as a butt for jokes.*

[24] He habitually indulged in incestuous relations with all his sisters and at a crowded banquet he would make them take turns in lying beneath him, while his wife lay above.* Of his sisters it was Drusilla whose virginity he is believed to have violated while still a boy. Indeed, it is believed that their grandmother Antonia, who was at that time responsible for their joint upbringing, once actually caught them in bed together. Not long afterwards, when Drusilla was married to the ex-consul Lucius Cassius Longinus, Caligula abducted her and openly treated her as if she were his lawful wife. When he was ill he made her heir both to his property and to the empire. When she died, he declared a period of mourning, during which it was a capital offence to laugh, wash, or dine with one's parents, spouse, or children. Unable to bear his grief, he fled from the city one night all of a sudden, sped through Campania and made for Syracuse. As soon as he arrived he set out again on his return journey, unshaven and with hair unkempt. From that time onwards he refused to take any oath, no matter how important the business, even before an assembly of the people or before the army, unless it was by the godhead of Drusilla. His feelings for his other sisters were not marked by the same passion or reverence but he often prostituted them to his catamites. Thus, during the trial of Aemilius Lepidus it was all the easier for him to condemn them as adulteresses involved in the plot against him. He publicized letters in the hand-writing of all of them which he had obtained through deception and sexual intrigue, and even made an offering in the Temple of Mars the Avenger of three swords intended for his murder, along with an inscription.

[25] As regards marriage, it is difficult to decide whether he behaved worst in acquiring wives, in getting rid of them, or during his marriages. When Livia Orestilla was marrying Gaius Piso* and he himself was a guest at the wedding he gave orders that the bride be taken to his own residence. After a few days he divorced her, then, a couple of years later, had her relegated on the grounds that, in the

mean time, she had resumed relations with her previous husband. According to another story, Caligula, during the wedding banquet, had sent an order to Piso, who was reclining across from him, saying: 'Get your hands off my wife!' He had then left the party taking the bride with him and the next day issued an announcement that he had found himself a wife following the precedent set by Romulus and Augustus.* Happening to hear that Lollia Paulina's grandmother had been in her day a very beautiful woman, he had the granddaughter at once summoned back from the province where she was accompanying her husband, the ex-consul and army commander, Gaius Memmius. Having separated her from her husband he married her but soon afterwards set her aside—with the orders that she was never again to have sexual relations with anyone. As for Caesonia, though her looks were not striking and she was hardly in her first youth (she had already had three daughters by an earlier husband), she was a woman devoted to luxury and sexual excess and he loved her with all the more passion and constancy. Indeed, he would often show her off to the soldiers decked out with cloak, shield, and helmet and riding by his side, while to his friends he would even display her naked. He did not honour her with the title of wife until the day she gave birth, announcing simultaneously that he was her husband and the father of her baby girl. As for the child, whom he named Julia Drusilla, he carried her around to the temples of all the goddesses, placing her in the lap of the statue of Minerva, entrusting her with the care for the child's growth and education. Her temper seemed to him the surest indication that she was his own daughter, for even then she was so savage that she would try to hurt the little children who played with her by scratching at their eyes and faces.

[26] It would be trivial and superfluous to add to this the manner in which he treated his relatives and friends, Ptolemy, son of King Juba, his cousin (for Ptolemy was the grandson of Mark Antony through his daughter Selene)* and especially Macro and Ennia who had helped him to secure the empire. All these were rewarded for their kinship and for their loyal services with a bloody death. And he was no more respectful or merciful towards the senate. Some who had held the highest offices he allowed to run in their togas alongside his military chariot for several miles, and, when he was eating, to wait upon him, sometimes at the head of the dining-couch, sometimes at his feet, dressed in short linen tunics.* Some, when he had

secretly had them killed, he would repeatedly summon as if they were still living. Then a few days later he would announce falsely that they had taken their own lives. When the consuls forgot to make an edict concerning his birthday, he stripped them of their office so that for three days the state was without its supreme magistrates. A quaestor who was alleged to have been involved in a conspiracy he had flogged.* The clothes which had been stripped off him were placed under the soldiers' feet to give them a firmer grip as they beat him.

He treated the other orders with similar arrogance and cruelty. When he was disturbed in the middle of the night by people trying to secure the free seats in the Circus he had them all driven away with cudgels. In the confusion more than twenty Roman knights and the same number of ladies, along with a vast number of others, were trampled to death. At the theatrical shows, trying to stir up fights between the common people and the Roman knights, he distributed the free tickets early so that the places for the knights were taken by the commonest people. At a gladiatorial show, he had the awnings drawn back when the sun was at its fiercest and would allow no one to leave. He would have the usual equipment taken away and then set the most useless and ancient gladiators against mangy wild animals and have mock fights between respectable family men who were known to be of good reputation but conspicuous for some physical disability. And sometimes he would condemn the people to hunger by closing the granaries.

[27] Through these acts he made the clearest demonstration of his cruel character. When the cattle to feed the wild beasts he had provided for a show were rather expensive, he instead selected criminals for them to devour; he looked over the row of prisoners, without any regard for their individual records, and, from his position in the middle of the colonnade, announced that those 'between the bald-heads' were to be led away. The man who had promised he would fight as a gladiator if the emperor were restored to health, he obliged to fulfil his vow,* looking on as he struggled in combat and not letting him off till he had won his fight and pleaded repeatedly for delivery. Another, who had offered his own life in the same cause but had hesitated to fulfil his pledge, he handed over to his slaves who were to drive the man, wearing sacred wreathes, through the streets, demanding fulfilment, then finally hurl him from a rampart. Many

men of honourable rank he first had disfigured with the marks of
branding irons and then condemned to the mines, to road-building,
or to the beasts or else he would force them into cages on all fours
like animals, or have them sawn in half.* Nor was this always for
some serious offence but sometimes merely because they had not
liked one of his shows or because they had never sworn by his
Genius. He obliged parents to witness the execution of their own
children and when one man excused himself on the grounds of ill
health he had a litter sent to collect him. Another man he forced
from the spectacle of torment direct to a banquet at which, all
charm, he tried to make him laugh and joke. The manager of the
games and beast fights he had beaten with chains for days on end,
while he himself looked on, and only had him killed when the smell
of the man's rotting brains made him ill. He had a composer of
Atellan drama burnt to death in a fire in the middle of the arena
because one of his lines of verse contained a doubtful joke.* When a
Roman knight who had been thrown to the wild beasts shouted out
that he was innocent, he had him taken out, then, his tongue cut out,
thrown back into the arena.

[28] He once asked a man, back after a long period in exile, how he
had spent his time there. The man answered, in an attempt to flatter:
'I kept praying to the gods that Tiberius would die, as indeed happened, and that you would come to power.' Thinking that those now
in exile were similarly praying for his own death, he sent people
around the islands to kill them all. When he had conceived a desire to
have one of the senators torn apart, he arranged for some men to
accuse him of being a public enemy as soon as he entered the senate,
and to stab him with their writing implements before handing him
over to the other senators to be torn to pieces. Nor was he satisfied
until the man's body parts, limbs, and entrails were dragged through
the streets and heaped up together in front of him.

[29] The most appalling deeds he made still worse by what he
said. He used to say he loved to praise and admire no aspect of his
own nature more than, to use his own words, his *adiatrepsia*, that is
to say his shamelessness.* When his grandmother, Antonia, tried to
give him some advice, he not only disobeyed her but said: 'Remember, I can do anything I please and to anybody.' When he was about
to kill his brother,* whom he suspected of taking remedies through
fear of being poisoned, he said: 'Do you think you can take a remedy

against Caesar?' When he exiled his sisters, he warned them that
he possessed swords as well as islands. A man of praetorian rank,
who had withdrawn to the resort of Anticyra on account of his
ill health and had written frequently asking for an extension to
his leave, he had killed, with the comment that bloodletting was
the cure for one who had got no benefit from hellebore* in all this
time. When he signed the list every tenth day of those from
among the prisoners who were to be put to death, he used to say
he was clearing his accounts. One time when a number of Greeks
and Gauls had been condemned, he boasted that he had beaten
Gallograecia.*

[30] When he had people put to death it was almost invariably by
means of numerous minor wounds and always with the same familiar
order: 'Strike him so he feels his death!' When a man had been
executed in error, his name mistaken for that of the intended victim,
Caligula commented that the dead man, too, had deserved the
punishment.* He often declaimed that line from tragedy:

Let them hate, provided that they fear!*

He would frequently attack all the senators equally, as if they were all
guilty of supporting Sejanus, and of denouncing his mother and
brothers, bringing out the records, which he had pretended to have
destroyed,* and defending Tiberius' cruelty as unavoidable when
there were so many plausible accusers. He ceaselessly reviled the
equestrian order as being in thrall to the stage or the arena.* Roused
to anger by the crowd cheering on those who competed against his
favourites, he shouted out: 'If only the Roman people had a single
neck!' And when the crowd called for the brigand Tetrinius,* he
termed them Tetriniuses, too. Once five net-fighters in tunics, fighting as a group, surrendered to the same number of *secutores* without
putting up any resistance. When the order was given that they
should be put to death, one of them picked up his trident and killed
all the victors. This Caligula lamented in a proclamation as the cruel-
lest slaughter, and denounced those who had felt able to witness the
spectacle.

[31] He used to complain openly about the times he lived in as
being unmarked by public disaster. Augustus' reign had the Varian
tragedy,* that of Tiberius was memorable for the collapse of a theatre
at Fidenae,* while his own, when nothing seemed to go wrong, was in

danger of being forgotten. And every now and again he would express his desire for a terrible military defeat, a famine, a plague, a great fire, or an earthquake.

[32] Even when he was relaxing and taken up with entertainment and feasting, his words and actions were marked by the same cruelty. Often, while he was having his lunch or enjoying himself, the most serious judicial investigations, in which torture was used, were conducted in his presence or else a soldier adept at decapitation would cut the heads of a number of prisoners. When his bridge at Puteoli (the design of which I recounted above*) was being dedicated, he invited a large number of people who were on the shore to come out to him, then at once had them all pushed into the sea. Some managed to get hold of the rudders but he had them pushed back into the sea with poles and oars. In Rome, at a public banquet, finding a slave had stripped off some silver from the couches, he at once handed him over to an executioner to have his hands cut off and hung in front of him around his neck, and he was led around among the banqueters, preceded by a placard indicating the nature of his offence. Once, when he and a *murmillo* from the gladiatorial school had been having a fight with wooden swords and the latter deliberately fell to the ground, he ran the man through with a real dagger and rushed about wearing a palm, as victors do. Another time, when a sacrificial victim was brought to the altar, he, dressed in the robes of a *popa*, raised his mallet high, then brought it down killing the *cultrarius*.* At a rather elegant dinner he suddenly roared with laughter and when the consuls, who were lying nearby, politely asked him why he was laughing, replied: 'Why else than because just a nod on my part would be enough to have either of you slaughtered at once?'

[33] Among his other jokes, he once asked the actor Apelles, when he was next to a statue of Jupiter, which of them was the greater and when Apelles hesitated to answer, he had him flayed with scourges, praising the quality of his voice, as he cried out for mercy, as delightful even when groaning. Whenever he kissed the neck of a wife or a mistress, he would add: 'This lovely neck would be severed the minute I gave the order.' Indeed, from time to time he would exclaim that he might even have to use torture on his own Caesonia to find out from her why he loved her so very much.

[34] The envy and malice with which he regarded persons of almost every period were no less than his arrogance and cruelty.

Some statues of famous men which Augustus had moved from the Capitoline precinct to the Campus Martius because of lack of space, he had overturned and broken up in such a manner that it was impossible to reassemble them with all their inscriptions. And he issued orders banning the future erection of any statue or image to a living man unless authorized or initiated by himself. He even thought of banning the poetry of Homer, remarking that there was no reason he should not be allowed to do as Plato had done,* in banning the poet from his ideal city. Indeed he came close to removing the writings and portraits of Virgil and Livy* from all the libraries, complaining that one had no talent and very little learning, while the other's history was long-winded and sloppy. As regards lawyers, he acted as if he was going to abolish the profession, often threatening that he would make sure, by Hercules, that none of them could give an opinion that went against his own.

[35] From all the greatest nobles he confiscated their family insignia, taking the collar from Torquatus, the lock of hair from Cincinnatus, and from Gnaeus Pompey, the *cognomen* of his ancient line, 'The Great'. Ptolemy, whom I mentioned earlier,* he summoned from his kingdom and welcomed with honour, then executed, for no other reason than because, when he himself was giving some gladiatorial games, he noticed that as Ptolemy entered the splendour of his purple cloak attracted the attention of the crowd. Whenever he came across men with a good head of hair, he had the backs of their heads shaved to spoil their appearance.* There was a man called Aesius Proculus, son of a chief centurion, who was known as the Giant Lover because of his impressive size and appearance. This man was at once dragged from the audience and taken into the arena, where Caligula matched him first with a Thracian, next with a heavy-armed gladiator, then, when the man had twice beaten his opponents, he ordered that he be bound in chains without delay and led about the streets, dressed in rags, to be shown to the women, before being put to death. To sum up, there was no one, however humble his rank, however wretched his lot, whose advantages Caligula did not resent. Since the King of Nemi had held his priesthood for many years, he procured a stronger man to supplant him.* When, one day during the games, an *essedarius* called Porius, who had freed his slave after a victory, was warmly applauded, Caligula rushed from the games in such haste that he trod on the hem of his

toga and fell headlong down the steps in a state of fury shouting that
the people who ruled the world gave more honour to a gladiator for
the smallest act than to their deified emperors or to himself, their
present one.

[36] He had regard neither for his own chastity nor for that of
others. He is said to have had sexual relations with Marcus Lepidus,
the actor Mnester, and a number of hostages—giving and receiving
pleasure in turn. Valerius Catullus, a man of consular family, proclaimed publicly that he had buggered the emperor and was quite
exhausted by his sexual demands. In addition to his incestuous relations with his sisters and his notorious affair with the prostitute
Pyrallis, there was hardly any woman of distinguished family he did
not make advances to. Most of them he invited to dinner, along with
their husbands, and as they passed by the foot of his couch, he would
appraise them carefully—as if he were buying slaves, sometimes
raising their faces with his hand, if they had cast their eyes modestly
downwards. Then, as often as he felt like it, he would leave the
dining-room, having called to him whichever woman he found most
attractive. Not long afterwards he would return,* making no attempt
to conceal the signs of his recent sexual activity, and would offer
criticism or praise of his partner, listing in detail the good or bad
features of her body and her sexual performance. To some women he
himself sent a divorce notice, in the name of their absent husbands,
and gave orders that these notices were to be entered in the public
records.

[37] His ingenuity in extravagant expenditure outdid that of all
other prodigals ever; he invented a new kind of bath and the most
outlandish varieties of food and drink—he used to bathe in hot and
cold perfumed oils and would drink the most precious pearls dissolved in vinegar* and offer his guests loaves of bread and savouries
made out of gold. He used to remark that a man should either be
frugal or be Caesar. Indeed for several days in a row he scattered
among the people coins of larger denominations from the roof of the
Basilica Julia. He had constructed some Liburnian galleys, their
prows studded with jewels, their sails of many colours, whose ample
interiors housed baths, porticoes, and dining-rooms as well as a large
variety of vines and fruit-trees, so that lounging on these vessels he
might travel by day along the shores of Campania entertained by
choirs and orchestras. In the construction of his palaces and villas,

with no regard for expense, he desired nothing more ardently than to achieve whatever was impossible. Great structures were built up in hostile and deep waters, mountains of the hardest flint were tunnelled through, while plains were raised to the level of mountains and excavations levelled mountain peaks flat.* The speed with which these measures were effected was incredible, for delay was punished by death. Thus, to save recounting all his projects in detail, he spent vast sums, including the two thousand seven hundred million sesterces built up by Tiberius Caesar, in the space of less than one year.

[38] In need of money, his funds exhausted, he turned his mind to robbery by means of a variety of cunningly devised false accusations, auctions, and taxes. He claimed that Roman citizenship had been illegally acquired by persons whose ancestors had been granted it for themselves 'and their descendants', except in the case of sons, for the term used, *posteri* ['descendants'], should be understood as covering no one beyond that degree of relationship. When certificates of citizenship issued under the Deified Julius and the Deified Augustus were presented to him he dismissed them as old and out of date. He also accused people of having made false census returns, if they happened to have subsequently acquired any addition to their estates.* Any wills of chief centurions made since the beginning of the reign of Tiberius which failed to specify either Tiberius or himself as heirs he annulled on the grounds of ingratitude. And he declared null and void also the wills of others, if someone said they had intended to make Caesar their heir when they died. Having stirred up this fear, when he was then named as heir alongside relatives by men he did not know and alongside children by their parents, he would claim that men were making a fool of him when they carried on living after having named him heir and to many he sent poisoned sweets.* He himself presided at the trials of such cases, beforehand stipulating the sum he planned to raise during the sitting and only drew business to a close once that sum was raised. Unable to suffer the slightest delay, he once passed a single sentence on forty men who had been arraigned on different charges and boasted to Caesonia of how much he had achieved while she had been having her afternoon nap. Having arranged an auction, he put up and sold all that was left over from the games, himself soliciting bids and exaggerating them to such an extent that some people,

bankrupted by the huge sums they had been forced to pay for goods, opened their veins. In one notorious incident, when Aponius Saturninus had nodded off on one of the seats and Caligula urged the auctioneer not to overlook the man of praetorian rank who kept nodding his head, the bidding did not come to an end until the man had unknowingly acquired thirteen gladiators for nine million sesterces.

[39] And while he was in Gaul he sold for vast sums the jewellery, household goods, slaves, and even the freedmen,* belonging to his condemned sisters. Then, spurred on by the profits he was making, he gave orders that all the furniture of the old palace was to be brought from Rome. Hire vehicles and draught animals from the bakeries were requisitioned for their transport with the effect that there were bread shortages in Rome and many people who were involved in court cases lost them, because they were unable to get to court and thus failed the terms of their bail. In his attempts to offload this furniture he resorted to every kind of deception and flattery, sometimes complaining about the avarice of particular individuals who were not ashamed of being richer than himself, sometimes pretending to feel regret that the property of the imperial family was falling into the hands of ordinary people. When he discovered that a wealthy man of the provinces had paid two hundred thousand sesterces to his secretaries in order, through bribery, to secure an invitation to a dinner party, he was not in the least annoyed that the honour of dining in his company should be valued at such a high price. The next day when the man was attending his auction, he sent a messenger to hand over to him some insignificant object for the price of two hundred thousand sesterces and to tell him that he was to dine with Caesar by personal invitation.

[40] His new and unheard-of taxes were exacted first through the tax-collectors, then, because they were making so much money, through centurions and tribunes of the praetorian guard. There was no kind of object or person which was not subject to some kind of tax. A fixed tax was imposed on all ready-cooked food sold throughout the city. With regard to all lawsuits and court cases, wherever they took place, a levy of one-fortieth of the sum at issue was charged, and a punishment imposed if anyone was found compromising with their opponents or giving up their suit. Porters were taxed an eighth of their daily earnings. Those who profited from

prostitution were taxed whatever they charged for one act of inter-
course. To the law's preamble was added the stipulation that anyone
who had ever been a prostitute or a pimp was liable for this tax and
that even their marriages were not exempt.

[41] When these laws had been announced but not issued in written form and many offences had been committed because of people's
ignorance of the exact provisions, in response to popular protest the
legislation was at last posted. However, the lettering was so small and
the position so awkward that no one was able to read any of it. So as
not to leave any method of plundering untried, Caligula set up a
brothel on the Palatine, designating a number of rooms and having
them furnished in a manner appropriate to the dignity of the location, and installed in them respectable married women and free-born
boys. He then sent around the forums and basilicas heralds who
invited young men and old to take their pleasure. Those who came
were lent money on interest and officials were at hand who openly
took down their names as contributors to Caesar's revenue. He was
not ashamed to make money even from games of dice where he
made a profit through lying and even perjury. And, one time, having
given up his turn in the game to the man sitting next to him, he
went out into the front hall of his house where, seeing two wealthy
Roman knights ride by, he gave orders that they should be seized and
their wealth confiscated without delay. He went back triumphantly
boasting that he had never had a luckier play.

[42] When his daughter was born, however, he lamented his poverty still more, complaining that he now had to bear a father's burdens as well as those of an emperor, and received contributions to the
girl's upbringing and dowry. He announced that he would be accepting New Year's presents at the start of the year and stood in the
temple vestibule on New Year's Day in order to take the donations
which a crowd of all sorts of people heaped upon him with overflowing hands and togas.* Finally, seized with a passion for handling
money, he would often walk with bare feet on the huge heaps of gold
pieces he had piled up in the most public places and sometimes he
would even roll about in them with his whole body.

[43] He only once got involved in war or military affairs—and
even then without having planned to do so. He was on a journey to
Mevania to see the grove and river of Clitumnus* when he was
advised that he ought to supplement the troop of Batavians who

accompanied him, and he was seized by the urge to undertake a German campaign. He allowed no delay but summoned legions and auxiliary forces from all over the place (the levy was everywhere enforced with great severity) and ordered supplies of all kinds, in quantities greater than ever before. Sometimes he embarked upon the journey and made for his destination with such haste and speed that the praetorian cohorts, against their usual custom, were obliged to load their standards onto pack animals and thus follow him. So lazy and luxurious was his style of travelling, at other times, that he was borne in a litter by eight bearers and the inhabitants of towns along the way were ordered to sweep the roads and sprinkle them with water in order to damp down the dust.

[44] On arriving at the camp, in order to make a show of his strictness and severity as a leader, he dismissed with dishonour the legates who had been too late in gathering together auxiliary troops from different regions. During his review of the troops, he demoted from their posts as chief centurion, on the grounds that they were old and infirm, quite a few men who were now of advanced years, some of them only a few days off retirement. Then, rebuking the rest for their greed, he cut the reward for completion of military service to six thousand sesterces.* All that he achieved was to accept the surrender of Adminius, son of the British king Cynobellinus, who, after he had been thrown out by his father, came as an exile with a tiny band of followers. Acting as though this signified the surrender of the entire island, Caligula sent a grandiose message to Rome, commanding the couriers to ride in their carriage right into the Forum* to the senate house and not to deliver it except to the consuls, in front of a crowded meeting of the senate in the temple of Mars the Avenger.*

[45] Later, not having anyone to fight with, he gave orders for some of his German bodyguards to be taken across the Rhine and hidden, then that after lunch news should be brought in a great commotion that the enemy had appeared. These orders fulfilled, he rushed out into the nearby woods, accompanied by his friends and some of the praetorian cavalry, where they cut down trees and decked them out like war trophies before returning by torchlight. Those who had not come with him he berated as cowards, while those who had accompanied him and participated he rewarded with crowns to mark this novel and unprecedented kind of victory. These,

decorated with images of the sun, moon, and stars, he termed 'the scout's crown'. Another time, some hostages were taken from an elementary school and sent secretly ahead. Then, suddenly abandoning a dinner party, he rushed after them with a body of cavalry as if they were escaped prisoners, seized them, and brought them back in chains. This charade, too, exemplified his extraordinary excesses. Having returned to the dinner, when messengers announced that the troops were drawn up, he urged that they should come and join the party just as they were, though they were dressed in their cuirasses. He also advised them, in Virgil's words, to 'endure and save themselves for better times'.* While all this was going on, he issued a ferocious edict cursing the senate and people in their absence, on the grounds that while Caesar was at war and exposed to such great dangers, they were enjoying regular parties, the circus, the theatre, and pleasant resorts.

[46] Finally, as if he was about to embark upon a war, he drew up his battle lines and set out his catapults and other artillery on the ocean shore. When no one had the least idea what he intended, he suddenly gave the order that they were to gather sea shells, filling their helmets and the folds of their tunics. These were what he termed spoils owed by the Ocean to the Capitol and Palatine. And, as a monument to his victory, he had a very high tower constructed, which would, like the Pharos,* send out beams of light to guide the course of ships by night. As if he had exceeded all previous models of generosity in announcing a donative for the troops of a hundred denarii per man, he told them, 'Depart in happiness, depart in wealth.'

[47] From this he turned to consideration of his triumph. Besides the captives and barbarian refugees, he selected all the tallest men of Gaul, men 'fit for a triumph' as he himself would say, as well as quite a few of the princes, who were to take part in the procession, and forced them not only to dye their hair red and grow it long, but also to learn some words of German and take on barbarian names. He even gave orders that the triremes, in which he had set forth on the Ocean, should be transported to Rome—though most of the journey was overland. He issued written instructions to the procurators to make preparations for a triumph, with the lowest possible outlay, but on a scale grander than ever before—for they had at their disposal the property of all.

[48] Before he left the province, he conceived the most appalling plan—to slaughter those legions which had tried to mutiny after the death of Augustus, on the grounds that they had trapped his father Germanicus, who was their leader, and himself, then a small child.* Only with great difficulty was he dissuaded from this reckless proposition and he could in no way be prevented from carrying through his wish to decimate them.* The legions were summoned, without their weapons, even their swords left behind, to attend an assembly where they were surrounded by armed cavalry. However, when he saw that quite a few of the legionaries, suspecting that something was going on, were slipping away to arm themselves in case violence broke out, he fled from the assembly and at once made for the city, where all his ferocity was displaced onto the senate whom he publicly threatened, in order to divert attention from rumours concerning the extent of his own shameful behaviour. He asserted among his other complaints, that he had been deprived of his merited triumph—though he himself, not long before, had given orders that no honours were to be offered him, on pain of death.

[49] Thus when on his journey home he was approached by legates representing that most distinguished order who begged him to hasten his return, he shouted at the top of his voice, 'I shall come, I shall come and this will be my companion', all the while banging the hilt of the sword he was wearing. He pronounced that he would return—but only to those who wanted him—the equestrian order and the people, for to the senate he would never more be either fellow citizen or prince. He even forbade any senators to come to meet him. Then, having either abandoned or postponed his triumph, he entered the city on his birthday with an ovation. Within four months he was dead, having dared to commit terrible crimes and planning worse ones. For he had proposed to move, first to Antium, later to Alexandria,* having first put to death all the best men of the senatorial and equestrian orders. There can be no doubt about this for amongst his secret papers were found two little books with different titles, one 'The Sword', the other 'The Dagger'. Both contained the names and details of those whom he intended to have killed. A chest full of different poisons was also found, which, when they were soon afterwards on Claudius' orders thrown into the sea, are said to have so polluted its waters that many fish died, their corpses washed up by the tide on neighbouring beaches.

[50] He was tall of stature, very pallid of complexion. His body was ill formed, his neck and legs very thin. His eyes and temples were sunken, while his brow was broad and intimidating. His hair was sparse, his crown being completely bald, while the rest of his body was hairy. Because of this he pronounced it a crime meriting death if, when he was passing, anyone should look down on him from above, or if, for whatever reason, the word 'goat' was mentioned. Though nature had made his face hideous and repulsive, he deliberately tried to make it more so by practising all kinds of terrifying and dreadful expressions in the mirror. His health, both of body and of mind, was unstable. When he was a boy he suffered from epilepsy. When he was a little older he was capable of some endurance but sometimes he would suddenly become weak and be unable to walk, stand, think straight, or hold himself up. He himself was aware of his state of mental health and sometimes thought of taking a rest cure to clear his brain. It is thought he was drugged by his wife Caesonia when she administered a love potion which had instead made him mad. He suffered terribly from insomnia for he could never sleep for more than three hours in a night and even this was not calm and peaceful but troubled by strange visions. One time, for instance, he thought he saw an image of the sea speaking with him. Thus, for most of the night, bored of lying awake in his bed, he would sometimes lounge on his couch and sometimes wander through long porticoes, calling out, every now and again, for daylight and longing for it to come.

[51] That such opposed vices, both the greatest arrogance and the greatest timidity, were to be found in the same person, I have no doubt in attributing to his mental infirmity. For this man, who had so little respect for the gods, would, at the slightest hint of thunder or lightning, close his eyes and cover his head, while a bigger storm would make him spring out of his bed and hide under it.* On a tour of Sicily, he greatly mocked the local wonders, then, one night, suddenly fled from Messana, terrified by the smoke and rumbling coming from the peak of Mount Etna. Despite the threats he would utter against barbarians, when he was travelling by chariot, on the farther side of the Rhine, with a tightly grouped body of men through a narrow passage and someone remarked what a panic there would be if the enemy made an appearance somewhere, he immediately mounted a horse and hurried back towards the bridges. And when he

found them crowded with serving men and baggage, he would not tolerate delay but had himself passed from hand to hand over people's heads. Soon afterwards, hearing of an uprising in Germany, he made plans to flee, making ready the fleet as his means of escape from the city. His only comfort was the thought that, even if the enemy took control of the Alps, as the Cimbri had done, or even the city of Rome, as the Senones* had once done, at least he would be left with the overseas provinces. It was this, I think, which later gave his assassins the idea of pretending to the rioting soldiers that he had taken his own life, terrified by the report of a military defeat.

[52] In his clothes, his footwear, and other aspects of his personal adornment his practice never conformed to the traditional manner of Roman citizens, sometimes departing from what was appropriate to his sex, sometimes even from what was right for a mortal. Often he would dress himself in a patterned cloak set with precious stones, a long-sleeved tunic, and bracelets, before making a formal appearance in public. Sometimes he dressed in silk or in women's clothes. For shoes he sometimes wore actor's slippers or platforms,* sometimes soldier's boots or feminine pumps. He was often to be seen with a gilded beard, holding a thunderbolt, a trident, or a *caduceum*— the emblems of the gods—and sometimes even in the regalia of the goddess Venus.* He frequently sported the robes of a triumphant general, even before he went on campaign, and sometimes the breastplate of Alexander the Great, which he had taken from his sarcophagus.*

[53] As regards the liberal arts, he had little time for learning but much for oratory, and was as fluent and quick as could be, especially if he was delivering an accusation against somebody. When he was angry, words and concepts came easily to him and his voice and enunciation were strong. Such was his enthusiasm that he could not keep still and even those standing far away could hear him. When he was about to make a speech, he would threaten that he was going to draw the sword forged by his late-night labours. He had so much contempt for more subtle and refined kinds of writing that he described Seneca—then very much in fashion—as the author of 'mere school essays' and 'sand without lime'.* He was also in the habit of writing responses to the successful pleas of orators and he would compose speeches for the prosecution and for the defence of high-status defendants on trial in the senate. Depending on how his own

compositions turned out, he made his judgements in condemnation or acquittal of each defendant, while the equestrian order, too, was summoned by edict to come and listen to him.

[54] When it came to other sorts of arts, he devoted himself with great enthusiasm to the widest variety. Taking on the roles of Thracian gladiator or charioteer, sometimes even those of singer or dancer, he would engage in battle with real weapons, and drove a chariot in circuses built in various locations. He was so transported by the pleasure of singing and dancing that he could not sit through public spectacles without singing along with the tragic actor as he delivered his lines, and openly imitating the actor's poses, as if praising or criticizing the performance. And indeed, the very reason for which he ordered an all-night festival on the day he died was so that the licence of the occasion might provide an auspicious opportunity for his stage debut.* Sometimes he even used to dance at night. Once, he summoned three men of consular rank to the Palatine at the second watch, then, when they arrived in great fear and dreading the worst, he made them sit on a platform. All at once, and with a great noise of flutes and castanets, he leapt out, dressed in a cloak and ankle-length tunic, and performed a dance, before going away again. However, despite being so multi-talented he never learned to swim.

[55] In relation to all those who were his favourites, his behaviour constituted madness. He used to kiss the pantomime actor Mnester even in the middle of the games. And if, when Mnester was performing, anyone made the slightest noise, he had him dragged from his seat and flogged him himself. When a Roman knight caused a disturbance, he sent a centurion to him with the message that he should go without delay to Ostia and thence travel on to King Ptolemy in Mauretania, carrying a message: 'Do nothing good or bad to the man I have sent you.' He put some Thracian gladiators in charge of his German bodyguards, while he reduced the armour of the *murmillones*.* When a certain Columbus won a victory but was slightly wounded, he gave orders that the wound be rubbed with a kind of poison, which he thereafter termed Columbinum. This was certainly how he recorded it amongst his other poisons. He was so wildly keen on the Green Faction* in the circus, that he used often to take his dinner in the stable and stay overnight there. At one of his parties, he gave the driver Eutychus two million sesterces in going-

home presents. As for his horse Incitatus, to prevent whose disturbance he used to send his soldiers, the day before the circus games, to demand silence in the surrounding area, apart from the marble stable, the ebony manger, the purple blankets and the gem-studded collar, he also gave him a house and a household of slaves and furniture, so that guests he invited in his name might be entertained in a more refined manner. It is said, too, that he meant to make him consul.*

[56] While he was running riot and laying waste in this way, a number of people had the idea of making an attempt on his life. However, when one or two conspiracies had been detected and others were hesitating, having so far lacked a favourable opportunity, two men devised a plan and carried it through—not without the complicity of the most powerful freedmen and the praetorian prefects. For the latter had themselves been accused, though falsely, of conspiring in some plot and felt themselves suspected and hated by the emperor. He had aroused great hatred against them by once taking them aside and asserting, his sword drawn, that if they thought he merited death he would take his life himself, and from that time he was constantly making accusations about one to the other and setting them all against each other. When they had decided to make their attempt on him during the Palatine games, at midday, as he made for the exit, Cassius Chaerea, tribune of a praetorian cohort, requested the leading part. For, though he was an older man, the emperor used to taunt him by calling him soft and effeminate* in the most abusive manner, sometimes, when he asked for the watchword, giving him 'Priapus' or 'Venus', and sometimes, when, for some reason, he gave the emperor thanks, offering his hand to be kissed, then moving it in an obscene gesture.

[57] Many prodigies foretold his violent end. The statue of Jupiter at Olympia, which he had decided to have taken apart and brought to Rome, suddenly gave out a such a laugh that the scaffolding collapsed and the removal men ran away; and at once a man called Cassius approached claiming that he had been ordered in a dream to sacrifice a bull to Jupiter. The Capitol in Capua was struck by lightning on the Ides of March; and on the same day the same thing happened at Rome to the Palatine doorman's booth. There were some who speculated that the latter omen portended danger to the Palatine's master from his guards, while the former signified the

violent death of a distinguished man in repetition of that which had taken place years ago on the same day.* The astrologer Sulla, when Caligula made inquiries about his star signs, assured him that certain death was very close. The lots of Fortune at Antium warned him to beware Cassius. He thus gave orders that Cassius Longinus,* who was then proconsul of Asia, should be put to death, forgetting that Chaerea, too, was called Cassius. The day before he met his death, he dreamt that he was standing in the heavens next to Jupiter's throne and that Jupiter pushed him with the big toe of his right foot so that he fell headlong to earth. Some other events are also regarded as prodigies which took place a little earlier on the day itself. When he was making a sacrifice he was sprinkled with the blood of a flamingo. And Mnester the pantomime performed the same tragedy which the tragedian Neoptolemus had produced at the games during which King Philip of Macedon was killed; and in the farce 'Laureolus'—in which the lead actor in trying to run away falls and vomits blood— several of the understudies sought most keenly to show off their talents, so that the stage was overflowing with blood.* Besides this, preparations were being made for a night-time show in which Egyptians and Aethiopians acted stories from the Underworld.

[58] On the ninth day before the Kalends of February,* at around the seventh hour, having delayed getting up for lunch since his stomach was still disturbed by the previous day's overeating, he finally went out, in response to his friends' persuasion. Since there were young aristocrats from Asia, who had been summoned to perform on stage, getting themselves ready in the covered passage through which his route lay, he paused to look them over and give them encouragement. If the leader of the troop had not complained of a cold, he would have gone back and had the show put on at once. There are two versions of the rest of the story. Some say that while he was speaking to the boys Chaerea from behind gave his neck a deep cut with his sword, shouting 'Take this!';* then that the tribune Cornelius Sabinus, the other conspirator, ran his chest through from in front. Others report that Sabinus, having got some centurions who were in on the plot to get rid of the crowd, asked Caligula for the password following usual military practice and, when Caligula replied 'Jupiter',* Chaerea shouted out 'Let it be so!' As Caligula looked behind him, Chaerea split his jaw with a blow. As he lay with his limbs twisted up, repeatedly calling out that he was alive, others

finished him off with thirty wounds. All acted on the signal 'At it again!' Some even applied the sword to his private parts. As the commotion began, his bearers came running to his aid with their litter-poles and the German bodyguards not far behind. They slaughtered several of the conspirators, together with some senators who had not been involved.

[59] He lived twenty-nine years and ruled for three years, ten months and eight days. His corpse was secretly transported to the Lamian gardens* and, partially burnt on a makeshift pyre, was buried under turf in a shallow grave. Afterwards, his sisters, back from exile, exhumed it and had it cremated and entombed. It is generally known that prior to this, the caretakers of the gardens were disturbed by ghosts and in the house, too, where he had slept, no night passed without some alarming apparition, until the house itself burnt down in a fire. His wife Caesonia died with him, run through by a centurion's sword, as did his daughter, who was dashed against a wall.

[60] Anyone might gauge the state of those times from the following circumstances, too. For when news broke of his assassination no one would believe it at first, and people suspected that the story had been devised and spread by Caligula himself in order to discover by this means how people felt about him. Not even the conspirators wanted anyone to succeed to supreme power, while the senate so heartily agreed on re-establishing liberty that the consuls summoned the first meeting not in the Senate house, which was called 'Julian',* but on the Capitoline, while some, when expressing their opinions, even proposed to wipe out all memory of the Caesars and pull down their temples. It was however particularly observed and noted that all the Caesars with the forename Gaius died by the sword, starting with the one who was murdered in the time of Cinna.*

THE DEIFIED CLAUDIUS

[1] The father of Claudius Caesar was Drusus, who first had the forename of Decimus, then later that of Nero. Livia, having married Augustus when she was pregnant, gave birth to Drusus less than three months later and it was suspected that he was the child of his stepfather, conceived in adultery.* Certainly the following line was soon circulating:

> The lucky ones have children in just three months.

This Drusus, during his quaestorship and praetorship,* led the army in the war in Raetia, then later in Germany. The first Roman general to cross the Northern Ocean, he had constructed, with enormous labour and trouble, the canals on the other side of the Rhine which even now are known by his name. He also killed many of the enemy and forced them far back into the most remote places of the interior, not leaving off his pursuit until an apparition, in the form of a barbarian woman but of greater than human size, gave a warning, in the Latin language, that the victor should not press further on. Because of these achievements, he secured the right to an ovation and the triumphal ornaments.

After his praetorship he at once embarked on the consulship and resumed his campaign, but died of an illness, while stationed in the summer camp, which became known as the Accursed from that time. His body was transported by the foremost men of the towns and colonies to Rome, where it was received by the divisions of the scribes* and buried in the Campus Martius. The army, too, raised a mound in his honour, around which soldiers would run every year thereafter on a particular day, while the Gallic cities would offer public prayers and sacrifices. Besides this, the senate among many other honours voted him a marble arch, decorated with trophies, on the Appian Way, and bestowed the title 'Germanicus' on him and his descendants.

Indeed, he is held to have been a man whose spirit was equally keen on military glory and on citizen government. Besides his victories over the enemy, he is also said to have wanted to win the opimian spoils* and to have often pursued the leaders of the

Germans all over the field, putting himself in great danger. Nor did he ever conceal the fact that, if it were in his power, he would restore the old republic. It is for this reason, I think, that some have been so bold as to record that Augustus did not trust him, recalling him from his province and, when Drusus delayed, having him killed with poison. However, I include this rather for completeness than because I hold it to be true or even likely. For Augustus was so attached to him while he lived, that he always specified him as co-heir with his own sons, and he once declared this in the senate; when Drusus was dead he so praised him before the crowd that he even prayed to the gods that they would make his Caesars* like Drusus and grant him as glorious a death as Drusus had been given. And not content with having a eulogy in verse, which he himself had composed, inscribed on Drusus' tomb, he also composed a memoir of his life in prose. With the younger Antonia* Drusus produced numerous children, though only three survived him: Germanicus, Livilla, and Claudius.

[2] Claudius was born at Lugdunum, when Iullus Antonius and Fabius Africanus were consuls, on the Kalends of August,* the anniversary of the day that the altar to Augustus was first dedicated there. He was named Tiberius Claudius Drusus. Later, when his older brother was adopted into the Julian family, he took the *cognomen* Germanicus.* He lost his father, however, when he was an infant, and throughout his boyhood and adolescence he suffered from various persistent illnesses to such a degree that his mental and physical development was impaired and, even when he reached the right age, he was not considered suitable for any public or private duties. Even after he had come of age,* he was treated as a minor and continued to be under the supervision of a tutor, a barbarian superviser of goods transport, as he himself complains in certain writings, who had been chosen deliberately to chastise him as brutally as possible on the slightest provocation. Again, because of his state of health, when he presided over the gladiatorial games which he was providing together with his brother in memory of their father, he was dressed in a Greek cloak, an unprecedented sight.* When he assumed his toga of manhood, he was taken to the Capitoline in a litter in the middle of the night, without the usual escort.

[3] From his earliest youth, however, he displayed an unusual devotion to the liberal arts and often even published some of his attempts in different genres.* Nevertheless, even by this means, he

was quite unable to secure any public position or create the hope that he might prove better in future.

His mother, Antonia, used to refer to him as a monstrous specimen of humanity, whom Nature made a start on but never completed. And if she wanted to emphasize anyone's stupidity, she would describe him as a bigger fool than her son Claudius. His grandmother Augusta* always had the greatest contempt for him, speaking to him only on the rarest occasions and giving him instructions in a brief and peremptory note or else via an intermediary. His sister Livilla, when she heard he was to become emperor, expressed her regrets publicly and unambiguously for the harsh and undeserved fate which was befalling the Roman people. As for his great-uncle Augustus, I include some extracts from his letters to make clear what opinion he had of Claudius:

[4] I have, as you instructed my dear Livia, consulted Tiberius as to what we should do with your grandson Tiberius* for the Games of Mars.* Indeed, we are both of the opinion that we should decide once and for all what plan we are to adopt in his case. For if he is sound and, so to speak, all there, have we any reason to suppose he may not advance along the same path by the same steps as his brother has done? If, however, we suspect that he is lacking and impaired in the wholeness both of his mind and of his body, we should not provide those people who are apt to mock and laugh at such things with opportunities to ridicule both him and ourselves. For if we make a separate decision for each occasion and do not determine in advance whether or not he is capable of fulfilling public duties, we shall always be in a quandary. As for the current issue about which you ask my advice, I am content that he should be in charge of the priests' banquet at the Games of Mars, so long as he allows himself to be guided by Silvanus' son, a connection of his by marriage, and does not do anything to make himself conspicuous or an object of ridicule. However, I do not wish him to watch the circus games from the imperial box, for he would be conspicuous, exposed at the front of the spectators. Nor do I wish him to go to the Alban mount or to be present in Rome on the day of the Latin festival. For if he is capable of going to the mount in attendance on his brother, why should he not be made prefect of the city?* So you have my views, dear Livia: we should decide the entire matter once and for all, so that we are not always vacillating between hope and anxiety. You may, if you wish, give this part of my letter to our Antonia to read.

And again in another letter:

Indeed, while you are away, I shall invite young Tiberius to dinner every day, so that he won't be dining on his own with Sulpicius and Athenodorus.* For I'd like him to make a more careful and sensible choice of someone whose gestures, walk, and behaviour he could take as models. The poor boy is unlucky; in important matters, when his mind doesn't wander, his nobility of character is clear enough.

And then in a third letter:

My dear Livia, I'm damned if I'm not filled with wonder that your grandson Tiberius is capable of making speeches that please me. For I can't see how someone who talks such nonsense in conversation speaks such sense in declamation.

There is, however, no doubt as to what Augustus subsequently decided, leaving Claudius with no experience of public office beyond being a member of the college of Augurs,* and not even instituting him as an heir except in the third degree,* and to a sixth part of his estate along with those who were virtually strangers, while the legacy he left was only eight hundred thousand sesterces.

[5] His uncle Tiberius responded to his request for public office by granting him the insignia of a consul but when Claudius pressed more strongly for the office itself all Tiberius did was to write him a note, saying that he had sent him forty gold pieces for the Saturnalia and Sigillaria.* Finally, at that point, giving up all hope of a magistracy, he hid himself away in retirement in Campania where he kept company with some very vulgar people and, already notorious for being slow, he acquired a further reputation for drinking and gambling. Despite this behaviour, however, he still continued to receive attention from individuals and respect from the public.

[6] The equestrian order twice chose him as their advocate to make a deputation on their behalf, once when they put in a request to the consuls that they be allowed to carry the body of Augustus to Rome on their shoulders, and again when they wished to send the consuls their congratulations on the fall of Sejanus.* Indeed, they would even rise up and take off their cloaks, to mark his arrival at the games. The senate, too, voted to appoint him as an additional member to the priests of Augustus,* who were generally selected by lot, and, when he later lost his house in a fire, to have it rebuilt at public expense, and also to grant him the right to state his opinion in the senate among those of consular rank.* This decree was rescinded,

when Tiberius insisted that Claudius was too infirm and promised that he would compensate his loss* through his own generosity. He, however, when he died, left Claudius as an heir only in the third degree, to a third part of his estate, although he also gave him a legacy of around two million sesterces and included his name in the list of family members commended to the armies and the senate and people of Rome.

[7] It was only under his brother's son Caligula, who early on in his reign attempted to secure popularity by every possible means, that he finally embarked on a public career, when Claudius held the consulship as his colleague for two months. And it happened that the first time he entered the Forum with the fasces, an eagle which was flying by landed on his right shoulder.* He secured by lot a second consulship, to be held four years later. On a number of occasions, when Caligula was away, he presided at the games and the people would cheer, some greeting him with 'Long live the emperor's uncle!', some with 'Long live the brother of Germanicus!'

[8] He remained nevertheless a butt for insults. If he arrived a little later than the appointed time for dinner, he only managed to find a place with difficulty after searching around the dining-room. And whenever he dropped off to sleep after eating, which happened quite frequently, he would be pelted with olive- and date-stones. Sometimes jokers would wake him with a whip or a cane, for their amusement. People would put slippers in his hands as he lay snoring, so that if he was suddenly woken up he would rub his face with them.

[9] Nor did he escape actual dangers. First of all, during his consulship he was almost removed from office on the grounds that he had been too slow in making arrangements to commission and set up statues to Nero and Drusus, the emperor's brothers.* Besides this, his position was also often endangered on various occasions when a stranger or even someone from his household made an allegation against him. Moreover, when the conspiracy of Lepidus and Gaetulicus was discovered* and Claudius was sent as part of the delegation to offer congratulations to Caligula in Germany, even his life was in danger, for Caligula was resentful and complained that his uncle had been purposely chosen to come to him as though to take charge of a boy. Indeed, his fury was such that there are some who record that Claudius was actually pushed into the river in the

robes he had arrived in. And from that time there was no occasion on which he was not the last of the consulars to give his opinion, for, in order to humiliate him, he was asked after everyone else. There was also a court case investigating the forgery of a will to which Claudius had been a witness. Finally, forced to spend eight million sesterces in order to become a member of the new priesthood,* he so undermined his family finances that he was unable to meet his obligation to the treasury and, by order of the prefects, his property was put on sale to make up the difference.*

[10] The greater part of his life had been passed in this way, when, in his fiftieth year, he became emperor in the most curious circumstances. Those conspiring against Caligula had shut him out along with everyone else, when they cleared people out of the way, pretending the emperor wanted privacy.* Claudius had retreated to a chamber, known as the Hermaeum. Shortly afterwards, terrified by rumours of the assassination, he crept to an adjacent balcony and concealed himself among the curtains which hung by the door. By chance, a common soldier who was wandering about, noticed his feet, as he hid there, and pulled him out, meaning to ask who he was. When he recognized Claudius, who had fallen to his knees in fear, he hailed him as emperor. The soldier led him from there to his comrades, who were by this time uncertain what to do and complaining. The soldiers put him in a litter and, since his own attendants had run off, took it in turns to carry him, in a state of misery and fear, on their shoulders to the praetorian camp; people they met on the way felt sorry for him, assuming he was an innocent man being rushed off for execution. He was received into the compound and passed the night under military guard, feeling relief rather than anticipation. For the consuls, along with the senate and the city cohorts, had taken control of the Forum and the Capitoline, with the intention of asserting civic liberty.* Claudius himself was summoned through the tribunes of the plebs to come to the senate meeting and advise what action he thought should be taken, but he replied that he was being held by force against his will. On the next day, however, when the senate was proving rather slow in executing its plans, since there was much disagreement between those advocating different courses, and the crowd of people standing around were by now demanding a single leader and calling for Claudius by name, he allowed the armed assembly of soldiers to swear allegiance to him and promised fifteen

thousand sesterces to each man. He was the first of the Caesars to have won the loyalty of the soldiers with bribery.

[11] Once his control was established he considered it most important to expunge all memory of the two days during which the restoration of the republic had been contemplated. He decreed therefore that everything which had been said and done during that time would be forgiven and forgotten in perpetuity. And this was what he actually did except in the case of a few of the tribunes and centurions who had conspired against Caligula. These he had executed both as an example and because he had discovered that they had demanded his own death also. From this he turned his attention to the observance of family duties, stipulating that his most sacred and frequent oath was to be 'By Augustus'. He had divine honours voted to his grandmother Livia, as well as a chariot drawn by elephants in the circus procession, like that for Augustus.* For his parents he arranged public funeral offerings and, besides these, for his father circus games to take place every year on the anniversary of his birth and for his mother a carriage to transport her image through the Circus, and also the title Augusta which she had refused when living. To commemorate his brother,* which he did at every opportunity, he staged a Greek comedy in the competition at Naples and awarded it the crown in accordance with the opinion of the judges.* He did not even leave Mark Antony forgotten and unacknowledged, swearing, in one of his edicts, that he was all the keener to ensure people celebrated the birthday of his father, Drusus, as the same day was also the birthday of his grandfather, Antony. He completed a marble arch dedicated to Tiberius next to Pompey's Theatre, which had once been voted by the senate but then forgotten. As for Caligula, though he rescinded all his acts, yet he would not allow the day of his murder to be celebrated as a festival, despite the fact that it marked the beginning of his own reign.

[12] In promoting himself, he was restrained and unassuming, refraining from taking the forename 'Imperator'* and refusing excessive honours. He held no public celebrations for the betrothal of his daughter or the birth of his grandson, which he marked only with family ceremonies. He recalled no one from exile without the authority of the senate. He requested the senate's permission, before bringing with him to the senate house the prefect of the praetorian guard and the military tribunes, and also sought their ratification of the

judicial acts of his agents in the provinces. He petitioned the consuls for the right to hold markets on his private estates. He frequently attended as one of the advisers at court cases heard by the magistrates. And when they gave games, he would rise up with the rest of the crowd to greet them, paying his respects with word and gesture. When the tribunes of the plebs came to see him, he apologized that, because of the lack of space, he could only hear them if they were standing. Because of this behaviour, in a short time he secured so much affection and support that when it was reported that he had been ambushed and killed as he was travelling towards Ostia, the people were greatly upset and, with horrible curses, insistently attacked the soldiers as traitors and the senators as parricides, only stopping when first one, then another, then numerous magistrates appeared on the rostra to confirm that the emperor was safe and on his way home.

[13] He did not, however, manage to avoid plots completely but was subject to attack by individuals, by factions, and, finally, in civil war. A man of the common people was apprehended in the middle of the night, just by his bed-chamber, armed with a dagger. Two men of the equestrian order were caught ready to ambush him in public places, one armed with a sword-stick to attack him as he came out of the theatre, the other with a hunting knife to set upon him as he was sacrificing in the Temple of Mars. Besides this, Asinius Gallus and Statilius Corvinus, the grandsons of the orators Pollio and Messala, plotted rebellion against him, winning over quite a number of his own freedmen and slaves. Furius Camillus Scribonianus, the governor of Dalmatia, began a civil war against him. However, within five days, Camillus was defeated by the legions who had sworn allegiance to him but then changed their minds, moved by religious feeling. For, as they responded to the order to join the new emperor, the eagles, through some divine intervention, could not be decorated* nor the standards pulled up and moved.

[14] He was consul on four further occasions, in addition to the earlier one. The first two he held in succession, the latter two, in each case after an interval of four years.* On the last occasion he held the office for six months, while the others were all for two months. The third time he held the office as suffect in place of a man who had died—a new departure for an emperor. He took immense trouble in administering justice both as consul and when out of office, even on

his personal festival days and those of his family, not infrequently, too, on long-established feast days and days of ill omen. He did not always follow what was set down in the laws but would often moderate their harshness or leniency, in accordance with his sense of equity and justice. He authorized a new trial in the case of some who had lost their suit, in a hearing before private judges, by demanding more than the law laid down, and he exceeded the penalty prescribed by law when he condemned to the wild beasts those who were found guilty of especially serious crimes.

[15] In hearing and deciding cases, he displayed astonishing inconsistency, however, being sometimes judicious and wise, sometimes ill-advised and hasty, and occasionally capricious and like a lunatic. When revising the lists of the divisions of jurors, he dismissed a man who had presented himself without revealing he was immune because of the number of his children,* on the grounds that he was eager to pass judgement. Another man, when challenged in relation to a suit he had brought himself by his opponents (who asserted this was not a matter for a hearing before the emperor but for a regular court), Claudius at once compelled to defend his case before him, claiming that the man would make clear when defending his own interests how fair he would be in judging the affairs of others. When a woman refused to acknowledge a man who claimed to be her son and it was unclear which of them had justice on their side, he forced her into a confession by demanding that she marry the young man. When one party to a dispute was absent, he would frequently rule in favour of those present, regardless of whether their opponent's absence was a matter of choice or of necessity. When someone declared that a forger ought to have his hands cut off, Claudius at once demanded that an executioner be summoned with his cleaver and chopping-block. In the case of a man whose citizenship was in dispute, a trivial argument arose among the lawyers as to whether he should offer his defence dressed in a toga or a Greek cloak; Claudius, as though to show his impartiality, made him change his clothes repeatedly, depending on whether the plaintiffs or the defence were speaking. In one case, he is even thought to have offered a written judgement as follows: that he decided in favour of whichever side was speaking the truth. For these reasons he lost respect to such a degree that he was held in universal and open contempt. One man, making excuses for a witness whom the

emperor had summoned from the provinces, claimed that the man could not appear but for a long time would not give the reason. Eventually, after repeated questioning, he declared: 'He's dead; I think that's a legitimate excuse.' Another, offering thanks that the emperor had allowed him to defend an accused man, added: 'Though that is the usual practice.' I myself used to hear older men claim that advocates would abuse his patience to such an extent that, when he was leaving the tribunal, they would not only call out for him to return but would even hold him back by grabbing the fringe of his toga or taking hold of his foot. And in case this should cause any surprise, I might add that a little Greek lawyer came out with the following comment in his own language in the midst of a heated exchange: 'You are an old man and a fool.' It is common knowledge that a Roman knight, who was accused, on a false charge trumped up by ambitious rivals, of improper conduct towards women, when he saw common prostitutes summoned as witnesses against him and their testimony admitted,* threw the writing implement and tablets he had in his hand at the emperor's face, causing a serious cut on his cheek, and at the same time reviled his stupidity and cruelty.

[16] He also held the office of censor, which had been in abeyance for a long time since the censorship of Plancus and Paulus,* but here too he was unpredictable and inconsistent both in his intentions and in his decisions. During the inspection of the knights,* he let off a young man of bad character without official stigma, because his father claimed he was very happy with him, on the grounds that he had a censor of his own. Another, who was notorious for corruption and adultery, he dismissed with nothing more than a warning: 'That he should give rein to his youth with greater restraint or at least with greater discretion.' He added, too: 'For why should I know what girlfriend you have?' In another case, in reponse to the entreaties of the man's friends, he removed the mark of ignominy which had been placed by his name but commented, 'Let the erasure be seen, however.' A most eminent man who was a leading figure in the province of Greece but lacked knowledge of the Latin language, he not only dismissed from the list of judges but deprived of his Roman citizenship. He obliged everyone to speak in their own defence as best they could, without the use of advocates. He imposed marks of disgrace on many, some quite unexpectedly for the novel offence of going out

of Italy without informing him and seeking his permission. To one man he gave a black mark, however, because, when he was in his province, he had been the companion of a king, and Claudius referred back to earlier times when a charge of treason was brought against Rabirius Postumus because he had followed Ptolemy to Alexandria to recover a loan.* As a result of the carelessness of his investigators, he attempted to impose marks on a number of people whom he then discovered to be innocent—much to his own shame. He accused some of not being married, not having children, or having insufficient resources, who then showed themselves to be married, or to be fathers, or to have ample means.* One man, who was accused of having stabbed himself, tore off his clothes to show that his body was unscathed. Notable acts of his censorship also included the following: he had a finely crafted silver chariot, which was on sale in the Sigillaria,* bought and then cut into pieces in his presence.* And in one single day, he issued twenty edicts, including one which prescribed that, since the harvest from the vineyards was ample, the wine-jars should be well sealed with pitch, and another which declared that the juice of the yew tree was the best remedy for a snake bite.

[17] He undertook just one military campaign and even that was a modest one. When the senate voted him the triumphal ornaments and he considered the honour insufficient to an emperor's dignity, wishing for the glory of a full triumph, he chose Britain on the grounds that it offered the greatest potential as a place to win it, for no one had made the attempt since Julius Caesar and the island was currently in a state of unrest because some deserters had not been returned. He set sail for that destination from Ostia but was twice almost lost at sea due to violent winds from the north-west, once off Liguria and once near the Stoechades islands. For this reason he travelled from Massilia as far as Gesoriacum by land.* Without a battle or a drop of blood being shed, part of the island surrendered within a very few days and, in the sixth month after setting out, he returned to Rome and held a triumph of the greatest splendour. To witness the spectacle, he permitted not only the provincial governors but even some people who had been exiled to stay in Rome. Among the enemy spoils was a naval crown which he had fixed to the gable of the imperial palace alongside the civic crown, to show that he had traversed and, as it were, conquered the Ocean. His wife, Messalina,

followed his chariot in a carriage. Also following him in the triumphal procession were those who had won triumphal ornaments in
the same war but, while the rest went on foot and wore purple-
bordered togas, Marcus Crassus Frugi rode a horse with special
trappings and wore a tunic embroidered with palms because he was
receiving the honour for a second time.

[18] He was always most scrupulous in undertaking responsibility
for the city of Rome and for the corn supply. When the Aemilian
area was afflicted with a rather stubborn fire, he stayed for two nights
in the Diribitorium,* and, when the assistance supplied by the soldiers and his own slaves was not enough, he had the magistrates call
on the common people from every area of the city and, with chests
full of money in front of him, he urged them to give help, paying
each person on the spot a suitable reward for their services. On one
occasion, after repeated poor harvests had led to a shortage of corn,
he was held up in the Forum by a mob who, hurling insults as well as
crusts of bread, attacked him so fiercely that he was scarcely able to
escape into the Palace. He then left no means untried of importing
supplies even in the winter season. For he offered traders guaranteed
profits by undertaking to cover any losses himself, if there should be
an accident as a result of bad weather, and to those constructing
merchant ships he offered large incentives, corresponding to each
person's status: citizens were to be given immunity from the
requirements of the Augustan marriage law;* those of Latin status
were to be given the privileges of citizenship; women were to
be given the privileges of those with four children.* [19] These
prescriptions are still in force today.

[20] He undertook many public works which were magnificent
rather than necessary. The principal ones were the completion of the
aqueduct begun by Caligula, as well as the canal from the Fucine
lake and the harbour at Ostia, although he was well aware that
Augustus had refused to undertake the canal, despite the repeated
requests of the Marsians, while the Deified Julius had several times
planned the harbour but abandoned it because of the difficulties
involved. By means of the stone-built Claudian aqueduct he brought
to the city the cold and plentiful waters of two springs, one known as
the Caeruleus, the other as the Curtius and Albudignus,* as well as
the waters of the new Anio, and divided their flow among a number
of highly ornamented basins. He tackled the Fucine lake, hoping for

profit as much as glory, since some people had undertaken to drain it at their own expense, if they could have the land which was thereby reclaimed. He only just managed to complete the canal in eleven years, with works partly to level and partly to tunnel through a mountain over a distance of three miles, though he had thirty thousand men working on the project continuously and without a break. At Ostia he had the harbour deepened, surrounding it with moles to the left and right and placing an artificial island in the deep water across from the entrance. In order to give this a more secure foundation, he first sank the ship in which the great obelisk had been transported from Egypt,* then, having built up piles, he crowned them with a tower of enormous height, on the model of the Pharos of Alexandria, so that at night time ships might be guided by its lights.

[21] He gave out presents to the people with some frequency and also provided a large number of splendid shows, not according to the accustomed pattern or in the usual places but some which were novel and some which were revived from ancient times and in places where no one before him had held shows. The games celebrating the dedication of Pompey's Theatre, which he had restored after a fire, he inaugurated from a raised seat placed in the orchestra, after first offering sacrifices in the temples at the top* and then coming down through the auditorium, while everyone sat in silence. He also held Secular Games,* claiming that Augustus had held them early, not waiting for the proper time, though he himself wrote in his 'Histories' that, when the games had been in abeyance for a long period, Augustus had revived them after a very exact calculation of the timing. Thus there was laughter when the herald's announcement, with the usual words, invited people to the games 'which no one had seen before and no one would see again', since a number of people were still living who had seen them before and indeed some actors made an appearance who had performed in the earlier games. He often gave circus games in the Vatican Circus, too, sometimes with animal hunts between every five races. The Circus Maximus, however, he adorned with marble starting-stalls and gilded goals,* replacing the earlier ones which were in both cases made of tufa and wood. He also constructed seating reserved for the senators, who had previously watched the games sitting amongst everyone else. Besides the chariot races, he also staged the Troy

game* and showed panthers, which were hunted down by a squad-
ron of mounted praetorian guardsmen, led by the tribunes and the
prefect himself. He gave a display of Thessalian horsemen, too, who
drive wild bulls around the Circus and, when they are tired out, leap
onto them and pull them to the ground by their horns.

He gave numerous gladiatorial shows in many different places. To
celebrate the anniversary of his accession, he gave shows in the praetorian camp, though without animal hunts or fine equipment, and
others in the Saepta following the regular and usual pattern. He also
gave other additional shows in the same place, lasting only a few
days, which he was the first to call 'little presents',* since, when he
was about to give them for the first time, he announced that he was
going to invite the people 'as though to a spur-of-the-moment supper party'. At these shows in particular he was friendly and relaxed,
even, when the gold pieces were presented to the visitors, bringing
out his left hand to count them off out loud on his fingers, as the
common people do.* He would frequently urge the crowd to enjoy
themselves with encouragements and exhortations, sometimes calling them 'masters', and adding an occasional sprinkling of feeble and
obscure jokes. For example, when people called out for the 'Dove',
he said he would hand him over, 'if he could be caught'. The following, however, was very good and appropriate to the occasion: when
with everyone's support he had granted the wooden sword* to an
essedarius whose four sons had pleaded on his behalf, he sent around
a placard straight away advising the people 'How they really ought to
have children, when they could see what a support and favour they
brought even to a gladiator'. In the Campus Martius he staged the
siege and destruction of a town, in the manner of an actual war, and
also the surrender of the kings of the Britons, while he presided
dressed in a general's cloak. Indeed, he even staged a sea-battle on
the Fucine lake, when he was about to drain it. However, when those
who were to fight called out: 'Hail emperor! Those who are about to
die salute you', he replied: 'Or not.'* After that pronouncement, none
of them was prepared to fight, arguing that he had thereby spared
them. Claudius debated for some time as to whether he should subject them all to fire and the sword before finally leaping out of his
seat and running all around the lake, despite the embarrassment of
his limp, and, offering a mixture of threats and encouragement,
compelling them to fight. In this spectacle a Sicilian fleet fought

against a Rhodian one, each made up of twelve triremes. The signal
was sounded on a horn by a silver Triton, which, thanks to a
mechanical device, rose up from the middle of the lake.

[22] As regards sacred rites and both civil and military pro-
cedures, and similarly as regards the standing of all the orders both
at home and abroad, he corrected various practices or reinstated
those which had fallen into disuse, or else instituted new arrangements. When co-opting priests into the colleges, he would nominate
no one without himself first taking an oath. Whenever there were
earth tremors in the city, he was scrupulous in observing the custom
that the praetor should call an assembly and proclaim a holiday;
similarly, that a supplication should be offered, whenever a bird of
ill-omen was seen on the Capitol. He himself would conduct the
supplication in his capacity as Pontifex Maximus, taking the lead in
pronouncing the formula to the people from the rostra, once all the
workmen and slaves had been sent away.

[23] The conduct of legal business, which had previously been
divided between a winter and a summer season, he ran together into
one session. In cases of trust, which it had been usual to assign on
an annual basis and only to magistrates in the city, he delegated
jurisdiction permanently and extended it to provincial governors.
He annulled a clause Tiberius Caesar had added to the Augustan
marriage laws, which implied that men of sixty were not capable of
fathering children. He sanctioned the exceptional allocation of
guardians to wards by the consuls. He also made it the law that those
who were banished from a province by a magistrate should also be
removed from Rome and Italy. He himself imposed a new kind of
punishment on some people, forbidding them to go more than three
miles outside the city. When he was about to conduct more serious
business in the senate house, he would take his place between the
seats of the consuls or else on the tribunes' bench. The business of
granting permission to travel,* which had previously been done by
the senate, he took over for himself.

[24] He favoured even middle-grade procurators with consular
insignia.* From those who turned down the offer of senatorial rank he
removed their equestrian rank as well. Although he had earlier
agreed that he would choose no one for the senate who was not the
great-grandson of a Roman citizen, he even made a grant of the right
to wear the broad stripe* even to the son of a freedman, though with

the condition that he first be adopted by a Roman knight. Fearing criticism for this, he declared that Appius Claudius the censor,* an ancestor of his family, had also selected the sons of freedmen for inclusion in the senate, for he was not aware that in Appius Claudius' day and for some time afterwards the term *libertini* was used not for those who had been freed from slavery but for the free-born children they produced.* He removed from the college of quaestors responsibility for the paving of roads, instead putting them in charge of a set of gladiatorial games. Taking away their duties at Ostia and in Gaul as well, he gave them back responsibility for the treasury of Saturn* which had for a while been under the charge of the praetors or, as now, ex-praetors.

He made a grant of triumphal ornaments to Silanus, who was engaged to his daughter, though he was still just a boy, and to so many older men, for such slight reasons, that a joint letter was circulated in the name of the legions, requesting that triumphal ornaments also be conferred on consular legates at the same time as they were given their armies, to prevent them from seeking any kind of pretext for war. He even decreed an ovation for Aulus Plautius and, as Aulus Plautius entered the city, he went to greet him and proceeded to walk on his left as he went to the Capitol, and then again as he came away from it.* Gabinius Secundus, who had conquered the Cauchi, a German tribe, he permitted to take the *cognomen* 'Cauchius'.

[25] He arranged the military service of Roman knights in such a way that they first had charge of a cohort, then of a division of cavalry, and then served as tribune of a legion. He also instituted various military positions and a kind of fictitious service, termed 'supernumerary', which could be fulfilled in name only by men who were absent. He even had passed a senatorial decree barring soldiers from entering the houses of senators to pay their respects. He confiscated the property of freedmen who passed themselves off as Roman knights. Those whose ingratitude caused their patrons to complain he forced back into slavery, insisting to those who acted as their advocates that he would refuse to hear cases against their own freedmen. As certain people were abandoning their sick and debilitated slaves on the island of Aesculapius, to avoid the expense of having them cured, he passed a law that all who were thus abandoned were to have their freedom and would not be subject to their

masters' power, if they recovered, and that if anyone decided to kill a slave rather than abandon him, they were to be liable for murder.* He also issued an edict banning travellers from passing through the towns of Italy unless they were on foot or in a chair or litter.* He stationed a cohort each at Puteoli and Ostia to guard against fires.

Persons of non-citizen status he forbade to use Roman names, at least the gentile ones.* Those who usurped Roman citizenship he had executed with an axe in the Esquiline field. The provinces of Achaea and Macedonia, which Tiberius had transferred to his own control, he returned to that of the senate. Because of the hideous disputes which had arisen amongst them he deprived the Lycians of their citizenship. To the Rhodians, because of their remorse for their earlier offences, he returned theirs. To the people of Ilium he granted perpetual exemption from tribute on the grounds that they were the founders of the Roman race,* having first read out a letter in Greek from the senate and people of Rome promising King Seleucus friendship and alliance but only on condition that he render their kindred, the people of Ilium, free of any taxation in perpetuity. The Jews he expelled from Rome, since they were constantly in rebellion, at the instigation of Chrestus.* The envoys of the Germans he allowed to sit in the orchestra, charmed by their simplicity and boldness, for when, having been directed to the ordinary seating, they discovered that the Parthians and the Armenians were sitting with the senators, they at once moved over to join them, declaring that their own virtue and status were in no way inferior.* He imposed a complete ban on the religion of the Druids among the Gauls which, under Augustus, had merely been forbidden to Roman citizens. In contrast to this, he made an attempt to have transferred from Attica to Rome the sacred mysteries of Eleusis and, when the temple of Venus Erycina in Sicily collapsed through decrepitude, it was rebuilt at the expense of the Roman treasury on Claudius' initiative. He forged treaties with kings in the Forum, sacrificing a sow and reciting the ancient formula of the fetial priests. However, both these and his other acts and indeed the greater part of his reign he conducted not so much according to his own judgement but rather according to that of his wives and freedmen. His behaviour for the most part was such as to suit their interests and pleasure.

[26] While still a youth he was betrothed on two occasions, once to Aemilia Lepida, great-granddaughter of Augustus, and the second

time to Livia Medullina who also had the *cognomen* Camilla and was
from the ancient family of the dictator Camillus. He broke off his
engagement to the former as her parents had offended Augustus.
The latter he lost to illness on the very day they were to have married. Later on he married Plautia Urgulanilla whose father had
received a triumph, and then Aelia Paetina whose father was an
ex-consul. He divorced both of them, Aelia Paetina for trivial
faults but Urgulanilla on the grounds of her scandalous love affairs
and the suspicion of murder. After these, he took as his wife Valeria
Messalina, the daughter of his cousin Messala Barbatus. However,
when he discovered that in addition to her other misdemeanours and
improper acts she had actually married Gaius Silius, with a contract
formally signed in front of witnesses, he had her put to death and
affirmed before an assembly in the praetorian camp that, since his
marriages had turned out so badly, he would remain unmarried and,
if he did not keep his word, he would not object to them killing him
with their own hands. Yet he could not resist entering at once into
negotiations for another marriage, and that, too, with Paetina, whom
he had earlier rejected, and also with Lollia Paulina who had once
been married to Caligula. However, his affections were secured
by the allurements of Agrippina, daughter of his own brother
Germanicus, who took advantage of a relative's right to give kisses
and opportunities for flattery. At the next senate meeting Claudius
put up some senators to propose that he should be made to take her
as his wife, on the grounds that it was very much in the interests of
the state, and also that marriages of this kind,* which were previously considered incestuous, should now be permitted. And scarcely
had a day passed before the marriage was concluded, though none
could be found to follow their example, with the exceptions of a
certain freedman and also of a chief centurion, whose weddings the
emperor himself attended, accompanied by Agrippina.

[27] He had children by three of his wives; Drusus and Claudia by
Urgulanilla, Antonia by Paetina, and, by Messalina, Octavia and the
boy first known as Germanicus and later as Britannicus. Drusus he
lost just as the boy was nearing adulthood, when he choked on a pear
which he had thrown up into the air in play and caught in his open
mouth. This happened a few days after he had been betrothed to the
daughter of Sejanus, so I am all the more surprised at those who
relate that he was murdered through Sejanus' scheming. Claudia,

although she was born less than five months after the divorce and
Claudius had initially accepted her, was exposed naked at her
mother's door on his orders and disowned, on the grounds that she
was the child of his freedman Boter. He married off Antonia to
Gnaeus Pompeius Magnus and, later, to Faustus Sulla, both young
men of the highest rank, while Octavia he married off to his stepson
Nero (she had earlier been engaged to Silanus). Britannicus was
born on the twenty-second day of his reign, when he was consul for
the second time.* While he was still very small, Claudius would
commend him to assemblies of soldiers, taking him in his arms, and
to the people at the games, holding him on his lap or in front of him,
and he would invoke good omens for him, with the approval of the
applauding crowd. As for his sons-in-law, Nero he adopted but
Pompeius and Silanus he did not; but rather he had them put to
death.

[28] Of his freedmen, he had particular respect for the eunuch
Posides. On the occasion of his British triumph, he even presented
him with the silver-tipped spear,* as he did men who had done military service. He had like regard for Felix, whom he put in charge of
cohorts and cavalry divisions as well as the province of Judaea, and
married him off to three queens. Similarly, he favoured Harpocras,
to whom he gave the right to travel through Rome in a litter and to
give public games. In addition to these, there was Polybius, minister
in charge of archives, who often walked between the two consuls,
but above all Narcissus, who was in charge of correspondence, and
Pallas, who was in charge of accounts. He willingly allowed those two
to be honoured by senatorial decree not only with huge gifts but also
with the insignia of quaestors and praetors—and indeed to
appropriate and embezzle so much that when, on one occasion, he
complained of the inadequacy of his funds, it was wittily observed
that he would have more than enough, if he were taken into
partnership by his two freedmen.

[29] At the mercy of these freedmen and his wives, as I said, he
acted not as an emperor but as a servant, dispensing magistracies,
military commands, immunities, and punishments, according to the
interests and indeed the passions and loves of one or other of them,
while he for the most part remained unaware and ignorant. To avoid
recounting minor matters individually, I note only that his gifts were
recalled, his judgements were rescinded, his official letters were sub-

stituted or blatantly altered. He put to death his father-in-law,
Appius Silanus,* Julia, the daughter of Drusus* and Julia daughter
of Germanicus, on unsupported charges and allowing them no
opportunity to defend themselves, as well as Gnaeus Pompeius, the
husband of his elder daughter, and Lucius Silanus, who was engaged
to his younger daughter. Of these, Pompeius was stabbed while making love to his young boyfriend, while Silanus was forced to give up
his praetorship four days before the Kalends of January* and then,
at the start of the new year, to kill himself on the day of the wedding
of Claudius and Agrippina. He imposed the death penalty on thirty-
five senators and more than three hundred knights in such an
unconcerned manner that when a centurion, announcing the death
of an ex-consul, reported that his orders had been carried out, he
replied that he had given no orders but that the deed was nevertheless well done, since his freedmen confirmed that the soldiers
were doing their duty in hurrying to avenge the emperor without
being asked. Credulity is, however, strained by the claim that, when
Messalina married her lover Silius, he himself signed the contract
for the dowry, having been led to believe that the arrangements were
a deliberate ruse, meant to avert and deflect the danger which was
foretold from certain portents as a threat to the emperor.

[30] His appearance was not lacking in authority and dignity when
he was standing, sitting, and particularly when he was lying down,
for his frame was tall and not thin, his face was handsome, as was his
white hair, and he had a full neck. However, when he started to walk
his rather feeble knees would fail him and he had numerous
undignified characteristics both when he was relaxing and when he
was engaged in business. His laughter was unbecoming, while his
anger was a worse source of embarrassment, for he would foam at
the mouth and his nose would run. Besides this, he had a speech
impediment and his head twitched all the time, but especially when
he made even the slightest movement. [31] Just as his health had once
been very poor, it was excellent when he was emperor, with the
exception of a stomach complaint. When he suffered from that, he
said, he had even contemplated ending his own life.

[32] He gave frequent and lavish dinner parties, generally in
spacious settings, so that there were often six hundred guests taking
their places at once. He even gave a dinner party just by the outlet of
the Fucine lake and was almost drowned when the water came out in

a great rush and overflowed. To every dinner he would also invite his own children, along with the sons and daughters of noble families, who would take their meals sitting in the old-fashioned manner at the ends of the couches. When a guest was suspected of having stolen a golden bowl one day, he invited him the next and had him served from an earthenware one. He is even said to have considered issuing an edict by which he would pardon those who broke wind discreetly or noisily at dinner, having learnt of a man who had endangered his health when he held back through embarrassment.

[33] He was very greedy for food and wine, no matter what the time or the place. Once, when he was hearing court cases in the Forum of Augustus, he was suddenly struck by the smell of the food which was being prepared for the Salian priests* in the adjacent temple of Mars, and left the tribunal, going up to join the priests with whom he lay down to dine. He hardly ever left the dinner table without being stuffed with food and overflowing with wine. He would at once lie down on his back, going to sleep with his mouth open, and a feather would be put into his throat in order that he could relieve his stomach. He never slept for very long at once and was usually awake before midnight but this caused him to nod off from time to time, not infrequently as he was giving judgement, so that he could scarcely be wakened, even when the advocates deliberately raised their voices. His passions for women were most ardent but he had no relations at all with males. He was quite devoted to playing dice, even publishing a book on the subject. He would even play while travelling, having his carriage fitted with a board so that the game would not be disrupted.

[34] That he was cruel and bloodthirsty by temperament was evident from major and very minor incidents. He would require and demand the immediate use of torture in interrogations and the punishment of parricides* to be carried out in his presence. When he was at Tibur and desired to witness an execution in the ancient manner* and, though the criminals were bound to the stake, there was no executioner available, he took great pains to have one summoned from Rome and persisted in waiting till nightfall for him to arrive. Whenever he was watching gladiatorial games, whether he himself or someone else was providing them, if any fighters fell to the ground even by accident he would give orders for them to be killed, particularly in the case of net-fighters, so that he could see their faces

as they died.* Once, when a pair of fighters struck one another and fell together, he gave orders that their two swords should without delay be made into small knives for his own use. He would take such pleasure in the beast-fights and in the midday entertainments that he would go down to the games at dawn and, at midday, would send away the people to take refreshment, while he carried on sitting there, and, in addition to those already committed to fight, he would condemn more men on trivial pretexts found on the spur of the moment, even from among the carpenters and attendants or others of that type, if a mechanism or piece of apparatus or something of that kind did not function correctly. He actually sent on one of his own ushers, just as he was, in his toga.*

[35] But above all he was cowardly and suspicious. In the earliest days of his reign, although, as I noted,* he boasted of his unassuming manners, he did not even dare to join a dinner party, unless guardsmen armed with lances were stationed around and soldiers took the place of servants. Nor would he visit anyone who was sick, unless their bedroom had first been searched, the pillows and covers checked over and thoroughly shaken out. For the rest of his reign, he would have those coming to offer him their respects inspected by officials who were very strict with everyone. He only relaxed this to a small degree and considerably later, to the extent that ladies and young boys and girls were no longer manhandled and boxes for writing equipment were not confiscated from people's attendants and scribes. When Camillus was in rebellion against him and, having no doubt that he could intimidate Claudius without going to war, sent him an offensive, bullying, and insulting letter in which he ordered him to surrender the empire and lead a life of leisure as a private citizen, Claudius summoned the leading men of the state and debated as to whether he ought to go along with this.

[36] He was so terrified by ill-founded reports of conspiracies, that he attempted to abdicate. And when a man with a sword was apprehended close by him as he was offering a sacrifice, as I noted above,* he hastily had his heralds summon the senate and, with tears and wailing, deplored his own situation, claiming that nowhere was safe for him, and for some time he kept away from public places. He put aside his own most ardent love for Messalina not so much through humiliation at the insulting way she had treated him as through fear of danger, since he was convinced she was seeking to acquire the

empire for Silius. It was then that he fled fearfully and shamefully to the praetorian camp, throughout the journey asking nothing but whether his position was safe.

[37] Indeed, even the most insignificant suspicion or the most untrustworthy informant would provoke some minor anxiety which would compel him to take precautions or to avenge himself. One man, who was party to a lawsuit, came to pay his respects and, addressing him privately, asserted he had had a dream in which Claudius was murdered by a certain person. Then, shortly afterwards, as though he recognized the murderer, he pointed to his opponent as the man was handing over his petition. This latter was at once hauled off to be executed, as though he had been caught in the act. It is said that Appius Silanus was disposed of in a similar way. When Messalina and Narcissus conspired to do away with him, they organized it so that Narcissus burst into Claudius' bedroom before dawn, pretending to be shocked and claiming that he had had a dream in which Claudius was violently attacked by Appius. Then Messalina, feigning surprise, recounted that she herself had had the very same dream a few nights previously. Shortly afterwards it was announced, as had been arranged, that Appius was forcing his way in (he had received orders the previous day to come at that time). As if this showed the truth of the dream, orders were at once issued that he should be accused and put to death. And the next day Claudius had no hesitation in recounting the affair to the senate and thanking his freedman for being alert to his safety even when asleep.

[38] He was aware of his own tendency to anger and irascibility and, in an edict, made excuses for both, drawing a distinction between them with the promise that his irascibility was brief and harmless, while his anger was not without justification. He gave a fierce reprimand to the people of Ostia on the grounds that they had not sent boats to meet him when he entered the Tiber, and with such vehemence that he claimed they had brought him down to the level of an ordinary citizen, but he forgave them, almost going so far as to apologize. When some people approached him in public at an ill-chosen moment he pushed them away with his own hand. He also banished unheard and innocent a quaestor's clerk and, similarly, a senator who had served as a praetor, the former on the grounds that he had been rather overbearing when he appeared in a court case against Claudius before he became emperor, the latter because he

had imposed fines on tenants on Claudius' estates when they were selling cooked foods in contravention of the law and had flogged a bailiff when he tried to intervene. For this reason Claudius even took jurisdiction over the cookhouses away from the aediles.*

He did not, indeed, keep silent on the subject of his own stupidity but asserted in several little speeches that he had deliberately pretended to be stupid when Caligula was in power, since otherwise he would not have survived and risen to his present station. However, he did not convince people, for shortly afterwards a book appeared, under the Greek title 'The Rise of Idiots', which argued that no one would make a pretence of stupidity.

[39] Amongst other things, people marvelled at his absentmindedness and lack of observation, or, to put it in Greek terms, his *meteoria* and *ablepsia*. When Messalina had been executed he asked, just after taking his couch in the dining room, why the lady of the house did not appear. In the case of many whom he had condemned to death, he would, on the following day, request them to appear both at his council and at his games of dice, and, as if they were late, he sent messengers taking them to task for sleeping late.* When he was planning to take Agrippina for his wife, in defiance of natural law, in every speech he made he would insistently refer to her as his daughter and pupil, born and brought up under his wing. And when he intended to endow Nero with his name, as if it were not bad enough (when his own son was already full grown) to adopt his stepson, he repeatedly announced that no one had ever been included in the family of the Claudii through adoption.

[40] Indeed, in his speech and in his actions he often showed such great insensitivity that he was thought neither to realize nor to care to whom or with whom or at what time or in what place he was speaking. When there was a debate about butchers and winemerchants he shouted out in the senate: 'I ask you, who can live without a nibble?'* and he gave an account of the wares of the old taverns where he himself had once been in the habit of buying wine. Regarding a man who was a candidate for the quaestorship, Claudius noted, as one of reasons why he was lending him his own support, that the man's father had once given him a drink of water at just the right time when he was ill. When a witness was brought before the senate, he observed: 'This person was my mother's freedwoman and hairdresser but she has always regarded me as her patron. I say this

because there are some even now in my own household who do not think me their patron.'* When some people from Ostia were addressing a petition to him in public, he exploded with rage on the tribunal itself and shouted out that he had no reason to do them a favour; if anyone was free, it was him. And the following comments were the kind he would make every day, indeed virtually every hour, even every minute: 'What, do you think I'm Telegenius?'* and: 'Your words don't touch me', and many similar comments which would be inappropriate even in a private citizen, let alone an emperor, especially one who was not inarticulate or uneducated but rather assiduously devoted to liberal studies.

[41] When he was a youth he began to write a history with the encouragement of Titus Livy,* and the direct assistance of Sulpicius Flavus. On the first occasion he gave a reading from this to a crowded hall, he scarcely managed to get through it and often interrupted himself. For at the start of the reading a number of chairs had broken under the weight of a fat man, provoking a burst of laughter, and, although the disruption had subsided, Claudius could not avoid recalling the incident every now and again and lapsing into laughter. During his reign, too, he wrote a good deal and frequently gave recitations via a reader. Though he first took up his history from the assassination of the dictator Caesar, he passed on to later times and began from the end of the civil war, since he felt that he could not enjoy the freedom to write openly and truthfully about the earlier period, for he was often criticized by his mother and his grandmother.* He left two volumes covering the earlier period and forty-one covering the later one. He also composed eight volumes on the subject of his own life—rather inappropriate but not lacking elegance—as well as quite a learned 'Defence of Cicero against the Writings of Asinius Gallus'. He even came up with three new letters of the alphabet* which he added to the existing ones, claiming that they were essential. He had already published a book giving the reasoning behind this when he was a private citizen and, as emperor, was easily able to bring about their common use. Examples of this lettering may still be seen in numerous books, in the daily record and in inscriptions on monuments.

[42] He devoted no less attention to Greek studies, on every occasion professing his love for the language and its excellence. When a barbarian made a speech in both Greek and Latin, Claudius

commented: 'Since you have come equipped with both our lan-
guagcs . . .'* And, when commending Achaea to the senate, he would
note that this province was dear to him because of the exchange of
shared culture. Often he would reply to Greek envoys to the senate
with a set speech.* Moreover, when he was on the tribunal he would
even come out with lines from Homer. Whenever he prescribed
punishment for an enemy or someone who had plotted against him,
he generally gave the tribune of the guard the following line, when
he was asked for the usual password:

> Ward off the man who first makes his attack.*

Besides this he actually wrote histories in Greek, twenty books on
Etruscan history and eight on Carthaginian. Because of these works,
a new museum was added in his name to the ancient museum at
Alexandria* and it was established that every year on set days his
works in their entirety were to be read out as if at a public recitation,
the Etruscan history in one museum, the Carthaginian in the other,
by various readers taking it in turns.

[43] Towards the end of his life, he gave some unambiguous indications that he regretted both his marriage to Agrippina and his
adoption of Nero; when his freedmen were noting with praise the
judgement he had given the previous day in condemning a woman
guilty of adultery, he declared that in his own case, too, the fates had
allotted wives who were unfaithful but not unpunished. Shortly
afterwards, encountering Britannicus, he embraced him and advised
him that, growing up, he would receive from his father an account of
all that he had done. And he added the following words, in Greek:
'The one who made the wound will heal it.'* When he decided to give
Britannicus the toga of manhood, for he was tall enough, though still
young and immature, he added: 'so that the Roman people may
finally have a true Caesar.'

[44] Not long after this he made his will, too, and had it sealed
with the seals of all the magistrates. At this point, before he could go
any further, he was cut short by Agrippina, who was motivated not
only by these actions but also by the accusations of her own
conscience—as well as those of informers—which reproached her
for many crimes. It is commonly agreed that Claudius was killed by
poison.* There is, however, disagreement as to where and by whom it
was administered. Some record that, when he was at a feast with

priests on the citadel,* it was given to him by his taster, the eunuch Halotus, others that it was given him at a family dinner by Agrippina herself, offering him the drug in a dish of mushrooms, a kind of food to which he was very partial. There are different versions even of the next part of the story. Many claim that immediately after consuming the poison he was rendered speechless and, wracked with pain throughout the night, died just before dawn. Some say that he first lost consciousness, then vomited up from his overflowing stomach all he had consumed but that he was given a second dose of poison. This may have been added to some porridge, with the pretence that he needed food to revive him in his weakened state, or else introduced in a syringe, adminstered on the grounds that his stomach was overloaded and might be relieved by that form of evacuation as well.

[45] His death was concealed until all arrangements were in place with regard to his successor. And so, as if he were still ill, vows were offered and, to reinforce the illusion, actors were brought in as if to provide the entertainment he was asking for. He died on the third day before the Ides of October, when Asinius Marcellus and Acilius Aviola were consuls, in his own sixty-fourth year and in the fourteenth year of his reign.* His funeral was celebrated with customary imperial ceremony and he was included among the ranks of the gods. This honour was neglected and then cancelled by Nero but was later restored by Vespasian.*

[46] The main omens foretelling his death were as follows. A star with a mane appeared, the kind people call a comet. The tomb of his father Drusus was hit by lightning and, in the same year, of all the holders of the different magistracies, a great many died. There are several indications that he himself seemed not unaware that the end of his life was approaching nor concerned to conceal it. For when he appointed the consuls, he made appointments only for the period up until the month he died, and, the last time he attended the senate, he warmly encouraged his children to be reconciled, then with feeling commended each of them, young as they were, to the care of the senators. On the occasion of his last appearance on the tribunal as judge, he pronounced, and repeated his pronouncement, despite the prayers of those who heard him, that he was approaching the end of his mortal life.

NERO

[1] Of the Domitian family, two branches achieved fame, the Calvini and the Ahenobarbi. The Ahenobarbi have as the founder of their branch and origin of their name Lucius Domitius. Two young men, twins of impressive bearing, are said to have appeared to him once, as he was returning from the countryside, and to have given him orders to announce to the senate and people victory in a battle whose outcome was at that time awaited.* And, as a sign of their divinity, they are said to have stroked his cheeks, turning his beard, which was black, a red colour like bronze.* This distinctive feature continued even among his descendants, many of whom had red beards. Between them, they achieved seven consulships, a triumph, two censorships, and promotion to the patricians, all the while continuing to use the same *cognomen*. And they took no other forenames than Gnaeus and Lucius. This usage they practised with remarkable variation, sometimes giving each name to three people in a row and sometimes one name alternating with the other. For we learn that the first three Ahenobarbi were all called Lucius, while the next three were all called Gnaeus, after which they alternated between Lucius and Gnaeus. I have decided to report on a number of members of the family to make clearer how Nero lapsed from the virtues of his ancestors yet reproduced each one's legacy of vice.

[2] To begin a little further back, his great-grandfather's grandfather, Gnaeus Domitius* was, as tribune, furious with the *pontifices*, because they had co-opted someone other than himself into the place his own father had occupied, and transferred the right of selecting priests from the colleges of priests to the Roman people. When he was consul and had defeated the Allobroges and the Arverni, he travelled through the province seated on an elephant and accompanied by a crowd of soldiers, as if in a triumphal procession.* The orator Licinius Crassus said against him that it was no wonder he had a beard of bronze when his face was made of iron and his heart of lead. The son of this Ahenobarbus, when he was praetor, called Julius Caesar to a senate inquiry at the end of his consulship, on the grounds that he had conducted himself in office contrary to the auspices and the laws.* Not long afterwards, when he himself was

consul, he dared to deprive Caesar of the command of the Gallic armies. Then, named as Caesar's successor thanks to the support of a faction, he was taken prisoner at Corfinium* at the start of the civil war. Released from there, he went to the support of the people of Massilia, who were besieged and struggling, but suddenly abandoned them for no apparent reason and finally met his end fighting at Pharsalus.* He was an indecisive man, though his temper was savage; having in desperation attempted suicide, he was so overcome by fear of dying that he regretted his decision, vomited up the poison he had taken, and rewarded the slave-doctor with his freedom on the grounds that, knowing his master well, he had been prudent enough to administer an insufficiently powerful dose.* When Gnaeus Pompey asked for advice on how to deal with persons who had remained neutral and taken neither side during the civil war, he was the only one who thought they should be treated as enemies.

[3] He left a son,* who, without doubt, was far superior to the rest of the family. He, though he was innocent, had been condemned under the Pedian law* as one of Caesar's assassins, and so joined cause with Brutus and Cassius, being closely related to them. After their deaths he kept the fleet which had been entrusted to him and increased it. Only when his side was utterly defeated everywhere did he hand the fleet over to Mark Antony—on his own initiative and as if he were conferring a great favour. And he alone, of all those who had been condemned by that same law, had his civil rights restored to him and fulfilled the highest offices. When, later, civil war broke out again and he was made a legate by that same Mark Antony, he was offered the supreme command by those of his side who were ashamed of the alliance with Cleopatra but, suffering from a sudden illness, dared neither to accept it nor to turn it down, instead going over to Augustus' side. A few days later he was dead, with his own reputation in doubt, for Antony asserted that he had changed sides through desire to be with his mistress, Servilia Nais.

[4] This Domitius was father of the man who was later well known for being named as executor in Augustus' will. He was no less famous in his youth for his skill in chariot driving than he was to be later for the triumphal ornaments he won in the war against Germany. However, he was an arrogant man, profligate and cruel, who, when he was merely an aedile, forced the censor Lucius Plancus to make way for him on the street. When serving as praetor

and as consul, he organised farces performed in the theatre by Roman knights and matrons. He provided animal shows in the Circus and in all parts of the city, as well as a gladiatorial show of such cruelty that Augustus, having offered him a discreet warning to no effect, was obliged to restrain him by edict.*

[5] He and the elder Antonia* were the parents of Nero's father, a man loathsome in every respect. As a young man, on a trip to the east accompanying Gaius Caesar,* he killed his own freedman, on the grounds that the man would not drink as much as he was ordered, and was himself dismissed from the entourage, yet made no attempt to regulate his lifestyle. Indeed, going through a village on the Appian Way he whipped up his team and knowingly ran over a boy, while at Rome in the middle of the Forum he gouged out the eye of a Roman knight who had been arguing with him too warmly. Moreover, his dishonesty was such that he not only cheated the banker intermediaries of the price of goods he had obtained but, when praetor, he even defrauded the chariot race winners of their prize money. When his own sister's jokes brought him into public disrepute for this and the team managers complained, he issued an edict* that prizes should subsequently be handed over on the spot. Shortly before Tiberius died, Domitius was accused of treason, adultery, and incest with his sister Lepida but escaped prosecution because of the change of regime. He died at Pyrgi of dropsy, after acknowledging his son Nero, whose mother was Agrippina, Germanicus' daughter.

[6] Nero was born at Antium, nine months after Tiberius died, on the eighteenth day before the Kalends of January,* just as the sun was rising, so that he was touched by its rays almost before he could be laid on the ground.* Many people made numerous and sinister predictions about his birth-signs. Among the warnings was even the pronouncement of his father, who responded to his friends' congratulations saying nothing could be born of himself and Agrippina that would not inspire loathing and bring disaster for the state. Another sign of his unhappy future occurred on the day of his purification.* For the emperor Caligula, when his sister asked him to give whatever name he chose to the child, looking upon his uncle Claudius—by whom, when he was emperor, Nero was later to be adopted—said that they should give the child *his* name.* However, he did not do this seriously but as a joke and Agrippina turned down the suggestion, for at that time Claudius was a figure of fun at court.

At three years old he lost his father. Heir to a mere third part of the estate, he did not even get that much, for his co-heir, Caligula seized everything.* When soon afterwards his mother was relegated he was left virtually penniless. His aunt Lepida brought him up, placing him in the care of two tutors, one a dancer, the other a barber. However, when Claudius succeeded to the empire, Nero not only got back his father's property but increased his wealth with an inheritance from his stepfather, Crispus Passienus. When his mother was recalled to Rome and re-established, his position was so improved by the favour and influence she exercised that, according to a popular rumour, Claudius' wife Messalina sent some men to strangle him during his siesta, on the grounds that he was a rival to her son, Britannicus. According to the same story, these men encountered a snake emerging from the couch and were so terrified they ran away. The story seems to have arisen because some snake-skins were found in his bed around the pillow. However, at his mother's request, these were set in a gold bracelet and for some time he wore them on his right arm until, tired of being reminded of his mother, he threw it away—though later on he asked in vain to have it back, when his affairs reached their final crisis.

[7] When he was still only a young boy he participated most enthusiastically and successfully in the Troy game at the Circus. In his eleventh year,* he was adopted by Claudius and handed over for his education to Annaeus Seneca, who was already a senator. People say that on the next night Seneca dreamed that he was teaching Caligula* and soon afterwards Nero provided confirmation of the dream, revealing his monstrous nature at the earliest possible opportunity. For when, after his adoption, his brother Britannicus, through habit, continued to address him as Ahenobarbus, he tried to convince his father* that Britannicus was not really his child but a substitute. When his aunt Lepida was on trial he publicly gave evidence against her in order to please his mother who was striving to undermine her position.

On the occasion of his first public appearance in the Forum, he promised gifts for the people and money for the soldiers and announced a parade of the praetorian guard, which he himself led, holding his shield before him. Then he spoke in the senate expressing his gratitude to his father. During his father's consulship, he gave speeches in Latin on behalf of the people of Bononia and in

Greek on behalf of the people of Rhodes and of Ilium. For his first
appearance as judge, he acted as prefect of the city during the Latin
festival,* when, although Claudius had forbidden it, many of the best
known advocates competed to present to him not the usual short and
conventional cases but a large number of highly important ones. Not
long after this he took Octavia* as his wife and gave circus games and
animal shows as offerings for the health of Claudius.

[8] When the death of Claudius was publicly announced, Nero,
who was then seventeen, approached the guards between the sixth
and the seventh hour, for in consequence of the terrible omens which
had occurred throughout the day, no earlier time had seemed suitable for embarking on his reign. In front of the steps to the Palatine,
he was saluted emperor then taken by litter to the praetorian camp,
where he addressed the soldiers briefly before returning to the senate
house, where he remained until evening. Of all the great honours
which were heaped upon him he refused just one—the title 'Father
of the Fatherland' which he deemed unsuitable for one of his age.*

[9] Beginning with a display of filial respect, he provided Claudius
with a most magnificent funeral at which he gave the official eulogy
and declared him to be a god. He paid the highest honours to the
memory of his father Domitius and allowed his mother the greatest
influence over all matters private and public. Even on the first day of
his reign, he gave as the password to the tribune of the watch 'the
best of mothers' and afterwards he often rode about the city with her
sharing a litter.* He made Antium a colony, enlisting veterans of
the praetorian guard and, besides them, the richest of the chief
centurions through residential transfer. He also had constructed
there a port on a most lavish scale.

[10] In order to provide a more certain measure of his disposition,
he declared that he would rule according to the prescriptions of
Augustus and he let slip no opportunity to demonstrate his generosity, his clemency, or his affability. More onerous taxes he reduced or
did away with. He cut to a quarter of their original rate the rewards
paid to informers under the Papian law.* He gave four hundred
sesterces to each man of the people and, in the case of senators of
noble family who had lost their ancestral fortunes, he provided
annual salaries of as much as five thousand sesterces.* He also distributed free grain every month to the praetorian cohorts. And
when, following usual procedure, he was asked to sign his consent to

the punishment of a man condemned to death, he replied, 'How I wish I had never learned to write!' He used to greet members of all the orders accurately and without prompting.* To votes of thanks, he replied, 'When I've deserved them.' He permitted even the common people to witness his exercises in the Campus Martius and often declaimed in public. He would recite his poems, not only in his home but also in the theatre, causing such widespread delight that a public thanksgiving* for his recitation was announced and passages from his composition which had been recited were inscribed in letters of gold and dedicated to Capitoline Jupiter.*

[11] He provided a great many games* of different kinds: Youth Games, circus games, theatrical performances and gladiatorial contests. In the Youth Games* he included old men of consular rank and respectable old women as participants. In the circus games, he assigned separate seating to Roman knights* and even ran chariots drawn by teams of camels. At the games which, since they were undertaken for the everlasting future of the empire, he wished to be termed 'The Greatest', a significant number of men and women from both the senatorial and the equestrian orders took on the parts of actors.* A very well-known Roman knight rode down a rope mounted on an elephant. When a play by Afranius* called 'The Fire' was put on, the actors were allowed to snatch the furnishings of the burning house and keep them for themselves.* Every day gifts of all kinds were thrown to the crowds: a thousand birds each day of every kind, different sorts of food, tokens to be exchanged for grain, clothes, gold, silver, jewels, pearls, pictures, slaves, working animals and even tame wild ones and finally ships, blocks of apartments, and farmland.

[12] He would watch these games from the top of the proscenium. At the gladiatorial games, which he gave in a wooden amphitheatre constructed in less than a year in the Campus Martius part of the city, he had no one put to death, not even criminals. However, he put on show as fighters four hundred senators and six hundred Roman knights, some of whom were wealthy men of good reputation.* Even those who fought the wild beasts and served as assistants in the arena were drawn from the senatorial and equestrian orders. He also gave a naval battle on sea water which had monsters swimming in it. He put on shows of young Greeks as Pyrrhic dancers* and after the games he gave each of them a diploma of Roman citizenship. In one

of these Pyrrhic dances, a bull mounted Pasiphae* concealed within a
wooden model of a heifer in such a way that many of the spectators
believed it was no mere show. In another, an Icarus on his first
attempt fell immediately to the ground* right next to the emperor's
couch, splashing him with blood. For he would rarely sit in state on
these occasions, preferring to recline, at first watching through a
small gap in the hangings but later with the whole of the balcony on
view. He was also the first to establish at Rome a five-yearly competition, in the Greek manner, made up of three events, musical, gymnastic, and equestrian, which he termed the Neronia. He also dedicated his baths and gymnasium,* distributing gifts of oil to each
senator and each knight. He put in charge of the whole competition
ex-consuls, chosen by lot, who occupied the seats of the praetors.*
Then he went down into the orchestra, where the senators sit, and
accepted the crown he was offered for oratory and verse in Latin.* All
the most distinguished men had competed for it but all agreed it was
rightly his. However, when the judges also offered him the crown for
lyre-playing, he paid it reverence and gave orders that it should be
taken as an offering to the statue of Augustus. At the gymnastic
contest, which was held in the Saepta, while a magnificent offering
of oxen was sacrificed, he placed the first shavings of his beard* in a
golden casket set with the most precious pearls which he dedicated
on the Capitol. To the athletic contests he even invited the Vestal
Virgins, on the grounds that the priestesses of Ceres were permitted
to be spectators at Olympia.*

[13] I am, I believe, justified in recording among Nero's spectacles
the entry of Tiridates into the city.* The king of Armenia had been
induced to come with great promises and, though Nero had dismissed the crowd because of bad weather on the day when his edict
had announced he would be showing Tiridates, he did bring him
forth at the earliest opportunity. Armed cohorts stood around the
temples in the Forum and he himself was seated in a curule chair on
the rostra, dressed in the robes of a triumphant general and surrounded by military standards and flags. When Tiridates approached
up the sloping platform, Nero first let him fall at his feet but then
raised him up with his right hand and kissed him. Next, while the
king made the speech of a suppliant (which was translated and
relayed to the crowd by a man of praetorian rank), Nero removed
from his head the turban and replaced it with a diadem. Then the

king was led from the Forum to the theatre where he again made
supplication and Nero placed him in a seat at his own right hand.
Acclaimed 'Imperator'* for this Nero offered laurels on the Capitol*
and closed the gates of the temple of two-headed Janus, to show
there were no longer any wars being waged.*

[14] He held the consulship on four occasions. The first time he
held it for two months, the second and fourth for six months, and the
third for four months. The second and third were held in successive
years, while a year's interval separated these from the first and
fourth.*

[15] When it came to dispensing justice, he was not keen to give
replies to those presenting cases unless in written form and on the
following day. His method of taking cognizance was to have each
party present each point in turn, instead of continuous pleadings.
And whenever he withdrew to take advice, he never debated anything openly among all present but would request separate written
opinions from each person which he then read silently and in private
before announcing whatever verdict he himself preferred as if it were
the one generally agreed. He refused for a long time to admit the
sons of freedmen into the senate* and denied offices to others who
had been admitted by previous emperors. Candidates for whom
there was not yet room in the senate were given charge of legions as
compensation for the postponement and delay. He generally
appointed people to the consulship for six months at a time. When
one of the consuls died just before the last day of December, he
appointed no one as substitute, citing with disapproval the old case
of Caninus Rebilis and his one-day consulship.* The triumphal
regalia* he conferred even on men with the rank of quaestor and, in a
few cases, on equestrians too, and not always in recognition of military achievement. When he sent speeches on certain matters to the
senate, he would often overlook the quaestors (who had responsibility for reading them) and have them delivered by a consul.

[16] He devised a new arrangement for buildings in the city and
prescribed that there should be arcades along the front of apartment
buildings and houses, whose flat roofs would provide a vantage point
for fighting fires.* And he had these constructed at his own expense.
His plan was to extend the city walls as far as Ostia and to have
excavated a canal to bring sea water from there to the old city.*

Under his rule, many practices were reproved and subject to controls and many new laws were passed.* A limit was imposed on expenditure. Public feasts were reduced to food handouts. With the exception of beans and vegetables, the sale of hot food in taverns was prohibited*—previously all kinds of delicacies had been available. Punishments were imposed on the Christians—adherents of a new and dangerous superstition. A ban was placed on the diversions of the charioteers, who for a long time had taken advantage of the freedom they enjoyed to wander about the city playing tricks on people and robbing them. At the same time, the pantomime actors and their associates were outlawed from the city.*

[17] To counter forgery, a new measure was introduced at that time stipulating that tablets must have holes bored through them and be bound three times before being signed. And it was to be ensured that, in the case of wills, two waxed leaves inscribed with nothing but the testator's name would be presented for signing by the witnesses, and that no one who was writing a will for some one else should include a legacy for himself. It was also provided that litigants should pay a set and fair fee for legal representation, but nothing for the benches which would be provided free by the treasury. And it was prescribed that cases involving the treasury were to be transferred to the Forum* and a different form of jury, while all appeals from the juries were to be taken to the senate.

[18] Nero was never moved by the slightest desire or hope to extend or add to the empire, and he even considered withdrawing the army from Britain but was dissuaded by the shame which he would have incurred in seeming to detract from the glory won by his own parent.* He merely made the kingdom of Pontus* a Roman province, when Polemon ceded control, and similarly, on Cottius' death, the latter's Alpine territory.*

[19] He undertook only two tours, to Alexandria and to Achaea. But on the very day he had set sail he suspended his Alexandrian trip, disturbed both by religious feeling and by a sense of danger. For when, at the end of a tour of the temples, he had sat down in the Temple of Vesta, first the flap of his toga got caught as he tried to rise and then a great darkness fell, so that he could make nothing out. In Achaea, he undertook to cut a canal through the Isthmus* and addressed the praetorian soldiers, encouraging them to begin the task. Then when the trumpet sounded the signal, he himself was the first to strike the earth with his mattock and to carry off a basketful

on his shoulders. He also undertook preparations for an expedition
to the Caspian Gates,* with a new legion of conscripts from Italy, all
six feet tall, whom he called the phalanx of Alexander the Great.*
These deeds, some of them meriting no reproach, others even
deserving some praise, I have gathered together to separate them
from the shameful deeds and crimes with which I shall henceforth be
concerned.

[20] Amongst the other attainments of his youth, he was also
very knowledgeable about music so that, as soon as he became
emperor, he summoned Terpnus, the leading lyre-player of the
time and as he sat, while the latter sang after dinner day after day
late into the night, he began himself to study and practise little by
little, omitting none of those exercises by which artists of that kind
preserve and strengthen their voices. Rather, he would lie on his
back, holding a lead tablet on his chest, and cleanse his system
with a syringe and with vomiting, and he would abstain from fruits
and other foods harmful to the voice. Finally, pleased by his progress, although his voice was thin and indistinct, he conceived a
desire to go on the stage, from time to time repeating to his companions the Greek proverb that hidden music has no admirers.*
Indeed, he made his first appearance in Naples and, though the
theatre was shaken by a sudden earthquake, he did not leave off
singing until he had come to the end of the song he had begun. In
the same city he sang often and over many days. And even when
he had taken a short break to rest his voice, he could not bear
being apart from his audience. After bathing he went to the
theatre, where he took his dinner in the middle of the orchestra,
with a great crowd present. Speaking in Greek, he promised that
once he'd had a drop to drink, he'd give them some hearty singing. The Alexandrians, who had come in large numbers to Naples
with a recent convoy, delighted him with their rhythmic applause
and he summoned more from Alexandria. And with no less
enthusiasm he selected some youths of the equestrian order and
more than five thousand of the strongest young men of the common people from all over, who were divided into groups and
taught different methods of applauding—they called them buzzers,
hollow tiles and flat tiles—which they were to employ vigorously
when he was singing. These men were remarkable for their sleek
hair-styles and most refined appearance—and for their left hands,

bare and without rings. Their leaders received four hundred thousand sesterces apiece.

[21] Since he set great store by singing even in Rome, he gave orders for a Neronian competition in advance of the regular date and, when everyone called out for his divine voice, he replied that, for those who wished to come, he would put on a good show in his gardens. However, when the entreaties of the crowd were supported by those even of a guard of soldiers,* who were then on duty, he willingly promised them he would put on a performance at once. Without delay he gave orders that his name should be included in the list of those who had entered as lyre-players and, along with the rest, he placed his lot in the urn. When his turn came, he made his entrance, accompanied by the prefects of the praetorian guard bearing his lyre, and following them, military tribunes, along with his close friends. When he had taken his position and the introduction was made, he announced, through the ex-consul Cluvius Rufus, that he was going to sing the role of Niobe.* He then held the stage until the tenth hour, before declaring that the award of the crown and the rest of the competition was to be deferred until the following year, so that there would be more frequent opportunities for singing. And when that seemed too long a delay, he did not hesitate to put on a show in the interim. He even debated whether to take the stage with professional actors in private performances when one of the praetors offered a million sesterces.* He also wore a mask and sang tragedies in the roles of heroes and gods and even of heroines and goddesses, having the masks made so that their features resembled his own or those of whatever woman he happened to be in love with. Among other parts, he sang those of Canace giving birth, Orestes the matricide, Oedipus blinded, and Hercules insane.* The story goes that, when he was playing the part of Hercules, a recent recruit who was standing guard by the exit, seeing the emperor laden and bound with chains—as the play required—rushed forward to rescue him.

[22] From his earliest youth he was passionate about horses and was always talking about the games in the circus, although he was told not to. On one occasion, when he and his fellow pupils were bemoaning the fate of the Greens' charioteer, who had been dragged around the arena, and his teacher reproved him, he pretended they had been talking about Hector.* In the early part of his reign, he used to play every day with ivory chariots on a gaming board and

would leave his country retreat to attend even the most insignificant
of circus races, first secretly and then quite openly so that everyone
knew he would be there on that day. He did not try to conceal his
wish that the number of prizes be increased. In consequence of the
greater number of races, the spectacle lasted late into the evening
and the faction leaders disdained to bring their adherents unless it
was for a whole day's racing. Soon he himself wanted to drive a
chariot and even to do so frequently in front of an audience; once he
had made his beginning in his own gardens watched by slaves and
poor common people, he offered himself as a spectacle to the entire
populace in the Circus Maximus, with some freedman giving the
starting signal usually provided by magistrates. Not satisfied with
giving displays of such talents in Rome, as I have reported,* his
principal motive for going to Greece was the following. Those city
states whose custom it was to organize musical competitions decided
to award all the prizes for lyre-playing to him. He received these
with such pleasure that the messengers who brought them were not
only given precedence but were even made welcome at his private
supper parties. When some of them requested that he sing after
dinner, he accepted with alacrity and declared that only Greeks knew
how to listen and that only they were worthy of him and his talents.
He did not delay his departure and, as soon as he had crossed to
Cassiope,* he at once embarked on his singing at the altar of Jupiter
Cassius and then went off on his tour of all the competitions.

[23] For he had given orders that competitions normally held at
quite different times should be made to take place in the space of one
year, causing some to be repeated, and he instructed, against
all precedent, that a musical competition was to be added to the
Olympic games.* And, so that nothing should distract or detain him
while he was engaged in these games, though he was warned by his
freedman Helius that affairs in Rome required his presence, he wrote
in reply: 'Although you now advise and wish my swift return, you
ought rather to counsel and desire that I return worthy of Nero.'

When he was singing, it was not permitted to leave the theatre
even for the most pressing of reasons. Thus, it is alleged that women
gave birth during his shows and many who were tired of listening
and applauding, when the entrance gates were all closed, either
jumped furtively off the wall or else pretended to be dead and were
carried out for burial. You could scarcely believe how nervous and

anxious he was in competitions, or how he competed against his rivals, or how he feared the judges' verdict. He would pay attention to his competitors and seek their favour, as if they were his equals, then cast aspersions on them behind their backs. Some he would insult to their faces. He would even bribe those who were especially talented. Nevertheless, he would address the judges most reverently before he began, assuring them that he had done all that he could but the outcome would be determined by Fate.* They, as wise and learned men, were to ignore what was fortuitous. And when they encouraged him to take heart, he would withdraw somewhat calmer but not altogether without concern, interpreting the silence and restraint of some as moroseness and ill-nature and saying he could not trust them.

[24] During his competition performance, he followed the rules most strictly, never daring to cough and wiping sweat from his brow with his arm.* And once when he was performing a tragedy and he dropped his sceptre and picked it up again, he was fearful and anxious that he might be disqualified for this fault and could only be reassured by the accompanist's assurance that no one had noticed it amid the rapturous cheers of the audience. However, it was he himself who proclaimed his own victory. For he was also an entrant in the competition for public heralds. And so that no memory or trace should remain anywhere of any other victor in the sacred games, he gave orders that all their statues and images should be overturned and dragged by a hook to the lavatories where they would be disposed of.* He also entered the chariot races on many occasions, even driving a ten-horse team at Olympia, although in one of his songs he had criticized this very thing in King Mithridates.* However, he fell from his chariot and although he resumed his post he was unable to finish, abandoning the race before the end. He received the victory crown, none the less. Then, on his departure, he bestowed freedom* on the entire province, at the same time giving the judges Roman citizenship and substantial sums of money. He himself announced these benefits, standing in the middle of the stadium on the day of the Isthmian games.

[25] He returned from Greece to Naples and, because this was where he had made his first public appearance on stage,* he entered drawn by white horses where the wall had been breached—this is the custom for victors in the sacred games. In a similar manner he made

his entries into Antium, then Albanum, and then Rome. In Rome, however, he made use of the very chariot in which Augustus had once conducted his triumphs; wearing a purple robe, picked out with stars of gold, a Greek cloak, and, on his head, the Olympic crown, his right hand holding the Pythian, he was preceded by a procession displaying his other crowns, labelled to indicate whom he had defeated and with which songs or dramas. Following his chariot came the applauders shouting rhythmic praise and proclaiming that they were the Augustiani and the soldiers of his triumph. Then, through the Circus Maximus, where an arch had been pulled down, he made his way via the Velabrum and the Forum to the Palatine and the Temple of Apollo.* Everywhere he went, sacrificial victims were slain, perfume was sprinkled in all the streets, and countless gifts of songbirds, victor's ribbons, and sweetmeats were made to him. He placed the sacred crowns in his bed-chambers around the couches and did the same with statues of himself in the costume of a lyre-player. He also had coins minted with the same device. And after this, far from restraining or putting aside his passion, he was so keen to preserve his singing voice that he refused ever to address the Roman army, unless by letter or with someone else speaking his words.* Nor would he undertake any business, serious or frivolous, unless a voice-coach was standing by to give advice, relax his wind-pipe, and apply a towel to his mouth. And many were those who became his friends or enemies, according to whether they had praised him lavishly or sparingly.

[26] At first the signs he showed of insolence, lust, luxury, greed, and cruelty were gradual and covert and could be put down to the errors of youth, but even then it was clear to all that these vices were due not to his age but to his nature.* As soon as night had fallen, he would throw on a freedman's cap or a wig* and would go around the cook-shops and wander about the streets looking for amusement— though putting himself at some risk, for he was in the habit of setting upon people returning home from dinner and would hurt anyone who fought back, throwing them into the drains, and he would even storm into the taverns and pillage them, setting up a market in his palace, where the spoils he had acquired were divided up for auction and he squandered the proceeds. And often in the course of these brawls, he would endanger his eyes or even his life. Indeed, he was almost killed by a man of the senatorial class whose wife he had

molested. After that he would never venture forth at that hour without a secret escort of tribunes following at a distance. From time to time also he would have his sedan chair covertly transported to the theatre where, from the upper part of the proscenium, he would look on and incite the pantomime actors as they quarrelled. And when they came to blows and were fighting with stones and bits of the seating, he himself threw many missiles into the crowd and even cracked open a praetor's head. [27] Gradually, however, as his vices took root, he left off jokes and disguises and, taking no care to conceal his actions, moved on to greater misdeeds.

He would draw out his banquets from noon to midnight,* refreshing himself with warm baths or, in the heat of summer, with ice-cold ones. Sometimes he would even dine in public, having drained the Naumachia or in the Campus Martius or in the Circus Maximus, while around him the prostitutes and singing girls of all the city were plying their trade. Whenever he sailed down the Tiber to Ostia or cruised around the Bay of Baiae, on the banks and shores taverns were set out and made ready along the way, remarkable for their feasting and their traffic in respectable ladies, who would imitate tavern women and would solicit him from this side and that to summon them.* He would also invite himself as a dinner-guest to the houses of his friends, one of whom spent four million sesterces on a dinner where people wore turbans, while another spent even more on one accompanied by roses.

[28] Besides his seduction of free-born boys and his relations with married women, he also forced himself on the Vestal Virgin Rubria. He came very close to making the freedwoman Acte his lawful wife, having bribed some men of consular rank to swear falsely that she was descended from kings. He had the testicles cut off a boy named Sporus and attempted to transform him into a woman, marrying him with dowry and bridal veil and all due ceremony, then, accompanied by a great crowd, taking him to his house, where he treated him as his wife. Someone made a rather clever joke which is still told that it would have been a good thing for humanity if Nero's father had taken such a wife. This Sporus, decked out in the ornaments of an empress and carried in a litter, he took with him around the meeting places and markets of Greece and later, at Rome, around the Sigillaria, kissing him from time to time. And all were convinced that he had desired to sleep with his mother but was frightened off by her

detractors, who were concerned lest this ferocious and power-hungry woman acquire greater influence through this kind of favour. This was all the more plausible when afterwards he added to his concubines a prostitute who was famous for her resemblance to Agrippina. People claim that at one time, whenever he travelled in a litter with his mother, his incestuous lusts were betrayed by the stains on his clothing.*

[29] He prostituted his own body to such a degree that, when virtually every part of his person had been employed in filthy lusts, he devised a new and unprecedented practice as a kind of game, in which, disguised in the pelt of a wild animal, he would rush out of a den and attack the private parts of men and women who had been tied to stakes, and, when he had wearied of playing the beast, he would be 'run through' by his freedman Doryphorus.* With this man he played the role of bride, as Sporus had done with him, and he even imitated the shouts and cries of virgins being raped. From quite a few sources I have gathered that he was fully convinced that no one was truly chaste or pure in any part of their body but that many chose to conceal their vices and hid them cleverly. And so when any confessed to him their sexual misdeeds, he forgave them all other faults.

[30] He believed that the proper use for riches and wealth was extravagance and that people who kept an account of their expenses were vulgar and miserly, while those who squandered and frittered away their money were refined and truly splendid. He praised and admired his uncle Caligula, above all because, in so brief a period, he had worked his way through the vast fortune left him by Tiberius.* Accordingly there was no limit to his gift-giving or consumption. On Tiridates—which might seem scarcely credible—he lavished eight hundred thousand sesterces in one day and, when he left, made him a gift of a hundred million.* On the lyre-player Menecrates and the gladiator Spiculus he bestowed fortunes and homes fit for triumphant generals.* For the monkey-faced Paneros, a money-lender with extensive property holdings in Rome and in the country, he provided a funeral almost fit for a king. He never wore the same robe twice. When gambling he would lay bets of four hundred thousand sesterces for each point. He went fishing with a net of gold interwoven with purple and scarlet threads. It is said that he always travelled with at least a thousand carriages, the mules shod with

silver and mule-drivers clothed in Canusian wool, and with a train of
Mauretanian horsemen and couriers, decked out with bracelets and
breast-plates.

[31] There was, however, nothing in which he was more prodigal
than in construction, extending from the Palatine as far as the
Esquiline the palace which he called first the House of Passage,* then,
after it had been destroyed by fire and rebuilt, the Golden House. It
should suffice to relate the following concerning its extent and
splendour. There was a vestibule area in which stood a colossal
statue, one hundred and twenty feet tall, in the image of the emperor
himself.* So great was its extent that its triple colonnade was a mile in
length. There was also a lake, which resembled the sea, surrounded
by buildings made to look like cities. Besides this, there were
grounds of all kinds, with fields and vineyards, pasture and woodland, and a multitude of all sorts of domestic and wild animals.*
Other areas were all covered in gold and picked out with jewels and
mother-of-pearl. The banqueting halls had coffered ceilings fitted
with panels of ivory which would revolve, scattering flowers, and
pipes which would spray perfume on those beneath. The principal
banqueting chamber had a dome which revolved continuously both
day and night, like the world itself. There were baths running with
sea water and spa water. When the house was brought to completion
in this style and he dedicated it, he said nothing more to indicate his
approval than to declare that he had at last begun to live like a human
being.*

In addition to this, he began work on a pool stretching from
Misenum to Lake Avernus, which was roofed over and surrounded
with an arcade, and into this he meant to channel all the hot springs
of every part of Baiae; also a canal from Avernus all the way to Ostia,
so that one could travel by ship without traversing the sea.* It was to
be one hundred and sixty miles in length and broad enough to
accommodate ships with five banks of oars passing one another. In
order to complete these works, he gave orders that prisoners everywhere should be transported to Italy and that even those who were
found guilty of heinous crimes should have no other punishment
than hard labour.

He was spurred on to this frenzy of extravagance, not only by his
confidence in the empire's riches, but also by the expectation of vast
hidden wealth to which he was suddenly prompted by information

from a Roman knight, who asserted as a fact that a wealth of ancient treasure, which Queen Dido had brought with her when she fled from Tyre, was concealed in huge caverns in Africa and could be extracted with only the smallest trouble.* [32] However, when this hope was dashed he was penniless and so wretched and desperate that it was necessary to defer and put off payment even of the soldiers' pay and veterans' pensions, so he put his mind to profiting from false accusations and robbery.

First of all he made it law that, instead of one-half, five-sixths of the property of a deceased ex-slave should pass to him, if the person had, without good reason, borne the name of any family to whom he himself was related. He also prescribed that the property of persons who had, in their wills, failed to recognize their obligations to the emperor, should pass to the treasury and that the lawyers who wrote or dictated such wills should not escape punishment either.* Moreover, he ensured that any word or deed which fell within the scope of the treason law, so long as an informer was not lacking, should be punished.* He demanded back the gifts he had made in recognition of the crowns he was awarded in competitions by different cities.* Having banned the use of amethystine and Tyrian purple, he sent a man to sell a small quantity on market day, then closed down all the stalls.* It is said that once, during one of his performances at the games, he noticed a woman wearing a forbidden colour and pointed her out to his agents, who dragged her out and stripped her on the spot not only of her robe but also of her property. He never gave someone a task without saying: 'You know what I need' or 'The object of the exercise is to leave no one with anything.' Finally, he looted many temples of their ornaments and melted down statues made of gold or silver, amongst them the Roman Penates, which were later restored by Galba.

[33] The murder of family members and general slaughter began with Claudius. For even if he was not responsible for his death he was certainly complicit and did not pretend otherwise, inasmuch as he was afterwards in the habit of praising the kind of mushrooms with which Claudius had ingested the poison as, in the words of a Greek proverb, the food of the gods.* Certainly, after his death he attacked him with every kind of insulting word and deed, harping sometimes on his stupidity, at others on his cruelty. And he would often joke that Claudius had ceased to 'be a fool' [*morari*] among

mortals, lengthening the first syllable,* and many of his decrees and pronouncements he disregarded on the grounds that they were the decisions of a raving idiot. Finally, he failed to provide anything but a low and insubstantial wall as the enclosure for the place where Claudius had been cremated.*

Against Britannicus he employed poison, no less because of the competition he posed in singing (he had a much pleasanter voice), than through fear that one day he would prevail in public favour through memory of his father. He obtained the poison from a certain Lucusta, who was an expert poisoner, and, when it took longer than he expected and Britannicus had merely vomited, he summoned her and beat her with his own hand, claiming that she had given him medicine rather than poison. When she replied that she had used only a small quantity in order to prevent the crime becoming known and making him unpopular, he exclaimed, 'Of course, *I'm* afraid of the Julian law!'* and at once forced her into a chamber to concoct a dose in his presence that would have the most rapid and immediate effect. He then tried it on a young goat, whose death throes lasted five hours. And then, having concentrated it further, on a pig. When this animal died instantly, he gave orders that the substance be brought to the dining-room and given to Britannicus as he dined with him. When Britannicus collapsed at the first mouthful, he pretended to his other dining companions that he was suffering from one of his usual epileptic fits. The next day, amid heavy rainstorms, Britannicus was taken out to be disposed of in a summary funeral. Nero rewarded Lucusta for the services she had rendered with immunity from prosecution and an ample estate. He even sent her pupils.

[34] His mother so irritated him by applying sharp scrutiny to his words and deeds and correcting him, that, to begin with, he tried to make her unpopular by threatening to give up the empire and retire to Rhodes because of her.* Later he stripped her of all honours and powers, depriving her of her guard of Roman and German soldiers and making her move out of the Palatine. Thereafter he let slip no opportunity for harassing her, secretly arranging that people annoy her with lawsuits when she was at Rome, and disturb her when she was resting on her country estates, making her the butt of jokes and abuse, as they travelled past by land and sea. Then, terrified by her violence and threats, he made the decision to do away with her. And

when he had three times made attempts on her life with poison and realized that she had protected herself in advance with antidotes, he prepared to adapt the ceiling of her bedroom, which by a special device would collapse and fall on her at night while she slept. When this plan became known, through the indiscretion of those involved, he devised a collapsible boat, which would suffer either shipwreck or the caving-in of its cabin. Then, in a pretence of reconciliation, he invited her in a letter of great warmth to come to Baiae to celebrate the festival of Minerva* in his company. He gave his captains the task, on her arrival, of wrecking the boat on which she had come, as if by accident. The banquet was then drawn out until late in the night and, when she wanted to set out for Bauli,* he offered her, in place of her disabled craft, the specially devised boat, cheerfully escorting her and even kissing her breasts in farewell. The rest of that night he lay awake with great anxiety, awaiting the fulfilment of his plans. But news came that matters had turned out otherwise—she had swum to safety. Not knowing what to do, he secretly dropped a dagger next to Lucius Agermus, Agrippina's freedman, who had joyfully reported her safe and sound, and gave orders that he be arrested and bound, on the grounds that he had been engaged to attack the emperor, while his mother was to be killed to make it look as if she had taken her own life when her criminal plot was discovered. Worse is reported by quite good authorities who claim that the emperor rushed to view his mother's corpse and handled her body, criticizing some parts of it and praising others, in the mean time drinking to quench a sudden thirst. Yet, although he was reassured by the congratulations of the soldiers, the senate, and the people, neither in the immediate aftermath nor ever after could he bear his feelings of guilt, often confessing that he was haunted by his mother's ghost and by the blows and blazing torches of the Furies. Indeed, he even had rituals performed by mystics in an attempt to call up and appease her shade. When he made his journey to Greece, he did not dare to participate in the Eleusinian mysteries, where a herald pronounces that criminals and the impious are banned.

To matricide he added the murder of his aunt: when he was visiting her, as she had taken to her bed with a stomach complaint, and she, stroking the downy cheek of her nearly grown-up nephew, as was her habit, said to him affectionately, 'When I have your first beard, I can die happy,'* he turned to his companions and said, apparently in jest, he would shave it off at once. He then gave instructions to the doctors to give the sick woman an excessive dose of laxatives and, before she was even dead, took over her property, suppressing her will so that everything would come to him.

[35] Besides Octavia he later married two other wives, Poppaea Sabina, a quaestor's daughter who had previously been married to a Roman knight, and then Statilia Messalina, great-great-granddaughter of Taurus, who had been consul twice and celebrated a triumph. In order to get possession of her, he put to death her husband Atticus Vestinus actually during his consulship. He quickly tired of Octavia's companionship and, when his friends criticized his behaviour, he replied that she should be content with the insignia of wife.* Soon, having tried in vain to strangle her on a number of occasions, he divorced her on the grounds that she could not have children, but when the common people did not hesitate to express their disapproval of the divorce in public complaints, he sent her into exile. Then he had her killed on a charge of adultery which was so patently false that everyone denied it during the trial and Nero had to set up his old tutor Anicetus as the witness who was to make up a story and confess that he had raped her through trickery. He had a great passion for Poppaea,* whom he married on the twelfth day after his divorce from Octavia. Yet he killed her, too, by kicking her when she was pregnant and ill, because she had scolded him when he came home late from the chariot-races. He had a daughter by her, Claudia Augusta, but she died in infancy.

His treatment of every one his relatives was characterized by criminal abuse. When, after Poppaea's death, he wanted to marry Claudius' daughter Antonia, and she refused him, he had her executed for involvement in a plot, and a similar fate afflicted everyone who was related to him by blood or marriage. Among them was the young Aulus Plautius* whom, before he was put to death, Nero had subjected to oral rape, with the comment: 'Now let my mother go and kiss my successor'—for he alleged that she loved the man and encouraged him to hope for the empire. His stepson Rufrius Crispinus, Poppaea's child, Nero had drowned on a fishing trip at sea by his own slaves, though he was just a boy, on the grounds that he was said to play at being general and emperor. He sent into exile Tuscus, the son of his nurse, because, when he was procurator of Egypt, he had washed himself in the baths built for Nero's visit. He forced his adviser Seneca to kill himself, even though, when Seneca requested that he be allowed to retire and give up his properties, he had sworn that Seneca's suspicions were unfounded and that he would sooner die than harm him. To his prefect Burrus* he sent poison in place of the medicine for his mouth which he had promised. As for the imperial freedmen,* now elderly and rich, who had supported and aided his adoption and his coming to power, he dispatched them with poisoned food in some cases and drink in others.

[36] He was no less cruel outside his household, and made attacks on many who were not his relatives. A comet—which is commonly supposed to portend the death of great rulers—had started appearing on successive nights.* He was worried by this and when he learned from the astrologer Balbillus that it was the custom among kings to expiate such omens by means of the death of someone important and thus displace the danger from themselves to their nobles, he was bent on death for all the most illustrious—all the more so when two conspiracies were discovered which might serve as an excuse. Of these the first and more important was the Pisonian conspiracy at Rome,* while the second, that of Vinicius, was hatched and discovered at Beneventum.* The conspirators made their defence, bound in triple sets of chains; some confessed of their own accord, quite a few boasting that death was the only remedy for one so corrupted by every kind of crime as Nero. The children of the condemned were expelled from the city and died through poison or starvation. It is recorded that some were killed at a single meal, along with their tutors and attendants, while others were prevented from securing daily sustenance.

[37] After this he showed neither discrimination nor restraint in putting to death whoever he wished and for whatever reason. To give just a few examples: the fault of Salvidienus Orfitus* was that he had let out three apartments in his house near the Forum to serve as offices to some cities; that of Cassius Longinus, the blind jurist, that he kept the image of Gaius Cassius, the assassin of Caesar, in his old family tree;* and that of Thrasea Paetus, that he had the miserable expression of a teacher.* To men condemned to die he never allowed more than an hour's respite. And lest there be any delay, he provided doctors who were to 'take care' at once of any laggards. For that was how he described killing them by opening their veins. It is believed

that he even conceived a desire to throw men still living to be torn up and devoured by a fiend from Egypt who would consume raw meat and whatever was given him. Excited and thrilled by these enormities, which he regarded as achievements, he declared that not one of his predecessors had known what he might do. And he often gave clear indications that he would not spare the remaining senators but would dispose of the entire order, sending out Roman knights and freedmen to govern the provinces and command the armies. Certainly, when he arrived in the city or set out on a journey, he would never kiss any of the senate nor even return their greetings. And when he inaugurated the Isthmus project, in the presence of a great crowd, he clearly expressed his wishes that it might turn out well for himself and the Roman people, without mentioning the senate.

[38] Yet he spared neither the people nor the fabric of his ancestral city.* When someone in general conversation quoted the Greek phrase 'When I am dead, let earth go up in flames', he responded, 'Rather, "while I live"', and acted accordingly. For, as if he were upset by the ugliness of the old buildings and the narrow and twisting streets, he set fire to the city,* so openly indeed that some ex-consuls, when they came upon his servants equipped with kindling and torches on their property, did not stop them. He greatly desired some land near the Golden House, then occupied by granaries, and had them torn down and burnt using military machinery because their walls were made of stone. For six days and seven nights destruction raged and the people were forced to take shelter in monuments and tombs. During that time, besides the enormous number of apartment blocks, the houses of great generals of old, together with the spoils of battle which still adorned them, the temples of the gods, too, which had been vowed and dedicated by Rome's kings and later in the Punic and Gallic wars, and every other interesting or memorable survival from the olden days went up in flames. Nero watched the fire from the tower of Maecenas,* delighted with what he termed 'the beauty of the flames' and, dressed in his stage attire, he sang of 'the Fall of Troy'. And lest he should lose any opportunity of securing spoils and booty even from this, he undertook to have the corpses and ruins cleared at his own expense, allowing no one to come near the remains of their own property.* Not merely receiving contributions but extorting them, he bled dry both the provinces and the fortunes of private individuals.

[39] Besides the terrible evils caused by the emperor, there were others which struck by chance: one autumn there was a plague which added thirty thousand victims to Libitina's portion;* in Britain, a great disaster struck when two of the foremost towns suffered a massacre of citizens and allies* and, in the East, humiliation when an army was sent to secure Armenia and had difficulty holding on to the province of Syria.* Amid these trials it was striking and remarkable that Nero bore nothing with greater patience than people's insults and mockery and indeed he was especially tolerant of those who had attacked him with quips or pasquinades.* Many of these, such as the following, in both Greek and Latin, were posted up or circulated by word of mouth:

> Nero, Orestes, Alcmeon, killed their mothers.*
>
> A new equation. Nero murdered his own mother.*
>
> Who disagrees that Nero is of the great line of Aeneas?
>   One carried off his mother, the other his father.*
>
> Since our leader strings his lyre, the Parthian his bow,
>   Ours will be musical Apollo, theirs the great archer.*
>
> Rome is becoming one house; run off to Veii, citizens!
>   Unless that house takes over Veii, too.*

But he made no attempt to seek out the authors and when some were denounced to the senate by informers he instructed that they were not to suffer harsh penalties. Once, when Nero was passing by, Isidorus the Cynic reproved him quite clearly and publicly, saying that 'he sang well of the ills of Nauplius, but used his own goods ill'.* And the Atellan actor Datus, when he sang the song 'Goodbye father, goodbye mother!' mimed the actions of drinking and swimming, thus seeming to refer to the deaths of Claudius and Agrippina. When he came to the final line:

> Orcus guides your steps.*

he gestured to indicate the senate. The actor and the philosopher Nero merely banished from Rome and Italy, either because he was beyond all insults or to avoid provoking further witticisms by revealing his displeasure.*

[40] Having endured a ruler of this sort for a little less than fourteen years, the world at last shook him off. The process was begun when the Gauls revolted under Julius Vindex who at that time

governed the province as propraetor.* Astrologers had predicted for
Nero that one day he would be rejected. Hence that famous saying of
his, 'My art keeps us going', a comment apparently intended to
secure greater tolerance for his study of the art of lyre-playing, as
being a diversion for him when emperor but a necessity for him
when a private citizen. However, some of them promised him power
in the East after his repudiation, several specifying the kingdom of
Jerusalem, and a number the restitution of all his earlier powers.
Inclined to this hope, when both Britain and Armenia had been lost
and then won back, he imagined he had had all his share of ill-
fortune. Indeed, when he received an answer from Apollo's Delphic
oracle (in response to his inquiries) that he should beware the
seventy-third year, believing that he himself would die at that age, he
made no connection with the age of Galba* and anticipated with great
confidence not only living to an old age but even perpetual and
exceptional good fortune, so that when he lost many precious possessions in a shipwreck he did not hesitate to assure his friends that the
fish would bring them back to him. He learned of the Gallic revolt at
Naples on the anniversary of his mother's murder, but took the news
so calmly and confidently that he gave the impression of being
pleased on the grounds that he would have an opportunity, in
accordance with the laws of war, to despoil these most wealthy provinces. He went at once to the gymnasium where with the greatest
enthusiasm he watched athletes in competition. And when he was
interrupted by a more disturbing message while at dinner, he was
angered but no more than so as to threaten vengeance on the rebels.
For the next eight days he made no attempt to send a reply to anyone
or to give any message or instructions and passed over the affair in
silence.

[41] Finally, disturbed by the frequent and abusive pronouncements of Vindex, he sent a letter to the senate urging them to take
vengeance for himself and the state, and claiming that a throat ail-
ment prevented him from being present in person. But nothing
annoyed him more than that Vindex criticized his poor lyre-playing*
and called him Ahenobarbus instead of Nero. He declared that he
meant to put aside his adoptive name and resume the one he was
born with and which had been used as a reproach against him. As for
the other charges, the only argument he used to demonstrate their
lack of foundation was that he was being accused of ignorance of

the art which he had brought to such a peak of perfection and refinement—and he would repeatedly ask people one by one if they knew of anyone to whom he was inferior. But, as more and more urgent messages arrived, he returned to Rome in great fear—though on the journey his spirits were restored by a trivial and foolish occurrence: he observed a monument inscribed with the image of a Gallic soldier, defeated by a Roman knight and being dragged by his hair, and at this sight he jumped for joy and gave thanks to heaven. Without even then summoning any public gathering of the people or the senate, he called a few of the leading men to his palace and held a brief conference before wasting the rest of the day on some water-organs, of a new and unprecedented kind, which he showed off one by one, discussing the workings and difficulty of each, and promising that he would produce them all in the theatre—with Vindex's permission.

[42] After this, when he learnt that Galba and the Spanish provinces had also revolted,* he was badly affected and collapsed and for a long time lay half dead, unable to speak. When he came to his senses, he tore his clothes and beat his head, proclaiming that it was all over for him. In response to his nurse who reminded him by way of consolation that other rulers had experienced the same, he replied that his sufferings were unheard of, unprecedented, and worse than all others, for he was losing power while still alive. Yet nevertheless he did not give up or curtail any of his usual luxuries or indulgences but rather, whenever he had some good news from the provinces, he would hold a most lavish dinner and sing obscene songs, mocking the leaders of the rebellion, which he would accompany with gestures (these became publicly known). He would make secret visits to the theatre during the games and, when an actor's performance was a popular success, he sent a message saying the man was taking advantage of the emperor's distraction.

[43] It is thought that in the early days of the revolt he had formed many cruel plans—though nothing inconsistent with his own nature—to send agents to depose and dispatch those who were commanding the armies and provinces on the ground that they were united in a conspiracy; to slaughter all exiles everywhere and all Gauls in Rome, the former in case they should join the rebels and the latter as supporters and co-conspirators of their countrymen; to let the armies lay waste the provinces of Gaul; to murder

the entire senate at poisoned banquets; to set fire to Rome, having let wild animals loose on the people so that they could not properly defend themselves. Then, overcome with fear and not so much regret as despair of ever bringing matters to a close, he came to believe that a military expedition was required and, ousting the consuls before the end of their term, he himself entered upon a sole consulship in their place, on the grounds that fate prescribed that Gaul could be defeated only by consuls. He took up the fasces and, as he left his dining-room after a banquet, leaning on the shoulders of his friends, asserted that, as soon as he had reached his new province, he would appear to the armies without weapons and simply show them his tears, then the next day, when the rebels had been brought to recant, he would, a happy man amongst happy men, sing a victory ode—which he really ought to be composing at that moment.

[44] In preparing for the expedition, his first concern was selecting vehicles for carrying his stage machinery and having the prostitutes, whom he meant to bring with him, shorn in a mannish fashion and equipped with the axes and shields of Amazons.* Then he urged the city voting tribes to join up and, when no one suitable responded, he obliged masters to provide a certain number of slaves, demanding the very best from each household and not even excepting accountants or secretaries.* He gave orders that men of every census rating were to hand over a proportion of their wealth and, in addition to this, that tenants of private houses and apartments should present a year's rent to the emperor's fund.* He was most strict and exacting in his demands for newly minted coins, refined silver, and pure gold, so that many openly refused the entire levy and joined together in calling for him to take back first whatever rewards he had given to the informers.

[45] Resentment increased when he sought to take advantage of the corn-supply system. For it became widely known that at a time of general food shortage, the ship from Alexandria had brought a cargo of sand for the court wrestlers. Thus the hatred of all was aroused against him and there was no insult of which he was not the object. A lock of hair was placed on the head of his statue, with a Greek inscription: 'Now finally there is real competition and you must give in at last.'* A sack was tied to the neck of another together with the tag 'I did what I could but you deserve the sack.'* People

wrote on columns that he had even roused the Gauls* with his singing. And at night quite a few would pretend to fight with their slaves
and call repeatedly for a Defender.*

[46] His fears were also increased by the clear portents which he
had received earlier and more recently from dreams, auspices, and
omens.* Though he had never before been in the habit of dreaming,
after the murder of his mother he dreamt that he was steering a ship
through quiet waters when the helm was snatched from him, that he
was being dragged by his wife Octavia into the blackest darkness
and covered with a swarm of winged ants, and then that he was
surrounded and prevented from moving by the statues of nations
which had been dedicated at Pompey's Theatre, and that an Asturian
horse, in which he took particular pleasure, had its body trans-
formed, taking on the shape of a monkey, while its head, the only
part which was unchanged, gave forth musical whinnies. The doors
of the Mausoleum* opened of their own accord and a voice was
heard, calling him by name. On New Year's Day, when the household gods had been decorated they collapsed in the middle of
preparations for the sacrifice. As he was taking the auspices, Sporus
offered him the gift of a ring, whose stone bore an image of the rape
of Proserpina.* When a large crowd of all the orders had assembled
for the ceremony of making vows,* the keys to the Capitol were only
found after much searching. And when a speech, in which he
attacked Vindex, asserting that the criminals would pay the penalty
and that they would soon meet the end they deserved, was being
read to the senate, everyone shouted out, 'It will be you, Emperor!' It
had even been noticed that the piece he had most recently performed
in public was 'Oedipus in Exile'* of which the final line was:

Wife, mother, father, goad me to my death.

[47] When news came, while he was having lunch, that the other
armies had also rebelled, he tore up the letters brought to him,
overturned the table, and hurled to the ground two of his favourite
goblets which he called his Homerics, as they were decorated with
scenes from Homer's poems. Then, having acquired some poison
from Lucusta* and hidden it in a golden box, he went over to the
Servilian gardens where he attempted to persuade the tribunes and
centurions of the praetorian guard to join him in escaping with the
fleet, which his most trusted freedmen had been sent to Ostia to

make ready. But when some were evasive and others openly refused, one even shouting out 'Is it really so hard to die?',* he debated various possibilities, whether he should present himself as a suppliant to the Parthians or Galba, or whether he should appear in public on the rostra dressed in black and beseech forgiveness for his past offences, appealing as much as he could to their pity, or, if he could not win them over, whether he should not beg them at least to give him the prefecture of Egypt. Later on, a speech addressing these matters was found in his desk. It is believed he was too frightened to carry out his plan, in case he was torn apart before he could reach the Forum.

Having then put off these deliberations till the following day, he woke up in the middle of the night and, realizing that the guard of soldiers had withdrawn, he leapt out of bed and sent for his friends. When he heard nothing back from any of them, he himself went with a handful of attendants to their sleeping-quarters. The doors were all closed and no one answered. Returning to his bedroom he found that the caretakers, too, had run away, having even dragged off the bedclothes and removed the box of poison. At once he called for Spiculus the gladiator or some other executioner, at whose hands he might obtain death, but could find no one. 'Am I a man without friends or enemies?' he cried, and rushed out as if to throw himself in the Tiber.

[48] Then when he had checked this impulse and conceived a wish for some secret hiding-place where he might collect his spirits, his freedman Phaon suggested his own villa, located between the Salarian Way and the Nomentan Way* about four miles outside the city. Nero, just as he was, unshod and wearing just a tunic, wrapped himself in a dark-coloured cloak, covered his head, and held a handkerchief to his face, then mounted his horse with only four attendants, one of whom was Sporus. All at once an earth tremor and a flash of lightning in his face filled him with terror and he heard the shouts of soldiers from a camp nearby prophesying doom for himself and success for Galba—and even one of those they met on the road was heard saying, 'These men are after Nero', while another kept asking, 'Is there any news from Rome about Nero?' But when his horse shied at the stench of a dead body someone had thrown onto the road, Nero's face was uncovered and he was recognized and saluted by a man who had served in the praetorians. When they came to the byway they let the horses loose and he made his way with great

difficulty, even when a robe was laid out for him to walk on, through the thickets and brambles along an overgrown path, eventually reaching the back wall of the villa. There the same Phaon urged him to hide for a while in a hole where sand had been dug out, but he replied he would not descend into the earth still living. As he waited for a short time while preparations were made for him to enter the villa unobserved, he scooped up a handful of water to drink from a pool nearby and said, 'This is Nero's essence.'* Then, though his cloak had been torn by thorns, he picked the twigs out of it and crawled on all fours through a narrow passage they had dug until he was inside the villa. There in the little room he came to first he lay down on a couch with an ordinary mattress and an old cloak thrown over it. Despite pangs of hunger and renewed thirst, he refused the coarse bread which was offered to him but did drink a small amount of tepid water.

[49] Then, as every one of his attendants urged him to place himself beyond the reach* of the abuses which were imminent, he gave orders that a trench be made at once, of a size which would accommodate his own body, and that at the same time fragments of marble should be collected, if any could be found, and water and firewood should be brought for the disposal of the corpse-to-be, weeping as each instruction was fulfilled and repeating 'What an artist dies with me!' During the delay caused by these preparations, a runner brought a message to Phaon which Nero grabbed, learning from it that he had been judged a public enemy by the senate and was the object of a search, so that he might be punished according to ancestral custom. He asked what manner of punishment this might be and when he discovered it meant that a man was stripped naked, his neck being placed in a fork, then his body beaten until he died, he was overcome with terror and snatched up two daggers which he had brought with him, but, having tried the blade of each one, he put them away again, on the grounds that the fatal hour had not yet arrived. And he would at one moment beseech Sporus to commence weeping and lamenting, and at another beg that someone should help him to die by setting an example. At the same time he berated his own procrastination with these words: 'My life is shameful—unbecoming to Nero, unbecoming—in such circumstances, one must be decisive—come, rouse yourself!' At that moment some horsemen drew near, under orders to bring him back living. Aware of

this, he hesitantly said: 'The thunder of swift-footed horses echoes around my ears,'* then drove the dagger into his throat with the help of his secretary Epaphroditus. Half-conscious, when the centurion burst in and, holding a cloak to his wound, pretended he had come to give assistance, Nero said only 'Too late' and 'This is loyalty'. And with these words he died, his eyes staring widely to the horror and dread of those looking on. The first and most insistent request he had made of his companions was that no one should be able to get possession of his head but that he should in some way be completely consumed by fire. This was allowed by Icelus, a freedman of Galba, who had just recently been released from the chains with which he had been bound at the start of the revolt.

[50] His funeral cost two hundred thousand sesterces and his body was dressed in the white robes, embroidered with gold, which he had worn for the Kalends of January. His nurses, Egloge and Alexandria, together with his mistress, Acte, buried his remains in the ancestral monument of the Domitii, which is located on top of the Hill of Gardens* and can be seen from the Campus Martius. The monument is made up of a sarcophagus of porphyry, on which is an altar of Luna marble, and with an enclosure of Thasian stone.

[51] He was of a good height but his body was blotchy and ill-smelling. His hair was fairish, his face handsome rather than attractive, his eyes bluish-grey and dull, his neck thick, his stomach protruding, his legs very thin, his general health good—for despite his luxurious and most excessive way of life, he was only ill three times in fourteen years, and even then not so as to have to abstain from drinking or his other habits. He was so very shameless in his concern for dress and the care of his person that he would always have his curls arranged in a pile on his head and, on his trip to Greece, even had them flowing down behind. He was often to be seen in public dressed in a dinner robe, with a handkerchief around his neck, his tunic unbelted* and his feet bare.

[52] In his youth he applied himself to almost all the liberal arts. However, his mother dissuaded him from taking up philosophy, warning that it was incompatible with imperial power.* His teacher, Seneca, kept him from getting to know the orators of old, hoping thus to prolong his admiration for himself.* Hence his inclination towards poetry, which he himself composed so freely and easily that many are of the opinion he passed off someone else's work as his

own.* I have had access to some notebooks and papers on which were written some of his best-known works in his own hand. These clearly show that his composition was not transcribed or taken from another's dictation but worked out with thought and creativity. For there are many crossings out and insertions and additions in the work.* He also had a keen interest in painting and sculpture.

[53] Above all, however, he was moved by a passion for popularity and was envious of anyone who in any way inspired the enthusiasm of the common people. It was widely believed that after his victories in the theatre, he would, at the next set of games, compete with the athletes at Olympia, for he was a keen wrestler and had looked on at the athletic contests all over Greece in the same way as the judges, sitting down at the level of the stadium, and if any pairs of wrestlers withdrew too far he would push them forward himself with his own hands. Since he was praised as equal to Apollo in song and the Sun in chariot-racing, it was inevitable that he would also emulate the achievements of Hercules. They say that a lion was trained for him to kill naked in the arena, with the people watching, either by means of a club or with the force of his arms. [54] Near the end of his life, indeed, he publicly made a vow that, if his regime survived, he would perform at the victory games on the water-organ, the flute, and the bagpipes and that on the last day he would appear as an actor and dance the story of Virgil's Turnus. Some people say that he had the actor Paris put to death because he was a dangerous rival.

[55] He had a desire to secure eternal and perpetual fame but his method was ill-advised. For he abolished the old names of many things and places and gave them new ones based on his own, so that he termed the month of April 'Neroneus'* and he had a plan to give Rome the name of Neropolis.

[56] He had great contempt for all cults with the single exception of that of the Syrian goddess* and even her he soon so despised that he polluted her with urine, when he became an enthusiast for another superstition—to which alone he remained most faithful. For he had received as a gift from some unknown commoner a small image of a girl which was said to be a protection against plots and, since a plot was immediately uncovered, he persisted in worshipping this image as the greatest of divinities with three sacrifices a day and he wanted it to be believed that it could give signs imparting knowledge of the future. A few months before he died he was

present at an examination of entrails but could not succeed in obtaining a favourable reading.

[57] He met his end in his thirty-second year on the anniversary of Octavia's death, thereby provoking such great public joy that the common people ran throughout the city dressed in liberty caps.* Yet there were also some who for a long time would decorate his tomb with spring and summer flowers, and would sometimes display on the rostra statues of him dressed in a toga or post his edicts as if he were still alive and would soon return to avenge himself on his enemies. Indeed, even Vologaesus, king of the Parthians, when he sent ambassadors to the senate to renew his alliance, also made an earnest appeal that the memory of Nero should be honoured. Moreover, twenty years later, when I was a young man, there was an individual of unknown origins who boasted that he was Nero, and the name was so popular with the Parthians that they gave him vigorous support and could scarcely be made to surrender him.*

GALBA

[1] With Nero, the descendants of the Caesars died out.* While the signs foretelling this were many, two in particular were quite unmistakable. Once, when, right after her marriage to Augustus, Livia was on a visit to her villa at Veii, an eagle flew by and snatched a white hen, which was clutching a sprig of laurel in its beak, and at once dropped the bird into her lap.* She decided to rear the hen and to plant the sprig. The hen produced such a quantity of chicks that today the villa is known as 'The Henhouse', while the laurel grew to such a size that, whenever the Caesars were about to celebrate a triumph, they would gather their laurels from it. It was also their practice when they held a triumph to plant other laurel branches in the same spot and it was noted that when each one's death was near the tree he had planted would droop. Now, in the final year of Nero's reign, the entire grove withered away completely, while every single chicken there died. Moreover, when immediately afterwards the temple of the Caesars* was struck by lightning, the heads fell off all the statues at once, while the sceptre was shaken from the hands of the statue of Augustus.

[2] Galba, who succeeded Nero,* was in no way related to the house of the Caesars, though he was, without doubt, of very eminent birth and his own line was a great and ancient one, for he would always have it included in the inscriptions on his statues that he was the great-grandson of Quintus Catulus Capitolinus,* and when he was emperor he even had in his entrance hall his family tree put on display, in which he traced back his father's origins to Jupiter and those of his mother to Pasiphae* the wife of Minos. [3] To describe the ancestral portraits* and accompanying inscriptions of the entire house would take too long, so I shall confine myself to sketching his immediate family. It is not clear why the first of the Sulpicii to have the name Galba* acquired it, nor by what means. Some people think that, having for a long time besieged a town in Spain without success, he eventually set fire to it with torches smeared with *galbanum*.* Others think it was because during a lengthy illness he made repeated use of *galbeum*, that is, remedies wrapped in wool. There are some who believe that it was because he looked very fat,

which the Gauls term *galba*, while others take the opposite view that it was because he was very thin, so that he resembled the insect which lives in oak trees and is called the *galba*.

Servius Galba, who attained the consulship, brought distinction to the family. He was the most eloquent of his contemporaries. The story goes that, when he was governing Spain as propraetor, he brought about the war of Viriathus, after thirty thousand Lusitanians were treacherously slaughtered.* His grandson took against Julius Caesar (whose legate he had been in Gaul) when he failed to gain the consulship, and joined the conspiracy of Cassius and Brutus. For this he was condemned under the Pedian law.* His son was the grandfather and his grandson the father of the emperor Galba. The emperor's grandfather was more distinguished as a scholar than as a magistrate, since he did not rise beyond the rank of praetor but produced an extensive and carefully written history. His father attained the consulship* and, though his person was slight—he was a hunchback, too—and his abilities as a speaker were only moderate, he argued cases frequently and conscientiously. He was married to Mummia Achaica, the granddaughter of Catulus and great-granddaughter of Lucius Mummius, who sacked Corinth; and later to Livia Ocellina, a woman of outstanding wealth and beauty but who, nevertheless, is thought to have taken the initiative in pursuing him because of his noble family—and the more zealously, too, after (in response to her advances) he privately bared his deformity to her, so that it would not be thought she had been deceived. With Achaica he had two sons, Gaius and Servius, of whom the elder, Gaius, having dissipated his resources, left Rome and, when Tiberius would not permit him to take part in the allocation of provinces for proconsuls in his year,* took his own life.

[4] Servius Galba, who became emperor, was born on the ninth day before the Kalends of January in the consulship of Marcus Valerius Messala and Gnaeus Lentulus,* in a villa on a hill near Terracina, on the left as you travel toward Fundi. He was adopted by his stepmother Livia and took on her name and the additional *cognomen* of Ocella, at the same time changing his forename.* From early on right up to the time he was emperor he was known as Lucius rather than Servius. It is common knowledge that, when he was still a boy and, along with his contemporaries, was paying his respects to Augustus, the emperor pinched his cheek and said: 'You, too, child,

will have a taste of our imperial power.' Tiberius, however, learning that Galba would become emperor but only as an old man, commented: 'Let him live, since it will make no difference to me.' And, when Galba's grandfather was conducting an expiatory sacrifice after a bolt of lightning and an eagle snatched the entrails out of his hands, carrying them to an oak tree covered with acorns, the prediction was made that the family would attain the highest power—but only late. He, smiling, replied: 'Yes, when a mule gives birth.' Nothing gave so much encouragement to Galba later, when he was trying to seize power, as the fact that a mule gave birth, which everyone else perceived as a dreadful omen but which he was greatly cheered by, remembering his grandfather's comment on the occasion of that sacrifice.

When he took on the toga of manhood, he had a dream that Fortune spoke, saying she was standing exhausted before his door and if he did not quickly welcome her, she would be picked up by whoever came along. On waking and opening the front door, he found beside the threshold the bronze image of a goddess, larger than a cubit in size. This he carried away in his arms to his villa at Tusculum, where he used to spend the summer. Here he consecrated it in a particular corner of the house and honoured it with supplications every month and a nightlong vigil once a year.*

Although he was not yet of mature years, he insisted unswervingly on the old national custom, which had fallen out of use and was observed nowhere other than in his house, that his freedmen and slaves should attend him in a group twice a day, to offer their greetings in the morning and to bid him goodnight in the evening, one by one.*

[5] Among other liberal studies, he applied himself to the law. He also took on the duties of a husband, though after he had lost his wife Lepida and the two children he had with her, he remained single and could not by any means be induced to marry again, not even by Agrippina,* who, left a widow by the death of Domitius, sought with all her powers to attract Galba (though he was not yet available, being still married) with the result that at an assembly of ladies Lepida's mother rebuked her sharply and even slapped her. He was especially respectful toward Livia Augusta, whose particular favour he enjoyed during her lifetime and through whose will, when she died, he almost inherited a fortune, for, of all her legatees, he was left

the largest bequest, fifty thousand sesterces. However, because the sum was given in figures rather than words, Tiberius, who was her heir, reduced it to five thousand—and Galba never actually received even that.

[6] He secured magistracies before the official age and, when praetor with responsibility for arranging the games for the goddess Flora, he provided a spectacle of a kind not seen before in which elephants walked on tightropes.* After that he governed the province of Aquitania for nearly a year. Shortly thereafter he held an ordinary consulship for six months.* By coincidence he took over the consulship from Lucius Domitius,* the father of Nero, while he himself was succeeded by Salvius Otho, the father of Otho. This was an omen of what was to happen later, when he would be emperor between the reigns of their two sons. Appointed governor of Upper Germany by Caligula as replacement for Gaetulicus, the day after he arrived to take charge of the legions he prevented them from applauding at the festival which happened to fall at that time, by giving written orders that they should keep their hands under their cloaks. Immediately the following verse circulated in the camp:

Soldiers, learn to be soldiers. Galba's no Gaetulicus.

With equal strictness, he prohibited the practice of buying leave. He took great care to train up both the veterans and the new recruits and quickly checked the barbarians, who had by then broken through as far as Gaul. And when Caligula was visiting,* Galba and his army made such a favourable impression that of the countless troops brought together from all the provinces none secured greater recognition nor greater rewards. Galba himself particularly stood out, since, while directing the deployment of men in the field, shield in hand, he had actually run alongside the emperor's chariot for twenty miles.*

[7] When news came of Caligula's assassination and many people urged him to take advantage of the opportunity, Galba preferred to take no action. Because of this he particularly endeared himself to Claudius and was made a member of his circle of friends; he was treated with such deference that the expedition to Britain was postponed to a later date when he quite suddenly fell ill, though it was not serious. He was specially chosen* to be proconsular governor of Africa for two years with the task of bringing order to a province

troubled by internal dissension and by barbarian revolt. And order he brought, with particular concern for strictness and justice even in the smallest matters. When a soldier was accused, during a time of great scarcity, of having sold (while on campaign) a *modius* of wheat, the remains of his rations, for a sum of one hundred denarii, Galba ordered that when his food ran out no one should help him, and the man died of hunger. When he was dispensing justice and a case came up concerning the ownership of a farm animal, since the arguments and witnesses on neither side had much authority, which made it difficult to arrive at the truth, Galba gave orders that the animal was to be taken with its head covered to the lake where it normally satisfied its thirst and, after its drink, that it should belong to whichever party it chose to go to, once its head was uncovered.

[8] Because of his achievements at that time in Africa and earlier in Germany, he was awarded triumphal ornaments and co-opted to be a member of three priesthoods, the Board of Fifteen,* the brother-hood of Titius,* and the priests of Augustus.* And from that time until about the middle of Nero's reign he lived his life largely in retirement. He would never undertake any journey, even to take the air, unless accompanied by a second carriage containing a million sesterces in gold, until at last, as he lingered in the town of Fundi, an offer came of the governorship of Nearer Spain.* It happened, after his arrival in his province, that when he was making a sacrifice in a public temple, there was among the attendants a young boy holding an incense box, whose hair suddenly went white all over his head. Not a few people interpreted this as a sign that there would be a change of regime and that an old man would succeed a young man— that is to say Galba would succeed Nero. Not long afterwards a thunderbolt hit the lake of Cantabria* and twelve axes were found there—a clear portent of imperial power.

[9] For eight years, he governed the province in a changeable and inconsistent manner, being at first fierce, severe, and even excessive in punishing certain offences. For when a money-changer was found to be fraudulent in his dealings, Galba had the man's hands cut off and nailed to his counting-table and, when a guardian was found to have poisoned his charge, whom he was to succeed in his inheritance, he had the man crucified.* When the man appealed to the laws and swore he was a Roman citizen, Galba, as though he were making the punishment more bearable by adding the comfort of some dignity,

gave orders that his cross be changed for one raised up much higher than the others and painted white. Little by little, however, he sank into sloth and idleness, in order to avoid giving Nero any grounds for concern; as he used to remark: 'No one is ever obliged to give an account of his indolence.'

He was presiding over court cases in New Carthage, when news came that the Gauls were in a state of rebellion* and the governor of Aquitania was calling for help. Not only that but letters arrived from Vindex urging that he should offer himself as the liberator and leader of humanity. He did not hesitate long but agreed to the task with a mixture of fear and hope. For he had earlier intercepted instructions secretly sent by Nero to his procurators, ordering Galba's death, while his hopes were encouraged not only by the most favourable auspices and omens, but also by the predictions of a noble virgin— the more so since the priest of Jupiter at Clunia,* prompted by a dream, had brought out from the inner part of the temple exactly the same verses delivered in the same way by a prophetic virgin two hundred years previously. The verses made clear that one day the prince and lord of the world would come forth from Spain.

[10] Thus he ascended the tribunal, as if he were about to conduct the usual manumission of slaves.* Placed in front of him were as many portraits as were available of those whom Nero had condemned and killed, while at his side was a boy of noble birth whom he had summoned from his place of exile on the nearest of the Balearic islands* for this very purpose. Galba voiced his deep concern at the current state of affairs and, when he was acclaimed as emperor, declared himself merely the legate of the senate and people of Rome. He then announced a suspension of public business and from among the common people of the province conscripted legions and aux- iliary forces, to add to his existing army of one legion, two squadrons of cavalry, and three cohorts. From those of the leading men who were distinguished for their wisdom and years, he set up a kind of senate, which he would consult on more important matters when- ever necessary. He also selected young men of the equestrian order, to be called volunteers, retaining entitlement to the use of the gold ring,* who were to keep watch around his bed-chamber in place of soldiers. He also issued edicts throughout the provinces, exhorting everyone, individually and collectively, to join together in the common cause, each contributing whatever help he could.

Around the same time, as defences were being constructed for the town which he had chosen as his headquarters, a ring was found of ancient workmanship and on the stone was carved a figure of Victory with a trophy. And straight after that an Alexandrian vessel reached the quayside at Dertosa,* loaded with arms but without captain, sailor, or any passenger, so that no one had any doubts that war was being undertaken justly, dutifully, and with the favour of the gods. Then, all of a sudden, the entire undertaking almost came to grief. One of the two cavalry squadrons, regretting that it had changed allegiance, attempted to desert Galba just as he was approaching the camp and was only just prevented from abandoning his cause. Besides this, some slaves, who had been given to Galba, and were primed for treachery by one of Nero's freedmen, would have succeeded in a plan to kill him as he passed through a passageway into the baths, if their urging one another to seize the opportunity had not prompted questions as to what they were talking about, so that a confession was extracted by torture.

[11] These dangers were exacerbated by the death of Vindex.* Galba was overwhelmed and almost abandoned hope—indeed, he came near to taking his own life. When he learnt, however, from messengers who had arrived from Rome that Nero was dead and that everyone had sworn allegiance to himself, he set aside the title of 'legate', took on that of 'Caesar',* then set forth, wrapped in a general's cloak and with a dagger hanging before his chest, suspended from his neck.* Indeed, he did not resume wearing his toga until those who were plotting revolt were suppressed—the praetorian prefect Nymphidius Sabinus in Rome, in Germany the governor, Fonteius Capito, and in Africa another governor, Clodius Macer.

[12] He was preceded by a reputation for both cruelty and avarice, for it was said that he had punished those communities of Spain and Gaul which did not come over to his side until a late stage with the imposition of a heavy tribute and, in some cases, with the destruction of their fortifications also, while on their commanders and procurators, along with their wives and children, he imposed capital punishment.* And when a fifteen-pound golden crown from the ancient temple of Jupiter was offered to him by the people of Tarraconensis, he had it melted down and, finding it three ounces short, demanded that these be forthcoming. This reputation was confirmed and increased immediately on his arrival in Rome. For,

when he gave orders that the marines, whom Nero had appointed
from the ranks of the oarsmen to be regular troops, should return to
their previous position and the men protested, insistently demanding their eagle and standards, not only did he send in horsemen to
break up the group but he even had every tenth man executed. In a
similar manner he sent back to their homeland, without any reward,
the cohort of Germans which had at one time been set up as a
bodyguard for the Caesars and whose immense loyalty had been
proven on many occasions, claiming that they favoured Gnaeus
Dolabella, next to whose gardens their camp lay. Other stories, too,
whether true or false, were bandied about, in mockery of him: that
he had let out a groan when a particularly refined dinner was placed
before him; and, when his official steward presented a summary of
accounts, he offered him a dish of beans to reward his conscientious-
ness and diligence; and that, when the flute-player Canus had pleased
him with an amazing performance, he gave him with his own hand
five denarii* from his private purse.

[13] For these reasons his arrival was not particularly welcomed,
as became clear when the games were next held, for as the Atellan
players began the well-known chorus:

> Onesimus is coming from his farm

all the audience, with one voice, together chanted the rest of it and,
starting again from that line, went through it repeatedly with the
accompanying gestures.* [14] Indeed, he enjoyed greater support
and authority when he came to power than when he ruled, although
he gave many indications of being an excellent emperor.* But these
did not bring him sufficient favour to outweigh the hostility earned
by his actions of a different character. He was controlled by the wills
of three men, who lived with him within the Palace and without
whom he was never seen, so that they were popularly referred to as
his tutors. The three were: Titus Vinius, one of his officers from
Spain, a man of immense greed; Cornelius Laco, who had risen from
the rank of legal assistant to become prefect of the praetorian guard,
a man of intolerable pride and indolence; and the freedman Icelus,
who had only a short time previously been honoured with the gold
ring* and the *cognomen* Marcianus but was already hoping to attain
the highest equestrian rank. By these men, each giving rein to
his particular vices, he let himself be so manipulated and taken

advantage of that he himself became quite inconsistent in his behaviour, being sometimes more severe and frugal and at other times more relaxed and careless than was proper for an elected emperor and one of his age.

He condemned without a hearing, on the slightest suspicion, certain distinguished men of the senatorial and equestrian orders. He rarely bestowed Roman citizenship and only made grants of parental privilege* on one or two occasions, and even then only for a fixed and limited period. When the judges begged him to add a sixth panel to their number, he not only refused but revoked a privilege granted by Claudius,* that they would not be summoned to pass judgement in the wintertime or at the start of the year.

[15] It was thought, too, that he planned to limit the tenure of senatorial and equestrian posts to two years and only to bestow them on men who were unwilling to take them or who turned them down. He appointed a commission of fifty Roman equestrians to revoke and recover at least nine-tenths of the gifts made by Nero,* prescribing that even if actors or athletes had sold something that had once been given to them, it was to be confiscated from the purchasers, if the original recipients had spent the money and could not produce it. Yet at the same time there was nothing he would not allow his companions and his freedmen to sell for money or give as a favour: exemptions from taxation, penalties to be imposed on the innocent, immunity for the guilty. Indeed, when the Roman people demanded punishment for Halotus and Tigillinus,* he singled out these two, the most evil of all Nero's agents, not merely leaving them unpunished but even honouring Halotus with a most powerful procuratorship, while on Tigillinus' behalf he actually issued an edict, criticizing the people for their savagery.

[16] As a result of these measures, he provoked the hostility of every section of Roman society, but above all of the soldiers, who hated him intensely. For although the officers had, in his absence, promised to those swearing loyalty to him a larger than usual donative,* he would not ratify this and repeatedly boasted that he was in the habit of levying soldiers, not of buying them. He thereby alienated all soldiers, wherever they were stationed. Even among the praetorians he provoked fear and indignation by dismissing a number of them at intervals on the grounds that they were suspected of favouring Nymphidius.* But it was particularly the soldiers of Upper

Germany who were filled with fury that they had been cheated of the rewards for the services they had rendered against the Gauls and Vindex. These, then, were the first who dared to abandon their allegiance and refused to swear their oath on the Kalends of January* unless it was in the name of the senate. Forthwith they resolved on a delegation to the praetorians in Rome with the message that they did not like the emperor who had been chosen in Spain and the praetorians themselves should choose another who would be approved of by all the armies.

[17] When Galba heard this news, taking the view that it was not so much his old age as his childlessness which counted against him, he suddenly picked out from among a group of people offering their respects Piso Frugi Licinianus, a distinguished young man of aristocratic family who had enjoyed his highest approval for some time, and who had always been designated in his will to succeed to his name and his property. Addressing him as his son, he escorted him into the camp of the praetorians and adopted him before the assembled soldiers—though without any reference to a donative even on this occasion, which made the task of Marcus Salvius Otho much easier, when he made his bid for power less than six days after the adoption.

[18] Even from the beginning of his rule there had been great and numerous portents predicting the manner in which he actually met his end. When all the towns were slaughtering sacrificial victims on the right and on the left as he passed through on his journey to Rome, it happened that an ox, enraged by the blow of the axe, broke its chain, attacked his carriage and, rising up on its hind legs, completely soaked him with its blood.* Then, when Galba alighted, he was almost wounded by the thrust of a bodyguard's lance, as the crowd pushed forward. As he entered Rome and then the Palace, he was welcomed by an earth tremor and a sound like cattle lowing. These signs were followed by others much clearer. From all the imperial treasure he had selected a necklace of intertwined pearls and gems as an ornament for the image of Fortune he kept in his villa at Tusculum.* This necklace he suddenly decided to dedicate to the Capitoline Venus, thinking it deserved a more elevated place. The next night he had a dream that his image of Fortune complained she had been cheated of the gift meant for her and threatening that she in her turn would take away what she had given him. Terrified,

he set out at first light for Tusculum to avert the evil spoken of in the
dream, sending on ahead attendants to make ready a sacrifice. But
when he arrived he found nothing but some warm ashes on the altar
and next to it an old man, dressed in black, holding the incense in a
glass dish and the wine in an earthenware cup.* It was noted, too, that
on the Kalends of January, when he was offering a sacrifice, the
crown fell from his head and, when he was taking the auspices, the
chickens flew away;* and that on the day of the adoption, when he was
about to address the soldiers, his chair was not placed in its usual
position before the tribunal, through the forgetfulness of his servants, while in the senate his official seat was also in the wrong place.
[19] When he was offering a sacrifice on the morning of his murder,
a seer repeatedly warned him to look out for danger, since assailants
were not far away.

Not long after this he discovered that Otho had control of the
praetorian camp, and, though several people tried to persuade him to
go there himself as quickly as possible, assuring him that he could
prevail by his authority and presence, he decided merely to stay
where he was and to reinforce his defence by bringing together a
guard of legionaries, whose quarters were spread all over the city. He
did, however, put on a corslet—but one of linen, and he made no
secret of the fact it would offer little protection against so many
swords. Nevertheless, he came forth, misled by false rumours which
the conspirators had deliberately spread in order to make him appear
in public. A few people rashly affirmed the business was concluded
and that those who had revolted were brought to order, while a large
crowd of others had come to offer their congratulations and were
ready to obey all his commands. Galba went forth to meet them with
such confidence that, when a soldier boasted that he had killed Otho,
he asked on whose authority, and made his way into the Forum. The
cavalrymen, who were entrusted with the task of killing him, driving
their horses through the streets and pushing aside a crowd of civilians, caught sight of him there from a distance and paused for a short
time before rushing in and slaughtering him, abandoned as he was by
his attendants.

[20] There are those who report that, as the disturbance erupted,
he cried out: 'What are you doing, my fellow soldiers? I am yours
and you are mine', and that he even promised a donative.* More,
however, favour the tradition that, of his own accord, he bared his

throat and urged them to do their work and strike, if that seemed right to them. One fact was notable, that of those present no one attempted to give the emperor any help and all who were summoned disdained the message, with the exception of a detachment from the German army. These, thanks to his recent and great kindness toward them when they were sick and wounded, hurried to his assistance but, not knowing the place, they came by a roundabout route and arrived too late.

He was slaughtered beside the lacus Curtius* and left lying just as he was, until a common soldier, returning from the corn distribution, put aside his load and cut off Galba's head. Then, since he could not grasp it by the hair,* he hid it under his clothing but later he stuck his thumb into the mouth and thus carried it off to Otho. The latter made a present of it to the army servants and followers, who impaled it on a lance and carried it around the camp, with jeers, shouting out repeatedly: 'Pretty boy Galba, make the most of your youth!' This insolent joke took its particular inspiration from an incident a few days previously, when a report was commonly circulated that Galba, in response to the praise someone made of his appearance as still youthful and vigorous, replied:

Steadfast my strength continues still.*

A freedman of Patrobius Neronianus* bought it from them for a hundred gold pieces and threw it away in the place where, on Galba's order, his master had been executed. Finally, later on, Argivus, Galba's steward, gave the head and the rest of the corpse a proper burial in Galba's gardens on the Aurelian Way.

[21] He was of medium height, very bald, with blue eyes, a hooked nose, and hands and feet so crippled by arthritis that he could not endure wearing shoes for long, nor could he unroll books or even hold them. On his right side, too, his flesh had grown out and hung down so far that it could hardly be kept in place with a bandage. [22] It is said that he was a heavy eater and in the wintertime would even have something before first light, while at dinner he would take so much that he would give orders for his leftovers to be carried round in big handfuls to be distributed among the attendants. His sexual preference inclined toward males, but only those who were especially tough and full grown.* They say that when Icelus, one of his long-standing favourites, came to him in Spain bringing news of

the death of Nero, Galba not only welcomed him publicly with the most ardent kisses but begged him to have his body hair plucked at once, then took him aside.

[23] He died in his seventy-third year* and in the seventh month of his reign. The senate, as soon as it was permitted to do so, had decreed him a statue to stand on a column with ship's beaks in that part of the Forum where he had been massacred. But Vespasian countermanded this decree, believing that Galba had secretly sent assassins against him from Spain to Judaea.*

OTHO

[1] Otho's ancestors came from the town of Ferentium;* the family was an ancient and illustrious one, descended from the rulers of Etruria. His grandfather was Marcus Salvius Otho, whose father was a Roman knight, while his mother was of humble birth, perhaps not even free-born. Thanks to the favour of Livia Augusta,* in whose household he grew up, he was made a senator, although he did not rise beyond the rank of praetor. Otho's father was Lucius Otho, who was of most distinguished birth with many important connections on his mother's side. Lucius was so dear to the emperor Tiberius and so closely resembled him in appearance that many believed he was the emperor's son. He discharged his city magistracies and his proconsulship of Africa, as well as some extraordinary commands, with great strictness. He even had the audacity, when in Illyria, to inflict capital punishment on certain soldiers in the middle of the camp,* and personally witnessed this, because, regretting their change of allegiance during Camillus' attempted coup,* they had killed their own officers, on the grounds that these men had instigated the rebellion against Claudius—though Otho was aware that Claudius had promoted the soldiers for that very reason. This deed enhanced his reputation as much as it detracted from his favour at court. However, he soon remedied this when he uncovered the deception of a Roman knight, who, Otho learned from his slaves' indiscretion, was planning to murder Claudius. Thus, the senate bestowed on him the rarest of honours, a statue to be placed on the Palatine, while Claudius appointed him to the ranks of the patricians and, praising him in the most lavish terms, concluded his speech thus: 'My friend, I could not hope that my own children could outdo you.' Albia Terentia, a lady of distinguished family, bore him two sons, Lucius Titianus and the younger one, Marcus Salvius Otho. They also had a daughter whom her father betrothed to Drusus, the son of Germanicus, when she was only just of marriageable age.

[2] The emperor Otho was born on the fourth day before the Kalends of May in the consulship of Camillus Arruntius and Domitius Ahenobarbus.* From his earliest youth he was extravagant and wild to such a degree that his father often beat him with a

thong.* It is alleged that he used to wander about by night and if he happened to meet someone who was weak or drunk, he would toss them into the air on a stretched-out blanket.* Later, after his father's death, there was an influential freedwoman of the court with whom he actually pretended to be in love, the better to secure her favour, though she was an old woman and virtually decrepit. It was through her that he secured easy access to Nero, becoming the foremost of his friends, since they were alike in character and, as some even allege, would take it in turns to use one another in satisfying their lusts. At any rate, Otho's influence was so great that, when an ex-consul had been convicted of extortion, he did not hesitate to bring the man into the senate to give thanks before he had actually secured his release, which he did with the promise of a large sum of money.

[3] He was party to all Nero's schemes and secrets, even arranging, for the day on which Nero planned to kill his mother, a most lavish and refined dinner party, to which both were invited in order to allay suspicion. It was Otho, too, who took on in a sham marriage Poppaea Sabina,* when she was already Nero's mistress. Nero induced her to leave her husband and entrusted her for the time being to Otho. Otho himself, however, seduced her and not content with this loved her so much that he could not with equanimity endure to have even Nero as a rival. It is certainly believed that not only did he shut out the messengers who were sent to fetch her but even on one occasion Nero himself, who stood before the entrance of the house vainly mixing threats with prayers and claiming back what he had handed over in trust.* And so it was that, after the marriage was dissolved, he was made provincial governor of Lusitania as a pretext to get him out of the way. This was deemed sufficient, since a more severe punishment might have made public the whole farce, though the matter was nevertheless well known through the following couplet:

> Why's Otho in exile in a specious post, you ask?
> He had become his own wife's lover.

For ten years, he governed the province as an ex-quaestor,* with notable moderation and restraint.

[4] When he finally had the chance of revenge, he was the first to support Galba's attempt to seize power. At the same time, though, he conceived an ambition for imperial rule for himself, encouraged

not only by the current state of affairs, but particularly by the assurances of the astrologer Seleucus. This man, who had once foretold that Otho would outlive Nero, unexpectedly came to see him of his own accord and promised in addition that he would shortly become emperor. Thus, Otho let slip no opportunity to perform services for or win popularity with anyone, giving a gold piece to each man in the praetorian cohort on guard whenever he invited the emperor to dinner. He took great care to put all the soldiers under an obligation in one way or another. When he was chosen as a judge in the case of one who was disputing the bounds of his property with a neighbour, he bought up the whole piece of land and made a present of it to the soldier.* Thus, when the time came there was scarcely a man among them who did not believe and declare that only Otho was fit to become emperor.

[5] He had, indeed, hoped to be adopted by Galba and expected news of this daily. But when Piso was elevated, he gave up on that hope and, instead, the seriousness of his debts adding to his indignation, turned to force. For he did not attempt to conceal that, unless he became emperor, he could not keep going, and that it did not matter whether he fell at the hands of an enemy on the battlefield or at the hands of his creditors in the Forum. A few days earlier, he had extorted a million sesterces from one of the emperor's slaves in return for securing the man a stewardship. This sum was the financial backing for his great undertaking. First he involved five members of his bodyguard in his project, then another ten, as each of the five brought in two more; each man was given ten thousand sesterces in ready money and promised a further fifty thousand. Through these men he secured the support of the rest, though they were not many, but he believed firmly that there would be more once the business was under way.

[6] He had planned to take immediate control of the praetorian camp after Piso's adoption and to attack Galba while he was at dinner on the Palatine. However, he decided against this out of concern for the cohort then on guard, not wishing to exacerbate ill-feeling against them, for the same cohort had been on duty when Caligula was killed and Nero was deserted. He did not exploit the intervening period, either, because of portents and on the advice of Seleucus.

And so, when the day was decided on, his conspirators primed to wait in the Forum, by the Golden Milestone,* just below the temple of Saturn, Otho went to offer his morning greetings to Galba, receiving a kiss from him, as was customary. He attended him too, as he made a sacrifice and listened to the predictions made by the seer. Then, when a freedman came with a message that the architects were waiting—this was the agreed signal—Otho left on the pretext that he was going to look over a house which was for sale, hurrying through the back of the Palatine to the agreed meeting-place. Others say that he pretended to have a fever and instructed his associates to offer that excuse if anyone was looking for him. Then, having quickly concealed himself in a lady's litter he rushed to the praetorian camp, getting out of the litter, when the bearers flagged, and starting to run. When he paused as his shoe came undone, his companions caught him up on their shoulders without delay and hailed him as emperor. Thus, accompanied by festive acclamations and drawn swords he arrived at the camp headquarters, where everyone he met joined in supporting him, as though all were aware of and party to the plot. From there, he sent agents who were to kill Galba and Piso.* As for winning over the minds of the soldiers with promises, he merely swore to their gathering that he would take that and only that which they left him.

[7] After this, when the day was already well advanced, he entered the senate and gave a brief account of events, giving the impression that he had been snatched from the street and compelled by force to take on the empire and that he planned to govern in consultation with all, before proceeding to the Palatine. As well as the other compliments offered by those seeking to congratulate and flatter him, he was hailed by the lowest of the common people as Nero—a title which he gave no indication of rejecting. On the contrary, as some report, he even added the *cognomen* Nero to his name on imperial certificates and on the first letters he sent to some provincial governors.* It is certainly true that he permitted portraits and statues of Nero to be restored and that he reinstated his procurators and freedmen to their former positions, while the first expenditure he authorized as emperor was fifty thousand sesterces to complete the Golden House.*

That very night, they say, he had a terrifying dream and let out loud groans. When his attendants came running, they found him lying on the floor beside the bed, where he was seeking to propitiate with every possible rite the shade of Galba,* by which he had dreamt he was ousted and expelled. On the following day, too, the story goes, as he was taking the auspices, a storm blew up and he fell heavily to the ground, repeatedly muttering: 'What have I got to do with long pipes?'*

[8] At around the same time, however, the armies in Germany swore their allegiance to Vitellius. When Otho discovered this, he got the senate to send a delegation with the news that an emperor had already been chosen and to urge calm and concord. However, he also sent agents with letters offering Vitellius a share in the empire and proposing to marry Vitellius' daughter. But when war became certain, as the leaders and troops sent on by Vitellius drew near, he had proof of the support and loyalty he enjoyed among the praetorians—an incident which almost involved the slaughter of the senatorial order. It had been decided that some weapons should be transferred by the men of the fleet and transported by ship. When these were being brought out in the praetorian camp towards night, some soldiers suspected a plot and started a riot. Almost at once all of them, with no one in control, rushed to the Palatine demanding the heads of the senate. They fought off those of the tribunes who tried to contain them—killing not a few of them—and were thus covered in blood, when they burst into the dining-room, demanding to know where the emperor was, and there was no holding them back until they had actually seen him.

Indeed, he began the campaign energetically and too hastily, without paying any regard to the omens, despite the fact that the sacred shields had been brought out but not yet replaced* (which was from earliest times regarded as inauspicious), and he started out on the day when the priests of the Mother of the Gods* begin their weeping and wailing, while the auspices themselves were very bad. For the signs were positive when he offered a victim to Father Dis,* a sacrifice in which adverse entrails are more favourable, and, when he was leaving the city, flooding from the Tiber hindered him. Then, at the twentieth milestone, the rubble from a collapsed building blocked his path.

[9] With similar rashness—though no one doubted he ought to have deferred the fighting, since the enemy was under pressure, running short of food supplies and disadvantaged by their restricted position—he resolved to fight a decisive battle as soon as possible,

whether because he could not tolerate continued uncertainty and
hoped to bring things to an early end before Vitellius' arrival, or
because he was not able to withstand pressure from the troops who
were clamouring for battle. He himself was not present at any of the
fighting, staying behind at Brixellum.*

Indeed, he won victories in three battles, though they were minor
ones, one near the Alps, one near Placentia, and one at Castor's
temple, as the place is called. But in the final battle, at Betriacum,* he
was defeated by trickery. Hope had been raised of talks and his
soldiers had been led out, thinking they were to hear the peace
terms, just as greetings were being exchanged when they were
unexpectedly forced to fight. Immediately Otho took the decision to
die, rather (as many believe and with good reason) from shame
because he could not bring himself to persevere in his claim to power
when it would place the state and human lives in such danger, than
from any desperation or lack of faith in his troops, for he still had
fresh and strong the forces he had kept back for a second battle, and
others were arriving from Dalmatia, Pannonia, and Moesia, while
even those who had been defeated were not so badly off that they
were not ready to face any battle of their own accord and even
without help, in order to avenge their disgrace.

[10] My father, Suetonius Laetus, took part in this war. He was an
equestrian tribune in the Thirteenth Legion. Later he would often
tell us how even before Otho became emperor he so loathed civil war
that, when someone mentioned over dinner the deaths of Brutus and
Cassius,* he shuddered with horror. Nor would he have made his bid
to oust Galba, if he had not been confident the business could be
accomplished without war. Later, my father said, he was moved by
the example of a common soldier to see his own life as dispensable.
When this man announced the defeat of his army and no one
believed him, accusing him of lying or else of cowardice, and suggesting he had deserted the battle line, he fell on his sword before
Otho's feet. When Otho saw this, my father would relate, he declared
he would not expose to any further danger such men, who had
deserved so well of him.

Having spoken words of encouragement to his brother, his
brother's son, and his friends one by one, advising each to look after
his own interests as circumstances permitted, he sent them all away
with an embrace and a kiss and retired to his private quarters where

he wrote two notes, a letter of consolation to his sister and another to Messalina, the widow of Nero,* whom he had planned to marry, entrusting her with his remains and with the preservation of his memory. Whatever other papers he had with him, he burnt, so they should not bring danger or harm to anyone by falling into the victor's hands. From the resources he had with him, he gave out sums of money to his household slaves.

[11] When he had made these preparations, he was fully intending to take his life, but a disturbance arose before he had done the deed and he realized that those who were beginning to depart and leave the camp had been seized and held as deserters. 'Let us', he said, 'add one more night to this life' (those same few words were his), and he gave orders that force was not to be used against anyone. He made himself available to anyone who wished to see him, his door open, late into the night. After this, having quenched his thirst with a drink of cold water, he took up two daggers and felt the blade of each, then hid one under his pillow before falling into a deep sleep, his chamber door closed. At last, around first light, he awakened and ran himself through with a single thrust, just below the left breast. At his first groan, people came bursting in. Now hiding, now revealing his wound, he lost consciousness. His funeral rites were conducted quickly, on his own instructions.* He died in the thirty-eighth year of his life and on the ninety-fifth day of his reign.*

[12] Otho's appearance and manner did not suggest a spirit of such greatness.* He was apparently of modest stature, with crooked feet and bandy legs, while in the care of his person he was almost feminine, plucking out his body hair and, as his hair was thinning, wearing a kind of wig fitted closely and carefully to his head, so that no one would notice it. Moreover, they say he would shave his face daily and apply wet bread to it—a practice he had taken up as soon as the first down appeared—so as to avoid ever having a beard. They say too that he would often celebrate the rites of Isis quite publicly, wearing the linen robe of the cult.* It was for this reason, I believe, that his death, so at odds with the manner of his life, caused the greater wonder. Many of the soldiers who were present wept greatly and fervently kissed his hands and feet as he lay there, declaring that he was the bravest of men, the one true emperor, before at once taking their own lives close to his funeral bier. Many even of those who were absent, when they heard the news, in their grief attacked

and killed one another.* Indeed, most people, though they detested him fiercely when he was living, sang his praises when he was dead, so that it was commonly asserted that he had had Galba killed, not to gain power but in order to restore the republic and liberty.

VITELLIUS

[1] Different authorities give quite separate accounts of the origins of the family of the Vitellii, some reputing it an ancient and noble line, others by contrast describing it as recent, obscure, and even disgraceful. I would attribute this to their respective enthusiasm for or hostility towards the emperor Vitellius, if it were not the case that there was already previously disagreement about the family's standing. A pamphlet written by Quintus Elogius survives, addressed to Quintus Vitellius, a quaestor of the Deified Augustus. According to this, the Vitellii were descended from Faunus, king of the Natives, and Vitellia,* who was worshipped as a divinity in many places, and they ruled over the whole of Latium; their surviving descendants came over from the Sabine country to Rome and were included among the ranks of the patricians. The Vitellian road, from the Janiculum right down to the coast, and the colony of the same name (which they had once claimed to defend against the Aequiculi with a force of their kinsmen) long served as reminders of the line.* Then, in the time of the Samnite war when a garrison was sent to occupy Apulia, certain members of the Vitellii family settled in Nuceria.* Many years later, according to this same document, their descendants returned to Rome and once again joined the senatorial order.

[2] More people maintain, on the other hand, that the founder of the family was a freedman, while Cassius Severus* and others, too, describe this individual as a cobbler, whose son acquired a more substantial fortune through auctions of confiscated goods and recovering state debts and married a commonplace woman, the daughter of a certain Antiochus who kept a bakery, in his turn producing a son who became a Roman knight. Let us not attempt to resolve these differences. Publius Vitellius did have his home in Nuceria and, whether he came from ancient stock or was of disreputable parents and ancestors, he was certainly a Roman knight and procurator of Augustus' property. He left four sons of high rank, with the same *cognomen*, distinguished only by their forenames,* Aulus, Quintus, Publius, and Lucius. Aulus died during his consulship, which he had entered with Domitius (father of the emperor Nero) as his colleague. He was a man of exquisite refinement,

notorious for the magnificence of his dinner parties. Quintus lost his senatorial rank when Tiberius decided to pick out less suitable senators and remove them from the order. Publius, who was on Germanicus' staff, prosecuted Gnaeus Piso, Germanicus' enemy and murderer, securing his condemnation.* After he had served as praetor, he was arrested for having conspired with Sejanus and given over to the custody of his brother. He slit his veins with a penknife but allowed his wounds to be bound up and taken care of, not because he regretted his decision to die but rather because of the protestations of his family. He died of an illness while still in custody. Lucius, after his consulship, became governor of Syria, where with consummate skill he succeeded in inducing Artabanus, the king of the Parthians, not only to enter into talks with him but even to pay homage to the legionary standards.* Soon after, with the emperor Claudius as his colleague, he secured two further regular consulships, as well as the censorship.* He also deputized for the emperor when the latter was absent on his British campaign. He was a man of integrity and industry but quite notorious for his love of a freedwoman. He would even mix her saliva with honey and rub this into his throat and jaws as a remedy, not secretly or occasionally but quite publicly and every day. His ingenuity in offering flattery was astonishing; he was the first to honour the emperor Caligula as a god. On his return from Syria he would only venture to come into the emperor's presence with his head veiled,* turning himself around and then prostrating himself. He omitted no measure which might secure him the favour of Claudius, who was at the mercy of his wives and freedmen. He asked Messalina, as an immense favour, to offer him her feet so he might take off her shoes, and when he had removed her right slipper he kept passing it between his tunic and his toga, from time to time kissing it. He also worshipped golden images of Narcissus and Pallas,* which stood among his household gods. It was he, too, who paid the famous compliment to Claudius, when he organized the Secular Games: 'May you do this often!'*

[3] He died the day after paralysis struck him, leaving two sons (their mother was Sestilia, a woman of great virtue and not undistinguished family), both of whom he saw reach the rank of consul—and in the same year,* indeed, since the younger succeeded the elder for six months. When he died the senate honoured him with a public funeral, as well as a statue on the rostra with the

following inscription: 'In honour of his unwavering piety toward the emperor.'

Aulus Vitellius, Lucius' son, who was to be emperor, was born on the eighth day before the Kalends of October (or, as some maintain, the seventh before the Ides of September), when Drusus Caesar and Norbanus Flaccus were consuls.* His parents were so horrified by the horoscope cast for him by astrologers that his father always maintained vigorously that, while he was living, his son would have charge of no province, while his mother, when he was sent out to the armies and acclaimed emperor, immediately lamented his miserable fate. His boyhood and earliest youth he spent on Capri among the favourites of Tiberius—ever after he was branded with the nickname 'tight-bum'* and it was thought that it was his physical charms which were the basis and reason for his father's rise.

[4] Over the next few years, too, corrupted by every kind of disgrace, he held a prominent place at court, sharing with Caligula a passion for chariot racing and with Claudius one for gambling.* However, he was still closer to Nero, both for these same qualities and also because of a rare service. For when he was presiding over one of Nero's contests* and the emperor, while desiring to compete among the lyre-players, did not dare to undertake a performance despite everyone's entreaties, he waited until Nero had left the theatre, then called him back in, claiming to be the conveyer of the people's demands, thus giving him the opportunity to be entreated by the crowd.

[5] Through the favour of these three emperors, he not only attained the highest magistracies and priesthoods but also subsequently governed the province of Africa and had charge of public works. He was, however, inconsistent in what he tried to do and in the reputation he acquired; in his province, he showed unusual integrity over two years in succession, staying on as an official when his brother succeeded him as governor. But during tenure of his city magistracy, he is alleged to have stolen gifts and ornaments from temples, in some cases changing them by substituting tin and brass for gold and silver.*

[6] He had as his wife Petronia, daughter of a man of consular rank, and with her produced a son, Petronianus, who was blind in one eye. Since the boy was made his mother's heir on condition that he be released from his father's power, Vitellius gave him his

independence and soon afterwards, as people believe, killed him, alleging that he planned to kill his father and, through guilt, had himself drunk the poison he had prepared for the deed. Not long afterwards, Vitellius took as his wife Galeria Fundana, whose father was of praetorian rank, and with her, too, produced children, one of each sex, but the boy was virtually mute and tongue-tied because of a stammer.

[7] To general surprise, he was sent by Galba to take command in Lower Germany. Some think that he was helped by the support of Titus Vinius,* who was at that time particularly influential and whose good opinion he had long enjoyed because of their common adherence to the Blue Faction.* Against this, however, is Galba's open declaration that no one was less to be feared than those who only thought about their stomachs and that even Vitellius could fill his deep gullet from the resources of that province, so that it was clear to anyone that his appointment was motivated by contempt rather than favour. It is well known that on his way out of Rome he even lacked supplies for the journey and that his domestic circumstances were so straitened that his wife and children, whom he left behind in Rome, lived obscurely in a rented apartment so that he could let out the house for the rest of the year, and he was obliged to pawn a pearl taken from his mother's ear in order to cover the expenses of his journey. He was only able to extricate himself from a throng of creditors who laid in wait to detain him (among them representatives of the peoples of Sinuessa and Formiae, whose tax revenues he had embezzled) by threatening them with prosecution for vexatious accusation. For when a certain freedman rather sharply demanded settlement of a debt, he had begun proceedings for damages against him, on the grounds that the freedman had kicked him, and he would not withdraw them, until he had extracted from him fifty sesterces.

On his arrival the army—which was ill-disposed towards the emperor and ready and willing for a change of ruler—welcomed him with hands raised to heaven, as if he were a gift from the gods, since he was son of a man three times consul, in the prime of life, and of easy-going and lavish disposition. Vitellius had managed to reinforce the support he already enjoyed with his recent behaviour, throughout the journey greeting any common soldiers he met with a kiss and being especially friendly to the muleteers and travellers at post-houses and inns. He would even ask them in the morning if they had had breakfast yet, before showing them with a belch that he had done so himself.

[8] Moreover, when he entered the camp itself, he denied no one's requests and, without being asked, relieved those who were in disgrace of their humiliations, those whose cases were undecided of their mourning garments* and those who were condemned of their punishments. And so it was that scarcely a month had passed when, with no regard to the day* and time (for it was already evening) he was carried off from his chamber by some soldiers, just as he was, in his off-duty clothes, hailed as emperor, and taken around the most crowded streets, bearing in his hand the drawn sword of the Deified Julius Caesar which someone had taken from the shrine of Mars and handed to him amid the first wave of enthusiasm. By the time he returned to his quarters, the dining-room was ablaze as the chimney had caught fire. To those who were greatly concerned and disturbed by this, seeing it as a ill omen, he announced: 'Be of good spirit! A light has shone for us!' This was the extent of his speech to the soldiers. Having then garnered the support of the army of Upper Germany, which had earlier defected from Galba to the senate, he willingly took on the title 'Germanicus' which was offered by all his supporters, but put off taking that of 'Augustus' and absolutely refused that of 'Caesar'.

[9] As soon as news came of Galba's murder, he settled his affairs in Germany and divided up his forces, planning to send some on ahead against Otho and lead the rest himself. An auspicious sign appeared to the troops which had been sent on ahead, when an eagle came from their right and flew towards them, circling the standards, then flew on just ahead of them as they continued with their march. By contrast, when Vitellius himself was on the move, some equestrian statues (which were being erected in his honour in a number of places) suddenly developed cracks in their legs and collapsed simultaneously, while the laurel wreath, which he had placed on his head with the greatest care, fell off into running water. Later, in Vienna,* when he was dispensing justice at the tribunal, a cock perched first on his shoulder and then on his head.* The mode of his death fully corresponded to these portents, for he himself was unable to keep hold of the empire which had been secured for him by his officers.*

[10] He heard news of the victory at Betriacum and the death of

Otho* while he was still in Gaul, and without delay gave orders in a
single edict that every section of the praetorian cohorts was to be
disbanded because of the appalling example they had set,* and that
they should hand over their weapons to their tribunes. Furthermore,
he gave orders that a hundred and twenty men, whose petitions to
Otho he had discovered, in which they demanded their reward for
completing the task of killing Galba, should be hunted down and
executed. This was an act of nobility and distinction which would
have given hope for his conduct as holder of supreme power, if he
had not otherwise behaved in ways more in accordance with his
character and actions before he took on imperial majesty. For, once
embarked on his journey, he was carried through the middle of
cities, as if in a triumphal procession, voyaging down rivers on the
most luxurious of vessels, decked out with different sorts of garland
and equipped with the makings of the most opulent banquets. He
exercised no discipline over his household or his soldiers, treating
the depredations and ungoverned violence in which they all engaged
as a joke—for they, not content with the official feasts which were
everywhere offered to them, set free whatever slaves they chose,
offering blows, beatings, sometimes injuries and occasionally death
to anyone who stood in their way. And when he arrived at the fields
in which the fighting had taken place and some of those with him
expressed their horror at the stench of the corpses, he made so bold
as to offer them reassurance with the following repulsive comment:
'The smell of a dead enemy is excellent—and even better in civil
war.' However, to lessen the effect of the smell, he knocked back a
large measure of wine in front of them and shared some all around.
He showed the same conceit and arrogance when he commented,
looking at the inscription on Otho's gravestone: 'That was the
Mausoleum he deserved.'* He also took the dagger with which Otho
had killed himself, and sent it to the colony of the Agrippenses,* to
be dedicated to Mars. He even held an all-night festival on the
heights of the Apennines.*

[11] Finally, he entered the city of Rome with a fanfare of trumpets, wearing the cloak of a general and girt with a sword. He was
surrounded by standards and ensigns, while his staff wore military
cloaks and his troops had their weapons bared.* Increasingly, he came
to neglect every law of gods and men, entering upon the office of
Pontifex Maximus on the anniversary of the Allia,* deciding the elec-

tions for the next ten years* and making himself consul in perpetuity.*
And lest any should doubt whom he had chosen as his model in
governing the empire, he made funeral offerings to Nero in the
middle of the Campus Martius, insisting on the attendance of state
priests, and at a ritual celebration he publicly urged a lyre-player
whose music pleased him to perform something from the Master's
Book.* When the man started playing some of Nero's songs, he was
the first to applaud, leaping from his seat in delight.

[12] Having begun in this manner, he conducted a significant part
of his rule according to the advice and counsel of the lowest of actors
and chariot-drivers and, in particular, his freedman Asiaticus. As a
youth Asiaticus had been his partner in mutual buggery but grew
tired of this and ran away. Later, Vitellius found him again, working
as a seller of cheap drinks in Puteoli,* and threw him in chains but
quickly released him and restored him to his former position as
favourite. Then, once more angry at him because of his insolence
and petty thefts, he sold him to a travelling trainer of gladiators, but,
when he was kept in reserve till the end of a gladiatorial show,
snatched him back again suddenly, giving the man his freedom,
when he himself was at last allocated a province. On the first day he
was emperor, he presented Asiaticus at dinner with the golden rings,*
even though that morning, when everyone had made entreaties on
Asiaticus' behalf, he expressed his extreme disgust at the idea of
imposing such a stain on the equestrian order.

[13] Above all, however, he was addicted to luxury and to cruelty,
always having at least three feasts, sometimes four in a day—
breakfast, lunch, dinner, and a drinking party—and easily finding
capacity for it all through regular vomiting.* Moreover, he would have
himself invited for each meal by a different host on the same day. No
one ever spent less than four hundred thousand sesterces in making
provision for one of these meals.* Among all his feasts the most
notorious was the one given by his brother to mark his arrival in
Rome as emperor, at which were served two thousand of the choicest
fish and seven thousand birds, so they say. But this, too, he himself
outdid when he dedicated the platter, which, because of its immense
size, he used to call the shield of Minerva the Protectress. In this he
blended the livers of scar-fish, the brains of pheasants and peacocks,
the tongues of flamingos, and the innards of lampreys which had
been sought out by ships' captains and galleys from Parthia to the

straits of Spain.* Yet characteristically for a man whose appetite was
not just insatiable but also immune to considerations of time or
decency,* he could not resist, when he was making a sacrifice, snatching bits of meat and sacrificial cake among the altars, almost from the
fire, and eating them up on the spot, or, when he was on a journey,
doing the same to titbits smoking hot or else left over from the
previous day and half-eaten in the inns along his route.

[14] It was his preference to impose death as a punishment on
anyone and for any reason. Men of consular family, comrades of his
whom he had known as a boy and whom he had induced to come to
court with offers of everything short of a share in the empire, he did
away with through deceptions of various kinds, even giving poison to
one man with his own hand in a drink of cold water which the other
had asked for when suffering from a fever. As for the money-lenders,
contractors, and tax-gatherers, he spared scarcely any who had ever
demanded from him repayment in Rome or taxes on his travels. It
was one of these whom he committed to punishment, just as the man
had come to pay his respects, then called him back. Everyone was
praising this act of mercy, when he gave orders that the execution
should take place in his presence, for he 'wanted his eyes to have a
feast'. In another case, he had a man's two sons executed with him
because they had tried to plead for their father. Moreover, when a
Roman equestrian called out, just as he was being taken away for
execution, 'But you are my heir!', Vitellius forced him to produce
the document and when he discovered that a freedman was instituted as joint heir with him, he ordered that the man and his freedman should both be killed.* He even executed some of the common
people, for the simple reason that they had shouted loudly against
the Blue Faction, thinking they were doing this because they despised him and were hoping for a change of ruler. However, there was
no one to whom he was more hostile than jokers and astrologers and
whenever an allegation was made against one he would have the man
executed without giving him a chance to defend himself. This was
because, when he had issued an edict ordering that astrologers were
to leave Italy by the Kalends of October, a placard was immediately
posted, reading: 'And the astrologers declare: For the good of the
state, by that same date let Vitellius Germanicus be no more!' He
was also suspected of involvement in his mother's death by ordering
that she should not be given food when she was ill, because a woman

of the Chatti,* to whom he listened as if she were an oracle, had predicted that his rule would be assured and long-lasting, provided he survived the death of his mother. Others record that it was she, weary of present evils and fearful of those to come, who demanded poison from her son—which he willingly gave her.*

[15] In the eighth month of his reign, the armies in Moesia and Pannonia defected from him, as did, among those overseas, the armies in Judaea and Syria. They swore allegiance to Vespasian, the latter in his presence, the former from afar. In order to retain the support and favour of the rest, Vitellius thereafter stopped short of nothing in distributing largesse both publicly and privately. He also recruited troops in Rome, promising volunteers that once victory was achieved they would not only be discharged but would even receive the rewards usually given to veterans who had fulfilled their regular term of military service. Later, coming under pressure from the enemy both by land and by sea, he stationed against them in one spot his brother with the fleet and a force of new recruits and gladi-ators, and in another, the forces and leaders who had fought at Betriacum. After he had been either defeated or betrayed on every front, he made a bargain with Flavius Sabinus, Vespasian's brother, to secure his own life and a hundred million sesterces. He at once made an announcement, on the steps of the Palatine, before a crowd of his soldiers, that he was giving up the empire which he had accepted with reluctance. But when everyone protested, he put the business off, letting a night go by. Then, appearing at first light in mourning garments, he went down to the rostra and, with many tears, he made the same declaration, this time from a written docu-ment. Again the soldiers and common people called out to him, exhorting him not to give up and promising their full support for his cause. This gave him new courage and in a sudden attack he forced Sabinus and the other Flavian supporters, who by this time were no longer on the alert, up onto the Capitol and into the Temple of Jupiter Best and Greatest, which he set on fire, thus putting an end to them.* He himself looked out over the battle and the fire from the House of Tiberius, as he was feasting.* Shortly afterwards, regret-ting what had happened and laying the blame on others, he called a public meeting, swearing and making others swear, too, that nothing was dearer to him than public order. Then, unsheathing the dagger he had at his side,* he held it out first to a consul, then, when he

refused, to other magistrates, then to each senator in turn. When none would accept it, he took it away, as though to dedicate it in the temple of Concord.* However, when some shouted out that he himself was Concord, he came back, declaring that not only would he keep the weapon but he would even take on the *cognomen* of Concord.

[16] He also persuaded the senate to send messengers, accompanied by the Vestal Virgins, to request either peace or time to negotiate. On the next day, as he was waiting for a reply, a scout brought news that the enemy was approaching. And so he at once hid himself in a closed sedan and with just two attendants, a baker and a cook, secretly made for the Aventine and his father's house, so that he might escape from there to Campania. But shortly afterwards, when there was slight and vague rumour that peace had been secured, he allowed himself to be taken back to the Palatine. When he found that it was quite deserted and those who were with him were slipping away, he put on a belt full of gold coins and took refuge in the porter's lodge, having chained up a dog at the entrance and blocked the door with a bed and mattress.

[17] Already the advance guard of the army had burst in and, meeting no one, were ransacking everything in the usual way. These men dragged him out of his hiding-place but when they questioned him as to who he was—for they did not know him—and whether he knew Vitellius' whereabouts, he managed to deceive them. But then, when he was recognized, he kept asking if he could be kept for a while under guard, even in the prison, pretending he had information concerning the safety of Vespasian, until finally with his hands tied behind his back, a noose around his neck, and his clothes torn, he was dragged half-naked into the Forum and, amid gross abuse, physical and verbal, along the whole length of the Sacred Way, his head pulled back by the hair, in the way of condemned criminals, and even his chin held up with the point of a sword, so that he should let his face be seen and not lower it. Some people threw dung and filth, others hurled abuse, calling him an arsonist and a glutton. Some of the common people even criticized his bodily defects, for he was unusually tall, his face was generally very red because of his drinking, and his belly distended. One of his thighs was crippled from being struck by a chariot once, when he was acting as attendant to Caligula as the latter was racing. Finally, he was butchered on the

Gemonian steps* with the smallest incisions and, when he was dead,
he was dragged from there with a hook to the Tiber.

[18] He died, along with his brother and his son, in his fifty-
seventh year, proving right the prophecies of those who interpreted
the portent at Vienna (set out above*) to mean nothing other than that
he would fall into the power of a man from Gaul. For he was finished
off by Antonius Primus, one of the enemy generals, who was born at
Tolosa* and in his youth was given the nickname 'Becco' which
means cock's beak.*

THE DEIFIED VESPASIAN

[1] With the uprisings of the three emperors and their violent deaths the empire had for a long time been in a state of disorder and almost of collapse when it was finally taken over and stabilized by the Flavian house, an unknown family without any ancestral portraits,* yet by no means a disgrace to the Roman state, although it is agreed Domitian was punished rightly for his lust and cruelty.

Titus Flavius Petro, a citizen of Reate,* was, during the civil war, a centurion or a volunteer veteran on Pompey's side. Having run away from the line of battle at Pharsalus* and retreated home, he later requested and obtained pardon and an honourable discharge, and went into business as a collector of payments at bankers' auctions. This man's son, whose *cognomen* was Sabinus, had no military experience (even if there are some who maintain that he was a senior centurion and others that he was in command of a cohort when he was relieved of his duties for health reasons) and collected the state tax of a fortieth* in Asia. There used to be some statues of him set up by the cities with this inscription: 'To an honest tax-collector.' Later on he was a money-lender among the Helvetii* and it was there that he died, leaving behind a wife, Vespasia Polla, and by her two children, of whom the elder, Sabinus, later achieved the urban praetorship, while the younger, Vespasian, actually became emperor. Polla came from an honourable family of Nursia.* Her father was Vespasius Pollio, who had served three times as military tribune and prefect of the camp, while her brother was a senator of praetorian rank. There is a place at the top of a hill, near the sixth milestone as you go from Nursia towards Spoletium, called Vespasiae, where there are many monuments to the Vespasii, a strong indication of the distinction and antiquity of the family. I would not deny that there are some who have spread the story that Petro's father came from the other side of the River Po and was a contractor for farm labourers (whose practice it is every year to go over from Umbria to the Sabine land to tend the fields), but settled in the town of Reate where he married. I myself, however, have found not the slightest evidence for this, though I have made a fairly thorough investigation.

[2] Vespasian was born in a little village in the Sabine land just

beyond Reate, known as Falacrina, on the evening of the fifteenth day before the Kalends of December, when Quintus Sulpicius Camerinus and Gaius Poppaeus Sabinus were consuls,* five years before the death of Augustus. He was brought up in the care of Tertulla, his paternal grandmother, on her estate at Cosa. Hence, even when he was emperor, he would frequently visit his childhood home, where the house was kept just as it had been so that he would not miss the sight of any familiar object. And he so cherished the memory of his grandmother that on religious and festival days he would insist on drinking from a small silver cup which had belonged to her.

Having assumed the toga of manhood, for a long time he refused to seek the broad-striped senatorial tunic,* though his brother had obtained it, and in the end no one but his mother could induce him to apply for it. She finally made him agree, not so much through entreaties or appeals to his respect for her as through teasing, for she repeatedly taunted him with being his brother's attendant. He served as military tribune in Thrace and was allotted Crete and Cyrene as his province when he served as quaestor. Shortly afterwards he stood as candidate for the aedilate and later the praetorship. The former post he only secured the second time he stood (having first been defeated) and even then he came sixth.* The latter post, though, he achieved at the first attempt, coming among those at the top of the list. When he was praetor, so as to lose no opportunity of gaining Gaius' favour at a time when the latter was hated by the senate, he proposed additional games to celebrate the emperor's victory in Germany, as well as recommending that the conspirators* should suffer the additional punishment of having their bodies thrown out without burial. In the presence of that illustrious order he even thanked the emperor because he had honoured him with an invitation to dinner.

[3] At around the same time, he took as wife Flavia Domitilla who had once been the mistress of Statilius Capella, a Roman knight of Sabrata in Africa. She was only of Latin status,* though afterwards she was declared free-born and a Roman citizen in a judicial hearing in response to the claim of her father, Flavius Liberalis. Originally from Ferentum, he had the rank merely of quaestor's clerk. By her Vespasian had three children, Titus, Domitian, and Domitilla. His wife and daughter he outlived, losing both of them before he became

emperor. After his wife's death, he asked Caenis, a freedwoman and secretary of Antonia,* whom he had once loved, to live with him again, and even when he was emperor he gave her the position almost of lawful wife.

[4] During the reign of Claudius he was sent to Germany as legionary legate through the influence of Narcissus. From there he was transferred to Britain* where he fought thirty battles with the enemy. He brought under Roman control two most powerful tribes, over twenty towns, and the island of Vectis,* which is very close to Britain, serving part of the time under the command of the ex-consul Aulus Plautius and part of the time under that of Claudius himself. As a consequence he was granted triumphal ornaments and soon afterwards received two priesthoods and, as well as this, the consulship which he held for the final two months of the year.* The period which elapsed before his proconsulship he passed virtually in retirement and at leisure, fearing Agrippina's continuing influence with her son, and her loathing of Narcissus' friends, even after the latter's death.

He was then allotted Africa as his province, which he governed with marked integrity and not a little honour, although during a disturbance at Hadrumetum* some turnips were thrown at him. Certainly he came back not at all richer, for his credit was so near collapse that he mortgaged his properties to his brother and was obliged to lower himself to trading in mules in order to keep up his position.* This was why he was commonly called 'the muleteer'. He is also said to have been convicted of extorting two hundred thousand sesterces from a young man for whom, against his father's wishes, he obtained a grant of the senatorial broad stripe, and to have been sternly reprimanded for this.

Travelling through Greece in Nero's entourage,* when the emperor was singing he would usually leave or, if he did stay, would fall asleep. Having thereby fallen into the deepest disfavour and been banished, not only from the emperor's inner circle but even from his public receptions, Vespasian retired to a small and out-of-the-way town where he hid, fearing the worst, until he was offered a province with an army.

According to an old and established belief widespread throughout the East, it was fated that at that time men coming from Judaea would take control of the world. This prediction, which events later revealed to concern the Roman emperor, the Jews took to refer to themselves and rebelled, killing the legionary commander, and, besides this, routing the governor of Syria who was bringing reinforcements, and seizing one of his eagles. Since to bring this disturbance under control required a bigger force and a leader of some energy—but one to whom such a great enterprise could be offered without risk, Vespasian was chosen above all others, for not only was his energy proven but also, being of modest name and family, he offered no threat.* Thus two legions, eight divisions of cavalry, and ten cohorts were added to his forces. Among his legates he included his elder son and, as soon as he arrived in his province, he attracted the attention of the adjacent provinces too, immediately re-establishing discipline in the camps and engaging in a couple of battles with such determination that in the assault on a fortress a stone wounded his knee and a number of arrows struck his shield.

[5] After the deaths of Nero and Galba, when Otho and Vitellius were struggling for the empire, Vespasian himself came to entertain an ambition to become emperor, which he had long ago conceived because of the following signs.* There was on a suburban estate of the Flavians an ancient oak tree which was sacred to Mars. On each of the three occasions Vespasia gave birth, it at once put forth a branch from its trunk which gave clear signs of the fate which would befall that child. The first branch was delicate and soon withered, just as the girl who was born did not see out the year. The second was very strong and abundant, portending great good fortune, but the third was like a tree itself. It was because of this, they say, that the father, Sabinus, receiving further confirmation from a *haruspex*, announced to his mother that a grandson had been born to her who would be a Caesar. She merely laughed, the story goes, expressing amazement that, while she was still of sound mind, her son should be losing his wits. Later, when Vespasian was aedile, Caligula was furious at him for neglecting his duty to keep the streets clean and gave orders that soldiers should cover him with mud, heaping it into the fold of his purple-bordered toga. There were some who interpreted this to mean that at some time the state would be trampled under foot and neglected in some civil strife but would come under his protection and, as it were, into his embrace. Once, when he was having lunch, a dog wandered in from the crossroads bringing a human hand* which it dropped under the table. Again, when he was dining, an ox that

was ploughing shook off its yoke and burst into the dining-room. It
frightened off the attendants but then, as if it were suddenly tired
out, fell right at Vespasian's feet, as he reclined, and bowed its neck.
Besides this, a cypress tree on his grandfather's estate was suddenly
uprooted and overturned, though there was no storm, but the next
day rose again, greener and stronger than before. When he was in
Greece, he had a dream that his own good fortune would begin the
moment Nero had a tooth removed. And the next day it happened
that a doctor walked into the hall and showed him a tooth which he
had just extracted. When he consulted the oracle of the god of
Carmel in Judaea, the lots were so encouraging as to promise that
whatever plan he was contemplating and turning over in his mind,
no matter how ambitious, would be fulfilled. And one of the captives
of noble birth, Josephus, when he was thrown into chains, insisted
that the same man would shortly set him free but that he would then
be emperor. Omens kept being reported from Rome, too: that during
his final days Nero received instructions in a dream to take the sacred
chariot of Jupiter Best and Greatest from the sanctuary to the house
of Vespasian and then into the Circus. And not long afterwards,
when Galba was on his way to the election for his second consulship,
a statue of the Deified Julius turned of its own accord towards the
East. Moreover, on the field of Betriacum,* before battle commenced,
two eagles had a fight, observed by everyone, and, when one of them
was beaten, a third appeared from the direction of the rising sun and
drove away the victor.*

[6] However, he did not attempt anything—despite the great willingness and even insistence of his own men—until he was induced
by the support he chanced to receive from others who were unknown
to him and far away. From the three legions which constituted the
army in Moesia, two thousand men had been sent to assist Otho.
When they were already on their way, news came that he had been
defeated and had taken his own life. Nevertheless, they pressed on to
Aquileia,* as they gave little credence to the rumour. There they took
advantage of the opportunity afforded by the lack of order to indulge
in every kind of plunder. Then, fearful that if they went back, they
would have to give an account of their actions and pay the penalty,
they hit upon the plan of making a man of their own choice emperor.
After all, they were by no means inferior to the Spanish army who
had brought Galba to power, nor to the praetorians who had made

Otho emperor, nor to the German army who had done the same for
Vitellius. The names of all the consular legates then in post anywhere were put forward and when, for one reason or another, they
had rejected the others, some men of the third legion, (which just
before the death of Nero had been transferred from Syria to
Moesia), commended Vespasian warmly; everyone concurred and
without delay they inscribed his name on all their banners. At that
point, however, their undertaking was brought under control, and
the detachments were soon afterwards recalled to their duties. But
the story spread and Tiberius Alexander, prefect of Egypt, was the
first to make his legions commit themselves to Vespasian on the
Kalends of July, which was later celebrated as the anniversary of his
principate. Then, on the fifth day before the Ides,* the army in Judaea
swore allegiance to him in person.

These undertakings were much advanced by the circulation of a
copy of a letter (genuine or a forgery) from the now-deceased Otho
addressed to Vespasian, begging him very earnestly to avenge his
cause and desiring that he should come to the aid of the state; also by
the story which went around that after his victory Vitellius intended
to change round the winter quarters of the legions, transferring the
German army to the East,* where service was less perilous and more
comfortable. Aid was also afforded by Licinius Mucianus* from
among the provincial governors, and from among the kings,
Vologaesus of Parthia. Licinius, having put aside the resentment
which he had hitherto openly borne against Vespasian through jeal-
ousy, promised the support of the Syrian army, while Vologaesus
promised forty thousand archers.

[7] And so, having embarked upon civil war, Vespasian sent
leaders and troops ahead to Italy, while he himself crossed over to
Alexandria to take possession of the gateway to Egypt. Here, wishing
to consult the auspices concerning the duration of his hold on the
empire, he dismissed all who were with him and entered the temple
of Serapis alone, and when, having made many offerings to the
god, he finally turned around, it seemed to him that the freedman
Basilides had brought him sacred branches, garlands, and cakes, as is
the custom there. Yet he was well aware that no one had let this man
in and, moreover, that he had for some time been scarcely able to
walk, because of a nervous disorder, and was indeed far away. And at
that very time letters arrived reporting that the troops of Vitellius

had been routed at Cremona and that Vitellius himself had been killed in Rome.

Recently and indeed unexpectedly made emperor, he still lacked a certain dignity and majesty. Yet these also came to him. A common man who had lost his sight and another who was lame approached him together as he sat before the tribunal, begging for the remedy for their ailments which Serapis had revealed in a dream; for he could heal eyes by spitting upon them and make whole a leg if he deigned to touch it with his heel. Although he had little faith that this could possibly succeed and indeed did not dare to put it to the test, finally, at the insistence of his friends, he undertook both actions in public before an assembly and met with success. At the same time, with the guidance of seers, some vessels of ancient workmanship were dug up in a sacred spot at Tegea in Arcadia, bearing an image very like that of Vespasian.

[8] Such was Vespasian and so great his renown when he returned to Rome where, having celebrated his triumph over the Jews, he added another eight consulships to his earlier one.* He also undertook the censorship and, throughout the entire duration of his rule, he considered nothing more important than bringing order to the empire, ravaged and collapsing as it was, and then improving it, too.

The soldiers, some made bold by their victory, others ashamed of their defeat, were indulging in every kind of licence and recklessness. Moreover, the provinces and the free cities and some of the kingdoms, too, were suffering from internal disorder. For this reason he discharged many of Vitellius' soldiers and punished many of them. Yet even to those who had had a part in his victory he was so far from showing particular indulgence that he was late in paying their standard rewards. He let slip no opportunity for reinforcing discipline; when a young man, perfumed with unguents, was thanking him for granting the military command he had requested, Vespasian drew away his head in disgust and reprimanded him in stern tones: 'I would rather you had smelt of garlic' then cancelled the commission. And when the marines who travelled in turns from Ostia and Puteoli to Rome on foot* put in a request that they be given an allowance to cover their shoes, as though it would not be enough to send them away without a reply, he gave orders that in future they would run unshod; and they have run thus ever since. He took away the freedom of Achaea, Lycia, Rhodes, Byzantium, and Samos, and made them into provinces, as well as Trachian Cilicia and Commagene which until then had been ruled by kings. He assigned more legions to Cappadocia because of the frequent barbarian incursions, giving the province a consular governor instead of an equestrian one.

The city of Rome was disfigured, as a result of the earlier fires and the collapse of buildings; he gave permission for anyone to move into and build on vacant lots, if the owners failed to do so. He himself undertook the restoration of the Capitol, with his own hand initiating the removal of the rubble, some of which he carried away on his own back.* He took charge of replacing the three thousand bronze tablets which had been destroyed in the temple fire, searching high and low for copies: these were the most ancient and precious records of the empire which contained decrees of the senate and acts of the people dating almost back to the foundation of the city, and relating to alliances, treaties, and special privileges granted to individuals. [9] He constructed new works also, the temple of Peace next to the Forum and that of the Deified Claudius on the Caelian hill,* for though work on this had been started by Agrippina it was virtually razed to the ground by Nero.* He also built an amphitheatre* in the heart of the city, learning that this had been the intention of Augustus.

The distinguished orders of senators and knights, which had been reduced in number as a result of the various massacres and debased by long-term neglect, he purged and reinforced, holding a review of the senate and the knights, in which the most unworthy were expelled, while the most distinguished of the Italians and the provincials were added to the orders.* Besides this, in order to make clear that the orders were distinguished from one another not so much by privileges as by position, once when there was an altercation between a senator and a knight he declared that senators should not be insulted but to return their insults was both proper and right.

[10] Everywhere the backlog of court cases had increased to an excessive degree, as the longstanding ones remained unresolved due to interruptions in the dispensing of justice, while new ones were added as a result of the turbulent nature of the times. He selected men by lot to take responsibility for the restoration of property seized in war and others to man the centumviral courts.* They were to exercise extraordinary jurisdiction and also to cut down the list as much as possible, since it seemed that the lifetime of the litigants

would hardly be long enough to get through the cases by means of regular proceedings.

[11] With no measures to curtail them, lust and luxury had flourished. At his instigation, the senate decreed that if any woman should have a relationship with someone else's slave, she was to be considered a slavewoman, and also that money-lenders should never have the right to enforce payment of money borrowed by those in the power of a family-head, not even after the family-head's death.*

[12] In other matters he was from the very beginning of his principate right up until his death unassuming and tolerant, never attempting to cover up his modest background and sometimes even flaunting it. Indeed, when some people attempted to trace the origins of the Flavian family back to the founders of Reate and a companion of Hercules, whose tomb stood by the Salarian Way,* he actually laughed at them. So far was he from desiring the outward trappings of power that on the day of his triumph, tired out by the slow and tedious procession, he had no hesitation in saying that it served him right for so foolishly wanting a triumph when he was an old man—as if it were due to his ancestors or had ever been his own ambition. At first he would not accept the tribunician power and refused the title 'Father of the Fatherland' until well on in his reign.* Indeed, even while the civil war was still going on, he had dropped the practice of having those who came to pay their respects searched.*

[13] He put up most patiently with the outspokenness of his friends and the insinuations of advocates, as well as the arrogance of philosophers.* When Licinius Mucianus, a man of notorious sexual impropriety, presuming on the services he had rendered,* treated Vespasian with little respect, the latter could only bring himself to criticize him privately and even then only to the extent that, when he complained of Licinius to a mutual friend, he would add, 'At least I am a real man.'* When Salvius Liberalis dared to say, in the course of speaking for a wealthy defendant, 'What is it to Caesar, if Hipparchus has a hundred million',* Vespasian himself praised him. And when he happened to meet Demetrius the Cynic, after his condemnation, and the latter did not deign to get up or to greet him but merely barked out some remark, Vespasian thought it enough simply to call him a dog.*

[14] He bore not the slightest grudge against those who had insulted or opposed him, arranging a splendid marriage for the

daughter of his enemy Vitellius and even providing her with a dowry and furnishings. When he had been fearful at being banned from Nero's court* and had asked what he should do and where he should go, one of the ushers has pushed him out and told him to go to hell. When this man later asked for forgiveness, Vespasian attacked him merely with words, using about the same number and to the same purpose. He was so disinclined to bring about anyone's downfall through some fear or suspicion that when friends warned him to beware of Mettius Pompusianus, because it was commonly believed that he had an imperial horoscope, he actually made him consul, promising that he would some day be mindful of the favour.*

[15] It cannot easily be shown that any innocent person suffered punishment, except when Vespasian himself was away and unaware of events—or at least against his wishes and through his being misinformed. Helvidius Priscus was the only man to greet him on his return from Syria by the private name of 'Vespasian' and, when praetor, made no honourable mention of him in any of his edicts,* yet he showed no anger against him until through the abusiveness of his retorts, Helvidius had virtually reduced him to the status of an ordinary citizen.* Moreover, while he gave orders, first that he be relegated and then that he be killed, Vespasian was so keen to save him that he sent messengers to recall the executioners and indeed would have saved him if he had not been falsely informed that the man was already dead. For he never took pleasure in anyone's death and would even shed tears over and lament well-deserved punishments.

[16] The only count on which he may justly be criticized is his love of money. For he was not content with reinstating the taxes abolished under Galba, but added swingeing new ones, increasing the tribute due from the provinces, in some cases to double the previous amount. He engaged openly in business deals which would have brought shame on a private citizen, buying up goods merely in order to sell them later at a profit.* He did not hesitate to receive money from candidates in return for magistracies, nor from defendants, whether innocent or guilty, for acquittals. He is even believed to have deliberately made it his practice to promote the most rapacious of his procurators to higher posts so that they would be the richer when he later condemned them. Indeed, he was commonly said to

treat these men as sponges, as it were, soaking them when they were dry and squeezing them when they were wet.

Some hold that he was very grasping by nature—such was the force of the criticism made by an old herdsman of his who had begged humbly for his freedom as a gift when Vespasian became emperor, but had been refused: 'The fox changes his coat but not his customs.' On the other hand, some argue that the drained resources of the treasury and the imperial fund absolutely compelled him to pursue spoil and plunder, and that he himself had borne witness to this at the start of his reign, declaring that forty thousand million sesterces were needed to set the state to rights. And this seems more plausible, for even when he acquired money improperly he always made excellent use of it.

[17] He was most generous to men of every rank, making up the property qualification for senators and supporting needy ex-consuls with annual grants of five hundred thousand sesterces.* He restored many cities throughout the world which had suffered damage through earthquake or fire. He gave particular encouragement to literary talent and the arts. [18] He was the first to establish a salary of a hundred thousand sesterces for teachers of Latin and Greek rhetoric, paid for from the imperial fund. He gave outstanding gifts and great rewards to eminent poets, as well as to artists, such as the restorers of the Venus of Cos and of the Colossus.* To an engineer who promised that he could transport some huge columns up to the Capitol at almost no cost, he gave a substantial reward for his device but declined to use it, remarking: 'I must be allowed to feed my poor common people.'

[19] For the games given to celebrate the dedication of the new stage in the theatre of Marcellus, he revived the old musical entertainments. To Apelles the tragic actor he gave four hundred thousand sesterces, to the lyre-players Terpnus and Diodorus* two hundred thousand each, and to several a hundred thousand. The smallest amount he gave was forty thousand and he also gave out a large number of gold crowns. He constantly threw parties, usually formal and lavish ones, in order to support the butchers. Just as he gave gifts to men on the Saturnalia, so too he gave presents to women on the Kalends of March.* Yet despite this, he could not shake off his longstanding reputation for avarice. The inhabitants of Alexandria persisted in calling him 'Cybiosactes'*—the name of one

of their kings, notorious for being mean. Even at his funeral, the leading mime actor Favor, who was wearing a mask of his face and imitating the actions and speech of the deceased during his lifetime, as is the custom, asked the procurators how much the funeral and the procession had cost and, hearing that it was ten million sesterces,* exclaimed that they should give him a hundred thousand and throw him into the river.

[20] His body was well proportioned, with strongly built limbs, while his facial expression suggested he was straining. A witty man made rather a good play on this when Vespasian asked him for a joke about himself. 'I'll tell one', he said, 'when you've finished relieving your bowels.' He enjoyed the most robust health, although he did nothing to maintain it beyond massaging his jaws and the rest of his body a regular number of times in the ball-courts and fasting for one day in each month.

[21] He kept his life pretty much to the following pattern. When he was emperor he would always rise early, while it was still dark. Then, when he had read his letters and the reports from all his officials, he would admit his friends and, while they were greeting him, he would put on his own shoes and cloak.* After he had dealt with whatever matters of business had arisen, he would take some air and then have a rest, lying with one of his mistresses (he had selected quite a few to take the place of Caenis* after her death). Then he would go from his private quarters to take a bath and thence to dinner. They say this was the moment when he was most amiable and indulgent, and the members of his household would take great trouble to seize this opportunity if they had any requests.

[22] Not only at dinner, however, but also at other times he was always very genial and settled many matters with a joke. For he had a great sense of humour, though with a taste for vulgar and dirty jokes, so that he did not hesitate to use obscenities. Quite a few of his witticisms have been preserved, however, including the following. When an ex-consul, Mestrius Florus, admonished him for saying 'plostra' instead of 'plaustra',* Vespasian greeted him the next day as 'Flaurus'. Pursued by a woman who claimed to be dying for love of him, he took her to bed and gave her four hundred thousand sesterces for sleeping with him. And when he was asked by his steward how the sum should be entered in his accounts, he replied: 'item: a passion for Vespasian.'

[23] He also quoted Greek poetry at quite appropriate moments,*
once remarking of a tall man with huge genitals:

> Striding along, bearing a lance that casts a long shadow.*

And referring to Cerylus, a freedman of great wealth, who, in order
to cheat the imperial fund of its dues when he died,* was trying to
pass himself off as a man of free birth and had changed his name to
Laches,* he said:

> O Laches, Laches, when you're dead,
> You'll straight away be Cerylus again.*

He was particularly inclined to make jokes about his improper
ways of making money so as to diminish their unpopularity with
humour and turn them into a source of amusement. When one of his
favourite attendants came to him requesting a position for a man he
pretended was his brother, he put him off, then summoned the candidate himself. Having extracted from him the sum of money he had
agreed to pay his intermediary, he appointed him to the post
immediately and when his attendant brought the matter up, he
observed: 'You'd better find yourself another brother. The one you
think is yours is mine.' Once when he was on a journey and suspected the mule-driver had got down to shoe the mules* so that the
delay would give someone with a lawsuit the chance to approach the
emperor, he asked him what his fee was for the shoeing and insisted
on a share of the money. When his son Titus criticized him for
putting a tax even on urine, he held up a coin from the first payment
to his son's nose and asked him if he was offended by its smell. When
Titus said no, he observed: 'But it comes from urine.' When messengers reported to him that a colossal statue had been publicly voted to
him at considerable cost, he gave orders that it should be set up at
once and, holding out his empty hand, said that the base was all
ready.* Even when he feared he would die and was in extreme danger, he would not leave off joking. For when, among other portents,
the Mausoleum* suddenly opened up and a comet appeared in the
sky, he declared that the former applied to Junia Calvina, a relative of
Augustus, and the latter to the king of the Parthians, who had long
hair.* When he felt the first onset of his illness he exclaimed: 'Alas! I
think I am becoming a god!'*

[24] During his ninth consulship he suffered a slight illness when

in Campania and, having at once returned to the city, he set out for Cutilae* and the countryside of Reate, where he used to spend every summer.* There, despite the fact that his illness was exacerbated by an intestinal disorder caused by excessive use of cold baths, he continued to perform his usual imperial duties just as before, even hearing embassies as he lay in bed. Suddenly stricken with an attack of diarrhoea so severe that he almost fainted, he said that an emperor should die on his feet. As he was struggling to rise, he died in the arms of those helping him, on the ninth day before the Kalends of July, at the age of sixty-nine years, one month and seven days.*

[25] Everyone agrees that he always had such faith in the astrological predictions made concerning himself and his sons that even after frequent conspiracies against him he still maintained to the senate that, if his sons did not succeed him, no one would. It is also said that once in a dream he saw a set of scales placed in the middle of the entrance hall of the Palatine residence and equally balanced, with, on one side, Claudius and Nero, and on the other, Vespasian and his sons. Nor was this misleading, since both reigned for the same number of years and the same space of time.*

THE DEIFIED TITUS

[1] Titus, who bore his father's *cognomen*,* was loved and doted upon by all humanity. Whether through innate disposition, policy, or good fortune, such was his success that he secured the goodwill of all and that too—a most difficult task—when he was emperor. For, when he was a private citizen and even during the reign of his father, he did not escape hatred, let alone public criticism. He was born three days before the Kalends of January, in the memorable year in which Gaius was killed,* in a lowly house near the Septizonium.* The room itself in which he was born was tiny and dark (it is still there and is on show).

[2] He was brought up and educated at court alongside Britannicus* in the same subjects and by the same teachers. They say that at that time a fortune-teller had been summoned by Narcissus, Claudius' freedman, to inspect the forehead of Britannicus and that he persistently asserted that it could not possibly be he but rather Titus, who was standing nearby, who would be emperor. Yet the boys were so intimate that Titus, too, who was reclining beside him, is believed to have tasted the same drink which Britannicus finished off and then died,* and to have been very ill for a long time. Later on, in recognition of all this, he set up a golden statue to Britannicus on the Palatine and dedicated another one of him on horseback, made of ivory, which even now is carried at the head of the circus procession, himself attending it on its first appearance.

[3] His qualities of mind and body at once stood out even when he was a boy but still more so as he advanced towards maturity. His appearance was striking, conveying authority as well as charm, and he was unusually strong, though not tall in stature, while his stomach protruded a little. He had an exceptional memory and a great gift for acquiring almost all the arts of war as well as those of peace. He was highly skilled in the use of weapons and in horsemanship and had a ready fluency in both Latin and Greek to such a degree that he could make a speech or compose a poem without preparation. Even in music he was not without talent and could sing and play the cithara with grace and skill. I have discovered from a number of sources that he used to write shorthand at great speed and for fun would play at competing with his secretaries and that he could imitate any

handwriting he had seen and often confessed he could have been the greatest of forgers.

[4] He served as military tribune both in Germany and in Britain, earning a great reputation for hard work and for integrity, as can be seen from the multitude of statues and images of him as well as the inscriptions on them, in both provinces. After his military service he worked as an advocate in the Forum, gaining a good reputation though he did not devote all his time to it. It was at that time that he married Arrecina Tertulla, whose father was indeed a Roman knight but had been prefect of the praetorian guard.* When she died, he married a woman from a noble family, Marcia Furnilla, whom he divorced after he had acknowledged the daughter she bore him. After serving as quaestor he was given command of a legion and conquered Tarichaeae and Gamala, two mighty cities in Judaea.* Though his own horse was killed under him in the midst of a battle he mounted another whose rider had fallen fighting by his side.

[5] When soon afterwards he was sent to congratulate Galba on becoming emperor, he attracted people's notice wherever he went as they believed he had been summoned so that he might be adopted as heir. However, when he realized that everything was again in a state of unrest, he returned from his journey, and having made a visit to the oracle of Paphian Venus, although he only asked for guidance concerning his voyage, he was also encouraged to hope he might be emperor. Soon confirmed in this expectation,* he was left to complete the conquest of Judaea, where in the final attack on Jerusalem he killed twelve defenders with as many arrows. He captured the city on his daughter's birthday, to the delight of the troops and so winning their devotion that they acclaimed him as 'Imperator'.* And when he was going to leave the province they tried to detain him, urging him with prayers and even with threats either to remain there or to take them all with him. It was this which provoked the suspicion that he had tried to rebel against his father and secure for himself rule over the East, a suspicion which he fuelled by wearing a diadem* when, on his way to Alexandria, he attended the consecration of the bull Apis at Memphis. Although this was in accordance with the customary rituals of the ancient cult, some put a worse interpretation on it. Because of this he hurried to Italy, putting in at Regium, then at Puteoli in a merchant-ship and hastening from there to Rome with the greatest dispatch. So as to show that the rumours were

unfounded, he announced, to his father's surprise: 'I have come, father, I have come.'

[6] And from that time he always acted as the emperor's partner and even his guardian. He celebrated a triumph together with his father and they held the censorship jointly.* He was his father's colleague, too, in holding tribunician power* and in seven consulships. Taking upon himself almost all the imperial duties, he dictated letters himself and signed edicts in his father's name, and even delivered his speeches in the senate, in place of a quaestor.* He also took on the command of the praetorian guard, which previously had always been held by a Roman knight. His tenure of this post was rather high-handed and violent. Whenever he had suspicions of someone he would send secret emissaries to the theatres and army camps to demand their punishment, as if by common consent, and then he would dispose of the suspect without delay. Among these was Aulus Caecina* a man of consular rank who had been invited to dinner. Titus gave orders that he should be run through when he was scarcely out of the dining-room—though this was a matter of urgency, since a speech had been found in the man's writing which was to be delivered to a gathering of the soldiers. While such measures were intended to ensure future security, they provoked a great deal of unpopularity at the time, and as a result scarcely anyone ever acceded to the principate with so bad a reputation and with everyone so against him.

[7] Besides being suspected of cruelty, he was also suspected of self-indulgence, on the grounds that he would engage in drinking bouts with the most dissolute of his companions which would go on until midnight. He was also suspected of lustfulness both because of his troupes of catamites and eunuchs and because of his great passion for Queen Berenice,* to whom he is even said to have promised marriage. There were also stories of his rapaciousness, for it was understood that when his father heard court cases, he was in the habit of selling his influence and taking bribes. To sum up, people thought of him and even publicly spoke of him as another Nero.* Yet this reputation turned out to be to his advantage for, when he was found to have no vices but instead the greatest virtues, it was succeeded by the greatest praise.*

The parties he gave were delightful rather than dissolute. The advisers he chose were ones whom later emperors also retained as indispensable both to themselves and to the public good, and made particular use of.* He sent Berenice away from Rome at once, though neither of them wished it. Some of the favourites he was most fond of, although they were such talented dancers that they later took to the stage, he not only ceased to hold dear but he would not even watch their public performances. He took nothing from any citizen. If ever anyone respected other people's property, it was he. He would not even accept permitted and customary gifts. Yet he was no less generous than any of his predecessors; at the dedication of the amphitheatre* and the baths which he had had rapidly constructed alongside, he put on the most splendid and lavish gladiatorial games. He also put on a sea-battle in the old Naumachia, and in the same place a gladiatorial combat, showing five thousand wild beasts of all kinds on a single day.

[8] He was indeed most good-natured and whereas other emperors, following the practice of Tiberius, would not ratify privileges granted by their predecessors unless they themselves had conferred the same ones on the same individuals, he was the first to confirm all previous grants in a single edict, without even being asked.* Moreover, in the case of other requests people made he was most careful never to send anyone away without hope. Indeed, when his staff criticized him for promising more than he could deliver, he replied that no one should go away from a conversation with the emperor feeling unhappy. On one occasion, recalling over dinner that he not given anyone anything during the course of the day, he came out with the memorable and rightly applauded comment: 'My friends, I have wasted a day.' Above all, he treated all the common people with such courtesy on every occasion that once, when he announced a gladiatorial show, he declared that he would give it in accordance not with his own wishes but with those of the spectators, and that is exactly what he did. Indeed, he never denied anything to a petitioner and of his own accord urged people to ask for what they wanted. Making much of his own enthusiasm for Thracian gladiators, he often engaged with the crowd in lively interchange with words and gestures like a real partisan, but without any loss of dignity or fairness.* He omitted nothing that would endear him to the people, frequently attending his baths when the common people were present.

During his reign a number of disasters happened, such as the

eruption of Mount Vesuvius* in Campania and a fire at Rome*
which lasted three days and the same number of nights, as well as a
plague of unprecedented severity. In the face of calamities of such
magnitude, Titus offered not just the concern of an emperor but the
love which only a parent can provide, giving consolation in his edicts
and as much practical help as his resources allowed. He appointed
officials to take charge of the restoration of Campania, chosen by lot
from among the ex-consuls. The property of those who had been
killed in the eruption and had no surviving heirs he set aside for the
reconstruction of the towns which had been damaged. During the
fire at Rome, his only public pronouncement was to declare that he
was ruined; he set aside all the ornaments from his country estates to
be used for the reconstruction of public buildings and temples and
put a number of men of the equestrian order in charge of the work to
ensure its more rapid completion.* He drew on all remedies, human
and divine, to restore people's health and cure their afflictions,
procuring sacrifices* and medical aid of all kinds.

Among the evils of the time were informers and their prompters
who had long been given free rein. On his orders these men were
thoroughly beaten in the Forum with whips and cudgels and finally
exhibited in the arena of the amphitheatre. Then some of them were
put up and sold as slaves, while others were deported to the most
inhospitable of the islands. To ensure that no one would undertake
anything similar at any time in the future, amongst other measures
he laid down that no one should be tried for the same offence under
different laws and that after a certain number of years no inquiry
could be made into the legal status of a deceased person.*

[9] Having declared that he would accept the office of Pontifex
Maximus* in order to keep his hands unpolluted, he kept his word,
never thereafter bringing about or condoning anyone's death,
(though he did not lack grounds to avenge himself), for he declared
he would rather meet his own end than cause someone else's. When
two men of patrician family were proved to have had designs on the
empire he merely advised them to refrain,* telling them that the
principate was in the gift of fortune, and promising to give them
anything else they might wish. Moreover, he at once sent his messengers to the mother of one of them, who was far away, to relieve
her anxiety with the news that her son was safe. Then not only did
he invite the men to a private dinner but, on the following day, when

there was a gladiatorial show, he deliberately had them seated near him and, when he was offered the weapons of the combatants, handed them over for their inspection.* It is even said that he investigated both of their horoscopes and declared that danger threatened them both but at some future time and from another source, and so it turned out.

When his brother continued to plot against him, soliciting the support of the army almost openly and planning his escape, he would not allow him to be killed or sent away or even to be held in less honour, but he continued to declare him his partner and heir, as he had done when he first came to power, and often, when they were in private, he would beg him with tears and entreaties to be willing at least to return his love.

[10] In the midst of this he was cut off by death, to the loss of humanity rather than his own. When the games were over, at whose conclusion he had shed many tears in front of the people, he went off to his Sabine estate, rather disheartened because when he was offering a sacrifice one of the victims escaped and because there had been thunder though the sky was clear. Then, at the very first stopping-place, he was stricken with a fever. Being transported from there by litter, he is said to have pushed back the curtains, looked up at the sky, and lamented greatly that life was being taken from him when he did not deserve to lose it, for he said that of all his deeds he regretted nothing, with a single exception. What this was he would not reveal at that time nor could anyone readily make it out. Some people believe that he was thinking of an affair he had with his brother's wife. But Domitia swore most solemnly that it had never happened and, if it had, she would not have denied it but rather boasted of it, as she was always most ready to do of all her scandalous behaviour.

[11] He died in the same villa as his father had, on the Ides of September, two years, two months and twenty days after succeeding him, in the forty-second year of his age.* When his death became known, everyone engaged in public mourning as if they had lost a member of their own family.* Before the meeting was called the senators hurried to the senate house, when the doors were still shut, and then, when they had been opened, gave such thanks for the dead man and heaped up such praises for him as they had never bestowed on him even when he was alive and present among them.*

DOMITIAN

[1] Domitian was born on the ninth day before the Kalends of November, when his father was consul designate* and about to embark upon office the following month, in the sixth region of the city, the Pomegranate, in a house which he subsequently converted into a temple to the Flavian line. He is said to have passed his adolescence and early youth in such poverty and shamelessness that his household had not a single silver dish in use. It is an established fact that a man of praetorian rank, Clodius Pollio, who was the object of an attack by Nero in a poem entitled 'The One-Eyed Man',* kept a note in Domitian's handwriting and would sometimes exhibit it, in which he promised to spend the night with Pollio. And there are those who claim that Domitian was even corrupted by Nerva, who was afterwards to be his successor. During the conflict with Vitellius, Domitian took refuge on the Capitol with his paternal uncle, Sabinus, and some of the troops they had with them, but when their opponents burst through and the temple caught fire, he secretly spent the night with the temple-keeper and, in the morning, disguised in the dress of an adherent of Isis, he joined a group of priests of that dubious superstition* and got away with one companion to the district across the Tiber, where he managed to hide in the home of a schoolfriend's mother, so that none of the searchers who had come after him were able to apprehend him. After victory was secured, he finally came forth and was saluted as Caesar.* Though given the office of urban prefect with consular power,* he took on only the title, transferring the judicial duties to his next colleague but taking advantage of his powerful position in so lawless a manner that it became clear even at that time what sort of a man he would become. Though I shall not go into detail, he harassed the wives of many men, even marrying Domitia Longina, who was the wife of Aelius Lamia.* In a single day he gave out more than twenty posts in the city and the empire, so that Vespasian remarked on a number of occasions he was surprised Domitian did not appoint the emperor's successor along with the others.

[2] He embarked upon a campaign in Gaul and the German provinces, although it was unnecessary and his father's friends counselled

against it, merely to emulate his brother in wealth and status. Taken
to task for this behaviour, he was obliged to live with his father to
make him more aware of his age and rank. Whenever his father and
brother went out in a sedan,* he followed in his litter and when they
both celebrated the triumph over the Jews he accompanied them on
a white horse. Moreover, of his six consulships only one was ordinary which his brother ceded to him, recommending his appointment.
He himself, too, gave an impressive appearance of modesty, as well as
of a particular enthusiasm for poetry, something which had been as
indifferent to him in earlier years as it would be despised and
rejected by him in years to come, and he even gave readings in
public. Yet despite this, when Vologaesus, the king of Parthia, sought
reinforcements and one of Vespasian's sons as their general in the
fight against the Alani,* Domitian made every effort to ensure that he
himself was sent rather than his brother. Then, when the project
came to nothing, he tried to solicit other eastern kings with gifts and
promises to make similar requests. When his father died, he debated
a long time as to whether he should give a double donative* to the
soldiers and he never hesitated to boast that he had been left a part-
share in the empire but had been cheated of it by means of a forged
will.* He never left off engineering plots against his brother both
secretly and openly until the time when Titus became very ill and
Domitian gave orders that he was to be left for dead, though he had
not yet breathed his last. After his death he offered him no honours,
apart from that of deification, and would often complain about him
indirectly in speeches and edicts.

[3] At the beginning of his principate he would spend hours every
day closeted on his own, occupied with nothing other than catching
flies and impaling them with a very sharp writing implement. Thus,
when someone once asked if there was anyone in with Caesar, Vibius
Crispus made the witty response that there was not even a fly.* He
gave the title Augusta* to his wife Domitia; he had had a son by her in
his second consulship, but lost the boy the second year after he took
power.* When she fell passionately in love with the actor Paris he
divorced her, but within a short time he could not bear the separation and took her back on the pretext that the people demanded it.
As regards the administration of the empire, for some time he was
unpredictable, displaying an equal mixture of faults and virtues until
his virtues also deteriorated into faults. So far as one may speculate,

it seems that it was poverty that had made him grasping and fear that had made him cruel, beyond what was in his nature.

[4] He constantly put on magnificent and lavish spectacles not only in the amphitheatre but also in the Circus, where, in addition to the ritual races of two-horse and four-horse chariots, he even put on two battles, one of cavalry and the other of infantry, while in the amphitheatre he also staged a naval battle. And he put on animal fights and gladiatorial combats even at night, when they were lit by torches, while the combats were not just between men but between women too. Besides this, so committed was he to attending the quaestors' games, which had been abolished but which he had reinstated, that he even granted the people the privilege of calling for two pairs of gladiators from his own school whom he would bring in at the end with full courtly splendour. And for the entire duration of the gladiatorial show a little boy dressed in red with a small and deformed head* would stand at his feet and he would talk with him a great deal, sometimes seriously. He was certainly heard to ask him if he knew why, amongst the latest appointments, he had put Mettius Rufus in charge of Egypt. He put on the naval fights with fleets of almost regular size on the lake which he had had dug out beside the Tiber and surrounded by seating, and he would watch these even in the most severe rainstorms. He also held Secular Games, having calculated the time period not from the year when Claudius had recently held them but from that when Augustus had done so.* As part of these, so that a hundred races could be completed in the course of the day of circus games, he reduced the number of laps from seven to five. He also established, to be held every five years, a three-part competition, in honour of Capitoline Jupiter, involving music, riding, and gymnastics, and with rather more prizes than are currently awarded. For there were competitions also in prose declamation* in both Greek and Latin and, besides those of the lyre-players, there were contests between singing lyre-players and those who only played the lyre, while in the stadium even girls ran races. Domitian presided over the contests, wearing high Greek shoes and clothed in a purple toga of Greek design, while on his head he wore a golden crown with images of Jupiter, Juno, and Minerva, and at his side sat the priest of Jupiter and the college of Flaviales,* dressed in the same manner except that their crowns also had images of the emperor. Every year, too, in Albanum, he would celebrate the

Quinquatria of Minerva,* for which he had established a college of priests, from amongst whom men were chosen by lot to act as officers, providing outstanding animal fights and theatrical shows as well as competitions for orators and poets.

He three times gave gifts to the people of three hundred sesterces each and during one set of gladiatorial games in honour of the sacred Seven Hills he provided a most ample banquet, the senators and knights receiving large baskets with delicacies and the common people smaller ones, the emperor himself beginning his first. On the next day, he had tokens for all kinds of gifts scattered, and because most of them had fallen among the common people, he gave orders that another five hundred tickets be thrown to each of the sections occupied by the senatorial and equestrian orders.

[5] A great number of splendid structures which had been destroyed by fire he rebuilt, including the Capitoline temple, which had burnt down again.* However, in all cases his own name was the only one inscribed and no mention was made of any of the earlier builders.* He also built a new temple on the Capitoline hill in honour of Jupiter the Guardian, as well as the Forum which now bears the name of Nerva and the Temple to the Flavian line, besides a stadium, an odeum, and a place for naval battles, the stones of which were later used to rebuild the Circus Maximus when it had been destroyed by fire on both sides.

[6] Some military campaigns he undertook through choice, others through necessity; by choice he fought against the Chatti,* while his campaign against the Sarmatians was made necessary after the slaughter of a legion together with its legate. He made two campaigns against the Dacians, the first after the ex-consul Oppius Sabinus had suffered a defeat, the second after the same fate had befallen Cornelius Fuscus, prefect of the praetorian cohorts, to whom he had entrusted the conduct of the campaign. After a number of battles (some more successful than others) with the Chatti and the Dacians, he celebrated a double triumph. After his Sarmatian campaign he merely brought a laurel crown for Capitoline Jupiter. Though not himself present he was able to bring the civil war begun by Lucius Antonius (the senior commander in Germany) to a conclusion with an amazing stroke of good fortune, for just as the battle was about to begin the Rhine suddenly thawed and cut off the barbarian forces which were about to cross over to join Antonius.

Domitian learnt of this victory through portents rather than messengers, for on the very day of the battle a splendid eagle enfolded in its wings his statue at Rome and gave forth exultant cries. Soon afterwards the rumour that Antonius was killed became so widespread that many claimed they had seen his head brought back.

[7] He also made many innovations in common practice, suspending the public distribution of food-baskets* but reinstating the practice of formal dinners.* He added two new circus factions to the four existing ones, one with gold and one with purple as their colours.* He banned actors from the stage but permitted them to put on performances within private houses.* He banned the castration of male persons and put a limit on the price of those eunuchs which were still held by slave-dealers.* On one occasion, when the vine crop was abundant but there was a shortage of corn, blaming the neglect of the crops on excessive devotion to viticulture, he decreed that no vines were to be planted in Italy and that in the provinces vines were to be torn up, leaving no more than half at most. However, he did not persist in enforcing this prescription. Some of the greatest offices he opened to both freedmen and Roman knights.* He prohibited the amalgamation of two legions into one camp, and ordered that no soldier could deposit more than one thousand sesterces at headquarters,* for it seemed that Lucius Antonius had planned his rebellion in the joint winter camp of two legions, relying particularly on the sum of money held as deposits. He increased the soldiers' annual pay by a quarter, adding three gold pieces.

[8] He applied himself conscientiously to the dispensing of justice, frequently holding additional hearings on the tribunal in the Forum. He overturned judgements of the centumviral courts* which had been influenced by bias. He repeatedly issued warnings against the arbiters not to validate unsubstantiated claims to free status. Jurors who took bribes he degraded along with all their colleagues. It was he who induced the tribunes of the plebs to prosecute a corrupt aedile for extortion and apply to the senate for judges. He devoted such concern to regulating the behaviour of both city magistrates and provincial officials that at no other time did they conduct themselves with more integrity and respect for justice, though since his reign we have seen many of them guilty of all sorts of crimes. Having undertaken the regulation of morals,* he curbed the disorder to be found in the theatres where the common people sat in the knights'

seats.* He put an end to the libellous verses commonly in circulation which blackened the characters of leading men and women, and imposed ignominious penalties on those responsible. He removed from the senate a man who had held the quaestorship because of his obsession with acting and dancing. To disgraced women he forbade the use of litters and made them ineligible to receive legacies and inheritances. He removed the name of a Roman knight from the list of jurors because he had taken back his wife whom he had previously divorced and accused of adultery.* He condemned a number of men of the senatorial and equestrian orders under the Scantinian law.* The desecration of Vestal Virgins, which had been overlooked by his father and brother, he punished through the application of different but severe penalties, at first through capital punishment, later on in the traditional way. For while he allowed the Oculata sisters and Varronilla to choose their own form of death and relegated their seducers, soon afterwards, when the senior Vestal Cornelia, who had been acquitted some time previously, was again, much later, accused and convicted, he ordered that she be buried alive and that her defilers should be beaten to death with rods in the Comitium, with the exception of a man of praetorian rank. This man, because he had confessed when the case against him was still doubtful and the exam- ination and torture of witnesses were inconclusive, Domitian let off with exile. And to show that no one could get away with defiling the cults of the gods, he had torn down by soldiers the monument which one of his freedmen had set up to his son, using stones intended for the construction of the temple of Capitoline Jupiter, and the bones and other remains which were in it were thrown into the sea.

[9] At the beginning he so abhorred any killing that while his father was still away from the city he would repeat a line of Virgil,

An impious race that slaughtered bullocks and feasted upon them,*

and give orders that no oxen should be sacrificed. He gave scarcely any grounds for being suspected of greed or avarice either before he became emperor or for some time during his reign. On the contrary, he often gave firm evidence not merely of integrity but even of liberality. Everyone around him he treated with generosity, advising them above all and with greatest insistence to do nothing meanly. When inheritances were left to him by people who had children, he would not accept them.* He even annulled a legacy in the will of

Rustius Caepio who had prescribed that his heir should every year give a particular sum to each senator as he entered the senate house. He dismissed the cases against those debtors whose names had been posted at the treasury for more than five years, and would only allow a case to be renewed within one year and on condition that an accuser whose suit was unsuccessful should himself be punished with exile. The scribes of the quaestors, who had been carrying on business which was in accordance with tradition but contrary to the Clodian law,* he pardoned for their past offences. Small plots of land, which were left over here and there after the assignment of farms to veterans, he ceded to their original owners by right of possession. False accusations which aimed at the confiscation of property he punished, imposing severe penalties on the accusers, and he is said to have remarked: 'The emperor who does not punish informers goads them on.'

[10] However, his disposition towards mercy and integrity did not continue, though his decline into cruelty was more rapid than his decline into greed. He had a pupil of the actor Paris killed, though he was still a boy and suffering from ill-health at the time, on the grounds that in appearance and in talent he had some resemblance to his teacher.* Hermogenes of Tarsus, also, because of some allusions in his 'History', he had crucified, even extending the punishment to those slaves who had written the work out. A householder, who had said that though the Thracian was a match for the *murmillo* he would not measure up to the giver of the games,* he had dragged from the audience and thrown to dogs in the arena, wearing the tag: 'A buckler-wearer with a big mouth.'*

He put to death many senators, including a number of consular rank, among them Civica Cerialis, who was at that very time pro-consul of Asia, also Salvidienus Orfitus and Acilius Gladrio, then in exile, on the grounds that they were planning a rebellion, while for the others the reason was in each case a trifling one: Aelius Lamia because of some suspicious jokes, though they were old ones and harmless; for when Domitian had stolen Lamia's wife* he had said, in reply to one who praised his voice: 'I practise continence'* and when Titus had urged him to marry again, he had replied: 'I hope you're not after a wife, too'; Salvius Cocceianus, because he had celebrated the birthday of the emperor Otho who was his paternal uncle; Mettius Pompusianus, because it was commonly reported that his birth-signs predicted empire and because he carried around a map of the world on parchment and copies of the speeches made by kings and generals in Livy, as well as giving two of his slaves the names Mago and Hannibal;* Sallustius Lucullus, a governor of Britain, because he had allowed a new variety of spear to be termed 'Lucullan'; Junius Rusticus, because he had published eulogies of Thrasea Paetus and Helvidius Priscus and called them the most virtuous of men.* When bringing this accusation, he also banished all philosophers from Rome and from Italy. He also had killed the younger Helvidius,* on the grounds that in a play he had written for the stage he had criticized Domitian's treatment of his wife through the characters of Paris and Oenone;* and Flavius Sabinus, a cousin on his father's side, on the grounds that on the day of the consular elections the herald had mistakenly announced him to the people as future emperor rather than consul.

However, after his victory in the civil war, his cruelty increased and, in order to track down any conspirators who were still in hiding, he had many of the opposing faction tortured, using a new kind of interrogation, inserting fire into their genitals; he even cut off the hands of a number of them. It is commonly agreed that he extended mercy only to two of the more prominent individuals, a tribune of senatorial rank and a centurion, who, in order to emphasize that they were not guilty of the crime, gave evidence that they had been used for other men's pleasures and for that reason could not command any respect on the part of the general or the soldiers.*

[11] But his cruelty was not only extreme but also ingenious and unpredictable. The day before he crucified one of his stewards, he invited the man into his bed-chamber, made him sit beside him on the couch, then sent him away happy and confident, having even deigned to share his supper with him. Intending to condemn on a capital charge a man of consular rank, Arrecinus Clemens, who was one of his friends and intermediaries, he favoured the man as much as before if not more, in the end asking him, as they were taking the air together and caught sight of the man who given information against him: 'Would you like us to hear this most wretched slave tomorrow?'

As a further abuse of people's endurance, he would never pronounce an especially dreadful sentence without first talking of clemency, so that there was no more certain indication of a hideous end

than the leniency of the preamble. Having brought certain men who
were charged with treason into the senate, he announced that he
would on that day discover how the senate valued him and thus
easily brought about the men's condemnation to the traditional
manner of punishment.* Then, alarmed at the cruelty of the penalty,
to lessen the ill-will which might result, he interceded with the
following words—for an exact quotation is of interest here: 'O senators, permit me to appeal to the respect you have for me, for I know
I am making a request you will grant with great difficulty, when I ask
that you allow these condemned men to choose the manner of their
deaths. For thus you will spare your own eyes and thus everyone will
know that I was present in this meeting of the senate.'

[12] Having exhausted his funds through expenditure on public
works and games, as well as his increases to the soldiers' pay, he
attempted to cut down military expenditure by reducing the number
of soldiers. But when he realized that this put him at the mercy of
the barbarians while he remained no less beset by financial burdens,
he had no hesitation in engaging in all manner of depredations.
Everywhere the goods of the living and of the dead were seized,
whatever the charge or the accuser. It was enough to allege some
kind of deed or word attacking the majesty of the emperor. The
estates of complete strangers were seized if one person could be
found who claimed to have heard the deceased, when living, say that
the emperor was his heir.* The tax on the Jews, in particular, was
exacted with the greatest rigour.* Those who lived as Jews without
being registered as such were indicted, as were those who concealed
their origins and did not pay the tax imposed on their race. I remember when I was a youth being present when an old man of ninety was
inspected by a procurator and a very crowded court, to see whether
he was circumcised.

From his youth his disposition was far from courteous; rather he
was presumptuous and unrestrained, both in his words and in his
deeds. When his father's concubine, Caenis, on returning from
Istria, went to kiss him as usual,* he offered her his hand. Angered
that his brother's son-in-law had attendants dressed in white as he
did, he pronounced:

Not good is a multitude of rulers.*

[13] Moreover, once he had become emperor he did not hesitate to

boast in the senate that it was he who had bestowed the empire on his father and brother* and they had simply returned what was his, nor to proclaim, when he took back his wife after their divorce, that she was recalled to his divine couch.* He was pleased to hear in the amphitheatre on the day of a banquet the cry: 'Blessings on our master and mistress!'* However, when during the Capitoline competition everyone joined with great accord in begging that he should restore Palfurius Sura, who had just won the crown for oratory, to the senate from which he had been removed some time ago, he did not deign to give any reply but simply had the herald demand silence.* With no less arrogance, when he was dictating a formal letter in the name of his procurators he would begin: 'Our master and god issues the following orders.' Thus after this it became customary for him always to be so addressed by everyone, even in writing and conversation. He would not allow statues of himself to be set up on the Capitol unless they were gold and of a particular weight. He put up so many vaulted passageways and arches on such a great scale, with four-horsed chariots and triumphal insignia, in every part of the city that on one of them someone wrote in Greek: 'Arci'.* He held the consulship on seventeen occasions,* which no one had done before him. Of these the seven middle ones were in successive years but all of them he held in name only, never continuing in office beyond the Kalends of May and often only until the Ides of January. After his two triumphs he took on the *cognomen* of Germanicus and changed the names of the months* of September and October to 'Germanicus' and 'Domitianus', using his own names, on the grounds that he had assumed power in the former and been born in the latter.

[14] By these means he made himself an object of terror and hatred to everyone and was finally brought down by a plot on the part of his friends and his most trusted freedmen, together with his wife. He had long ago had warning of the year and day of his death, and even of the hour and of the way he would die. When he was a youth Chaldaean astrologers had foretold all these things. Once, when at dinner he refused the mushrooms,* his father had openly laughed at him for being forgetful of his destiny in not rather fearing the sword. For this reason he was always fearful and anxious and the slightest grounds for suspicion disturbed him to an abnormal degree.* It is believed that he was induced to discount the edict he had made concerning the cutting down of vines* above all by the

pamphlets which appeared here and there with the following verse:

> Though you gnaw my roots, yet shall I still have juice,
> O goat, to pour on you, when you're the sacrifice.*

It was the same terror which made him refuse the senate's offer of a new and unprecedented honour, despite his usual passion for such things, when they decreed that whenever he held the consulship some Roman knights, chosen by lot, should precede him, along with his lictors and attendants, wearing the trabea* and carrying lances.

However, as the time when the danger was expected came closer, he became daily more anxious and had fitted with phengite stone* the walls of the porticoes where he used to walk, so that he would be able to see in the images reflected by the gleaming surface whatever was happening behind him. Most prisoners he would only hear in secret and alone, while keeping hold of their chains. And to convince the members of his household that a patron's death was not to be risked even on good grounds, he condemned to death Epaphroditus, his secretary in charge of petitions, because he was thought to have helped Nero to take his own life after the emperor was deserted.

[15] Finally, there was Flavius Clemens, his cousin on his father's side and a man of the most shameful idleness, whose young sons Domitian had only lately named publicly as his heirs, putting aside their former name, and calling one of them Vespasian and the other Domitian. He put Clemens to death all of a sudden, on the slightest grounds and when he had barely come to the end of his consulship. It was this deed in particular which precipitated his assassination.

Over a period of eight successive months so many lightning bolts occurred and were reported to him that he cried out: 'Let him now strike the man he wants.' The Capitol was struck and the Temple to the Flavian Line, as well as the Palatine residence and his own bed-chamber, while the inscription was torn from the base of his triumphal statue in a violent storm and fell onto a nearby tomb. The tree which had been thrown down when Vespasian was still a private citizen but had then put forth new growth, at that time suddenly fell down again.* Fortuna at Praeneste, who throughout his reign had been accustomed to give a favourable omen and always the same one, whenever he commended the new year to her, on the last occasion gave forth a most sinister omen, even including a reference to bloodshed.

He dreamt that Minerva, whose cult he most scrupulously observed, came out of her shrine and said that she could no longer watch over him, as she had been disarmed by Jupiter. However, nothing disturbed him more than the response he had from the astrologer Ascletarion and the man's subsequent fate. When this man was denounced by informers and did not deny that he had talked openly of things he had foreseen through his art, he was questioned by Domitian as to the manner of his own death. When he replied that he would shortly be torn apart by dogs, Domitian gave orders that he should be killed at once and that great care should be taken to see that he was cremated so as to prove his predictions unfounded. While these plans were being carried out it happened that the pyre was overturned by a sudden storm and the half-burnt body was torn to pieces by dogs. This, along with the other events of the day, was related to the emperor, as he dined, by an actor of Latin farces, who had happened to be passing by at the time.

[16] The day before he died he gave orders that the apples which had been brought to the table should be served on the following day, then added: 'If I shall be allowed to eat them.' He then turned to his neighbours and asserted that the next day the moon would be stained with blood in Aquarius and that an event would take place which people would talk of throughout the world. At around midnight he was so terrified that he jumped out of his bed. Then in the morning he heard the trial of a *haruspex*, sent from Germany, who when he was consulted about the lightning bolt had predicted a change of rulers, and condemned him. And when he was scratching an ulcerated wart on his forehead rather fiercely and blood flowed from it, he exclaimed: 'If only this were all!' Finally, when he asked what the time was, they told him deliberately that it was the sixth rather than the fifth hour, which was the one he feared. Delighted at these words, and thinking the danger past, he was hurrying off to take a bath when Parthenius, who was in charge of his bedchamber, made him change his mind, telling him there was a man who had come about some important matter which could not be put off. And so all his attendants withdrew and he retired into his bed-chamber where he was killed.

[17] The details which circulated concerning the manner of the plot and the assassination were essentially as follows. When the conspirators were undecided as to when and how they were going

to attack, whether when the emperor was washing or at dinner, Stephanus, Domitilla's steward,* who was at that time under suspicion of embezzlement, suggested the plan of action. In order to avert suspicion, he kept his left arm wrapped up in woollen bandages for a number of days as though it were injured, concealing a dagger in them when the appointed hour approached. Next, claiming to have evidence of a conspiracy, he gained admission to the emperor, stabbing the astonished Domitian in the stomach as he read the document which had been handed to him. As the emperor was wounded and struggling he was attacked by Clodianus, a centurion's adjutant, Maximus, Parthenius' freedman, and Satur, a senior member of the bed-chamber staff, together with someone from the gladiatorial school, who butchered him with seven wounds. A boy, who witnessed the assassination as he was going about his usual business in the bed-chamber, tending to the cult of the Lares, related the following additional details: as soon as the first blow was struck he had been ordered by Domitian to bring him the dagger which was hidden in the cushions and to call the servants, but he had found nothing but the hilt at the head of the bed, while all the doors were locked. In the mean time the emperor had laid hold of Stephanus and brought him to the ground, struggling with him for some time, while he tried now to wrest the weapon from him and now to gouge out his eyes, despite the lacerations to his fingers. He was killed on the fourteenth day before the Kalends of October in the forty-fifth year of his life and the fifteenth of his reign.* His corpse was brought out on a common bier by those who carry the bodies of the poor. His funeral was taken care of by his old nurse,* Phyllis, at her suburban villa on the Latin Way. However, she secretly brought his remains to the Temple of the Flavian Line and mixed his ashes with those of Julia, Titus' daughter,* whom she had also brought up.

[18] He was tall in stature, modest in his expression, and prone to blushing. His eyes were large, though his sight was not good. Indeed, especially in his youth, he was attractive and graceful in every particular, apart from his feet, for his toes were rather curled in. Later he was further disfigured as he went bald and acquired a large stomach, while his legs grew thin, weakened as a result of a long illness. He was so well aware of the advantage he gained from his modesty of expression that he once had boasted in the senate: 'Certainly, thus far you have approved both my disposition and my looks.' He was so

annoyed by his baldness that he took it as a personal insult if anyone else was teased or mocked on that account.* However, in an essay on haircare which he published and dedicated to a friend, he added the following words, as a consolation to his friend and himself: ' "Do you not see how tall and handsome I am, too?"* Yet the same fate lies in store for my own hair. With fortitude I endure the ageing of my hair while still young. Be sure that nothing is more pleasing than beauty or more transient.'

[19] He would not tolerate physical effort and rarely went about the city on foot, nor did he often ride a horse when on the march or in battle but would generally be carried in a litter.* He had no interest in exercises with arms but was very keen on archery.* At his Alban retreat many people witnessed him shoot a hundred animals of different kinds on numerous occasions and he would even deliberately shoot at the heads of some of them in such a way that two arrows seemed to make horns. Sometimes a slave would stand at a distance holding up the palm of his right hand as a target with the fingers outspread and Domitian would aim his shots with such skill that they would pass safely through the gaps between the boy's fingers.

[20] At the start of his reign he paid little attention to the liberal arts,* although when some libraries were destroyed by fire, he took care to have them restored at enormous expense, procuring copies of texts from all over the place and sending people to Alexandria* to make fresh copies and correct others. However, he never expended any effort on reading history or poetry or even on the writing demanded by his duties. He used to reread nothing beyond the notebooks and records of Tiberius Caesar.* For the composition of letters, orations, and edicts he relied on the skills of others. Yet his speech was not inelegant and sometimes he even produced noteworthy remarks: 'How I wish', he said, 'I were as handsome as Maecius thinks he is.' And he compared the head of a man whose hair was partly reddish and partly white to 'snow on which mead had been poured'. [21] He used to say that the situation of emperors was a most wretched one, for everyone thought their suspicions of conspiracy groundless until they were killed.

Whenever he was at liberty he enjoyed playing dice,* even on working days and during the morning. He would take baths early and lunched until he was full, so that often at dinner he would have no more than a Matian apple* and a drink of wine from a jug. He often threw large parties but quickly brought them to a close; certainly, he never continued them beyond sunset or followed them with drinking. For before he went to bed he would do nothing but walk about alone in a secluded place.

[22] A man of excessive lusts, he used to refer to his constant sexual activity as 'bed-wrestling', as if it were some form of exercise. There was also a rumour that he would himself depilate his mistresses and that he used to go swimming with the commonest prostitutes. After stubbornly refusing his brother's daughter who was offered to him in marriage, when she was still a virgin, because he was still caught up in his union with Domitia, he was ready enough to seduce her not long afterwards when she was married to someone else, even though Titus was still living at the time. Soon, when she had lost her husband and her father, he loved her passionately and openly and was even the cause of her death, when he forced her to abort a child she had conceived by him.

[23] His assassination was a matter of indifference to the common people but a source of gravest dismay to the soldiers who immediately called out for him to be deified and would have attempted to avenge him, if they had had leaders. Indeed, this objective was achieved not long afterwards following repeated demands that those responsible for the murder be punished. The senators, by contrast, were so delighted that they eagerly filled the senate house and did not refrain from attacking the dead man in the most abusive and ferocious outbursts, giving orders that ladders should be brought and his shields and images be torn down and dashed to the ground while they looked on, and finally they decreed that his names were to be everywhere erased and that all reminders of him were to be destroyed.*

A few months before he was killed a raven on the Capitol cried out: 'All will be well!' an omen which some people interpreted as follows:

> A raven sitting on the Tarpeian heights not long ago
> Could not cry out 'all is' but cried 'all will be well'.

They say that even Domitian himself dreamt that a golden hump grew out of his back and he understood this as a certain indication that the condition of the state would be happier and more prosperous after his time, as indeed happened shortly afterwards through the self-control and integrity of the subsequent emperors.

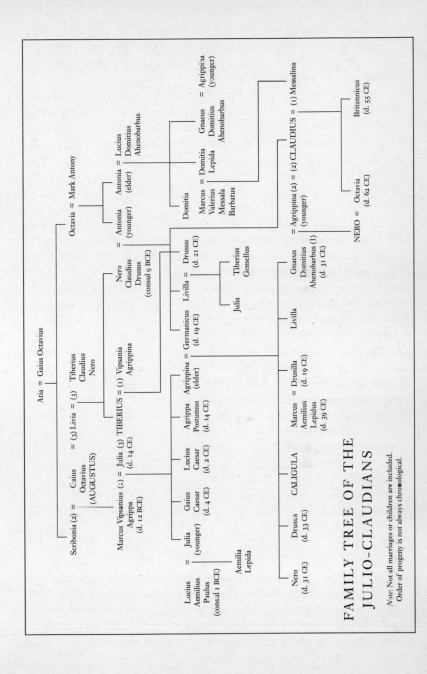

FAMILY TREE OF THE JULIO-CLAUDIANS

Note: Not all marriages or children are included. Order of progeny is not always chronological.

EXPLANATORY NOTES

The following abbreviations are used:

Aug.	*The Deified Augustus*
Cal.	*Caligula*
Claud.	*The Deified Claudius*
Dom.	*Domitian*
Jul.	*The Deified Julius Caesar*
Tib.	*Tiberius*
Vesp.	*The Deified Vespasian*
Vit.	*Vitellius*

For explanation of technical terms, ranks, etc. see the Glossary

THE DEIFIED JULIUS CAESAR

3 *lost his father*: according to Suetonius' chronology, Caesar was born in 100 BCE, while his father died in 85 or 84. There is considerable debate about his date of birth.

divorced Cossutia: the Flamen Dialis, was not permitted to divorce his wife and had to be married but it seems Caesar was never formally inaugurated into the office.

many Mariuses: the great general Marius, many times consul, had been Sulla's greatest rival and was married to Caesar's paternal aunt Julia.

Marcus Lepidus' measures: Lepidus, who with Catulus was consul in 78 BCE, tried to repeal some of Sulla's laws but was overthrown by Catulus and Pompey.

4 *a charge of extortion against Cornelius Dolabella*: members of the Roman élite regularly brought such charges against one another, in part, at least, as an opportunity to display their own rhetorical skills.

the leading teacher of oratory: probably 74 BCE. See ch. 55 below for Caesar's oratorical skills.

the punishment with which he had often jokingly threatened them: crucifixion, according to ch. 74 below.

after the consul's death: Sertorius and his supporters had held out in Spain for the cause of Marius 77–73 BCE.

his aunt Julia: the widow of Marius.

5 *Ancus Marcius*: Caesar's grandfather, C. Julius Caesar, was married to a Marcia. Ancus Marcius was the fourth king of Rome.

the profaning of rituals: the festival was that of the Bona Dea ('Good Goddess') from which men were excluded (see also ch. 74 below). Cicero was much exercised by Clodius' alleged sacrilege. Cf. his letter *To Atticus* 1. 12–16.

5 *Alexander had already conquered the world*: cf. *Aug.* 18.

some Latin colonies . . . full citizenship: the Gallic towns beyond the river Po (i.e. 'Transpadane'), including Verona, Comum, and Cremona.

Publius Sulla: nephew of the dictator, Lucius Sulla.

consular elections: held in 66 BCE to elect consuls for 65. A rather different version of the plot appears in Sallust, *Catiline* 18.

6 *the Ambrani and the Transpadanes*: the Ambrani were a tribe in Liguria. For the Transpadanes see note to p. 5 above.

displayed in great profusion: it seems to have been customary for aediles to erect such temporary structures around the Forum (though not on the Capitoline hill) to display materials associated with the games which they were responsible for providing.

termed ally and friend by the senate: according to Caesar himself (*Civil War* 3. 107. 2), Ptolemy did not receive this title, the regular term for a dependent king, until 59 BCE. Ptolemy's expulsion seems not to have occurred until 58 or 57.

7 *prosecutions for murder*: as *iudex quaestionis* (president of the court), an office held by Caesar between the aedileship and the praetorship.

proscriptions: under Sulla (partly in revenge for the massacres instigated by Marius in 87 and 82), many of his enemies had been declared outlaws, so that their property was confiscated and rewards were offered for their deaths in 82–81 BCE.

Gaius Rabirius: the accusation was brought under the ancient and practically obsolete form of trial by *duumviri perduellionis* (described by Livy 1. 26). In 63 BCE Rabirius was defended by Cicero (*On Behalf of Rabirius*). The details of the trial remain unclear.

the harshness of his judge: Caesar was one of a commission of two men appointed by lot to try cases of high treason. Appeals against his decision could be made to the people.

a province: presumably the special command of Egypt referred to in ch. 11.

he won more votes . . . overall: at this time, seventeen tribes (each associated with a particular region of Italy or part of Rome) were eligible to vote (there were thirty-five voting tribes in total). A candidate would generally count on the support of his own tribe.

When . . . than he had intended: as consul elect, Silanus would have been asked to give his opinion first. Senators were invited to speak in order of seniority. After the debate, different opinions were put to the vote. For a clear modern account see T. P. Wiseman, 'The Peasants' Revolt and the Bankrupts' Plot', in *Cambridge Ancient History*, ix (2nd edn., Cambridge, 1994), 346–58.

the consul: the famous orator, Marcus Tullius Cicero.

8   *the first day of his praetorship*: 1 January 62.

the restoration of the Capitoline: the temple of Jupiter had been damaged
in a fire of 83. The new temple, bearing Catulus' name as restorer, was
dedicated in 69.

someone else: Pompey, according to other sources.

their attendance . . . his measures: Caesar had taken advantage of the fact
that it was customary for friends of the new consuls to accompany them
to their homes, after they had offered the sacrifice with which they
embarked on their year of office on 1 January (thus they were not around
when he began his attack on Catulus).

decree of the senate: Suetonius is the only source to state that the decree
applied to Caesar.

9   *once he was out of office*: as magistrate or pro-magistrate (provincial
governor), Caesar would be immune from civil prosecution.

he was obliged . . . excluded from the consulship: as holder of *imperium* a
general had to wait outside the sacred boundary of the city (the *pomerium*) to be granted a triumph by the senate. Once he had given up his
imperium he could enter the city without waiting for permission—but
would no longer be eligible to celebrate a triumph.

Even Cato . . . the good of the state: Cato was famously opposed to the use
of bribery in elections. Cf. Plutarch, *Younger Cato* 44 and 49.

woodland and pastures: in charge of the woodland and pastures of Italy,
Caesar would, of course, have no army under his command.

10 *the lictors would follow behind him*: according to tradition there was
originally only one set of lictors which each of the consuls used in turn.
Later, it seems, each consul was given a set of lictors who would walk
before him. Caesar altered this procedure for those months in which his
colleague held the fasces and was therefore in charge of public business.

adverse omens: public business could be interrupted by a magistrate's
announcement that he had observed adverse omens in the sky.

did nothing . . . omens: thus technically nullifying all Caesar's subsequent
legislation.

tax-collecting contracts: the Roman state delegated the collection of taxes
to private tax-collectors who would bid for the contract. If they bid too
high in their attempt to secure the contract, they might have difficulties
recovering their costs.

his veto: other sources suggest he was objecting to Caesar's land laws.

11 *at the ninth hour of the same day*: that is, after the usual close of business.
Clodius, as a member of a patrician family, had not been eligible to stand
for election as tribune of the plebs. Cicero and Clodius fell out after
Cicero gave evidence against Clodius when he was on trial in 61 BCE for
appearing disguised as a woman at the Bona Dea festival in 62.

11 *'long-haired' Gaul also*: this term is sometimes used to refer to the area of Gaul outside Roman control. Here Suetonius appears to use it to mean Gaul beyond the Alps, as opposed to 'Cisalpine', on 'this' side of the Alps.

mounting on their heads: a claim which could also be take in an obscene sense, as the response indicates. Threats of oral rape were a regular feature of the Roman political vocabulary.

And when someone . . . a large part of Asia: for allegations that Caesar had taken a passive 'feminine' sexual role in relations with Nicomedes, cf. chs. 2, 49, and 52. Such claims were not uncommon against powerful Romans (see Introduction for further discussion of this). Suetonius also lists in ch. 45 details of Caesar's dress and self-presentation which might be construed as 'effeminate'. Semiramis was a famous queen of Assyria. The Amazons were a mythical race of female warriors associated with the region of Pontus.

12 *a candidate for the consulship*: for the year 55.

he added . . . the Alauda: such enrolments of non-citizens in the legions are not previously recorded.

After that . . . enemies and barbarous peoples: a very different view is offered in Caesar's own account, *The Gallic War*.

ought to be handed over to the enemy: on the grounds that his actions had been in breach of natural justice. According to Plutarch, Cato made this proposal in 55, claiming Caesar had breached an armistice (*Younger Cato* 51. 1). Caesar himself claimed it was the enemy who had broken the armistice (*Gallic War* 4. 1–16).

days of supplication: a supplication was a public thanksgiving which took the form of prayers at all the temples in Rome, often accompanied by processions.

nine years: 58–49 BCE.

Mount Cebenna: modern Cévennes.

13 *the murder of Publius Clodius*: early in 52 at the hands of thugs associated with his enemy, Milo.

he persuaded them . . . before the campaign was rounded off: returning to Rome as consul rather than as a private citizen, Caesar would be immune from prosecution for his actions while in Gaul.

a forum . . . a hundred million sesterces: the Forum Iulium, adjoining the Forum Romanum. This was later completed by Augustus.

something which no one had ever done before: previously only men had received such honours.

whenever famous gladiators . . . kept for him: this must refer to gladiators who were defeated and whom the spectators had not opted to save from death at the hands of their opponents.

14 *He doubled . . . in perpetuity*: probably a reference to the legions raised by

Caesar himself. The senate's authority would be needed for such a measure in relation to the state legions.

he offered him as wife Octavia, his sister's granddaughter: Pompey declined the offer.

15 *intervention on his behalf by the tribunes of the plebs*: when the senate decreed that Caesar should disband his army, the tribunes Mark Antony and Quintus Cassius vetoed it (cf. Caesar, *Civil War* 1. 2. 6–7). The senate ignored the veto and the tribunes were forced to flee.

16 *Others say . . . during his first consulship*: cf. chs. 20 and 21 above.

Milo: prosecuted for the murder of Publius Clodius, who was very popular with the poorer inhabitants of Rome. Pompey surrounded the court with armed men in order to secure Milo's conviction.

Asinius Pollio's account: Pollio was with Caesar at the crossing of the Rubicon and at Pharsalus. He wrote a history of the civil war in seventeen books which has not survived.

'On Duties': 3. 82. The quotation comes from Euripides' *Phoenissae* 524.

17 *It is even thought . . . four hundred thousand sesterces*: the gold ring was worn only by knights and senators. To qualify a man needed to own property of at least 400,000 sesterces.

Corfinium: a town of the Paeligni in central Italy, modern Pelino.

Brundisium: modern Brindisi.

18 *Pharsalus*: in central Thessaly.

sons of Pompey: Gnaeus and Sextus.

Gaius Antonius: brother of Mark Antony.

the same month: in 46 BCE.

19 *after the defeat of the sons of Pompey*: in 45.

the speed with which it was completed: cf. Suetonius' comments on the speed with which Caesar defeated Pharnaces in ch. 35.

In a gladiatorial fight . . . to the finish: public performance in gladiatorial and theatrical entertainments (though not circus races) was considered degrading and inappropriate for members of the élite, who might be punished with the loss of their privileged status. Some were nevertheless attracted to participate by the associated glamour—or money. Cf. Suetonius' remarks in *Aug.* 43, *Nero.* 4.

a Pyrrhic dance: a war dance in armour.

five hundred thousand sesterces and a golden ring: thus restoring the equestrian status Laberius had lost by appearing on stage.

the fourteen rows: since 67, it had been the privilege of knights (and senators) to sit in the front fourteen rows.

20 *the Troy game*: see Glossary.

20 *the lesser Codeta*: a marshy area on the banks of the Tiber across from the
Campus Martius.

the calendar . . . a long period of time: it was the duty of the *pontifices* to
ensure the calendar remained in sync with the seasons, by adding an extra
month from time to time (to compensate for the fact that the lunar
calendar year of 355 days was slightly shorter than the solar year). Since
magistracies coincided with the calendar year, the length of a particular
year was of material interest both to magistrates in power and to their
rivals.

He increased . . . the senate: both by adding new members and by restoring
those who had been expelled. According to Dio (43. 47. 2), he had raised
the number to 900 by 45 BCE.

made new appointments . . . patricians: presumably replacing families who
had died out. Certain priesthoods could only be held by patricians.

the number of . . . magistrates: the increased number of provinces requiring governors and other staff provoked a need for more ex-magistrates to
take these posts. By 44 the number of praetors was sixteen per year. The
number of quaestors had risen to forty by 45.

censors: for instance, in 50 when many had been struck from the senate by
the censor Appius Claudius (and had subsequently given their support to
Caesar).

electoral corruption: Pompey had introduced a new law on electoral
corruption in 52.

21 *to compete for office*: Sulla had passed a law debarring the sons of those he
proscribed from office. For the proscriptions, see note to p. 7 above.

which had been the third: this category of men had provided a third of the
judges since 70. The qualifications for the category remain unclear. Such
men were apparently of lesser status than Roman knights.

forty: 'ten' (the figure in the manuscript) makes little sense. Probably the
text is corrupt here. Scholars have suggested instead a more plausible age
such as 'forty'.

guilds . . . of ancient foundation: these were guilds, associations, or clubs
sometimes made up of those who worked in the same professions, sometimes for religious or burial purposes. They had been abolished in 64 on
the grounds that they were seedbeds of political disruption, then
reinstated by a law proposed by Publius Clodius in 58. The exception
here may refer to the synagogues of the Jews which were respected for
their antiquity.

according to Cicero: allusion unknown.

22 *a temple to Mars . . . just by the Tarpeian rock*: neither of these projects
was completed.

Marcus Varro: author of many books and with a reputation for great
learning. This project, too, was not fulfilled.

to drain the Pontine marshes . . . if he had first tested their forces: these projects also were not embarked upon. Augustus' extension of the via Salaria could be seen as carrying out Caesar's project here. Later, Caligula and Nero tried unsuccessfully to dig through the Isthmus of Corinth (cf. *Cal.* 21; *Nero* 19). The Parthians were to be approached with caution after the disaster suffered by Crassus in 53. Caesar was planning a campaign against them when he was assassinated in 44.

23 *had his body hair plucked out . . . disapproval*: for men to have their body hair removed was often seen as a sign of effeminacy (though a century after Caesar's time, the younger Seneca implies it was proper for men to have hair removed from their armpits but not from their legs; *Letters*: 114. 14).

fringed sleeves down to his wrists: both the length of the sleeves and the fringes were associated with effeminacy. Cf. Aulus Gellius, *Attic Nights* 7. 12. 1.

belted . . . rather loosely: a belt was not usually worn with the senator's broad-striped tunic. Belts were worn with ordinary tunics—but to wear a belt loose was regarded as a sign of effeminacy.

Subura: an area between the Forum and the Esquiline, largely, it seems, inhabited by the poor.

bread . . . different from that which was served to himself: Roman moralists regularly express disapproval of hosts who eat better food than that offered to their guests.

24 *I shall not discuss*: Suetonius' use of the trope of *praeteritio* (mentioning something while self-righteously claiming to be leaving it out) is particularly flagrant in this section.

as they march behind the chariot: the soldiers' mockery of their triumphant general has been seen as having the function of repelling the envy of the gods, on an occasion when Roman generals came close to assuming godlike status.

25 *having divorced . . . Aegisthus*: Pompey divorced his wife Mucia on the grounds of her unfaithfulness during his absence. The reference to Aegisthus implies that Caesar was one of her lovers, since, in Greek mythology, Aegisthus was the lover of Clytemnestra, wife of the great general Agamemnon who led the Greeks against Troy.

daughter in marriage: Julia, whom Pompey married in 59. Cf. ch. 21.

Tertia: in Latin, *tertia* means a third.

Bogud: one of the African kings supported by Caesar as opponents of Juba, who sided with Pompey.

Naso: M. Actorius Naso, also mentioned in ch. 9 above.

he welcomed her to Rome: other sources (e.g. Dio, *Roman History* 43. 27. 3) suggest Cleopatra arrived in Rome in 46.

The child . . . were aware of this: the child's name was Caesarion. His paternity became a more contentious political issue after Caesar's death.

Octavian (Caesar's heir and adopted son) and his supporters wished to deny Caesarion's claim to be Caesar's true son, while Antony, disputing Octavian's position, had a vested interest in backing Caesarion. Matius and Oppius were Roman knights who were agents of Caesar. Oppius' memoirs were used by both Suetonius and Plutarch in writing about Caesar.

25 *tribune of the plebs*: in 44 BCE.

26 *governor in Spain*: 61–60 BCE.

three thousand sesterces a pound: much less than the usual price, it seems.

During his first consulship . . . gilded bronze: this may be a version of the story told by Appian (*Civil Wars* 2. 41), according to which Caesar in 49 raided the Treasury of Saturn, taking gold deposited there at the time of the Gallic invasion in the early fourth century. There was a curse on anyone who used it except for a Gallic war.

Dolabella: see ch. 4 and note to p. 4.

Cicero . . . ample: Cicero, *Brutus* 261.

27 *Caesar Strabo*: a cousin of Julius. Aedile in 90 BCE, he was also a writer of tragedies.

common opponents: cf. ch. 16.

it was the latter . . . the Gallic war: apparently completing both books 7 and 8 of *The Gallic War*.

'The "Commentaries" . . . pen to paper': Cicero, *Brutus* 262.

'They are so much approved . . . how easily and quickly he did it': *The Gallic War* 8, preface 5–6.

28 *'On Analogy'*: this work survives only in a few fragments. Part of an ongoing debate about grammar, it seems to have argued in favour of standardization.

speeches in criticism of Cato: after the death of Cato at Utica, Cicero wrote a speech in praise of Cato. Caesar responded with a speech against. Only a few fragments survive.

across the scroll: the exact nature of this innovation is not clear.

letters to Cicero: a small number of these survive in Cicero's collection *To his Friends*.

Augustus prohibited publication of any of these works: Augustus, whose initial claim to power was largely based on his status as adopted son of the Deified Julius, seems to have taken some care to control Caesar's reputation.

29 *omens*: Caesar's disregard for omens indirectly causes his downfall in ch. 81 below.

his expedition against Scipio and Juba: cf. ch. 35 above.

the victim . . . sacrifice: this would normally be interpreted as a bad omen.

Salvito . . . he led: according to the elder Pliny, he was so named after a particular mime-actor (actors were considered very disreputable), *Natural Histories* 7. 54; 35. 8.

30 *military cloak*: the crimson cloak worn by commanders.

31 *dripping with perfume*: contrast *Vesp.* 8.

'*comrades*': contrast *Aug.* 25.

the Titurian disaster: see ch. 25 above.

Dyrrhachium: see ch. 36 above.

32 *a hundred and thirty thousand*: Caesar himself gives more modest figures; see *Civil War* 3. 52–3.

Cynegirus: at the battle of Marathon; see Herodotus, *History* 6. 114. Cynegirus was the brother of the playwright Aeschylus.

Placentia: modern Piacenza.

When the men . . . due to receive: this incident is described in detail by Appian 2. 92.

Masintha: the name seems to be Numidian. He may have been a son of King Hiarbas (an ally of the Marians) whom Pompey (on Sulla's orders) had deposed in favour of Hiempsal.

King Juba's son: Hiempsal was the son of Juba.

33 *after his praetorship*: that is, in 61.

the lictors with their fasces: the praetor setting out for his province would be attended by lictors as well as his own friends and clients.

when he sought the consulship: on Memmius, see ch. 49 above.

When Gaius Calvus . . . a letter of his own: Gaius Licinius Calvus was a friend of the poet Catullus. See ch. 49 above.

Mamurra . . . reputation: Mamurra was Caesar's *praefectus fabrorum* (overseer of works) and had allegedly acquired great wealth through Caesar's favour. See Catullus' poems 29 and 57.

the pirates . . . strangled first: see ch. 4 above.

during the time . . . delivered to Sulla: see ch. 1 above on Caesar's need to take refuge from Sulla.

without further punishment: a slave who tried to murder his master would normally be crucified.

34 *When he was summoned . . . free of crime*: see ch. 6 above and note to p. 7 above.

When conditions of surrender . . . committed against him: for a more detailed (and somewhat different) account of this, see Caesar, *Civil Wars* 1. 74–6.

none of the Pompeians . . . young Lucius Caesar: Faustus Cornelius Sulla was son of the dictator Sulla. Lucius Caesar was a distant relative of Julius. Other sources, e.g. Appian 2. 100 and Plutarch, *Caesar* 53. 3, record that many more were killed.

34 *which had been broken up by the common people*: when news came of the battle of Pharsalus (Dio 42. 18. 2).

35 *Pitholaus*: a freedman of Pompey.

one consulship after another: having already held the consulship in 59 and 48, Caesar was again consul in 46, in 45 (without a colleague), and in 44 (which was to have been first in a run of ten consulships).

responsibility for morals: conferred in 46 for three years (Dio 43.14), this effectively made him censor, a powerful post with particular responsibility for the composition of the senate.

a statue displayed with those of the kings: these statues were located on the Capitol, along with a statue of Brutus who had driven the last king out of Rome.

the procession for the circus games: the procession, which went from the Capitol via the Velabrum and Forum Boarium to the Circus Maximus, traditionally included litters on which statues of the gods were displayed.

a couch: of a kind on which statues of the gods were displayed.

a priest: Mark Antony held this priesthood.

an extra college of Luperci: there were previously just two colleges of Luperci, the priests responsible for the February festival in honour of the god Lupercus.

a month of the year named after him: the seventh month of the year was renamed July.

in each of these two years . . . during his absence: other sources give different accounts of these constitutional arrangements.

Rufio: a typical slave name.

Titus Ampius: one of Pompey's supporters, recalled from exile in 46.

36 *heart*: Caesar here plays on the double meaning of *cor*, 'heart', which was also regarded as the seat of intelligence. On Caesar's disregard for omens more generally, see ch. 59 above.

Pontius Aquila: later involved in the conspiracy against Caesar.

the Latin festival: an ancient festival of the Latin league in honour of Jupiter, held on the Alban Mount outside Rome.

a white ribbon: an emblem of royalty.

not King but Caesar: 'Rex'—'King'—was also a Roman family name.

the Lupercalia: on 15 February. The festival was by this time particularly associated with Caesar. See ch. 76 above.

the consul Antony . . . Jupiter Best and Greatest: other sources give somewhat different accounts of this incident. Appian (2. 109) and Plutarch (*Caesar* 61) record that Caesar twice refused the crown, Nicolaus of Damascus (21) that a man called Licinius first put the crown at Caesar's feet and Cassius put it on his knee. In Dio (49. 19. 4) Antony is made to offer the crown to Caesar as a way of forcing Caesar to turn it down. Shakespeare's *Julius Caesar* offers a memorable reworking of the incident.

37 *the Board of Fifteen*: the college of priests who had charge of the oracular Sibylline books.

the Parthians . . . 'king': Caesar was planning a campaign against Parthia in 44.

the broad stripe: an emblem of senatorial rank.

Lucius Brutus: famous for driving out the kings of Rome and becoming the republic's first consul.

the bridge: the raised gangway over which the voters passed.

on the Sacred Way: Caesar's official residence as Pontifex Maximus was located here.

Pompey's Senate Chamber: part of the theatre complex Pompey had constructed in 55 with the spoils of his eastern triumphs.

38 *the colony of Capua*: founded under Caesar's law of 59–58.

Capys: Virgil makes Capys a companion of Aeneas from Troy and founder of Capua (*Aeneid* 10. 145); Livy makes him king of Alba Longa (1. 3. 8).

a king's bird: probably a wren.

a dream . . . Jupiter: cf. the dream of Caligula described in *Cal.* 57.

pediment: usually only temples had pediments but one of the honours bestowed on Caesar (according to Florus, *Epitome* 4. 2. 91) was that of having one on his house.

the fifth hour: around 11 a.m.—the senate usually met earlier.

39 *into the Tiber*: cf. *Tib.* 75 and *Vit.* 17.

the Ides of September of the previous year: 13 September 45.

his sisters' grandsons . . . the rest: Gaius Octavius (later Augustus) was the grandson of Caesar's younger sister; Lucius Pinarius and Quintus Pedius were the grandsons of two different husbands of Caesar's elder sister.

40 *heirs of the second rank*: these would only inherit if the first-rank heirs died or refused the inheritance. Cf. *Aug.* 101 and note to p. 78.

Julia: Caesar's daughter and Pompey's wife (see chs. 21 and 50 above). Burial within the Campus Martius was a signal honour. That of Julia was apparently highly controversial (cf. Plutarch, *Pompey* 53).

the temple of Venus Genetrix: the temple in the Forum Julium, built by Caesar, whose family claimed descent from Venus.

some songs . . . from Atilius' 'Electra': the text is uncertain here. The author referred to may be Acilius or Atilius. The latter, known to have been a writer of plays, is perhaps more likely. Roman audiences were highly sensitized to the potential of plays, even those written long previously, to resonate with contemporary events.

40 *the flute-players and the actors*: musicians usually led the funeral procession, which would also include actors and dancers. For an example of the entertainment actors might offer on such an occasion see *Vesp*. ch. 19.

41 *the Jews*: Caesar had allowed the Jews special privileges, according to Josephus, *Jewish Antiquities* 14. 8–10.

Helvius Cinna: tribune of the plebs and a supporter of Caesar. Cf. ch. 52 above.

Xenophon: *Education of Cyrus* 8. 7. Cyrus was founder of the Persian empire.

the fifty-sixth year of his life: sources disagree about Caesar's exact age.

42 *the eleventh hour*: about an hour before sunset.

THE DEIFIED AUGUSTUS

43 *Velitrae*: about 20 miles south of Rome (modern name Velletri).

minor families: i.e. those who were not patricians but of plebeian rank.

The family . . . to the patriciate: Suetonius' account here is inconsistent with what is known of the senatorial élite in the earliest period of Roman history from other ancient sources. Livy's account implies that in the time of the kings only patricians could be senators. It is also highly unlikely that an entire family could change status from patrician to plebeian.

during the Second Punic War: 205 BCE.

44 *other services . . . elections in the Campus Martius*: presumably these related to the conduct of elections and were not wholly respectable.

the gang of runaway slaves . . . around Thurii: 60 BCE. Spartacus led a rebellion of slave gladiators in 73–71 BCE; the aristocrat Catiline was leader of a conspiracy suppressed 63–62.

Bessi: a mountain tribe in Thrace.

Cicero . . . our allies: Cicero, *To his Brother Quintus* 1. 2. 7.

displayed many senatorial portraits: a family with senatorial ancestors would display portraits of them in the entrance hall of the house.

the twenty-man commission . . . the Julian law: 59 BCE. Cf. *Jul*. 20.

45 *eight days before the Kalends of October*: 23 September 63. It is not known which part of the Palatine was known as Ox Heads.

the emperor: Hadrian.

46 *Ennius*: Quintus Ennius (239–169) was one of Rome's leading epic poets before Virgil. The line is from his *Annals* (502, Vahlen, edn. 2).

when his great-uncle . . . a serious illness: in 46.

47 *tribunes of the plebs . . . not a senator*: this magistracy was restricted to those of plebeian family. Since the time of Sulla only senators were eligible.

48 *he should be honoured then disposed of*: Cicero, *Letters to his Friends* 11. 20. 1. Cicero seems to have been punning on the double meaning of the Latin verb *tollo*, 'to raise' and 'to put out of the way'.

in two battles . . . Antony's wing: in 42.

mora: a game whereby one person suddenly raises his fingers and the other must at once guess how many.

49 *Perusia*: modern Perugia, a town in Umbria.

both before the war and during it: in 41.

the orders: i.e. senators and knights.

the capture of Perusia: in 40.

the Sicilian war: 43–35 BCE.

50 *Others criticize . . . festival procession*: it is no doubt relevant that Sextus Pompeius presented himself as the 'son of Neptune' according to Dio 48. 48.

Paulus' father: Marcus Lepidus the triumvir's elder brother, Lucius Aemilius Paulus, proscribed by the triumvirs in 43.

Circeii: a seaside town south of Rome.

51 *Gnaeus*: the name wrongly appears as Titus in the manuscripts.

Bononia: modern Bologna.

Actium: in 31.

the Ceraunian mountains: in northeastern Epirus.

Psylli: an African people known for their skill in dealing with snakes.

52 *Alexander the Great . . . for him to see*: compare the references to Alexander in *Jul.* 7, also *Aug.* 50 and 94.

Lepidus: Marcus Aemilius Lepidus, son of the triumvir Lepidus.

the emperor's granddaughter: Julia, daughter of Augustus' daughter Julia.

the foreign wars . . . the defeat of Antony: in 35–33 and 26–25.

53 *the River Albis*: the River Elbe.

Marcus Crassus and Mark Antony: Crassus lost his standards at Carrhae in 53, Antony his when his officers were defeated in 40 and 36.

on only two occasions: the doors of the temple of Janus Quirinus were believed to have been closed in the time of the legendary King Numa and in 235 with the conclusion of the First Punic War.

54 *Lollius . . . Varus*: in 17 or 16 BCE, and 9 CE respectively.

every tenth man . . . barley: 'decimation' was a traditional form of punishment in the Roman army. Soldiers' rations normally included wheat rather than barley.

ten-foot measuring poles or even a lump of turf: these were associated with the common soldiers' tasks of measuring off the camp or building the ramparts and thus would have been humiliating for officers.

55 *sons*: i.e. his grandsons, sons by adoption. See *Aug.* 64.

'comrades'. . . *the dignity of his own family*: contrast *Jul.* 67.

his naval victory: Agrippa and Augustus defeated Sextus Pompeius at Naulochus in 36 BCE.

'make haste slowly!'; 'A safe commander's better than a bold one': both these phrases are given in Greek.

The consulship . . . the army: in 43 BCE.

56 *His second consulship . . . the eleventh time*: 33, 31, 30–23 BCE.

he accepted it for the twelfth time . . . the thirteenth time: 5 and 2 BCE.

He did not begin them all in Rome: it was almost unprecedented for a consul to embark upon his period of office outside Rome.

he later raised . . . when the latter was proscribed: it was exceptional for an ex-slave to be given equestrian status.

57 *on one occasion and then another chose a colleague*: Agrippa and Tiberius.

the first and third times with a colleague: again, Agrippa and then Tiberius.

59 *Ariminum*: modern Rimini on the Adriatic coast.

Pontifex Maximus: in 13 BCE.

the calendar which had been brought to order by the Divine Julius: cf. *Jul.* 40.

he gave his own name . . . the month of his birth: cf. *Jul.* 76 and *Aug.* 100.

60 *the augury of Safety*: an inquiry as to whether prayers should be offered for the safety of the state.

he would risk incurring . . . the crime: the penalty would be applied to the accuser if the accused were acquitted.

61 *ducenarii*: these would be men whose property was valued at 200,000 sesterces (half that required for knights) or above.

twenty-five: the Latin text is most likely corrupt here. The manuscripts give the new minimum age as 30 but all other evidence suggests 30 was already the minimum, thus five years younger than the previous figure would be 25.

the punishment of being sewn in the sack: parricides were sewn up in a sack with a dog, a cock, a snake, and a monkey and thrown into the sea or a river.

the Cornelian law: under this law the witnesses to a forged will were liable to the same penalties as the forger.

allowing an exception of three years: so that those who were widowed were not obliged by the threat of legal penalties to remarry immediately.

increasing the rewards: the law regulating marriage passed in 18 BCE was modified in 9 CE. Those who did not marry were penalized (e.g. with regard to their capacity to inherit) as were, to a lesser extent, those without children. Those who were married and had three children were given a number of privileges such as the right to stand for election in advance of the usual age.

62 *the young man's example*: Germanicus was the son of Livia's son Drusus. With his wife Agrippina he produced numerous children. For details see Family Tree.

Orcini: a term used to denote slaves freed by their master's will, thus owing their status to a death. The implication is that it was the triumvirs who had swelled the ranks of the senate with the unworthy, though Caesar himself seems to have increased the number from around 600 to around 900.

63 *the centumviral court*: dealing with civil cases involving status, inheritance, and some other property rights referred to it by the praetor.

Board of Ten: these judged disputes of law.

praetors: from eight to ten.

 . *generous in honouring military achievements*: the triumph was the highest military honour which could be won by a Roman general. Despite Suetonius' claim, triumphs, at least after the first ten years of Augustus' reign, virtually disappeared. The last non-member of the imperial family to triumph was Lucius Cornelius Balbus in 19 BCE. After that the only triumphs to take place under Augustus were those of Tiberius in 7 BCE and 12 CE. One reason for this was that a general needed to be fighting under his own auspices to win a triumph and most major wars took place in provinces which were under Augustus' supreme command. It is not clear how many may have received the less prestigious triumphal ornaments.

64 *the Theatre Law . . . the equestrian census*: strictly speaking, to be a member of the equestrian order, one needed a fortune of at least 400,000 sesterces. The Julian Law on the Theatre reinforced the existing reservation of the front rows at the theatre for senators and knights.

restored the older arrangements for elections: presumably reversing the change instituted by Julius Caesar (*Jul.* 41).

65 *no matter what their degree of freedom*: normally a grant of 'legitimate freedom' would automatically entitle an ex-slave to citizenship.

Behold the Romans . . . the toga'd race!: Virgil, *Aeneid* 1. 282. Written in Augustus' own time, this epic poem was already playing an important role in the construction of national identity.

money tokens: these were tablets or balls distributed to the people which could be exchanged for the sums inscribed on them.

66 *nothing would be given to those to whom nothing had been promised*: because when the promise was made they were not citizens.

'Torquati': from *torquis* meaning 'collar'.

67 *Augustus would even employ . . . forbade the practice*: despite their high profile and sometimes glamorous associations, the social status of professional actors and gladiators was very low. For members of the élite to appear on stage and in the arena could be seen as humiliating.

67 *no one dressed in dark clothing should sit in the central rows*: thus, all who did not wear a toga had to sit in less conspicuous places.

though it had been the custom . . . together: apparently they had always sat separately at the theatre and circus.

68 *the praetor's tribunal*: the president at the games was normally a praetor.

Pontifex Maximus: cf. ch. 31 above.

the upper-storey apartments: that is, in nearby buildings which commanded a view of the circus.

of the Greek kind: perhaps meaning in Greek language and dress.

the three theatres: those of Pompey, Balbus, and Marcellus.

69 *pantomime actor*: Roman pantomime consisted in one actor presenting a dramatic scene to musical accompaniment through dance and gesture rather than words.

he gestured with his finger: this seems to be a gesture signifying the effeminacy of the victim. Cf. *Cal.* 56.

colonies: Here the term colony refers to the settlement of a number of veteran soldiers.

he even gave Italy . . . the election day: thus, parity with the city-dwellers was not complete as only the local councillors in the colonies were in a position to exercise their voting rights as Roman citizens.

allied cities: cities which enjoyed autonomy in their internal affairs.

Latin or Roman citizenship: Latin citizenship gave some but not all the rights of full citizenship.

70 *Calagurritani*: Calagurria was a town in northwestern Spain on the River Iberus (Ebro).

Alexander the Great: for the significance of Alexander see chs. 18 and 94, and also *Jul.* 7.

his clemency: though contrast ch. 27 above.

71 *young Agrippa*: Augustus' grandson.

to accept the dictatorship: in 22, the first year for some time when Augustus was not consul. Augustus' example in refusing honours is followed by a number of his successors. Cf. e.g. *Tib.* 24.

the title 'Master': the term *dominus* was associated with the master–slave relationship.

72 *so that people . . . pay him respect*: it was an established custom to greet or bid farewell to magistrates or commanders with a procession.

All and sundry . . . the common people: it was the custom for important men to receive visits daily from those who hoped for their patronage.

in the senate house: rather than them coming to his house. This account of Augustus' behaviour forms a contrast with that attributed to Caesar in *Jul.* 78.

each man selecting his own candidate: see ch. 35 above.

freedom of speech in wills: Romans often used the occasion of making a will to express their opinions of others. Cf. ch. 66 below.

73 *the conspiracy of Murena*: cf. ch. 19 above.

the lacus Curtius: a well or pool in an enclosure in the Forum which had powerful mythological associations. Cf. Livy, who gives two different versions of its origins in *History of Rome* 1. 12–13 and 7. 6.

destroyed by fire: around 3 CE.

guilds: probably of officials.

74 *'Father of the Fatherland'*: Augustus received this title (see Glossary) in 2 BCE. Contrast Suetonius' disapproving comment on Julius Caesar's acceptance of this title (*Jul.* 76).

a dangerous illness: cf. ch. 81 below.

Aesculapius: the god of healing.

begun long ago: allegedly under Peisistratus in the sixth century.

75 *dressed in togas . . . regal insignia*: their dress acknowledged that they were Roman subjects.

his sister Octavia: presumably Augustus' full sister. See ch. 4 above.

during his first consulship . . . his fifty-fourth year: 43 and 9 BCE respectively.

Mark Antony writes . . . for himself: such stories would have served Antony's purpose by showing Augustus' faithlessness in breaking an earlier engagement and his willingness to contract an alliance with a foreign ruler, as Antony himself had done.

76 *with penny and scales*: the purchaser had to touch the scales three times with a penny in the presence of the praetor. Augustus thus became their *pater familias*, acquiring important legal rights over them.

consuls: Gaius was consul designate in 5 BCE, assuming office in 1 CE. Lucius was consul designate in 2 BCE but died before assuming office.

working wool: a traditionally respectable feminine occupation, associated with the virtues of early Rome.

daily chronicles: probably the daily public bulletin of official news.

He himself taught . . . many other skills: usually a slave tutor would have taught them.

the lowest couch: the host's usual place.

He adopted . . . by a law passed by the assembly of the curiae in the Forum: this form of adoption was followed because both were at the time legally independent following the deaths of their fathers.

Surrentum: modern Sorrento, on the coast near Naples.

77 *her island*: Pandateria, off the coast of Latium.

77 *an island*: Planasia, a small island south of Elba.

Oh, that I . . . without children!: a variation on *Iliad* 3. 40.

78 *Murena's conspiracy had been discovered*: cf. ch. 19 above.

For, although he was for . . . gratitude and affection: Suetonius makes clear later that Augustus received a very substantial part of his income from this source; see ch. 101 below.

legacies or inheritances: it was customary in a Roman will to leave one's friends legacies or to institute them as second (or third) heir. In this case they would only inherit if the first (or second) heir was unable or unwilling. Thus, this was often simply a mark of honour.

effeminate: Roman politicians regularly made such charges, particularly against younger opponents. Cf. Cicero's speech *In Defence of Caelius* 6.

79 *to singe his legs*: for a man to depilate his legs was often associated with effeminacy.

the Mother of the Gods: the priests of the Great Mother, or Cybele, were themselves eunuchs and were known as *galli*.

rules the globe with his finger: the Latin is a pun, meaning also 'beats the drum'. Particular gestures of the finger were themselves seen as signs of effeminacy.

in front of her husband . . . dishevelled hair: the same story is told about Caligula; see *Cal.* 36.

Tertulla or Terentilla or Rufilla: these are all diminutives to parody the language of lovers.

the Twelve Gods: the worship of the Twelve Gods was Greek practice. Similar stories of audacious fancy-dress are associated with Antony (see e.g. Velleius Paterculus, *Roman History* 2. 83. 2).

Apollo: Augustus associated himself with Apollo through various means. Cf. ch. 18 above.

80 *As soon as . . . his golden throne*: these lines are obscure and have puzzled numerous editors. Mallia is perhaps the name of the house where the banquet took place.

My father . . . Corinthian: cf. ch. 3 above for comments on Augustus' father's profession.

murrine: perhaps agate or fluorspar. Whatever this substance was, it was highly prized in Rome.

in everyday use: the use of precious metals for everyday purposes was seen as a sign of tyrannical luxury on the part of Antony and Cleopatra. Augustus' own practice forms a conspicuous contrast.

December: there seems to have been a law against gambling which it was customary to ignore in December, when the festival of the Saturnalia took place.

a 'dog' . . . whoever threw a Venus scooped the lot: if all the dice showed one, this was a 'dog'; if they all showed different numbers, a 'Venus'.

81 *Quinquatria*: the festival of Minerva, 19–23 March.

Alban stone: several leading men of the late republic were criticized for importing marble pillars to decorate their homes.

82 *produced in his own household . . . granddaughters*: cf. ch. 64 above.

His togas . . . neither broad nor narrow: Julius Caesar had been criticized for his flowing toga; see *Jul.* 45. The stripe on Augustus' toga was midway between the broad stripe of the senator and the narrow stripe of the knight.

the defeat of Sextus Pompeius' fleet: an admiral of Sextus Pompeius, Menas had betrayed his forces to Octavian in 38 BCE.

a man in whose villa he used to stay: cf. ch. 72 on Augustus' visits to the villas of his freedmen.

Saturnalia: when it was customary to give presents.

83 *every couch*: usually at dinner parties guests reclined three to a couch.

his Sabbath fast: apparently Augustus misunderstood Jewish practice.

he would not touch a thing: Suetonius attributes eccentric eating habits to several emperors. Augustus' are excusable since they do not reflect an excessive interest in the pleasures of eating. Contrast e.g. *Claud.* 33.

very sparing in his consumption of wine also: constrast the excessive consumption attributed to Tiberius and to Claudius (*Tib.* 42, *Claud.* 33).

he would sleep no more than seven hours . . . in the course of those hours: Suetonius attributes to Vespasian a similar commitment to duty (*Vesp.* 21).

84 *His eyes . . . the sun's force*: cf. the superhuman gaze attributed to Alexander the Great (an important figure for Augustus, as Suetonius emphasizes, chs. 18, 50, and 94).

five feet nine inches tall: in Roman measures; about 5 feet 7 inches (imperial) or 1.7 metres.

strigil: an implement used to scrape off oil applied during the bathing process.

treatment with sand and reeds: perhaps a poultice of warm sand and pounded-up reeds.

85 *Antonius Musa*: cf. ch. 59.

his birthday: 23 September.

Praeneste or Tibur: towns only a short distance from Rome.

pass-ball and balloon-ball: the former term covers a variety of games played with a small ball, the latter a game played with a large, light ball.

86 *'Reply to Brutus concerning Cato'*: Marcus Brutus had written a panegyric of his father-in-law and uncle, Cato, who had chosen to kill himself rather than live under the rule of Caesar.

86 *'On his own Life'*: these memoirs are often quoted by Suetonius; see chs. 2, 7, 27, 42, and 43, for example.

   sponge: rather than, as in the legend, on his sword. A sponge was used to erase writing in ink.

87 *Annius Cimber*: his reputation for inflated oratory seems to have been notorious. Cf. Quintilian, *Institutes of Oratory* 8. 3. 28.

   which Sallustius Crispus took from Cato's Origines: Cato wrote in the early second century BCE and Sallust in the mid-first century. Several ancient authors criticize Sallust's obscure brevity and his use of archaic terms (Quintilian, *Institutes* 8. 3. 29; Seneca, *Letters* 114. 17).

   the high-flown style . . . in to our own language: on the distinction between plain 'Attic' and florid 'Asiatic' styles, see Quintilian, *Institutes* 12. 10. 1 and 16–20). Antony's alleged preference for the exotic Asiatic style is of a piece with allegations concerning his preference for eastern modes of dress and consumption, and of course, his alliance with the eastern ruler Cleopatra.

   Greek Kalends: there was no Greek Kalends (the Roman term for the first day of the month).

88 *Apollonia*: cf. ch. 8 above.

   Metellus' . . . in earlier days: both of these men were consuls in the mid- to late first century BCE though there is some dispute as to the exact identity of Metellus.

89 *a sealskin for protection*: cf. Pliny, who writes that seals are never struck by lightning (*Natural Histories* 2. 146).

   as I said earlier: ch. 29 above.

   he would beg from the people . . . put pennies in: this could be understood as an act of humility to ward off *invidia*, the ill-feeling which Romans believed posed a particular danger to the fortunate. Suetonius attributes a similar practice to Caligula (*Cal.* 42).

   palm tree: an omen of victory.

   Aenaria . . . the island: Aenaria is modern Ischia. The islands were exchanged in 29 BCE.

   market-day: the *nundinae*, or market-day, fell every eight days.

90 *the unlucky sound of the name*: *Nonis* could be understood as *non is*, 'you do not go'.

   the mysteries at Athens: of Ceres at Eleusis.

   Apis: the sacred bull of Memphis in Egypt.

   pay his respects in Jerusalem: to do so would have meant acknowledging the faith of the Jews.

   registered in the treasury: without which the decree would not be law.

91 *Liber*: another name for Bacchus.

Alexander the Great: for links with Alexander, cf. chs. 18 and 50 above.

Quintus Catulus: cf. *Jul.* 15.

93 *as they had to Romulus*: cf. Livy, 1. 7—an account written in Augustus' own time.

Eutychus . . . Nicon: the names mean 'fortunate' and 'victor' in Greek.

he was performing the rites: traditionally the censors performed rituals of purification to mark the conclusion of their period of office. Though not a censor, Augustus had undertaken many censorial duties.

94 *Beneventum*: modern Benevento.

traditional practice: in Greek settlements (including Naples, of whose territory Capri had been part), young men had regular gymnastic training as part of their education.

95 *'Ktistes'*: Greek for 'founder'.

his tomb was surrounded by a crowd of people and many lights: this seems to have been customary on the anniversary of someone's death.

Since the play . . . applause: the final lines of a comedy by Menander (*Poetae Comici Graeci* VIII. 925 (p. 275)). For Suetonius' emphasis here on the way the death corresponds to the subject's wishes, cf. *Jul.* 87.

96 *'euthanasia'*: Greek for 'good death'.

the fourteenth day before the Kalends of September: 19 August 14 CE.

Bovillae: about twelve miles from Rome on the Appian Way.

his bones . . . priests of the senior colleges: this was usually done by female relatives.

97 *three days before the Nones of April*: 3 April 13 CE.

secondary heirs: cf. *Jul.* 83 and *Aug.* 66.

tribes: since all Roman citizens were also members of tribes this distinction is unclear.

his two fathers: Octavius, his natural father, and Julius Caesar who had adopted him.

a list of his achievements . . . his Mausoleum: versions of this have survived It is referred to as *Res Gestae Divi Augusti*, 'The Achievements of the Deified Augustus'.

TIBERIUS

98 *Regilli*: location unknown.

six years after the expulsion of the kings: 504 BCE, according to traditional chronology.

Appius Caecus: consul in 312 BCE.

Claudius Caudex: consul in 264 BCE.

Appius Caecus . . . Hannibal: in 207 BCE.

98 *attempted . . . gratify his lust*: an incident traditionally dated to 451 BCE.

Claudius Russus: the name 'Russus' is a conjecture by Ihm. The manuscript has 'Drusus'.

Forum of Appius: a small town in Latium on the Appian Way.

Claudius Pulcher: son of Appius Claudius Caecus.

99 *When he was defeated . . . perilous situation*: mid-third century BCE.

Idaean mother of the gods: the Phrygian goddess Cybele, also known as the Great Mother. Her cult was introduced to Rome in 204 BCE. This Claudia was granddaughter of Appius Claudius Caecus. See also note to p. 79 above.

that other Claudia: daughter of Appius Claudius Caecus.

had himself adopted . . . younger than himself: in 60 BCE. Clodius could only be elected tribune of the plebs if he was of plebeian family. Cf. *Jul.* 6, 20, 24, 74.

veto his action or prevent him: to do so would have been sacrilege because of the presence of the Vestal Virgin.

consul a second time and censor: he was consul first in 219 BCE. After victory over the Illyrians he had been found guilty of dividing up the booty unfairly but was elected consul again in 207 BCE and censor in 204.

100 *Narbo and Arelate*: modern Narbonne and Arles.

on the sixteenth day before the Kalends of December: 16 November 42 BCE.

102 *He also gave other games, though without attending them himself*: note Suetonius' comment at ch. 47 below on Tiberius' attitude to games.

Caecilius Atticus: better known as Titus Pomponius Atticus, he took the name Quintus Caecilius Pomponianus Atticus after his adoption by Quintus Caecilius.

He also took back the standards . . . Crassus: 20 BCE (cf. *Aug.* 21.)

103 *Gallia Comata*: Transalpine Gaul. See note to p. 21 above.

Raeti and Vindelici: peoples from Raetia, a country to the north of Cisalpine Gaul.

Breuci: a people of Pannonia.

entered the city in a chariot: i.e. celebrating a triumph. This was in 7 BCE.

Augustus' children: see note to p. 55 above. The children are the Gaius and Lucius referred to in ch. 11 below.

104 *he did his duty . . . whatever gifts he had ever given her*: though cf. ch. 50 below.

105 *Nemausus*: a town in Gallia Comata of which he had been governor.

106 *Aponus*: a warm medicinal spring, modern Bagno d'Albano.

Carinae . . . Esquiline: Carinae was a smart residential area adjoining the Forum, ideally situated for prominent public figures, while the Esquiline was on the outskirts of the city.

Marcus Agrippa: also known as Agrippa Postumus.

107 *For he could neither . . . to his personal fund*: persons under their father's power, like slaves, could not own property but could be permitted to accumulate funds which, though not technically their own, might be treated as such.

108 *he took his food . . . without a tent for shelter*: in giving up the comforts to which his rank entitled him, Tiberius was aligning himself with the common soldiers.

Bructeri: a Germanic tribe occupying modern Westphalia.

he celebrated the triumph: 12 CE.

109 *Bato . . . installed at Ravenna*: usually the enemy leader would be led in the triumphal procession and then executed.

110 *'One man alone . . . our state'*: Ennius, *Annals* 370V2 (substituting *vigilando*, 'taking care', for the original *cunctando*, 'delaying').

'If only he should follow . . . very wise': Homer, *Iliad* 10. 246–7.

112 *he behaved in a very unassuming manner . . . an ordinary citizen*: Suetonius' comments at ch. 67 offer an additional perspective here.

an oath . . . to ratify his acts: an oath taken by all citizens to indicate approval for the emperor's deeds past and future.

Tiberius . . . Livius: on the model of the months already named after Julius and Augustus (cf. *Jul.* 76 and *Aug.* 100).

to take the cognomen . . . the civic crown: honours accepted by Augustus. See e.g. *Aug.* 58.

three consulships . . . until the Ides of May: 18, 21 and 31 CE.

113 *When a certain fellow . . . in this insulting way*: cf. *Aug.* 53.

in a free state minds and tongues should be free: contrast ch. 61 below.

mutual enemies: thus implying equal status. Cf. *Aug.* 56.

114 *with ambassadorial status*: thus able to use the imperial postal service established by Augustus.

the proper concluding formula: which included prayers for the welfare of the emperor.

115 *Corinthian vases . . . three mullets*: Corinthian vases and fish, especially mullet, often serve as emblems of luxury in the writings of Roman moralists. Cf. *Aug.* 70.

regulating inns and cook-shops: the cook-shops were often subject to regulation. They were perceived as places where the poor would gather and foment unrest.

half-eaten dishes . . . just as good as a whole one: this story may well have served to illustrate the emperor's meanness.

116 *Women of ill repute . . . the penalties specified by the law*: adultery had been made a criminal offence by the Julian law on adultery of 18 BCE.

116 *the restrictions . . . in the theatre and arena*: presumably earlier legislation stipulated harsher penalties than loss of senatorial or equestrian status for senators and knights who engaged in such activities.

so that he could rent a house in the city more cheaply after than date: rental contracts in Rome seem to have commenced 1 July.

because he married . . . the day afterwards: Augustus' marriage laws stipulated that married men should be given preference in the assignment of public posts.

Pollentia: in Liguria, modern Pollenza.

117 *the kingdom of Cottius*: in the Alps, between Italy and Gaul.

asylum: by which people sought refuge at temples or statues to avoid punishment for crimes.

Cyzicus: a city of northwest Asia Minor.

Antium: a coastal town near Rome.

Tarracina: a coastal town in Latium, modern Terracina.

118 *Fidenae*: a town in Sabine territory, to the north of Rome.

he had so long struggled to conceal: cf. ch. 33.

'Biberius' . . . for wine: from *bibo* drink, *callidus* hot, and *merum* unmixed wine. Contrast *Aug.* 77.

119 *a mushroom . . . and a thrush*: all luxury foodstuffs. Contrast Suetonius' comments on Tiberius' frugality at ch. 34.

'tight-bums': meaning a male who takes a 'passive', 'feminine' role in sexual relations.

Elephantis: a Greek author notorious for her lewd writings.

'the old goat's den' . . . the island: this played on the similarity between *caper*, goat, and Capreae, the name of the island.

Atalanta: in Graeco-Roman mythology, Atalanta was a huntress with no wish to marry who was pursued by Meleager.

. . . in his bed-chamber: Romans regarded the use of the mouth for sexual activity as especially degrading.

120 *his Greeks*: cf. ch. 56 below.

As emperor . . . many years later: contrast *Aug.* 28–30.

he was forced to buy the freedom of the comic actor Actius: presumably by the demands of the crowd. Contrast Tiberius' parsimony regarding games with the generosity of Augustus (*Aug.* 43).

121 *the plans of Sejanus*: Aelius Sejanus had been praetorian prefect, a position which he seems to have used to bring about the downfall of many leading Romans, but he fell from grace and was punished with death after plotting to take over the empire. Cf. 55, 61, and 65.

ready money: which could be seen as preparation for a revolution.

to restore liberty: presumably in the sense of senatorial government. Cf. *Cal.* 60.

122 *he also cheated her . . . in his will*: contrast ch. 11 above.

123 *Hector*: the mythical Trojan hero who died defending his city against the Greeks, according to Homer's *Iliad*.

124 *Gemonian steps*: the flight of steps leading from the Forum to the Capitoline hill where the bodies of executed criminals were exposed. Cf. ch. 61 below.

showed him the noose and the hooks: thus indicating that he was condemned to death, to be strangled with the noose and his body then to be dragged to the Tiber with the hooks.

125 *his savage and tenacious nature was not completely hidden*: cf. *Cal.* 11.

126 *ostensibly motivated . . . to improve morals*: Suetonius characteristically adds a new and more critical perspective on activities introduced earlier as praiseworthy (cf. ch. 34 above).

the hundred thousands . . . exile on Rhodes: to qualify as a knight one needed a fortune of 400,000 sesterces. As Augustus' adopted son, Tiberius could own no property while his father lived (cf. ch. 15 above). It is perhaps also relevant that Roman citizens sent into exile lost the rights of citizenship.

the golden age of Saturn . . . iron: Augustus had been associated by his supporters with the return of the proverbial golden age of Saturn. In myth the golden age was succeeded by one of silver and then one of iron, as human society deteriorated.

he drinks as greedily . . . wine without water: cf. ch. 42 above.

Sulla, fortunate for himself not for you: the dictator Sulla had taken the *cognomen* Felix, meaning 'fortunate'.

Marius . . . Antony: Marius was another great general, whose conflict with Sulla generated a civil war in the early first century BCE. Mark Antony's conflict with the young Augustus had also led to civil war (cf. *Aug.* 17).

'Let them hate me provided they respect me': cf. the comment Suetonius attributes to Caligula (*Cal.* 30).

127 *Agamemnon*: mythical king of Mycenae or Argos, in Homer commander-in-chief of the Greeks fighting at Troy. On his return home he was killed by his wife, Clytemnestra, aided by her lover, Aegisthus. The story was the subject of a play by the Greek tragedian Aeschylus.

Authors were attacked and books banned: constrast ch. 28, and cf. *Aug.* 54–6.

129 *Priam*: mythical king of Troy. In some versions of his story all his numerous children are killed by the Greek army before him.

the victim of insult: cf. ch. 66 below.

129 *the temple*: of Fortuna Primigenia at Praeneste.

131 *when he began his reign ... such great honours*: contrast Suetonius' treatment of this at ch. 26 above.

132 *Euphorion, Rhianus, and Parthenius*: Euphorion and Rhianus were both Alexandrians who lived in the third century BCE. The former, a follower of Callimachus, was proverbial for his obscurity; the latter was a composer of learned epic. Parthenius was a first-century Greek poet who is thought to have played a major part in promoting learned Alexandrian poetry in Rome.

Hecuba's mother ... on the death of his son: Hecuba was the wife of Priam, king of Troy at the time of the Trojan war according to Homer. The Greek hero Achilles had once sought refuge by disguising himself as a young girl. The songs of the Sirens who lured men to their deaths were among the perils threatening the hero Odysseus in Homer's *Odyssey*. Minos was a mythical king of Crete.

in the senate: contrast Suetonius' claim concerning Claudius, *Claud.* 42.

'monopolium': a Greek term meaning 'monopoly', transliterated into Latin.

'emblema': a Greek term (with no Latin equivalent) meaning inlaid figures (e.g. on cups).

133 *on the seventeenth day ... Gaius Pontius Nigrinus*: 16 March 37 CE.

134 *Apollo Temenites*: Temenos was a place in Syracuse sacred to Apollo.

the hook and Gemonian steps: cf. ch. 61 above.

Atella: a town north of Naples.

in the amphitheatre: perhaps to make a point about Tiberius' failure to provide entertainments during his lifetime?

CALIGULA

136 *Gaius Caesar's*: the emperor properly known as Gaius Caesar is more usually known as Caligula (see ch. 9). Since the name Gaius is a common one, I have often, though not exclusively, used 'Caligula' for clarity.

Germanicus ... his paternal uncle Tiberius: Suetonius does not include an account of earlier generations here since this is covered in *Aug.* and *Tib.* The account of Caligula's virtuous father, Germanicus, provides a strong counterpoint to Suetonius' portrait of Caligula himself.

went straight on to the consulship: without holding any of the usual intermediate offices (though five years elapsed between Germanicus' quaestorship and his consulship).

The plot to kill him ... condemned him to death: cf. Suetonius' treatment of this at *Tib.* 52.

137 *the Varian disaster*: three legions, under the command of Varus, were destroyed in 9 CE. Cf *Aug.* 23.

after his death: contrast these responses with those Suetonius attributes to the death of Caligula himself, ch. 60 below.

the king of kings: the term 'king of kings', originally used for the kings of Persia, was subsequently also applied to the Parthian king.

138 *the feast days in the month of December*: the Saturnalia. See Glossary.

only respect for Germanicus . . . the cruelty to which Tiberius soon gave rein: Suetonius does not advance this as an explanation of Tiberius' changing behaviour; see e.g. *Tib.* 61.

Tiberius was their accuser: cf. *Tib.* 54.

the day before the Kalends of September . . . were consuls: 31 August, 12 CE.

Gnaeus Lentulus Gaetulicus: consul in 33.

Pliny: Plinius Secundus, better known as the elder Pliny.

the rivers: the Rhine and the Moselle.

139 *earlier*: ch. 7 above.

puerae . . . puelli: in classical Latin the usual term for boys was *pueri* and for girls *puellae*.

the fifteenth day before the Kalends of June: 18 May.

sought to transfer to Antium the seat and capital of empire: cf. ch. 49 below.

'Caligula': meaning 'Little boot' from *caliga*, the term for a soldier's boot.

140 *even at that time . . . nature*: cf. Suetonius' comments on Tiberius, *Tib.* 57.

he showed the keenest interest . . . disguised in a wig and long cloak: for a similar story of disguise, see *Nero* 26. For allegations of cruelty, cf. *Claud.* 34.

Phaethon: the mythical figure Phaethon was a son of the sun-god Helios, who granted his request to be allowed to drive the sun chariot. Phaethon, not strong enough to control the divine horses, fell from the sky and scorched the earth.

141 *And as the royal house . . . that he himself might succeed*: cf. *Tib.* 61 and 65.

he himself . . . strangled him: cf. *Tib.* 73 where different versions are also given.

co-heir: cf. *Tib.* 76.

142 *others posted public notices in which they promised their own lives*: cf. ch. 27.

'Germanicus': cf. *Jul.* 76 and *Aug.* 100.

Prince of Youth: a title previously given by Augustus to his adopted sons Gaius and Lucius. Hence it might be taken as signifying Tiberius' position as heir.

143 *proposals of the consuls*: the consuls' proposals to the senate began with a set formula. Caligula's apparently admirable concern for his sisters would have an extra dimension for any reader familiar with the stories of his incestuous relations with them. Cf. ch. 24.

143 *he ordered tht the records . . . touched any of them*: for a similar act, cf. *Aug.* 32. However, see *Cal.* 30.

the 'tight-bums': cf. *Tib.* 43.

which had been banned by senatorial decree: contrast *Tib.* 61. These authors were well known for their unbridled attacks on prominent individuals.

he added . . . to the existing four: see *Aug.* 32.

Julia Augusta: i.e. Livia, Tiberius' mother.

144 *the Parilia*: a festival association with the foundation of the city, which was traditionally celebrated on 21 April.

the Kalends of July . . . the same month: 1 July 37 CE; 1 January 39; 13 January 40; 7 January 41.

Lugdunum: modern Lyons in France.

145 *the Troy game*: see *Jul.* 39.

three thousand six hundred paces: 5.22 km; *c.* 3½ miles.

Xerxes . . . Hellespont: for the significance of this comparison see Introduction, p. xx.

146 *Pompey's Theatre . . . by Tiberius*: see *Tib*: 47.

completed the former: see *Claud.* 20.

to dig a canal through the Isthmus of Greece: cf. *Jul.* 44 and *Nero* 19, and the note to the latter.

'Caesar Best and Greatest': an echo of the title of 'Jupiter Best and Greatest', whose temple on the Capitoline Hill was the most important in Rome.

Let there be one Lord, one King!: Homer, *Iliad* 2. 204.

the statue of Zeus from Olympia: a colossal statue of gold and ivory, reputed to be the masterpiece of the fifth-century Athenian sculptor, Phidias. At ch. 57 below the statue is said to foretell Caligula's assassination.

Jupiter Latiaris: Jupiter of Latium.

147 *Raise me up or you I'll . . .*: Homer, *Iliad* 23. 724 (the words are spoken by Ajax, when wrestling with Odysseus).

Tiberius: his brother by adoption.

148 *preserved as a butt for jokes*: cf. *Claud.* 7.

at a crowded banquet . . . while his wife lay above: Romans generally dined reclining on couches, each of which was designed to accommodate three people.

Gaius Piso: the central figure in a conspiracy against Nero of 62.

149 *the precedent set by Romulus and Augustus*: a reference to the story of the rape of the Sabine women (supposed to have been organized by Romulus in order to obtain wives for Rome's earliest inhabitants), and to Augustus' behaviour as recounted in *Aug.* 62 and 69.

Selene: Antony's daughter by Cleopatra.

short linen tunics: such short tunics were normally worn by young slaves to display their attractions.

150 *flogged*: corporal punishment was a humiliation normally reserved for slaves.

The man who had promised . . . fulfil his vow: cf. ch. 14 above.

151 *disfigured with the marks . . . sawn in half*: again, these were punishments normally reserved for slaves.

He had a composer . . . a doubtful joke: contrast the alleged tolerance of such licence by other emperors; see e.g. *Aug.* 55–6; *Nero* 39.

adiatrepsia . . . his shamelessness: stoic term meaning 'impassivity', here perverted by Caligula.

his brother: Tiberius Gemellus. See ch. 23 above, and note to p. 147.

152 *hellebore*: a traditional remedy, especially associated with the island of Anticyra in the Aegean.

Gallograecia: another name for Galatia in Phrygia, to which some Gauls had migrated.

the dead man, too, had deserved the punishment: Cf. *Claud.* 29.

Let them hate provided that they fear: Accius, *Tragedies* 203. Cf. the comment Suetonius attributes to Tiberius (*Tib.* 59).

which he had pretended to have destroyed: cf. ch. 15 above.

in thrall to the stage or the arena: an enthusiasm associated with the common people, though cf. *Aug.* 45.

called for the brigand Tetrinius: presumably to fight in the arena.

the Varian tragedy: see *Aug.* 23.

the collapse of a theatre at Fidenae: see *Tib.* 40.

153 *I recounted above*: ch. 19.

popa . . . cultrarius: the *popa*'s job was to strike the sacrificial victim with a mallet while the *cultrarius* would cut its throat.

154 *as Plato had done*: in the *Republic*.

Virgil and Livy: authors who were both staples of the curriculum.

Ptolemy, whom I mentioned earlier: ch. 26 above.

he had the backs of their heads shaved to spoil their appearance: Suetonius tells us at ch. 50 that Caligula himself was bald.

the King of Nemi . . . to supplant him: by tradition, the priest of Diana at Nemi was a fugitive slave who had killed the previous incumbent.

155 *he would leave the dining-room . . . he would return*: Suetonius tells a similar story about Augustus, *Aug.* 69.

the most precious pearls dissolved in vinegar: a manifestation of luxury typically associated with eastern rulers. Cf. Pliny's story about Cleopatra, *Natural Histories* 9. 120–1.

156 *Great structures . . . levelled mountain peaks flat*: Roman moralists were especially critical of such dramatic interventions in the natural landscape.

He also accused people . . . any addition to their estates: the estates were consequently forfeit.

when he was then named as heir . . . poisoned sweets: contrast Augustus' behaviour as described by Suetonius at *Aug*. 66.

157 *even the freedmen*: the freedmen were, of course, no longer their property.

158 *overflowing hands and togas*: the fold of the toga was often used by Romans as a pocket.

the grove and river of Clitumnus: a well-known beauty spot in southern Umbria. Cf. Pliny, *Letters* 8. 8.

159 *six thousand sesterces*: half the amount set by Augustus (according to Dio 55. 23).

to ride in their carriage right into the Forum: this was not normally permitted in the daytime.

in the temple of Mars the Avenger: see *Aug*. 29.

160 *'endure and save themselves for better times'*: *Aeneid* 1. 207.

the Pharos: at Alexandria.

161 *those legions which had tried to mutiny . . . a small child*: see ch. 9 above.

to decimate them: i.e. kill one in ten. This was a traditional military punishment.

Alexandria: Caligula's ancestor Mark Antony was alleged by his enemy Augustus to have planned transferring the capital to Alexandria.

162 *thunder and lightning . . . hide under it*: similar anxieties are attributed to Augustus (*Aug*. 90) and Tiberius (*Tib*. 69).

163 *Cimbri . . . Senones*: the Cimbri had been driven back by Marius in 101 BCE, while the Senones were a Gallic tribe who were said to have captured Rome itself in 390 BCE.

platforms: actors in tragedy traditionally wore high-soled shoes to enhance their size.

Venus: Venus was reputed to be the mother of the mythical hero Aeneas and through him ancestress of the Julii.

the breastplate . . . from his sarcophagus: other emperors, too, were linked with Alexander the Great, according to Suetonius; see *Jul*. 7, *Aug*. 18, 50, 94.

he described Seneca . . . 'sand without lime': cf. Suetonius' account of Augustus' literary criticism (*Aug*. 86).

164 *He was so transported . . . his stage debut*: actors were considered effeminate in their movements and their speech—hardly suitable models for an emperor. For an emperor to appear on stage seemed scandalous. Cf. *Nero* 21.

He put some Thracian gladiators . . . the murmillones: cf. ch. 30. The Thracians were Caligula's favourites, the *murmillones* their opponents.

Green Faction: one of the chariot-racing teams in the circus. There were at this time four 'Factions': the Whites, Reds, Blues, and Greens.

165 *to make him consul*: see Introduction, p. xxv.

effeminate: the accusation of effeminacy was especially humiliating for a military man.

166 *that which had taken place years ago on the same day*: i.e. the assassination of Julius Caesar—Caligula's namesake.

Cassius Longinus: cf. ch. 24.

several of the understudies . . . overflowing with blood: after the play, it seems to have been common for actors who played minor roles to entertain the audience by imitating the actions of the lead player.

the ninth day before the Kalends of February: 24 January 41 CE.

'Take this!': using a form of words which was part of the ritual pronouncements during a sacrifice. The emphasis on Caligula's neck could be seen as ironic in view of the emperor's threats to other people's necks, as recorded at chs. 30 and 33 above.

'Jupiter': Jupiter was the god of sudden death.

167 *the Lamian gardens*: an estate on the edge of the city, where Caligula had a villa.

'Julian': it had been completed by Augustus and named for his adoptive father Julius.

the one who was murdered in the time of Cinna: Gaius Julius Caesar Strabo, who was killed in 87 BCE (several other family members with the name Gaius died naturally, however).

THE DEIFIED CLAUDIUS

168 *gave birth to Drusus . . . conceived in adultery*: in 38 BCE. See *Aug.* 62.

his quaestorship and praetorship: on Augustus' initiative, Drusus was given a special dispensation by the senate to stand for these magistracies before he had reached the usual age. He was quaestor in 18 and praetor in 11 BCE.

the divisions of the scribes: probably the quaestor's clerks.

the opimian spoils: to secure this honour, a general in full command of an army had to kill the enemy leader in single combat.

169 *his Caesars*: his grandsons, Gaius and Lucius.

the younger Antonia: the younger daughter of Mark Antony and Octavia, sister of Augustus.

at Lugdunum . . . the Kalends of August: at modern Lyons, 1 August 10 BCE.

169 *when his older brother . . . Germanicus*: in 4 CE, Germanicus was adopted by Tiberius, while Tiberius himself was adopted by Augustus.

of age: at puberty, normally reckoned at age 14.

the Greek cloak, an unprecedented sight: on an official occasion such as this, a toga would have been expected. It seems the Greek cloak was the usual dress of invalids.

published . . . in different genres: see chs. 41 and 42 below.

170 *Augusta*: i.e. Livia.

Tiberius: i.e. Claudius.

Games of Mars: celebrated by Augustus in 12 CE in honour of Mars the Avenger whose temple was the focus of the Forum of Augustus (cf. *Aug.* 29).

Nor do I wish him . . . prefect of the city: the Latin festival was celebrated at the temple of Jupiter Latiaris on the Alban Mount, about 14 miles (20 km.) from Rome. Since the festival was attended by the urban magistrates, it was usual for a prefect of the city to be appointed to cover their absence, a position given to youths of prominent families, often of the imperial family itself.

171 *Sulpicius and Athenodorus*: presumably his regular attendants.

college of Augurs: one of Rome's four major colleges of priests.

not even instituting him as an heir except in the third degree: on Augustus' will see *Aug.* 101 and note to p. 78.

Saturnalia and Sigillaria: at the festival of the Saturnalia in mid-December it was usual to exchange gifts. Sigillaria was the last day of the Saturnalia when small gifts made of pottery were exchanged.

the fall of Sejanus: in 31. Cf. *Tib.* 55.

priests of Augustus: established by Tiberius as part of the cult of the Deified Augustus.

among those of consular rank: senators were called on to express their views in order of seniority by rank.

172 *his loss*: i.e. of his house.

an eagle . . . landed on his right shoulder: a circumstance which might readily be interpreted as portending his future rise to power. See e.g. *Tib.* 14.

the emperor's brothers: Caligula's older brothers both died during the reign of Tiberius, apparently as a result of the machinations of Sejanus.

the conspiracy of Lepidus and Gaetulicus was discovered: in 39 CE.

173 *the new priesthood*: associated with the worship of Caligula himself; see *Cal.* 22.

he so undermined . . . make up the difference: he had presumably borrowed money from the treasury with his property as security in order to pay the entrance fee for the new priesthood.

Those conspiring . . . privacy: Suetonius gives a fuller account of the conspiracy at *Cal.* 56–8. Caligula was killed 24 January 41 CE.

With the intention of asserting civic liberty: this is generally taken to mean that there was talk of restoring the republic in some form.

174 *a chariot drawn by elephants . . . like that for Augustus*: these chariots carried images of Augustus and Livia to the circus where they would be placed in positions of honour overlooking the games.

his brother: Germanicus.

a Greek comedy . . . the judges: it is presumed Germanicus was the author of this work. See *Cal.* 3.

refraining from taking the forename 'Imperator': cf. *Jul.* 76.

175 *decorated*: with garlands, part of the usual celebrations marking a new reign.

He was consul . . . four years: Claudius was consul in 42, 43, 47 and 51 CE.

176 *he was immune because of the number of his children*: Augustus' marriage laws of 18 BCE and 9 CE prescribed various privileges of this kind for parents of larger families.

177 *common prostitutes . . . their testimony admitted*: normally prostitutes were considered too disreputable to be admitted as witnesses.

the censorship of Plancus and Paulus: in 22 BCE. Claudius held the office in 48 CE.

the inspection of the knights: cf. *Aug.* 39.

178 *a charge of treason . . . to recover a loan*: Gaius Rabirius Postumus made large sums out of banking. When prosecuted in 54 BCE he was defended by Cicero in a speech which is still extant. Cf. *Jul.* 12.

He accused some . . . to have ample means: Augustus' marriage laws of 18 BCE and 9 CE imposed various penalties on the unmarried and those who did not have children. There was a minimum census requirement of 400,000 sesterces to be a knight and, since Augustus' time, of 1,000,000 sesterces to be a senator.

the Sigillaria: an area of the city of Rome.

cut into pieces in his presence: presumably as a warning to the luxurious. The policing of luxury was traditionally part of the censors' remit.

from Massilia as far as Gesoriacum by land: modern Marseille and Boulogne on the English Channel.

179 *Diribitorium*: a large building in the Campus Martius area.

the Augustan marriage law: see *Aug.* 34.

women . . . with four children: another provision of Augustus' marriage legislation was privileges for free-born mothers of three children and ex-slave mothers of four children.

179 *the Caeruleus . . . Curtius and Albudignus*: all springs in the Sabine country to the northeast of Rome.

180 *transported from Egypt*: by Caligula, to be set up in his circus near the Vatican hill.

the temples at the top: Pompey's Theatre had a temple to Venus at the top of the seating area.

Secular Games: cf. *Aug.* 31.

goals: these were the markers at each end of the central island, around which the chariots raced.

181 *the Troy games*: see *Jul.* 39.

'little presents': using the Latin term *sportula* which was normally used to refer to the presents of food which patrons often gave their clients.

bringing out his left hand . . . as the common people do: upper-class Romans normally kept their left hands covered under their togas.

granted the wooden sword: the sign that a gladiator was discharged.

those who were to fight . . . 'Or not': the combatants in such conflicts were usually condemned criminals. The point of Claudius' joke, presumably, was that not all would die in battle.

182 *permission to travel*: under a law of 45 CE, senators were not supposed to travel beyond a certain distance from Rome without permission.

procurators with consular insignia: procurators—a term which covered the governors of minor provinces, as well as imperial financial agents—were drawn from the equestrian order.

the right to wear the broad stripe: the broad purple stripe on the tunic was worn only by senators and those the emperor selected for future senate membership.

183 *Appius Claudius the censor*: a magistrate of the fourth century BCE of legendary moral severity.

the free-born children they produced: i.e. those children born to them after they had acquired their freedom. Other ancient sources do not concur with this definition.

treasury of Saturn: the state treasury located in the Temple of Saturn in the Forum.

to walk on his left . . . as he came away from it: these were marks of particular respect.

184 *liable for murder*: killing a slave did not normally count as murder. Indeed, under most circumstances a master could kill his own slave without running the risk of legal action (though few seem to have risked the moral condemnation and hostility such an action would bring).

unless they were on foot or in a chair or litter: i.e. not in carriages.

he forbade to use Roman names, at least the gentile ones: i.e. the names such as Claudius, Cornelius, or Tullius which Roman citizens had as the second of their traditional three names.

Ilium . . . the founders of the Roman race: Ilium was another name for Troy. Romulus and Remus were descendants of the Trojan Aeneas, according to legend.

at the instigation of Chrestus: scholars argue as to whether or not this might be a reference to Jesus Christ.

the envoys of the Germans . . . in no way inferior: Augustus' rules on seating arrangements in the theatre had excluded foreign envoys from sitting in the area reserved for senators, though special exceptions were made.

185 *marriages of this kind*: i.e. between uncle and niece.

186 *Britannicus was born . . . when he was consul for the second time*: in 42 CE— long after twenty-two days had elapsed since Claudius' accession.

   the silver-tipped spear: a military prize.

187 *Appius Silanus*: Silanus was married to Messalina's mother.

   Julia, the daughter of Drusus: otherwise known as Livilla.

   four days before the Kalends of January: 29 December.

188 *the Salian priests*: the feasts of the Salii were proverbial for their luxury (see e.g. Horace, *Odes* 1. 37. 2).

   parricides: see *Aug.* 33.

   an execution in the ancient manner: presumably along the lines described at *Nero* 49.

189 *net-fighters, so that he could see their faces as they died*: those who fought with nets did not wear helmets.

   He actually sent on . . . in his toga: the summary execution of someone whose toga clearly marked him as a Roman citizen was especially shocking.

   as I noted: ch. 12 above.

   as I noted above: ch. 13 above.

191 *Claudius even took jurisdiction over the cookhouses away from the aediles*: see note to p. 115 above.

   he would, on the following day . . . taking them to task for sleeping late: cf. *Cal.* 26.

   a nibble: presumably it was the use of the colloquial term *offula*, 'little bit', which was felt inappropriate.

192 *there are some . . . who do not think me their patron*: this could be taken as a reference, whether conscious or unconscious, to Claudius' manipulative freedmen.

   Telegenius: probably someone proverbial for his idiocy.

192 *Titus Livy*: the famous historian.

his mother and his grandmother: Antonia, daughter of Mark Antony, and Livia, wife of Augustus, who would no doubt have had their own particular perspectives on this period.

three new letters of the alphabet: these were the inverted digamma (to represent 'u' as a consonant), probably the anti-sigma (to represent 'bs') and the sign for the Greek rough breathing (to represent the Greek 'y').

193 *When a barbarian . . . in both our languages*: contrast *Tib.* 71.

a set speech: presumably in Greek. The use of Greek in the senate seems to have been avoided in earlier periods, with Greek ambassadors being required to speak in Latin.

Ward off the man . . . attack: this line occurs at *Iliad* 24. 369 and *Odyssey* 21. 133.

the ancient museum at Alexandria: a famous centre of learning.

'The one who made the wound will heal it': a proverbial saying, drawn from the story of Telephus who was told by an oracle that his wound could be cured only by Achilles who had inflicted it.

killed by poison: rumours of foul play are associated with most deaths in the imperial family. Virtually all sources, with the exception of Josephus (*Jewish Antiquities* 20. 151), relate that Claudius was poisoned.

194 *the citadel*: the part of the Capitoline Hill where the temple of Juno was located.

He died . . . the fourteenth year of his reign: 13 October 54 CE.

restored by Vespasian: cf. *Vesp.* 9.

NERO

195 *Two young men . . . a battle whose outcome was at that time awaited*: Plutarch (*Aemilius Paulus* 25) identifies the twins as Castor and Pollux. The battle in question was that of Lake Regillus fought against the Latins in 496 BCE, according to Roman tradition.

turning his beard . . . bronze: hence 'Ahenobarbus' from *aheneus*, 'bronze' and *barbus*, 'beard'.

Gnaeus Domitius: tribune of the plebs in 104 BCE he went on to be consul in 96 and censor in 92.

When he was consul . . . as if in a triumphal procession: actually, it was the tribune's father, also called Gnaeus Domitius, who defeated the Allobroges. For the motif of appropriating the triumph, cf. ch. 25 below.

The son of this Ahenobarbus . . . contrary to the auspices and the laws: see *Jul.* 23–4.

196 *Corfinium*: in central Italy.

Pharsalus: the battle which brought the defeat of Pompey by Julius Caesar. See *Jul.* 35.

He was an indecisive man . . . an insufficiently powerful dose: for similar indecision on the part of Nero himself, see chs. 47–9 below.

a son: Gnaeus Domitius Ahenobarbus, consul 32 BCE. This is the Aenobarbus of Shakespeare's *Antony and Cleopatra*.

the Pedian law: the law condemning the conspirators was proposed in 43 by the consul Quintus Pedius.

197   *He was no less famous . . . to restrain him by edict*: this ancestor foreshadows the emperor in his enthusiasm for chariot racing (22 and 24), cruelty (36 and 37) and humiliation of the Roman élite on stage (11). Suetonius is the only source to attribute these vices to the former.

the elder Antonia: Mark Antony's elder daughter.

Gaius Caesar: Augustus' grandson—his adopted son. Their respective ages make this story most unlikely but it serves Suetonius' purpose in emphasizing Nero's inherited vices.

he issued an edict: in his capacity as praetor, but the edict did not remedy his own previous action.

on the eighteenth day before the Kalends of January: 15 December 37 CE.

laid on the ground: it was the custom for a new-born baby to be laid on the ground. The father would then acknowledge it by picking it up.

purification: this ceremony, which for a boy took place nine days after his birth, entailed the child's purification by means of a sacrifice and the receipt of a name.

his name: either Claudius' forename, Tiberius or his *cognomen*, Nero. Both these names were later taken by Nero on being adopted.

198   *his co-heir, Caligula, seized everything*: cf. *Cal.* 38, also ch. 32 below.

In his eleventh year: Nero was adopted 25 February 50, when he was 12. His mother Agrippina had married Claudius in 49 (cf. *Claud.* 27).

teaching Caligula: Suetonius' account lays particular emphasis on similarities between Caligula and Nero.

his father: i.e. Claudius.

199   *the Latin festival*: see note to p. 170.

Octavia: Claudius' daughter by Messalina.

he refused just one . . . for one of his age: contrast the repeated refusal of honours by Augustus (*Aug.* 53).

sharing a litter: this apparent sign of filial respect takes on a new significance in the light of accusations of incest (see ch. 28 below).

the Papian law: of 9 CE, part of the Augustan marriage legislation. Cf. *Claud.* 19.

in the case of senators . . . five thousand sesterces: cf. *Tib.* 47 and *Vesp.* 17. Augustus, too, is said by the historian Dio to have helped needy senators (55. 13).

200 *without prompting*: cf. *Aug.* 53.

a public thanksgiving: an honour previously conferred only on generals after a great victory.

He would recite his poems . . . to Capitoline Jupiter: though this could be seen as foreshadowing the much less acceptable forms of self-display recounted in chs. 20 and 21 below.

He provided a great many games: cf. *Aug.* 43–5.

Youth Games: according to Dio (61. 19. 1) these celebrated the first shaving of Nero's beard. Cf. ch. 12 below.

he assigned separate seating to Roman knights: hitherto, equestrians had had separate seating only at the theatre.

took on the parts of actors: while this added to the lustre of the production it could also be seen as humiliating for the participants. Cf. note to p. 67.

Afranius: born *c*.150 BCE. None of his works have survived.

keep them for themselves: contrast citizens' experience at the time of the real fire, as recounted in ch. 38 below.

four hundred senators . . . of good reputation: members of the senatorial and equestrian orders seem to have appeared on stage and in the arena under other emperors as well, but generally, Suetonius implies, they chose to do so for the money (such activities were particularly associated with the profligate). Nero, Suetonius suggests, was exercising compulsion upon those who would not otherwise be making an exhibition of themselves.

Pyrrhic dancers: originally a dance of armed men, this seems later to have developed to include the performance of mythological stories.

201 *Pasiphae*: wife of the mythical king Minos and mother of the Minotaur.

an Icarus . . . fell immediately to the ground: trapped on Crete, the mythical inventor Daedalus is said to have made wings from feathers and wax to enable himself and his son Icarus to escape. Icarus flew too near the sun, the wax melted and he fell to his death.

his baths and gymnasium: in the Campus Martius area of Rome.

who occupied the seats of the praetors: thus indicating that these games ranked higher than those over which the praetors presided.

oratory and verse in Latin: part of the 'musical' phase of the competition.

the first shavings of his beard: these were celebrated as a mark of a young man's accession to adulthood.

To the athletic contests . . . Olympia: women had been excluded from watching athletics by Augustus.

I am, I believe, justified . . . into the city: Tiridates was the brother of Vologaesus I of Parthia who made him king of Armenia in 54 CE. Tiridates was temporarily displaced through Roman intervention then reinstated by his brother. After negotiations with the Roman general Corbulo, Tiridates agreed to come to Rome and receive the crown of Armenia ceremonially from Nero in 66, thereby allowing Romans the appearance at least of control over Armenia. There is perhaps some irony in Suetonius' suggestion that this was just a show. At ch. 30 below he criticizes the cost of this event.

202 *'Imperator'*: the term used to salute a victorious general. No mention is made of Corbulo who actually negotiated the agreement.

offered laurels on the Capitol: this was normally done only when a triumph was celebrated.

closed the gates . . . no longer any wars being waged: as Augustus had done; see *Aug.* 22.

He held the consulship . . . the first and fourth: 55, 57, 58, and 60. A fifth consulship in 68 is referred to in ch. 43 below.

He refused . . . into the senate: contrast *Claud.* 24.

his one-day consulship: see *Jul.* 76.

the triumphal regalia: previously conferred only on senior military commanders.

He devised a new arrangement . . . for fighting fires: presumably after the great fire which destroyed large swathes of the city and for which many believed Nero himself to be responsible. See ch. 38 below.

He devised . . . to the old city: it is striking that Suetonius gives no account of major public-works projects which Nero is known to have undertaken, such as his baths in the Campus Martius (alluded to in ch. 12 above). See also ch. 31 below.

203 *Many new laws were passed*: Suetonius' use of the passive in the rest of this chapter has been seen as an acknowledgement that Burrus (the prefect of the praetorian guard) and Seneca (Nero's tutor) rather than Nero himself initiated these measures.

the sale of hot food in taverns was prohibited: several emperors are said to have initiated measures of this kind. See e.g. *Tib.* 34 and *Claud.* 38.

the pantomime actors . . . outlawed from the city: the imposition of such controls is associated with several emperors (see e.g. *Tib.* 37). It fits oddly with the emphasis elsewhere in Suetonius' account on Nero's enthusiasm for the stage (e.g. ch. 26 below)

transferred to the Forum: rather than coming before the prefects of the treasury.

his own parent: i.e. Claudius. Suetonius does not seem to be critical of Nero's behaviour here. Cf. *Aug.* 21.

Pontus: a small client kingdom on the south coast of the Black Sea.

the latter's Alpine territory: the only remaining part of the Alps not already a Roman province.

the Isthmus: of Corinth. This project is also associated with Julius Caesar (*Jul.* 44). Caligula, too, according to Suetonius, hoped to dig through the isthmus (*Cal.* 21). Roman moralists often associated such interventions in the natural boundaries between land and sea with tyranny (see e.g. Horace, *Odes* 3. 1).

204　*the Caspian gates*: the name given to the chief pass through the central part of the Caucasus.

　Alexander the Great: other emperors, too, had linked themselves with Alexander: see *Aug.* 18, 50 and 94; *Cal.* 52.

　hidden music has no admirers: public performances of this kind were traditionally seen by Romans as degrading to the performer, however.

205　*supported by those even of a guard of soldiers*: soldiers in particular might have been expected to disapprove of such unmanly activities.

　Niobe: the mythological figure Niobe who had twelve children attracted the wrath of the gods for comparing herself favourably with Leda who had only two, Apollo and Diana. The latter, both archers, shot all her children dead. Niobe was the archetype of the bereaved mother. Nero's choice of a female role for his début accentuates the effeminate aspect of acting.

　one of the praetors offered a million sesterces: performance for payment was perceived as especially degrading—an added excitement for an emperor with perverse tastes?

　Canace . . . Hercules insane: four figures from mythology. Canace, the daughter of Aeolus, committed incest with her brother, Macereus. Orestes killed his mother Clytemnestra to avenge his father, Agamemnon, and was hounded by the Furies. Oedipus blinded himself after discovering that he had unwittingly killed his father and married and had children by his own mother. Hercules was driven mad by the goddess Hera and killed his own children. All these stories could be seen as relevant to Nero's own life.

　when he and his fellow pupils . . . Hector: see note to p. 164 above. After his death, the body of Hector, the Trojan hero of Homer's *Iliad*, was dragged by Achilles' chariot around the walls of Troy.

206　*as I have reported*: see ch. 19

　Cassiope: a harbour on Corcyra (modern Corfu).

　the Olympic Games: the major games in Greece (Pythian, Nemean, and Isthmian as well as Olympic) took place every four years.

207　*the outcome would be determined by Fate*: judges with a sense of their own safety would know better than to award the prize to anyone but the emperor.

　wiping sweat from his brow with his arm: it seems handkerchiefs were not permitted. Nero's scrupulousness here contrasts with his flagrant disregard of the conventions which normally governed the behaviour of emperors.

. . . disposed of: cf. *Cal.* 60 where the senate debates a similar fate for the statues of emperors.

Mithridates: several kings of Pontus bore this name.

freedom: i.e. local self-government and freedom from tribute. The grant was later cancelled by Vespasian when he made Achaea a province (*Vesp.* 8). Hence, perhaps, its inclusion here among Nero's bad deeds.

his first public appearance on stage: see ch. 20.

208 *through the Circus Maximus . . . the Temple of Apollo*: in contrast to the route of the usual military triumph which culminated at the Temple of Jupiter on the Capitol. Nero's procession could be interpreted as a parody of a triumph and might thus seem especially offensive to those who valued Rome's military traditions.

he was so keen . . . someone else speaking his words: another indication that Nero valued the theatre over the army.

. . . due not to his age but to his nature: cf. *Tib.* 57 and *Cal.* 11.

a freedman's cap or a wig: for the use of disguise cf. *Cal.* 11.

209 *He would draw out his banquets from noon to midnight*: banquets normally took place in the evening.

respectable ladies . . . to summon them: according to Suetonius, Caligula too was associated with the prostitution of respectable women; see *Cal.* 41.

210 *all were convinced that he had desired to sleep with his mother . . . his clothing*: cf. the allegations of incest relating to Caligula (*Cal.* 24).

he devised a new and unprecedented practice . . . Doryphorus: cf. the sadistic practices Suetonius attributes to Tiberius (*Tib.* 44).

the vast fortune left him by Tiberius: see *Cal.* 37.

Tiridates . . . a hundred million: see ch. 13 above.

On the lyre-player . . . fit for triumphant generals: again, Nero shows disrespect for traditional Roman values by rewarding entertainers as if they were triumphant generals.

211 *the House of Passage*: this structure linked the imperial residences on the Palatine with the gardens of Maecenas, an imperial property on the Esquiline, via the area later occupied by the Colosseum.

the emperor himself: this was later altered by Vespasian. See *Vesp.* 18.

There was also a lake . . . wild animals: the re-creation of rusticity in the heart of the city could itself be seen as an affront to natural propriety.

he said nothing more . . . like a human being: Nero might rather have been expected to compare his new house to that of the gods. Subverting this expectation, the joke emphasizes the huge gulf separating Nero's house from anyone else's. Contrast Augustus' conspicuous modesty (*Aug.* 72).

a canal from Avernus . . . the sea: the coastline was dangerous to shipping. But such activities can also be placed in the context of Nero's other interventions in the natural landscape, such as the Golden House and the Corinth canal. See note to p. 203 above.

212 *Queen Dido . . . with only the smallest trouble*: Dido, the mythical queen of Carthage, whose love for Aeneas is the subject of Virgil, *Aeneid* 4.

he made it law . . . should not escape punishment either: cf. *Cal.* 38.

punished: the penalty would include confiscation of property.

the gifts . . . different cities: see ch. 24.

closed down all the stalls: presumably confiscating their wares.

the kind of mushrooms . . . the food of the gods: cf. *Claud.* 44.

213 *lengthening the first syllable*: of *morari*. The word would otherwise have signified 'remain'.

he failed to provide . . . cremated: cf. *Claud.* 45. Contrast the respect for predecessors shown by some earlier emperors, e.g. *Jul.* 88 and *Aug.* 100.

the Julian law: 'Against Assassination', renewed by Julius Caesar.

. . . and retire to Rhodes because of her: cf. the story Suetonius tells about Tiberius' reasons for retiring to Capri (*Tib.* 51). Tiberius had himself retired to Rhodes in 6 BCE.

214 *festival of Minerva*: a four day festival in March.

Bauli: a small Campanian town between Misenum and Baiae.

'When I have your first beard, I can die happy': see note to p. 200.

215 *the insignia of wife*: just as the triumphal insignia might be granted in place of a triumph.

a great passion for Poppaea: Suetonius gives an account of this at *Otho* 3.

Aulus Plautius: it is not clear how he was related to Nero.

216 *Seneca . . . Burrus*: it is notable that Suetonius makes no mention of the strong influence both Burrus and Seneca are alleged by other sources to have had over Nero's administration, though cf. note to p. 203 above.

the imperial freedmen: Pallas and Doryphorus are mentioned by Tacitus (*Annals* 14. 65). On Pallas, see *Claud.* 28.

A comet . . . successive nights: cf. *Jul.* 88.

the Pisonian conspiracy at Rome: discovered in 65. Tacitus gives a lengthy account of it (*Annals* 15. 48–74). Suetonius does not list the prominent individuals who were killed in the aftermath.

Vinicius . . . Beneventum: nothing is otherwise known of this plot.

Salvidienus Orfitus: consul in 51.

Gaius Cassius . . . family tree: compare the similar charge made at *Tib.* 61.

Thrasea Paetus . . . a teacher: Thrasea was known for his commitment to Stoic philosophy. Stoic teachers were often criticized for affecting an over-serious demeanour.

217 *the fabric of his ancestral city*: contrast Suetonius' comments on Augustus' treatment of Rome, *Aug.* 28–30.

he set fire to the city: Rome was devastated by a great fire in 64. Nero's responsiblity for it is much less clear in, for example, Tacitus, *Annals* 15. 38.

the tower of Maecenas: presumably located in the Gardens of Maecenas on the Esquiline hill.

he undertook . . . their own property: this act could be seen as one of imperial beneficence.

218 *Libitina's portion*: records of deaths were kept in Libitina's temple.

a great disaster . . . allies: the revolt of Boudicca.

humiliation . . . Syria: cf. to p. 201.

was especially tolerant . . . pasquinades: though cf. ch. 32 on treason accusations.

Nero . . . killed their mothers: in Greek. On Orestes see note to p. 205. Alcmeon, another figure from myth, was the son of Amphiareus. He too killed his mother and was hounded by the Furies.

A new equation . . . mother: in Greek. The numerical value of the letters in Nero's name (1,005) is equivalent to that of the rest of the sentence.

Aeneas . . . his father: Aeneas rescued his father by carrying him on his back from the ruins of Troy.

. . . theirs the great archer: hence, perhaps, the Parthians will triumph.

Rome is becoming one house . . . Veii, too: when Rome was sacked by the Gauls in 390 BCE, there was allegedly a debate as to whether the Romans should leave their city for the neighbouring town of Veii. Nero thus appears as an enemy occupying the city of Rome.

Isidorus the Cynic . . . his own goods ill: Cynic philosophers, having no regard for material comforts, were traditionally outspoken even to the most powerful. Nauplius, the son of Odysseus' rival Palamedes, sought to avenge his father after the latter had been framed by Odysseus.

Orcus guides your steps: Orcus, a god of the underworld, was often used as a synonym for death. Roman audiences were well attuned to perceiving contemporary resonances in plays, sometimes with the encouragement of the actors. See e.g. Cicero, *To Atticus* 39. 3 (59 BCE) which describes an audience interpreting a line from a play as a reference to the ambitions of Pompey.

The actor and the philosopher . . . displeasure: contrast *Cal.* 27 and *Dom.* 10.

219 *Vindex . . . propraetor*: Gaius Julius Vindex (a Roman of aristocratic Gallic descent) rebelled against Nero in spring of 68.

the age of Galba: though Galba was actually 71 in 68 CE.

his poor lyre-playing: again, Suetonius presents Nero as valuing his achievements as a singer over everything else.

220 *Galba . . . had also revolted*: see *Galba* 9.

221 *shorn in a mannish fashion . . . Amazons*: cross-dressing characterizes even the military activities of Suetonius' Nero. On Amazons see note to p. 11 above.

not even excepting accountants or secretaries: the use of slaves in war was perceived as a last resort of the desperate.

to the emperor's fund: rather than to their landlords.

real competition . . . at last: in contrast to those of the games. The lock of hair was presumably a reference to Nero's practice of wearing his hair long. See. ch. 51 below.

the sack: part of the prescribed punishment for parricide.

222 *the Gauls*: a pun on *galli* which means both 'cocks' and 'Gauls'.

a Defender: i.e. *Vindex*, a pun on the name of the rebel leader.

His fears . . . and omens: cf. the dreams of Julius Caesar, *Jul.* 81.

the Mausoleum: constructed by Augustus for himself and his descendants. See *Aug.* 100.

Proserpina: she was carried off by Pluto, the god of the underworld. Thus her story could be understood as portending death.

vows: on New Year's Day, for the safety of the state and the emperor.

'Oedipus in Exile': on Oedipus, see note to p. 205 above. The line might be thought especially pertinent to Nero who was alleged to have been involved in poisoning his stepfather Claudius, to have committed incest with and murdered his mother, and to have had his wife Octavia sent into exile for a crime she did not commit.

Lucusta: see ch. 33 above.

223 *'It is really so hard to die?'*: Virgil, *Aeneid* 12. 646.

the Salerian Way and the Nomentan Way: two roads leading out of Rome to the west.

224 *'This is Nero's essence'*: apparently referring to a drink he was alleged to have devised (see Pliny, *Natural Histories* 31. 40).

beyond the reach: i.e. to commit suicide.

225 *'The thunder . . . my ears'*: Homer, *Iliad* 10. 535.

the Hill of Gardens: now known as the Pincio.

his tunic unbelted: the absence of a belt was often seen as a sign of effeminacy.

philosophy . . . incompatible with imperial power: some philosophical sects advocated a life of contemplation, which would mean rejecting active involvement in running the state.

Seneca . . . for himself: cf. the comments on Seneca's style which Suetonius attributes to Caligula (*Cal.* 53).

226 *many are of the opinion . . . as his own*: this has been seen as an attempt to refute Tacitus, *Annals* 14. 16. 1–8.

I have had access . . . in the work: this is one of the very few occasions on which Suetonius refers to an archive source later than the letters of Augustus.

'Neroneus': cf. *Jul.* 76, *Aug.* 100.

the Syrian goddess: Atargatis, widely worshipped in Syria.

227 *He met his end . . . dressed in liberty caps*: Nero died 9 June 68.

Yet there were also some . . . to surrender him: contrast the much less ambiguous responses to the deaths of Tiberius (*Tib.* 75) and Caligula (*Cal.* 60).

GALBA

228 *With Nero, the descendants of the Caesars died out*: subsequent emperors (apart from Vitellius, see *Vit.* 8) took the name 'Caesar' as a title.

an eagle . . . dropped the bird into her lap: eagle portents are very frequent in Suetonius, particularly in relation to the holding of supreme power. See e.g. *Aug.* 94, *Tib.* 14, *Claud.* 7.

the temple of the Caesars: it is not clear what building is referred to here.

Galba . . . succeeded Nero: in 68 CE.

Quintus Catulus Capitolinus: a leading figure of the late republic who acquired his title because he was given responsibility for rebuilding the temple of Jupiter on the Capitol after it was destroyed by fire in 83 BCE.

Pasiphae: see note to p. 201 above.

the ancestral portraits: see note to p. 44.

the name Galba: as a *cognomen*.

galbanum: the resin of a Syrian plant.

229 *Servius Galba . . . slaughtered*: governor of Further Spain 151–150 BCE. He is alleged to have promised peace to the Lusitani, then, when they had laid down their arms, to have captured a large number of whom all but a few were slaughtered. The survivors included Viriatius, who went on to lead the Lusitani and after whom the war was named.

the Pedian law: see note to p. 196.

the consulship: he was suffect consul in 5 BCE.

the allocation of provinces . . . in his year: under the principate, it became the practice that the governorships of Africa and Asia were awarded each year to the two most senior ex-consuls (the lot determining who got which province).

the ninth day . . . Gnaeus Lentulus: 24 December 3 BCE.

He was adopted . . . changing his forename: women in Rome could not formally adopt except in their wills. Before becoming emperor, Galba seems to have used the name L. Livius Ocella Sulpicius Galba.

230 *the bronze image of a goddess . . . once a year*: cf. the omen involving this
statue in ch. 18 below.

he insisted unswervingly . . . one by one: one of several ways in which Galba
is presented as excessively devoted to tradition.

Agrippina: the younger Agrippina, daughter of Germanicus and the elder
Agrippina, and mother of the emperor Nero. She subsequently married
the emperor Claudius (see *Claud.* 26).

231 *elephants walked on tightropes*: cf. *Nero*: 11.

for six months: in 33 CE.

Lucius Domitius: elsewhere Nero's father is referred to as 'Gnaeus' rather
than 'Lucius'.

when Caligula was visiting: see *Cal.* 43–4.

run alongside the emperor's chariot for twenty miles: cf. *Caligula* 26—though
with a rather different spin.

He was specially chosen: normally provinces were allocated by lot to
appropriately qualified ex-magistrates. See note to p. 229 above.

232 *the Board of Fifteen*: see note to p. 37.

the brotherhood of Titius: an ancient priesthood, origins uncertain.

the priests of Augustus: founded by Tiberius to serve the cult of Augustus
after his deification.

the governorship of Nearer Spain: in 60 CE.

the lake of Cantabria: in northern Spain.

crucified: crucifixion was regarded as punishment suitable only for slaves.

233 *a state of rebellion*: cf. *Nero* 40 and note to p. 219.

Clunia: a city in northern Spain.

manumission of slaves: part of Galba's duties as provincial governor would
have been granting requests to manumit slaves. The regular time for this
would have been an especially apt moment to declare his intention to free
the empire from Nero's slavery.

the nearest of the Balearic islands: Majorca.

retaining entitlement . . . the gold ring: normally equestrians who served as
legionaries or centurions would lose this.

234 *Dertosa*: a town near the mouth of the river Hebrus (modern Ebro) in
Spain.

the death of Vindex: defeated at the battle of Vesontio by Verginius Rufus,
the governor of Upper Germany, Vindex may have been killed or else
committed suicide.

'Caesar': originally the family name of Julius Caesar, the name 'Caesar'
had by this time effectively beome an imperial title, which could be taken
on even by someone quite unrelated to the Julio-Claudians. See note to
p. 228.

a dagger . . . suspended from his neck: the dagger was an emblem of the emperor's proconsular power.

capital punishment: in Roman law this might mean no more than exile, along with the forfeiting of property and citizen rights.

235 *five denarii*: a very meagre reward.

the well-known chorus . . . with the accompanying gestures: we should assume this chorus was a lament uttered by the city household on the unwelcome arrival of their severe elderly master from the country. For a similar incident see *Nero* 39 and note to p. 218.

he gave many indications of being an excellent emperor: Suetonius chooses not to include any specific instances of these.

the gold ring: one emblem of equestrian status; cf. ch. 10 above.

236 *parental privilege*: see note to p. 61 above.

by Claudius: see *Claud.* 23. The addition of a sixth panel of judges would presumably reduce the burden of service on the others.

the gifts made by Nero: see *Nero*: 30.

Halotus and Tigillinus: Halotus was a eunuch food-taster, allegedly involved in poisoning Claudius (see *Claud.* 44), while Tigellinus (as his name is spelled elsewhere) served as prefect of the praetorian guard under Nero.

a larger than usual donative: it was customary for a new emperor to make a gift of money to each soldier on his accession to power. Note Suetonius' apparently critical comment on an instance of such 'bribery' at *Claud.* 10.

Nymphidius: from 65 praetorian prefect. He had made an attempt to seize power for himself after Nero's death; see ch. 11 above.

237 *to swear their oath on the Kalends of January*: it had become customary for the armies to take an oath of loyalty to the emperor on his appointment and to renew this every New Year's Day. Cf. *Nero* 46.

an ox . . . soaked him with its blood: it was considered very unlucky for a sacrificial victim to run away.

the image of Fortune he kept in his villa at Tusculum: see ch. 4 above.

238 *some warm ashes . . . the wine in an earthenware cup*: for an auspicious sacrifice, the altar would have been blazing, the attendants young, and the vessels made of precious materials.

the chickens flew away: the chickens were supposed to stay and eat, the more greedily the better.

he even promised a donative: which he had hitherto refused them; see ch. 16 above.

239 *the lacus Curtius*: a spot in the middle of the Forum linked to several different myths associated with early Rome, as well as with vows for the emperor's welfare (cf. *Aug.* 57).

since he could not grasp it by the hair: Suetonius notes below (ch. 21) that Galba was virtually bald.

239 *Steadfast . . . continues still*: in Greek; a quotation from Homer, *Iliad* 5. 254 (the same line occurs at *Odyssey* 21. 426).

Patrobius Neronianus: as his name indicates, Patrobius was himself a freedman of Nero.

only those who were especially tough and full grown: Romans generally seem to have considered boys and younger men suitable objects for desire, while it was thought perverse to lust after mature men.

240 *in his seventy-third year*: this statement cannot be reconciled with the birthdate Suetonius gives in ch. 4 above.

believing that Galba . . . to Judaea: this echoes Suetonius' earlier statement that Nero was alleged to have sent orders that Galba should be killed (*Galba* 9).

OTHO

241 *Ferentium*: a town in south Etruria.

Livia Augusta: the wife of Augustus.

in the middle of the camp: executions usually took place outside the camp, under the supervision of more junior officers.

Camillus' attempted coup: Camillus Scribonianus, governor of Dalmatia from 40 CE, made a bid for power in 42. Cf. *Claud.* 13.

the fourth day . . . Domitius Ahenobarbus: 28 April 32 CE.

242 *a thong*: a kind of punishment more usually used for slaves.

he used to wander about by night . . . blanket: Suetonius tells similar stories about Nero; see *Nero* 26.

Poppaea Sabina: cf. *Nero* 35.

Nero himself . . . what he had handed over in trust: this scene evokes a situation frequently represented in Latin love-elegy where the would-be lover, shut out of his mistress's house, offers a poetic lament.

as an ex-quaestor: normally provincial governors had previously reached the rank of praetor at least.

243 *When he was chosen . . . to the soldier*: Otho's treatment of soldiers could be seen as excessively indulgent. Contrast *Galba* 16.

244 *the Golden Milestone*: a symbol of Rome's position as the centre of empire.

agents who were to kill Galba and Piso: see *Galba* 19.

he was hailed . . . some provincial governors: Suetonius has already emphasized their similarities of character; see ch. 2 above. On Nero's popularity even after his death, see *Nero* 57.

the Golden House: cf. Suetonius' comments on Nero's Golden House as the summit of his extravagance in *Nero* 31.

245 *to propitiate . . . the shade of Galba*: the shades of those who had been murdered were often thought to seek vengeance on the murderers.

'*What have I got to do with long pipes?*': in Greek. A proverbial expression which seems to have been used of those doing something for which they were not suited.

the sacred shields . . . replaced: the replacing of the shields was a ritual believed to be of great antiquity, performed by the Salii (priests of Mars) in March.

the Mother of the Gods: also known as the Great Mother or Cybele. The festival mentioned here included a day commemorating Cybele's grief at the loss of her beloved Attis.

Father Dis: the god of the underworld.

246 *Brixellum*: a town on the River Po in northern Italy, modern Brescello.

Betriacum: a settlement between Cremona and Mantua.

the deaths of Brutus and Cassius: at the end of the civil war which their assassination of Julius Caesar had triggered.

247 *Messalina, the widow of Nero*: Statilia Messalina was Nero's third wife.

His funeral rites . . . on his instructions: presumably to avoid his corpse suffering mutilation at the hands of his opponents as had been Galba's fate (*Galba* 20).

He died . . . his reign: contrast the noble manner of Otho's death, as described by Suetonius, with the details of Nero's inconsistent and cowardly last hours (*Nero* 47–9), a contrast all the more notable given the many respects in which the two are presented as similar (see chs. 2 and 7 above).

Otho's appearance . . . such greatness: Suetonius frequently implies that physiognomy ought to reflect character. See e.g. the descriptions of Caligula, Nero, and Domitian.

the rites of Isis . . . the cult: although Caligula had earlier established an official state cult of Isis, other emperors had not participated publicly in this exotic cult, originating in Egypt, whose priests were eunuchs.

248 *in their grief attacked and killed one another*: contrast *Cal.* 27 where people offer their lives for the emperor's safety but are not willing to fulfil their promises.

VITELLIUS

249 *Faunus . . . and Vitellia*: Faunus was rustic deity associated with fields and woods. Vitellia is not otherwise known.

The Vitellian road . . . reminders of the line: the road is not otherwise known. There seems to have been a colony called Vitellia in the fifth century BCE. The Aequiculi of ancient Latium lived east of Rome on the bank of the River Anio.

249 *Nuceria*: probably near Naples.

Cassius Severus: an author of the Augustan age, notorious for his attacks on prominent people's reputations.

distinguished only by their forenames: as sons of the same father they would automatically share the same family (middle) name Vitellius.

250 *Gnaeus Piso . . . his condemnation*: see *Tib.* 52 and *Cal.* 2 and 3.

he succeeded in inducing Artabanus . . . the legionary standards: Rome and Parthia had been in dispute over who should rule Armenia, and over Roman attempts to control the Parthian throne. Suetonius refers to this episode in *Cal.* 14.

the censorship: the most senior and prestigious magistracy of all.

with his head veiled: it was usual for Romans to cover their heads when offering homage to a divinity.

Narcissus and Pallas: these two freedmen were believed to have enormous influence over Claudius; see *Claud.* 28–9.

'May you do this often!': the games were held in 47 CE. The proper interval between Secular Games was thought to be 100 or 110 years.

in the same year: Aulus (later emperor) and Lucius were both consul in 48.

251 *on the eighth day . . . were consuls*: 24 or 7 September 15 CE.

'tight-bum': see *Tib.* 43.

chariot racing . . . gambling: for these imperial passions, see *Cal.* 54–5 and *Claud.* 33.

Nero's contests: for these, see *Nero* 12 and 21.

in his province . . . gold and silver: Suetonius presents Otho as similarly inconsistent; see *Otho* 2–3.

252 *Titus Vinius*: see *Galba* 14.

the Blue Faction: see note to p. 164 above.

253 *mourning garments*: it was usual for someone who was on trial to wear mourning clothes until their case was determined.

with no regard to the day: it was 2 January. Traditionally it was considered inauspicious to begin something on the day after the first of the month.

Vienna: modern Vienne, on the Rhône.

a cock . . . and then on his head: for the significance of this, see ch. 18 below.

his officers: presumably a reference to Caecina and Valens, legionary legates who had commanded his victorious armies at Betriacum.

254 *the death of Otho*: see *Otho* 9 and 11.

because of the appalling example they had set: presumably in deserting Galba and appointing Otho as emperor, without the authority of the senate.

'That was the Mausoleum he deserved': contrasting Otho's modest grave with the grandeur of the imperial Mausoleum in Rome (*Aug.* 100).

the colony of the Agrippenses: modern Cologne.

an all-night festival . . . Apennines: the implication seems to be that this was nominally a religious thanksgiving for his victory over Otho but was in fact some kind of orgy. It was generally thought inappropriate to celebrate too enthusiastically a victory over fellow Romans.

he entered the city . . . their weapons bared: traditionally such displays were associated only with the exceptional circumstances of a triumph, the celebration of which was rare and could only be granted by the senate. Again, this overt parade of force could be seen as both a tasteless assertion of Vitellius' victory over Otho and a threat against anyone in the city who might oppose him.

the anniversary of the Allia: 18 July was always regarded as a day of particular ill-omen since it was the anniversary of a terrible defeat suffered by the Romans at the hands of the Gauls in 390 BCE, by the River Allia near Rome.

255 *deciding the elections for the next ten years*: though the senate theoretically had the right to elect magistrates, in practice the candidates commended or nominated by the emperor secured posts as a matter of course, but it was not usual to specify magistrates so far in advance.

consul in perpetuity: among earlier emperors, only Nero had held a perpetual consulship (see *Nero* 43). It was more usual for any extended consulship to be fixed at five or ten years.

the Master's Book: apparently the name of a book containing Nero's compositions.

Puteoli: now Pozzuoli, a coastal town near Naples.

the golden rings: the sign of membership of the equestrian order.

finding capacity for it all through regular vomiting: it was usual Roman pratice to eat only lightly except at dinner.

No one ever spent less . . . one of these meals: cf. *Nero* 27.

256 *In this he blended . . . the straits of Spain*: Roman moralists were particularly critical of exotic foods sought out from distant places and of dishes which combined different foods together. Compare the unnatural dishes associated with Caligula, *Cal.* 37.

decency: cf. *Claud.* 33.

when he discovered . . . both be killed: cf. *Cal.* 38.

257 *the Chatti*: a German tribe.

He was also suspected . . . which he willingly gave her: the allegation of matricide again emphasizes Vitellius' resemblance to Nero.

which he set on fire, thus putting an end to them: Suetonius tells of how Domitian escaped from this conflagration at *Dom.* 1.

348 *Explanatory Notes*

257 *looked out . . . as he was feasting*: looking on while Rome burns could be seen as another echo of Nero. Cf. *Nero* 38.

the dagger he had at his side: this dagger symbolized the emperor's power of life and death over the people.

258 *the temple of Concord*: a temple on the slope of the Capitoline hill, overlooking the Forum. It had strong associations with the resolution of civil conflict.

259 *Gemonian steps*: see note to p. 124.

set out above: in ch. 9 above.

Tolosa: in Gallia Narbonensis, modern Toulouse.

cock's beak: there is also a play here on *gallus* meaning 'cock' and *Gallus* meaning 'Gaul'.

THE DEIFIED VESPASIAN

260 *without any ancestral portraits*: i.e. no members of the family had held curule magistracies which would have entitled the family to display their busts.

Reate: an ancient Sabine city.

Pharsalus: see *Jul.* 35.

a fortieth: a tax on imports and exports.

the Helvetii: a Gallic tribe.

Nursia: a Sabine town.

261 *the fifteenth day . . . consuls*: 17 November 9 CE.

the broad-striped senatorial tunic: a preliminary qualification for the senate, granted as a special privilege to some sons of equestrian fathers.

he came sixth: i.e. of all the six successful candidates he secured fewest votes.

the conspirators: presumably Aemilius Lepidus and Lentulus Gaetulicus, accused in 39 of plotting to usurp the empire. See *Cal.* 24 and *Claud.* 9.

Latin status: a form of citizenship with more limited rights than those of full Roman citizens. Many slaves who had been freed but not according to the prescribed rituals also fell into this category.

262 *Antonia*: daughter of Mark Antony and mother of the emperor Claudius.

Britain: cf. *Claud.* 17.

the island of Vectis: the Isle of Wight.

of the year: 51 CE.

Hadrumetum: a city near Carthage in North Africa.

to keep up his position: there was a property qualification for the senatorial order of 1,000,000 sesterces.

Nero's entourage: see *Nero* 22.

263 *being of modest name and family, he offered no threat*: an ironic comment
on Suetonius' part. Only those of aristocratic background could make a
plausible claim to the empire, it was believed—wrongly, as events turned
out.

the following signs: Suetonius' inclusion of omens and portents at this
point in his narrative effectively serves to increase the reader's suspense
as he builds up to the account of Vespasian's unexpected rise to power.

a human hand: the Latin for hand, *manus*, is often used to mean power.

264 *Betriacum*: see *Otho* 9.

two eagles . . . drove away the victor: the first two eagles could be taken to
represent Otho and Vitellius, the third Vespasian, who defeated Vitellius,
the vanquisher of Otho.

Aquileia: a town in northern Italy on the Adriatic coast.

265 *the fifth day before the Ides*: 11 July. The date is disputed.

transferring the German army to the East: and thus stationing the eastern
legions in less attractive locations.

Licinius Mucianus: governor of Syria, the neighbouring province.

266 *he added another eight consulships to his earlier one*: in 70, 71, 72, 74, 75, 76,
77, and 79.

the marines . . . on foot: they were stationed at Ostia and at Puteoli, the
two major ports serving Rome, to watch for fires and also had duties in
the city.

267 *on his own back*: cf. *Nero* 19.

that of the Deified Claudius on the Caelian hill: cf. *Claud.* 45.

virtually razed to the ground by Nero: presumably in the process of
constructing the Golden House; see *Nero* 31.

an amphitheatre: the Colosseum. The amphitheatre of Statilius Taurus,
also of stone, was constructed in Augustus' time but in the Campus
Martius, i.e. outside the city proper (as defined by the *pomerium*). In
general, Suetonius presents Vespasian's interest in the fabric of the city
as parallel to that of Augustus. Cf. *Aug.* 28–30.

The distinguished orders . . . to the orders: cf. the actions attributed to
Augustus, *Aug.* 35. Other emperors are presented as undermining the
senate. See e.g. *Tib.* 55, *Cal.* 49, *Claud.* 24 and 29, *Nero* 37.

the centumviral courts: see *Aug.* 36 and note to p. 63.

268 *money-lenders should never have the right . . . after the family-head's death*:
it seems to have been common for money-lenders to make loans to those
in their father's or grandfather's power (when legally they had no
property of their own) which were to be repaid on the father's or grandfather's death (when the borrower would acquire legal independence and
would probably have inherited property).

the Salarian Way: leading from Rome to Reate.

268 *At first . . . well on in his reign*: it is unclear what is meant here, as Vespasian's tribunician power seems to have been dated from the day he was acclaimed emperor, 1 July 69 (although perhaps he did not at first make use of it). Vespasian (like Nero) seems to have refused the first offer of 'Father of the Fatherland' (cf. *Nero* 8), while Tiberius had declined it altogether (*Tib.* 26, 67).

having those who came to pay their respects searched: contrast *Claud.* 35.

He put up most patiently . . . the arrogance of philosophers: cf. *Aug.* 54–5.

the services he had rendered: see ch. 6 above.

'At least I am a real man': presumably an allusion to Licinius' allegedly effeminate sexual preferences.

'What is it to Caesar if Hipparchus has a hundred million': thus implying that the notoriously avaricious Vespasian might be inclined to condemn a wealthy man in order to secure his property.

a dog: Cynic philosophers were called such since the extremely simple life they recommended was likened by some to that of a dog, the Greek for 'dog' being *kuōn*.

269 *fearful at being banned from Nero's court*: see the section on Vespasian's travels in Nero's entourage in ch. 4. above.

he would some day be mindful of the favour: an ironic comment to the effect that when Mettius was emperor he might return Vespasian's kindness.

his edicts: normally the emperor's name and titles of honour would be listed at the beginning of the praetor's edict, as well as on other official documents.

Helvidius Priscus . . . an ordinary citizen: the Stoic Helvidius Priscus (praetor in 70) was married to the daughter of Thrasea Paetus. Under Nero, Thrasea had been made to commit suicide and Helvidius had been banished (in 66). Helvidius' outspoken opposition to Vespasian is celebrated by the later Stoic writer, Epictetus.

He engaged openly . . . at a profit: the Roman élite generally expressed disapproval of transactions of this kind, claiming that agriculture was the only truly respectable way to make a living (cf. Cicero, *On Duties* 1. 42). Such actions were considered especially shameful for senators (though there is considerable evidence that senators actually engaged in all kinds of business deals, often through agents).

270 *supporting needy ex-consuls . . . sesterces*: cf. *Nero* 10.

the Colossus: the colossal statue of Nero (see *Nero* 31).

Terpnus and Diodorus: Terpnus had earlier taught Nero, according to Suetonius (*Nero* 20), while Diodorus had been defeated by him in a Greek musical contest (Dio 63. 20).

Saturnalia . . . Kalends of March: the festival of the Saturnalia (see Glossary) was traditionally associated with the giving of gifts; 1 March was the Matronalia, in honour of the goddess Juno Lucina (associated with childbirth), when gifts were traditionally given to women.

'*Cybiosactes*': literally, 'salt-fish vendor' in Greek.

271 *ten million sesterces*: contrast the alleged cost of Nero's funeral (*Nero* 50).

he would put on his own shoes and cloak: usually high-ranking Romans would have slaves help them dress. Another sign of Vespasian's unassuming nature.

Caenis: see ch. 3 above.

'*plostra*' *instead of* '*plaustra*': meaning 'wagons'. Vespasian was being criticized for his rustic pronunciation.

272 *at quite appropriate moments*: contrast for example Claudius' generally inappropriate use of language (*Claud.* 21).

Striding along . . . a long shadow: Homer, *Iliad* 7. 213. The Latin for spear, *hasta* was sometimes used as a synonym for 'penis'.

to cheat . . . when he died: an ex-slave's former owner was entitled to at least some part of his estate.

Laches: a curious choice, as Laches was a stock name for a slave in Greek comedy.

O Laches . . . Cerylus again: Vespasian is presented as adapting some lines from a play by Menander (fr. 223. 2, Koch) to suggest that, whatever name the man used, his estate would be treated as that of the freedman Cerylus on his death.

to shoe the mules: mules were not normally shod, but their hoofs might be given temporary protective coverings on difficult terrain.

the base was all ready: i.e. the pile of money was to be placed on his hand.

the Mausoleum: that of Augustus (*Aug.* 100). For the portent cf. *Nero* 46.

long hair: the Latin *comata* literally means 'long-haired star'. Comets were particularly associated with the deaths of rulers. Cf. *Jul.* 88 and *Nero* 36.

I think I am becoming a god: an ironic reference to the practice of deifying some emperors after their deaths.

273 *Cutilae*: a town in the Sabine country.

Reate, where he used to spend every summer: see ch. 2 above.

on the ninth day . . . one month and seven days: 23 June 79.

both reigned . . . the same space of time: Claudius and Nero reigned respectively 13 and 14 years; Vespasian reigned 10, Titus 2, and Domitian 15.

THE DEIFIED TITUS

274 *his father's cognomen*: Vespasianus. His brother took the *cognomen* Domitianus, from their mother's family.

three days . . . in which Gaius was killed: 30 December 41 CE.

274 *the Septizonium*: a seven-storey building. Location unknown.

Britannicus: son of the emperor Claudius.

. . . which Britannicus finished off and then died: see *Nero* 33.

275 *a prefect of the praetorian guard*: the highest office a knight might aspire
to.

conquered . . . two mighty cities in Judaea: in 67.

Soon confirmed in this expectation: by the accession of his father,
Vespasian.

they acclaimed him as 'Imperator': it had been customary for conspicuous
victories to be marked in this way under the republic. However, under the
principate it was almost unheard of for anyone other than the emperor
himself to receive such an acclamation. Cf. *Jul.* 76, *Claud.* 12.

a diadem: the wearing of a diadem suggested regal aspirations. Cf. Julius
Caesar's rejection of the diadem offered by Antony (*Jul.* 79).

276 *they held the censorship jointly*: in 73.

tribunician power: this clearly marked him as Vespasian's successor (cf.
Tib. 16). He was also consul in 70, 72, 74, 75, 76, 77, and 79.

in place of a quaestor: the quaestors appointed by the emperor were
normally responsible for reading out his communications to the senate.

Aulus Caecina: consul in 69 CE.

Queen Berenice: daughter of Agrippa I, king of Judaea.

another Nero: compare the vices Suetonius attributes to Nero (*Nero* 26).

this reputation . . . by the greatest praise: Suetonius' Titus, who turns out
to be good despite his reputation, is the mirror image of Tiberius,
Caligula, Nero, and Domitian who, though initially welcomed, are
gradually revealed as monstrous (cf. *Tib.* 57, *Cal.* 11, *Nero* 26, *Dom.* 1).

277 *later emperors also . . . made particular use of*: usually a change of regime
involved a change of advisers.

the amphitheatre: the Colosseum, on which work began under his father
(see *Vesp.* 9).

he was the first . . . without even being asked: the rights bestowed by
emperors on communities, classes, and individuals, such as exemptions
of various kinds, which had previously been regarded as invalid on the
death of the emperor who granted them.

without any loss of dignity or fairness: contrast Suetonius' attitude to the
preferences expressed by Caligula (*Cal.* 55) and Domitian (*Dom.* 10).
Similarly, Suetonius comments on Claudius' lack of dignity when
watching the games (*Claud.* 21).

278 *the eruption of Mount Vesuvius*: that of 79 which destroyed Pompeii and
Herculaneum.

a fire at Rome: in 80.

During the fire . . . its more rapid completion: contrast the response of Suetonius' Nero, who sings while Rome burns (*Nero* 38).

sacrifices: plagues were often seen as a sign of divine anger which might be propitiated by the appropriate sacrifices.

the legal status of a deceased person: if the dead person were proved a slave rather than of free status, the dispositions of their will would no longer be valid.

Pontifex Maximus: since 13 BCE all emperors had held this priesthood.

When two men . . . to refrain: Suetonius presents Julius Caesar as similarly lenient towards conspirators (*Jul.* 75).

279 *their inspection*: it was customary for the person giving the games to inspect the weapons to see if they were sharp enough. A similar story is told about the emperor Nerva (Dio 68. 3).

On the Ides of September . . . in the forty-second year of his age: 13 September 81.

everyone . . . a member of their own family: cf. Suetonius' account of the mourning for Germanicus (*Cal.* 5).

heaped up such praises . . . present among them: contrast the great joy which Suetonius attributes to the senate on the death of Domitian (*Dom.* 23).

DOMITIAN

280 *Domitian was born . . . consul designate*: 24 October 51 CE.

'The One-Eyed Man': perhaps with the added sense of penis.

that dubious superstition: Isis was an Egyptian divinity. The priests of Isis were eunuchs and might seem appropriate companions for a young man of apparently compromised masculinity.

as Caesar: see note to p. 228 above. The extension of 'Caesar' to an emperor's son is noteworthy.

the office of urban prefect with consular power: an unprecedented combination of powers (his father and brother were both away from Rome).

he harassed the wives . . . the wife of Aelius Lamia: compare Suetonius' comments on Augustus (*Aug.* 69) and Caligula (*Cal.* 36). On Aelius Lamia, see further ch. 10 below.

281 *sedan*: since Claudius chairs (in which the occupant sat upright) had been used by emperors in preference to litters (in which one reclined) to travel through the city.

Alani: in Scythia.

a double donative: i.e. twice what his brother gave, as the new emperor.

a forged will: we might note here the boast Suetonius attributes to Titus (*Titus* 3) that he could have been a master forger.

281 *not even a fly*: a proverbial way to describe a deserted place.

    Augusta: the title awarded to Livia after the death of Augustus.

    but lost the boy . . . power: the MSS readings are problematic here.

282 *a little boy . . . with a small and deformed head*: dwarfs and people with deformities were often chosen as favourites by emperors and members of the Roman élite.

    having calculated the time period . . . when Augustus had done so: the proper timing for the Secular Games (supposedly due to take place every 100 or 110 years) was much disputed. Cf. *Claud.* 21.

    prose declamation: i.e. as well as in poetry.

    the college of Flaviales: established for the worship of the deified Flavian emperors, as the Augustales had been for deified Julio-Claudians.

283 *the Quinquatria of Minerva*: see note to p. 81.

    which had burnt down again: in 80, having earlier been destroyed in 69 (see *Vit.* 15).

    no mention . . . the earlier builders: this was not the usual practice. Contrast Augustus' boast in the *Res gestae* ('Account of his Achievements') that he had refrained from inscribing his own name on buildings he had restored leaving only those of earlier builders. Dio makes a similar comment about Domitian's father, Vespasian (66. 10).

    the Chatti: a tribe living near the Rhine in Western Germany.

284 *food-baskets*: see *Nero* 16. Often, it seems, patrons gave money instead of food.

    formal dinners: cf. *Aug.* 74.

    two new circus factions . . . as their colours : see *Cal.* 55 and note to p. 164.

    He banned actors . . . private houses: measures to curb the licence of actors are attributed to many earlier emperors by Suetonius. See e.g. *Tib.* 37.

    He banned . . . still held by slave-dealers: widely celebrated as a positive feature of Domitian's reign.

    to both freedmen and Roman knights: presumably those positions which were held exclusively by freedmen until the time of Nero, such as secretary in charge of letters (*ab epistulis*). By Hadrian's time freedmen were excluded from such posts.

    deposit . . . at headquarters: for safe-keeping.

    centumviral courts: see note to p. 63.

    the regulation of morals: in 83.

285 *the knights' seats*: the fourteen rows, immediately behind those at the front which were occupied by the senatorial order.

    because he had taken back his wife . . . adultery: laws passed under Augustus in 18 BCE and 9 CE had made it a husband's duty to divorce and prosecute an adulterous wife (see *Aug.* 34). In ch. 3 above Suetonius presents Domitian himself as guilty of the same actions as those punished here.

the Scantinian law: the prescriptions of this law, as well as its history, have been much debated by scholars. It seems to have been aimed at punishing homosexual acts involving the penetration of a free-born male.

An impious race . . . and feasted upon them: Georgics 2. 537

he would not accept them: cf. *Aug.* 66.

286 *the Clodian law*: it is not known what law is referred to here.

some resemblance to his teacher: Domitian's wife allegedly had an affair with Paris; see ch. 3 above.

the Thracian . . . the giver of the games: Domitian was thought to favour the Thracians.

'A buckler-wearer with a big mouth': the buckler was part of the characteristic equipment of the Thracians. Cf. the treatment allegedly meted out by Caligula (*Cal.* 27.).

Domitian had stolen Lamia's wife: see ch. 1 above.

'I practise continence': would-be orators were advised to improve their voices by abstaining from sexual activity. Cf. Quintilian, *Institutes of Oratory* 11. 3. 19.

287 *Mago and Hannibal*: Hannibal and his younger brother Mago led the Carthaginian invasion of Italy in 218 BCE, initiating the Second Punic War. They were thus archetypal enemies of Rome.

Thrasea Paetus . . . the most virtuous of men: Thrasea Paetus was a notable Stoic senator, condemned for treason under Nero. Helvidius Priscus, his son-in-law, was also known for his Stoic views and was condemned under Vespasian. See *Vesp.* 15.

the younger Helvidius: son of Helvidius Priscus.

Paris and Oenone: in mythology Oenone was Paris' first wife, whom he deserted for Helen. Roman audiences were quick to perceive contemporary allusions at the theatre; cf. *Nero* 39.

they had been used for other men's pleasures . . . the soldiers: in taking on a 'feminine' receptive role in sexual relations, these men would be seen to have forfeited the respect normally due to their rank—and gender.

288 *the traditional manner of punishment*: see *Nero* 49.

The estates . . . was his heir: cf. *Cal.* 38. This behaviour forms a contrast though with what Suetonius says of Domitian's treatment of those making false accusations in ch. 9 above.

The tax on the Jews . . . with the greatest rigour: a tax of two drachmas per head imposed by Titus in return for freedom to practise their religion.

went to kiss him as usual: as though she were Vespasian's wife. It was customary for Roman women to kiss their relations and those of their husbands. On Caenis, see *Vesp.* 3.

288 *Not good is a multitude of rulers*: Iliad 2. 204.

289 *it was he who had bestowed the empire on his father and brother*: they had both been in the East when Vespasian's supporters, including Domitian, took control of Rome.

divine couch: the term *pulvinar*, used here, normally refers to the sacred couch on which images of the gods were displayed.

master and mistress: the term *dominus*, used here, had been shunned by previous emperors (see e.g. *Tib.* 27). Normally used in the context of the master–slave relationship, it could be taken to imply the enslavement of the Roman people.

he did not deign . . . demand silence: contrast Titus' behaviour at *Titus* 8.

'Arci': meaning 'enough' in Greek as well as sounding like an archaic form of the plural of the Latin *arcus*, arch.

on seventeen occasions: in 71, 73, 75, 76, 77, 80, 82–8, 90, 92, and 95.

changed the name of the months: cf. *Jul.* 76, *Aug.* 100, *Nero* 55.

he refused the mushrooms: the emperor Claudius had allegedly met his end eating poisoned mushrooms; see *Claud.* 44.

he was always fearful . . . to an abnormal degree: cf. the fear attributed to Tiberius, *Tib.* 63.

the edict . . . concerning the cutting down of vines: see ch. 7 above.

290 *Though you gnaw . . . you're the sacrifice*: an epigram by Evenus of Ascalon (in *Palatine Anthology* ix. 75).

the trabea: a toga with horizontal purple stripes, worn by knights on public occasions.

phengite stone: a hard, white translucent stone, according to Pliny, *Natural Histories* 36. 103.

the tree . . . suddenly fell down again: see *Vesp.* 5.

292 *Domitilla's steward*: she was a niece of Domitian.

on the fourteenth day . . . the fifteenth of his reign: 18 September 96.

his old nurse: cf. the role played by nurses at *Nero* 50.

Julia, Titus' daughter: an ironic detail given the events Suetonius describes in ch. 22 below.

293 *He was so annoyed by his baldness . . . on that account*: cf. *Jul.* 45 and *Cal.* 50.

"Do you not see . . . I am, too?": Iliad 21. 108.

He would not tolerate . . . in a litter: one might contrast the great energy Suetonius attributes to Julius Caesar (*Jul.* 57).

He had no interest . . . archery: contrast the all-round skills attributed to Titus (*Titus* 3).

At the start of his reign . . . the liberal arts: cf. ch. 2 above.

Alexandria: although it seems a part of the library's holdings were destroyed by fire when Caesar attacked Alexandria in 47 BCE, the great library of Alexandria remained an outstanding collection even in late antiquity.

Tiberius Caesar: a dubious choice of model.

playing dice: a pursuit Suetonius also attributes to Augustus and Caligula (*Aug.* 70, 71; *Cal.* 41).

a Matian apple: a variety named after Gaius Matius, a friend of Augustus and an expert on gardening.

294 *The senators, by contrast . . . to be destroyed*: cf. *Cal.* 60.

GLOSSARY

aedile magistrate ranking above a QUAESTOR and below a PRAETOR. Under the principate the functions of this post related largely to the city of Rome.

augur priest who performed divination from observing the flight of birds. One of the four major priesthoods (the others being the *PONTIFICES*, the Board of Fifteen and the Fetials), which tended to be held by magistrates and ex-magistrates.

auspices divination from observation of the flight of birds, officially practised at elections, inaugurations of office, and entrance to a province, as well as at the start of wars. The right to take the auspices was reserved to the commander-in-chief in time of war. Officers serving under him thus acted 'under his auspices'.

auxiliaries a permanent armed force, including infantry and cavalry, supplementary to the LEGION, commanded by Roman citizens but made up of non-citizen fighting men.

caduceum a staff carried by heralds as a token of peace; particularly associated with the god Mercury.

Capitol used variously to mean the hill in Rome; the temple to Jupiter Best and Greatest, housing the three deities Jupiter, Juno, and Minerva, which was located on that hill; by extension, temples to the same deities elsewhere.

civic crown a crown of oak leaves awarded for saving the life of one's fellow citizens.

cognomen a surname, family name, or epithet, usually the third element of a Roman citizen's name.

cohort unit of the Roman army. There were ten cohorts in a LEGION.

colony a settlement of Roman citizens, often veteran soldiers.

Compitalician Games see under *LARES COMPITALES*.

consul the most senior of Rome's annual magistrates. Consuls enjoyed and sometimes exercised extensive military powers. The office of consul was often held by the emperor. See further under ORDINARY and SUFFECT.

curule seat special seat used by CONSULS, PRAETORS, and curule AEDILES.

decurion member of the senate of a municipium or COLONY.

dictator a single chief magistrate elected for a period of six months in an emergency.

equestrian *see under* ROMAN KNIGHT.

essedarius type of gladiator who fought from a British chariot.

fasces the bundle of rods enclosing an axe which symbolized the senior magistrates' authority to impose punishment.

Father of the Fatherland an honorary title conferred on Augustus in 2 BCE. It was subsequently offered to numerous other emperors and accepted by most.

Flamen Dialis priest of Jupiter.

freedmen ex-slaves.

Genius the individual's guardian deity.

haruspices college of priests responsible for predicting the future by observing the entrails of sacrificial victims.

Ides the fifteenth day of March, May, July, and October and thirteenth in other months.

Imperator under the republic, term used to salute a victorious general. Augustus took 'Imperator' as a first name to designate his rank. Under the principate this term was used almost exclusively for the emperor.

imperial fund (*fiscus*) the imperial exchequer, officially distinct from the public TREASURY, theoretically controlled by the senate.

imperium supreme administrative power, involving command in war and the interpretation and execution of law (including the infliction of the death penalty).

Kalends the first day of the month.

knight *see* ROMAN KNIGHT.

Lares each Roman household had its own Lares, worshipped, along with the Penates, as guardian deities. The Lares were also guardians of crossways, including those in the city.

lares Compitales divinities associated with crossroads in whose honour the annual Compitalician Games were held. The shrines of the *lares Compitales* were the focus of an annual festival which was celebrated, it seems, particularly by Rome's humbler citizens and was regarded as a potential source of disorder by members of the upper classes.

Latin colony a settlement of persons with LATIN RIGHTS.

Latin rights on the model of the rights enjoyed by some Italian allies of Rome under the republic, these rights were more limited than those of Roman citizens but included the right to contract legal marriage with and to enter into contracts with citizens.

legate under the republic, the term used for a senatorial member of a provincial governor's staff. Under the principate the term is generally used for legionary commanders (normally of praetorian rank) and some provincial governors.

legion principal unit of the Roman army, comprising in theory 5,000 infantry and 120 cavalry.

lictor attendant whose function was to carry the FASCES.

Lupercalia festival held on 15 February involving the ritual beating of bounds and purification rites. It was associated with Rome's pastoral origins and particularly with wolves.

Master of Horse under the republic, a subordinate official nominated by a DICTATOR to be his representative either on the field of battle or in Rome.

military tribune an equestrian legionary officer. A position often held by a young man aiming for a senatorial career.

murmillo type of gladiator who wore a Gallic helmet and was often pitched against the NET-FIGHTER.

Naumachia vast tank used for staging sea-battles in Rome.

net-fighter type of gladiator who fought with a net and trident.

Nones the fifth day of most months, the seventh of March, May, July, and October.

optimates term sometimes used to refer to those who supported maintaining or increasing the power of the senate in relation to the people.

orders Roman citizens were divided into orders, the senatorial comprising senators and their families, the equestrian comprising Roman knights and their families, and the third order comprising everyone else.

ordinary consul officials who took office for a few months at the start of the year, their names were used for dating purposes (i.e. 'in the consulship of X and Y') and who enjoyed more prestige than those who occupied the office in the latter months of the year (SUFFECT CONSULS). From the time of Augustus it became increasingly unusual for a consul to hold office for the entire year; shorter consulships meant more men could reach the coveted office.

ovation a celebration of victory somewhat less prestigious than a TRIUMPH. The victorious general entered the city on foot, accompanied by a procession.

patrician member of one of the families who claimed to have been included in Romulus' original senate. Under Augustus and some other emperors further grants of patrician status were made.

Penates each Roman household had its Penates, the guardian deities of the store cupboard. The Roman Penates fulfilled a parallel role in relation to the state as a whole. Their cult was associated with the temple of Vesta in the Forum.

plebs in some contexts used to refer to all Roman citizens who are not patrician; in others to refer to the common people of the city of Rome.

Pontifex Maximus head of the *PONTIFICES*. The chief priest of the Roman state religion, he exercised disciplinary functions (among others). Under the late republic his official residence was the Regia in the Forum. From 12 BCE this priesthood was held by the emperor.

pontifices advisory board which presided over the state cult.

praetor the next most senior magistrate after a consul. Praetors enjoyed and sometimes exercised the right of military command, as well as some important legislative and judicial functions. Many legionary commanders and provincial governors were ex-praetors.

praetorian guard imperial bodyguard organized by Augustus in nine cohorts (more were added later).

proconsul provincial governor or military commander with the rank of consul.

procurator agent of the emperor in civil administration (a freedman or of equestrian status), for instance as the governor of a minor province such as Judaea, as a financial agent in a larger province governed by a legate (and indirectly by the emperor), or as agent responsible for imperial properties in a province governed by the senate.

propraetor provincial governor or military commander with the rank of praetor.

quaestor junior magistrate with financial responsibilities which brought membership of the senate.

relegation a milder form of exile which did not entail the loss of citizen rights.

Roman knight member of the second order of Roman citizens (the first being of senators), an order originally associated with cavalry service. Knights were expected to be the sons of free-born Romans and there was a property qualification of 400,000 sesterces. Some members of this order played an increasingly important part in the administration of the empire under the principate.

rostra platform in the Forum, decorated with the prows of defeated enemy ships, from which speeches were made.

Saturnalia a festival of several days falling in late December, associated with giving gifts and frivolous amusements, especially gambling (which was otherwise banned).

Secular Games theatrical games and sacrifices performed by the Roman state to celebrate the end of one *saeculum* and the beginning of the next. The *saeculum*, thought of as the longest span of human life, was fixed in the republic at 100 years but later different definitions were used, so that Augustus celebrated the games in 17 BCE and Claudius in 47 CE.

secutores gladiators armed with a sword, a shield, one greave, and a visored helmet

senator member of the Roman senate, the qualification for which was serving at least as QUAESTOR or TRIBUNE OF THE PLEBS. Emperors might also, through adlection, directly introduce new members to any senatorial rank. From the time of Augustus, there was a property quali-fication of 1,000,000 sesterces. Senators and their families formed the first and most prestigious order of Roman citizens.

sesterce silver coin; unit used to express large sums.

suffect consul officials who held the consulship for a few months only, not from the start of the year. Under the principate it became increasingly common for the consuls to occupy their posts for a few months rather than a year, thus allowing more men to hold this pres-tigious office. Those who held office from 1 January were termed ORDINARY CONSULS, gave their names to the year, and enjoyed greater prestige.

Thracian type of gladiator armed with a short sword and greaves. He was generally pitted against a *MURMILLO* who was heavily armed and carried a big shield.

toga of manhood the formal and official civilian dress of the male Roman citizen, a plain toga was taken on by boys on reaching the age of around 14, when they put aside the bordered toga worn by children.

treasury (*aerarium*) the state treasury, theoretically under the control of the senate.

tribune of the plebs a relatively junior magistrate (with membership of the senate) who nevertheless enjoyed the important right to veto any act performed by a magistrate, as well as elections, laws, and decrees of the senate. Tribunes of the plebs were responsible for enforcing decrees of the people and protecting their rights.

tribunician power assumed by Augustus and subsequent emperors, this power paraded the emperor's concern for the rights of ordinary cit-izens. It was also sometimes conferred on the emperor's close associates and his designated heir.

triumph the procession of a victorious Roman general, his army, and prisoners of war, accompanied by the senate, through the city of Rome to the temple of Jupiter on the Capitol. The prerequisites were a victory over a foreign enemy with at least 5,000 enemy dead by a magistrate with IMPERIUM and the right to take AUSPICES. The general waited outside Rome to be granted the senate's permission before embarking on the procession. This was a relatively rare honour which brought the triumphant general huge prestige. It rapidly became a monopoly of the imperial family.

triumphal ornaments granted to victorious generals as a substitute for a TRIUMPH, these brought nothing like the prestige and soon lost much connection with military achievements.

triumvirs term used to refer to the three members of a board with practically absolute powers, Mark Antony, Lepidus, and Octavian (later Augustus) appointed to bring order to the state in 43 BCE for five years.

Troy game an elaborate equestrian display involving, particularly, young members of the Roman élite. Cf. Virgil, *Aeneid* 5. 545–603.

INDEX OF PROPER NAMES

Note: individuals are generally listed under forms familiar in English in the case of well-known figures such as Cicero or Caesar but otherwise under the middle (gentile) of the three Roman names in the case of men and the first of their two names in the case of women. Roman usage is not, however, consistent.

became more hostile; eventually Octavian's forces defeated those of Antony and Cleopatra at Actium in 31. Thereafter he effectively controlled the state through his money and soldiers. While some provinces were returned to the control of the senate, those with any significant army presence were governed through his legates by Augustus himself (as he was called after 27 January BCE). Extensive military campaigns led to the reinforcement of eastern frontiers (20s BCE), the final submission of Spain in 27–25 BCE, and the annexation of Galatia (25 BCE). In 23 BCE Augustus resigned the consulship he had held continuously, obtaining instead an extensive range of powers including tribunician power for life. In 17 BCE, having no sons, Augustus adopted his grandsons Gaius and Lucius. In 12 BCE he became Pontifex Maximus. Heavily reliant on Agrippa until the latter's death in 12 BCE, Augustus subsequently derived considerable support from the military talents of Tiberius and Drusus (the sons of his wife Livia); their operations in Illyricum, Moesia, and Germany led to many successes. In the course of his reign Augustus reorganized many areas of Roman life including the senate, the army, and the city of Rome. His only child Julia was the daughter of his wife Scribonia, whom he divorced in order to marry Livia in 39 BCE. Augustus was subsequently viewed as the founder of the principate and many emperors liked to be compared to him: *Jul.* 55, 56, 88; *Aug. passim*; *Tib.* 4, 6, 7, 8, 10, 11, 12, 13, 15, 16, 17, 21, 22, 23, 42, 47, 48, 50, 51, 57, 58, 61, 68, 70; *Cal.* 1, 4, 7, 8, 9, 16, 23, 25, 31, 34, 48; *Claud.* 1, 3, 4, 6, 11, 20, 21, 25, 26; *Nero* 3, 4, 10, 25; *Galba* 1, 4; *Vit.* 2; *Vesp.* 2, 9, 23; *Dom.* 4

Aurelia, mother of Julius Caesar: *Jul.* 74

Aurelius Cotta: *Jul.* 1

(Aurelius) Cotta, Lucius: *Jul.* 79

Aurunculeius Cotta, Lucius, consul 65 BCE: *Jul.* 25

Autronius: *Jul.* 9

Balbillus: *Nero* 36

Basilides, freedman of the emperor Vespasian: *Vesp.* 7

Bato, leader of the Pannonians: *Tib.* 20

Berenice, daughter of Agrippa I, king of Judaea: *Titus* 7

Bibulus, Marcus Calpurnius, Julius Caesar's colleague in the aedileship, praetorship and finally, in 59 BCE, the consulship. He attempted, without success, to oppose Caesar's agrarian legislation: *Jul.* 9, 10, 19, 20, 21, 49

Boter, freedman of the emperor Claudius: *Claud.* 27

Britannicus, Tiberius Claudius Caesar (41–55 CE), son of the emperor Claudius and Messalina; given the name Britannicus after Claudius' campaign of 44 CE. When Agrippina persuaded Claudius to adopt her son (who took the name Nero), Britannicus, three years younger, yielded precedence to him and it was Nero who succeeded Claudius in 54. Responsibility for Britannicus' death in 55 CE was widely attributed to Nero: *Claud.* 27, 43; *Nero* 6, 7, 33; *Titus* 2

Brutus, Decimus Junius. After a distinguished military career serving as an officer under Julius Caesar, he later turned against him and was involved in

the conspiracy to assassinate him. He was eventually defeated in the ensuing civil war and put to death on Antony's orders: *Jul.* 80, 81, 83; *Aug.* 10
Brutus, Lucius, the first Roman consul: *Jul.* 80
Brutus, Marcus Junius, fought with Pompey in the civil war but was pardoned
by Julius Caesar after the battle of Pharsalus; notorious as a leading figure in
the conspiracy against Julius Caesar; defeated by Antony and Octavian in
the ensuing civil war; committed suicide in 42 BCE: *Jul.* 49, 50, 55, 56, 80,
82, 85; *Aug.* 9, 10, 13, 85; *Tib.* 61; *Nero* 3; *Galba* 3; *Otho* 10
Burrus, Afranius, prefect of the praetorian guard under Claudius and Nero:
Nero 35

Caecilius Metellus, Quintus, tribune of the plebs: *Jul.* 16, 55
Caecina, Aulus: *Jul.* 75
Caecina, Aulus, consul 69 CE: *Titus* 6
Caenis, mistress of the emperor Vespasian: *Vesp.* 21; *Dom.* 12.
Caesar, Gaius (20 BCE–4 CE), eldest son of Marcus Agrippa and Julia. He and
his brother were adopted by their grandfather Augustus in 17 BCE, presumably with the hope that one or both of them would eventually succeed him
as emperor. In 5 BCE, when Gaius assumed the toga of manhood, he was
designated consul for 1 BCE. He died after receiving a wound on campaign in
the east: *Aug.* 26, 29, 64, 65, 67, 93; *Tib.* 11, 12, 13, 15, 23; *Nero* 5
Caesar, Gaius Julius (100–44 BCE). In his youth he was closely associated with
the policies of the general Gaius Marius (who was married to his paternal
aunt Julia) and made a name for himself as an orator as well as on the
battlefield. Thwarted by the senate, Caesar formed a close compact with
Pompey and the wealthy Crassus (known as the 'first triumvirate') in 59
BCE. A supremely gifted military commander, he engaged in numerous
successful operations including his Gallic campaign of 58 to 49 (of
which he gives an account in *The Gallic War*); he refused to lay down his
command despite the instructions of senate, and embarked on civil war,
eventually defeating the Pompeian forces at Munda in 45. From 48 he was
dictator and even while engaged in military compaigns he kept close
control over the city of Rome through agents. At least some of his many
ambitious plans for the transformation of the city as well as other aspects of
Roman life such as the calendar were fulfilled. Suspected of aspiring to
tyranny, Caesar was assassinated in 44 BCE by a conspiracy which included
numerous young aristocrats, some of whom had been his own officers. In
his will, Caesar adopted his great nephew Gaius Octavius (later Octavian/
Augustus) and made him his heir. For later rulers, Caesar was a problematic precedent, his numerous far-sighted reforms counterbalanced by a lack
of sensitivity to the concerns of Rome's governing class such that they
would not tolerate his rule: *Jul. passim*; *Aug.* 8, 10, 13, 17, 35, 45, 48, 64,
95; *Tib.* 4; *Nero* 37
Caesar, Lucius, fought with Pompey in the Civil War: *Jul.* 75
Caesar, Lucius (17 BCE–2 CE), second son of Marcus Agrippa and Julia. He
and his brother were adopted by their grandfather Augustus in 17 BCE,

later generations and a great many of his speeches have survived, widely studied in antiquity and later periods: *Jul.* 9, 17, 20, 30, 42, 49, 50, 55, 56; *Aug.* 5, 37, 14, 94; *Tib.* 2, 7; *Claud.* 41

Cicero, Quintus Tullius, brother of the orator: *Jul.* 14; *Aug.* 3

Cincinnatus: *Cal.* 35

Claudia, a Vestal Virgin: *Tib.* 2

Claudia, daughter of Fulvia and Publius Clodius: *Aug.* 52

Claudia, daughter of Appius Claudius Caecus: *Tib.* 2

Claudia (Quinta), granddaughter of Appius Claudius Caecus: *Tib.* 2

Claudia, daughter of the emperor Claudius and Urgulanilla: *Claud.* 27

Claudia Augusta, daughter of the emperor Nero and Poppaea: *Nero* 35

Claudius (Tiberius Claudius Nero Germanicus) (10 BCE–54 CE), emperor. Younger son of the elder Drusus and the younger Antonia, he was in his youth in the shadow of his distinguished brother Germanicus. Claudius seems to have suffered from a variety of health problems and was, it appears, deliberately kept out of the public eye. He held no office until he became suffect consul with his nephew, the emperor Caligula, in 37 CE. After Caligula's assassination, the praetorian guard saluted Claudius as emperor, a choice reluctantly accepted by the senate, with whom Claudius never enjoyed good relations. His rule was perceived as inconsistent and excessively influenced by his powerful freedmen advisers (such as Narcissus and Pallas) and by his wives; these included Messalina (mother of Octavia and Britannicus), who was executed for conspiring to replace Claudius as emperor with her lover Silius, and Agrippina (Claudius' niece and mother of the future emperor Nero by an earlier marriage). Claudius adopted Nero in 50 CE. Agrippina is widely believed to have killed Claudius with poison to make way for Nero as emperor. Claudius had an extensive knowledge of history and was a prolific author; none of his works has survived: *Cal.* 15, 21, 23, 49; *Claud. passim*; *Nero* 6, 7, 8, 9, 33, 35, 39; *Galba* 7, 14; *Otho* 1; *Vit.* 2, 4; *Vesp.* 4, 9, 25; *Titus* 2; *Dom.* 4

Claudius Atta: *Tib.* 1

Claudius Caecus, Appius, consul 312 BCE; builder of the Appian Way: *Tib.* 2, 3; *Claud.* 24

Claudius Caudex, Appius, consul 264 BCE: *Tib.* 2

(Claudius) Nero: *Tib.* 2

(Claudius) Nero, son of Caecus: *Tib.* 3

(Claudius) Nero, Tiberius (d. 33 BCE), husband of Livia and father of Tiberius and Drusus; induced by Octavian (Augustus) to divorce his wife so the latter could marry her in 39 BCE: *Aug.* 62; *Tib.* 4

Claudius Pulcher, Appius, son of Caecus: *Tib.* 2, 3

Claudius Regillianus, traditionally believed consul 451 BCE: *Tib.* 2

Claudius Russus: *Tib.* 2

Clemens, slave of Agrippa: *Tib.* 25

Cleopatra (69–30 BCE), daughter of Ptolemy XII; became joint ruler of Egypt with Ptolemy XIII in 51 BCE. Expelled by Ptolemy's party in 48 she was reinstated with the help of Julius Caesar who allegedly became her lover.

celebrated Cicero, Brutus, and Cassius. Prosecuted for treason he committed suicide in 25 CE. Though his work was publicly burned it was known to later Roman writers (but has not survived to more recent times): *Aug.* 35; *Cal.* 16

Curio, Gaius Scribonius (d. 53 BCE), consul in 76 BCE; active in the lawcourts in the 60s and 50s where he often opposed Cicero: *Jul.* 9, 49, 50, 52

Curio, Gaius Scribonius, son of above; quaestor in 54 and tribune in 50 BCE. Initially hostile to Caesar, he later joined him, serving under him in 49 in the civil war. After occupying Sicily he crossed to Africa where he was killed: *Jul.* 29, 36, 50

Curius, Quintus: *Jul.* 17

Cybiosactes: *Vesp.* 19

Cynegirus: *Jul.* 68

Cynobellinus, king of the Britons: *Cal.* 44

Cyrus, king of Persia: *Jul.* 87

Dareus, Parthian boy: *Cal.* 19

Datus, actor: *Nero* 39

Demetrius Cynicus: *Vesp.* 13

Demochares: *Aug.* 16

Dido, mythical queen of Carthage: *Nero* 31

Diodorus, lyre-player: *Vesp.* 19

Diogenes, grammarian: *Tib.* 32

Diomedes, steward of Augustus: *Aug.* 67

Dionysius, son of the philosopher Areus: *Aug.* 89

Domitia, paternal aunt of the emperor Nero: *Galba* 5; *Nero* 34

Domitia Lepida, paternal aunt (younger) of the emperor Nero: *Nero* 6, 7

Domitia Longina, wife of the emperor Domitian. Divorced for adultery, she was later recalled: *Titus* 10; *Dom.* 1, 3, 22

Domitian (Titus Flavius Domitianus) (51–96 CE), emperor. Son of the emperor Vespasian, he succeeded his brother Titus, who died leaving no children in 81. He had earlier held several consulships but exercised no significant powers. He seems to have adopted an autocratic approach to imperial rule, appropriating complete control over membership of the senate. Numerous persons were executed for plotting against the emperor particularly in the final three years of his reign. A conspiracy involving his wife Domitia was eventually successful: *Vesp.* 1; *Titus* 9; *Dom. passim*

Domitianus, son of Flavius Clemens: *Dom.* 15

Domitilla, *see* Flavia

Domitius Ahenobarbus, Gnaeus, consul 96 BCE; ancestor of Nero: *Nero* 2

Domitius Ahenobarbus, Gnaeus, Nero's great-grandfather. Sharing his own father's hostility to Caesar, he fought on the republican side, continuing even after the deaths of Brutus and Cassius, but in 40 BCE he surrendered to Antony and was pardoned by Octavian in 39 BCE. Consul in 32 he returned shortly to Antony in the east, dying soon afterwards: *Aug.* 17; *Nero* 3

Ennius, Quintus, writer of Roman epic: *Aug.* 7
Epaphroditus, Nero's secretary: *Nero* 49; *Dom.* 14
Epidius Marullus, tribune of the plebs: *Jul.* 79, 80
Eunoe, Moorish queen: *Jul.* 52
Euphorion, Greek elegiac poet: *Tib.* 70
Euripides, Athenian writer of tragedy: *Jul.* 30
Eutychus, charioteer: *Cal.* 55
Eutychus, muleteer: *Aug.* 96

Fabius Africanus, consul 10 CE: *Claud.* 2
(Fabius) Maximus, Quintus: *Jul.* 80
Fannius Caepio: *Aug.* 19; *Tib.* 8
Faunus, mythical king of Laurentes: *Vit.* 1
Faustus Sulla: *Claud.* 27
Favonius, Marcus: *Aug.* 13
Favor, actor: *Vesp.* 19
Felix, freedman: *Claud.* 28
Flavia Domitilla, wife of Vespasian: *Vesp.* 3
(Flavia) Domitilla, daughter of Vespasian: *Vesp.* 3
(Flavia) Domitilla, wife of Flavius Clemens: *Dom.* 17
Flavian emperors: Vespasian, Titus, Domitian
Flavius Clemens, cousin of Domitian: *Dom.* 15
Flavius Liberalis, Vespasian's father-in-law: *Vesp.* 3
Flavius Petro, Titus, grandfather of Vespasian: *Vesp.* 1
Flavius Sabinus, father of Vespasian: *Vesp.* 1, 5
Flavius Sabinus, brother of Vespasian: *Vit.* 15; *Vesp.* 1; *Dom.* 1
Flavius Sabinus, cousin of Domitian: *Dom.* 10
Fonteius Capito, consul 59 CE: *Galba* 11
Fonteius Capito, Gaius, consul 12 CE: *Cal.* 8
Fulvia, wife of Mark Antony: *Aug.* 17, 62
(Furius) Camillus, dictator in 396 BCE: *Tib.* 3; *Claud.* 26
(Furius) Camillus Arruntius, consul 32 CE: *Otho* 2
Furius Camillus Scribonianus: *Claud.* 13, 35; *Otho* 1
Furius Leptinus: *Jul.* 39

Gabinius, Aulus: *Jul.* 50
Gabinius Secundus Cauchius: *Claud.* 24
Galba, Servius Sulpicius (*c.*3 BCE–69 CE), emperor. Closely associated with the imperial court from boyhood, he had a prominent political career (consul 33 CE, governorships of several provinces). In 68 Vindex, in revolt against the emperor Nero, invited Galba to take his place. With the support of others including the praetorian guard, Galba took the title of Caesar but failed to sustain his control over the military (as he was unwilling to give them the financial rewards they expected) and was assassinated in Rome by soldiers acting on the orders of Otho in January 69: *Nero* 32; *Galba passim*; *Otho* 4, 5, 6, 7, 10, 12; *Vit.* 7, 8, 9, 10; *Vesp.* 5, 6, 16; *Titus* 5

Laetorius, Gaius: *Aug.* 5

Lentulus, Gnaeus, consul in 3 BCE: *Galba* 4

Lentulus Augur, Gnaeus: *Tib.* 49

Lentulus Gaetulicus, Gnaeus: *Cal.* 8; *Claud.* 9; *Galba* 6

Lepida, wife of Quirinus: *Tib.* 49

Lepida, wife of Galba: *Galba* 5

Lepidus, *see* Aemilius *and* Domitius

Licinius Calvus, Gaius, Roman orator and poet; contemporary of Catullus: *Jul.* 49, 73; *Aug.* 72

Licinius Crassus, Lucius: *Nero* 2

(Licinius) Crassus, Marcus, general with vast personal wealth; member of unofficial 'first triumvirate' with Julius Caesar and Pompey: *Jul.* 9, 19, 21, 24, 50; *Aug.* 21; *Tib.* 9

(Licinius) Crassus Frugi, Marcus: *Claud.* 17

Licinius Mucianus: *Vesp.* 6, 13

Licinus, freedman: *Aug.* 67

Livia Drusilla (58 BCE–29 CE), wife of Augustus from 39 BCE; earlier married to Tiberius Claudius Nero by whom she had two sons, Tiberius and Drusus. A formidable person, she was believed to exercise considerable influence over Augustus (frequently acting as intercessor for suitors) and enjoyed a public profile unprecedented for a woman in republican Rome. She was said by some to have poisoned several members of Augustus' family to make way for her own descendants. Adopted into the Julian family under Augustus' will, she was renamed Julia Augusta. Her influence seems to have continued during the rule of her son Tiberius: *Aug.* 29, 40, 43, 49, 62, 69, 84, 99, 101; *Tib.* 4, 6, 14, 22, 50; *Cal.* 7, 10, 15, 16, 23; *Claud.* 1, 3, 4, 11; *Galba* 1, 5; *Otho* 1

Livia Medullina Camilla: *Claud.* 26

Livia Ocellina: *Galba* 3, 4

Livia Orestilla: *Cal.* 25

Livilla (Livia Julia), daughter of Drusus (Livia's son) and the younger Antonia; married to Gaius Caesar, then Drusus Caesar; suspected of adultery and conspiracy with Sejanus leading her to poison her husband Drusus: *Tib.* 62; *Claud.* 1, 3

Livilla (Julia) (18–*c.*42 CE), youngest daughter of Germanicus and the elder Agrippina; after the accession of her brother Caligula she received particular honours along with her sisters; executed under Claudius: *Cal.* 7; *Claud.* 29

Livy (Titus Livius) (59 BCE–17 CE), celebrated Roman historian. Substantial sections of his history of Rome have survived: *Cal.* 34; *Claud.* 41; *Dom.* 10

Livius Drusus, first to bear the name: *Tib.* 3

(Livius) Drusus, grandfather of the emperor Tiberius: *Tib.* 7

Livius Salinator, consul 219 BCE: *Tib.* 3

Lollia: *Jul.* 50

Lollia Paulina, wife of Caligula: *Cal.* 25; *Claud.* 26

Lollius, Marcus: *Tib.* 12, 13

Index of Proper Names

Tatius, a legendary Sabine king said to have shared the throne with Romulus: *Tib.* 1

Taurus, *see* Statilius

Tedius Afer: *Aug.* 27

Telephus, a slave: *Aug.* 19

Terentia, *see* Albia

Terentia, wife of Maecenas: *Aug.* 66

Terentilla: *Aug.* 69

Terpnus, a lyre-player: *Nero* 20; *Vesp.* 19

Tertia, sister of Marcus Brutus: *Jul.* 50

Tertulla, *see* Arrecina

Tertulla, grandmother of Vespasian: *Vesp.* 2

Tetrinius: *Cal.* 30

Thallus, a slave: *Aug.* 67

Theodorus Gadareus: *Tib.* 57

Theogenes, an astrologer: *Aug.* 94

Thermus, Marcus: *Jul.* 2

Thrasea, *see* Paetus

Thrasyllus: *Aug.* 98; *Tib.* 14, 62; *Cal.* 19

Tiberius, *see under* Claudius, emperor

Tiberius, grandson of the emperor Tiberius: *Tib.* 54, 62, 76; *Cal.* 15, 23

Tiberius Alexander: *Vesp.* 6

Tiberius Julius Caesar Augustus (b. 42 BCE), emperor 14–37 CE. Son of Tiberius Claudius Nero and Livia who divorced his father and married Octavian (later Augustus) in 38 CE. Tiberius' military career was conspicuous, with particular successes in Pannonia and Germany. In 12 BCE Tiberius was obliged to divorce his wife, Vipsania Agrippina (by whom he had a son, Drusus), in order to marry Agrippa's widow, Julia, the only child of Augustus. Having withdrawn to Rhodes in 6 BCE, he returned to Rome in 4 CE to be adopted by Augustus and received a range of powers in recognition of his position as Augustus' likely successor. Proclaimed emperor on the death of Augustus in 14 CE, Tiberius seems not to have been a popular ruler. A series of treason trials alienated many. In 27 he withdrew to Capri, never to return to Rome: *Aug.* 40, 51, 63, 65, 71, 76, 85, 86, 92, 97, 100, 101; *Tib. passim*; *Cal.* 1, 2, 4, 6, 7, 10, 11, 12, 13, 14, 15, 16, 19, 21, 28, 30, 31, 37, 38; *Claud.* 4, 5, 6, 11, 23, 25; *Nero* 5, 6, 30; *Galba* 3, 4, 5; *Otho* 1; *Vit.* 2; *Titus* 8; *Dom.* 20

Tiberius Nero, sometime husband of Livia and father of the emperor Tiberius: *Aug.* 62; *Tib.* 4

Tigillinus, an agent of Nero: *Galba* 15

Tigranes: *Tib.* 9

Tillius Cimber: *Jul.* 82

Tiridates I, king of Armenia and brother of Vologaesus I: *Nero* 13, 30

Titianus, *see* Salvius

Titisenia, *see* Salvia

Titurius (Sabinus), one of Caesar's generals; *Jul.* 25

GENERAL INDEX

absent-mindedness *Claud.* 39
accession *Tib.* 22–3; *Cal.* 12; *Claud.* 10;
  Nero 8; *Galba* 10; *Otho* 6; *Vit.* 8; *Vesp.* 6
acting and the theatre (*see also* games)
  Jul. 39; *Aug.* 43–5; *Tib.* 35; *Cal.* 11,
  54–5, 58; *Nero* 16, 20–1, 26; *Dom.* 7, 10
adoption *Jul.* 83; *Aug.* 64–5; *Tib.* 6, 15,
  21; *Cal.* 4; *Claud.* 27; *Nero* 7; *Galba* 17;
  Otho 5
adultery *Jul.* 6, 48, 50–2, 74; *Aug.* 34, 69,
  71; *Tib.* 11, 35; *Cal.* 11, 24–5, 36;
  Claud. 1, 26, 43; *Nero* 28, 35; *Otho* 3;
  Vesp. 11; *Titus* 10; *Dom.* 1, 3, 8
advisers *Aug.* 35; *Tib.* 55; *Claud.*
  28–9; *Nero* 35, 52 ; *Galba* 14; *Vit.* 12;
  Titus 7
affability *Nero* 10; *Vesp.* 22; *Titus* 8
ancestry *Jul.* 6; *Aug.* 1–4; *Tib.* 1–4; *Cal.*
  23; *Nero* 1–5; *Galba* 2–3; *Otho* 1; *Vit.*
  1–3; *Vesp.* 1
anger *Claud.* 38
arrogance *Jul.* 76–9; *Tib.* 68; *Cal.* 22–35;
  Dom. 12
assassination *Jul.* 81–2; *Cal.* 56–8; *Galba*
  19–20; *Dom.* 17
astrologers *Aug.* 94; *Tib.* 14, 36, 69; *Cal.*
  57; *Nero* 36, 40; *Otho* 4; *Vit.* 3, 14; *Vesp.*
  14, 25; *Titus* 9; *Dom.* 14, 15
avarice (*see also* meanness) *Jul.* 54; *Aug.*
  70–1; *Tib.* 46–9; *Cal.* 38–42; *Nero* 26,
  32; *Galba* 12, 15; *Vesp.* 16–19, 23; *Titus*
  7; *Dom.* 3, 9, 12

birth *Aug.* 5, 94; *Tib.* 5; *Cal.* 8; *Claud.* 2;
  Nero 6; *Galba* 4; *Otho* 2; *Vit.* 3; *Vesp.* 2;
  Titus 1; *Dom.* 1
building activities (in Rome) *Jul.* 26, 44;
  Aug. 28–31; *Tib.* 20, 47; *Cal.* 21–2;
  Claud. 11, 20–1; *Nero* 16, 31; *Vesp.*
  8–9; *Titus* 7, 8; *Dom.* 5; (outside Rome)
  Jul. 28, 44; *Aug.* 16, 46; *Cal.* 21; *Claud.*
  20; *Nero* 31; *Vesp.* 17

calendar, interventions in *Jul.* 40, 76;
  Aug. 31, 100; *Tib.* 26; *Nero* 55; *Dom.* 13
censorship *Aug.* 27, 37; *Tib.* 3, 21; *Claud.*
  16, 24; *Vesp.* 8; *Titus* 6
character *Jul.* 30; *Tib.* 21, 33, 57, 67; *Cal.*

11, 29; *Nero* 19, 26; *Galba* 14; *Otho* 2;
  Vit. 4, 7, 10; *Vesp.* 16; *Titus* 1, 3, 8;
  Dom. 1, 3, 19
chariot-racing (*see also* games) *Jul.* 39;
  Cal. 19, 55; *Nero* 16, 22, 24, 53; *Vit.* 4
childhood *Aug.* 8, 94; *Tib.* 6; *Cal.* 8–10;
  Claud. 2; *Nero* 6–7, 22, 52; *Galba* 4;
  Vit. 3; *Titus* 2–3; *Dom.* 1
circus, *see* chariot racing
city, administration of *Jul.* 44; *Aug.* 30;
  Claud. 18; *Nero* 16, 38; *Vesp.* 8–9
civil war *Jul.* 3–4, 30–6, 68–70, 75; *Aug.*
  9–13, 15–17; *Tib.* 4; *Nero* 2–3; *Galba*
  9–11, 19–20; *Otho* 4–11; *Vit.* 8–10,
  15–18; *Vesp.* 1, 5–8; *Dom.* 1, 6
civility *Aug.* 51–6; *Tib.* 26–32; *Vesp.*
  12–15; *Titus* 8; *Dom.* 9, 12–13
clemency *Jul.* 14, 73–5; *Aug.* 51–6; *Cal.*
  15; *Claud.* 11; *Nero* 10; *Vesp.* 12–15;
  Titus 8; *Dom.* 9
conspiracies against emperors *Jul.* 75,
  80–2, 86; *Aug.* 19; *Tib.* 25, 63, 65;
  Cal. 24, 56–8; *Claud.* 9, 13, 36; *Nero*
  36; *Otho* 6; *Titus* 9; *Dom.* 2, 14,
  16–17
constitutional change *Aug.* 28, 37
consulship *Jul.* 18–23, 26, 76; *Aug.* 26;
  Tib. 9, 26; *Cal.* 17; *Claud.* 5, 7, 14;
  Nero 14; *Vit.* 11; *Vesp.* 4, 8; *Titus* 6;
  Dom. 2, 13
criticism, responses to *Jul.* 22, 75; *Aug.*
  27, 51, 54–6; *Tib.* 28, 61, 66; *Cal.* 16,
  27; *Vit.* 14; *Vesp.* 13–14
cruelty *Aug.* 13, 15, 27; *Tib.* 50–62; *Cal.*
  6, 10, 22–35; *Claud.* 34; *Nero* 5, 26,
  33–8; *Galba* 9, 12; *Vit.* 10–11, 13–14;
  Titus 6–7; *Dom.* 9–11
cult, imperial *Jul.* 88; *Aug.* 52; *Tib.* 26,
  51; *Cal.* 22, 52; *Claud.* 45; *Vesp.* 23;
  Dom. 4–5, 23

dancing *Cal.* 54
death, manner of *Jul.* 81–2, 86–7; *Aug.*
  97–100; *Tib.* 72–3; *Cal.* 56–8; *Claud.*
  44–6; *Nero* 2, 47–9; *Galba* 19–20; *Otho*
  10–11; *Vit.* 17–18; *Vesp.* 23–4; *Titus*
  10–11; *Dom.* 14–17
deification, *see* cult, imperial

	Classical Literary Criticism
	The First Philosophers: The Presocratics and the Sophists
	Greek Lyric Poetry
	Myths from Mesopotamia
APOLLODORUS	The Library of Greek Mythology
APOLLONIUS OF RHODES	Jason and the Golden Fleece
APULEIUS	The Golden Ass
ARISTOPHANES	Birds and Other Plays
ARISTOTLE	The Nicomachean Ethics Physics Politics
BOETHIUS	The Consolation of Philosophy
CAESAR	The Civil War The Gallic War
CATULLUS	The Poems of Catullus
CICERO	Defence Speeches The Nature of the Gods On Obligations The Republic and The Laws
EURIPIDES	Bacchae and Other Plays Medea and Other Plays Orestes and Other Plays The Trojan Women and Other Plays
GALEN	Selected Works
HERODOTUS	The Histories
HOMER	The Iliad The Odyssey

A SELECTION OF   OXFORD WORLD'S CLASSICS

THOMAS AQUINAS	Selected Philosophical Writings
FRANCIS BACON	The Essays
WALTER BAGEHOT	The English Constitution
GEORGE BERKELEY	Principles of Human Knowledge and Three Dialogues
EDMUND BURKE	A Philosophical Enquiry into the Origin of Our Ideas of the Sublime and Beautiful Reflections on the Revolution in France
CONFUCIUS	The Analects
ÉMILE DURKHEIM	The Elementary Forms of Religious Life
FRIEDRICH ENGELS	The Condition of the Working Class in England
JAMES GEORGE FRAZER	The Golden Bough
SIGMUND FREUD	The Interpretation of Dreams
THOMAS HOBBES	Human Nature and De Corpore Politico Leviathan
JOHN HUME	Selected Essays
NICCOLO MACHIAVELLI	The Prince
THOMAS MALTHUS	An Essay on the Principle of Population
KARL MARX	Capital The Communist Manifesto
J. S. MILL	On Liberty and Other Essays Principles of Political Economy and Chapters on Socialism
FRIEDRICH NIETZSCHE	Beyond Good and Evil The Birth of Tragedy On the Genealogy of Morals Twilight of the Idols

A SELECTION OF   **OXFORD WORLD'S CLASSICS**

THOMAS PAINE	**Rights of Man, Common Sense, and Other Political Writings**
JEAN-JACQUES ROUSSEAU	**The Social Contract** **Discourse on the Origin of Inequality**
ADAM SMITH	**An Inquiry into the Nature and Causes of the Wealth of Nations**
MARY WOLLSTONECRAFT	**A Vindication of the Rights of Woman**

Bhagavad Gita

The Bible Authorized King James Version
   With Apocrypha

Dhammapada

Dharmasūtras

The Koran

The Pañcatantra

The Sauptikaparvan (from the
   Mahabharata)

The Tale of Sinuhe and Other Ancient
   Egyptian Poems

Upaniṣads

ANSELM OF CANTERBURY	The Major Works
THOMAS AQUINAS	Selected Philosophical Writings
AUGUSTINE	The Confessions On Christian Teaching
BEDE	The Ecclesiastical History
HEMACANDRA	The Lives of the Jain Elders
KĀLIDĀSA	The Recognition of Śakuntalā
MANJHAN	Madhumalati
ŚĀNTIDEVA	The Bodhicaryāvatāra

A SELECTION OF OXFORD WORLD'S CLASSICS

<table>
<tr><td></td><td>Women's Writing 1778–1838</td></tr>
<tr><td>WILLIAM BECKFORD</td><td>Vathek</td></tr>
<tr><td>JAMES BOSWELL</td><td>Life of Johnson</td></tr>
<tr><td>FRANCES BURNEY</td><td>Camilla
Cecilia
Evelina
The Wanderer</td></tr>
<tr><td>LORD CHESTERFIELD</td><td>Lord Chesterfield's Letters</td></tr>
<tr><td>JOHN CLELAND</td><td>Memoirs of a Woman of Pleasure</td></tr>
<tr><td>DANIEL DEFOE</td><td>A Journal of the Plague Year
Moll Flanders
Robinson Crusoe
Roxana</td></tr>
<tr><td>HENRY FIELDING</td><td>Joseph Andrews and Shamela
A Journey from This World to the Next and
   The Journal of a Voyage to Lisbon
Tom Jones</td></tr>
<tr><td>WILLIAM GODWIN</td><td>Caleb Williams</td></tr>
<tr><td>OLIVER GOLDSMITH</td><td>The Vicar of Wakefield</td></tr>
<tr><td>MARY HAYS</td><td>Memoirs of Emma Courtney</td></tr>
<tr><td>ELIZABETH HAYWOOD</td><td>The History of Miss Betsy Thoughtless</td></tr>
<tr><td>ELIZABETH INCHBALD</td><td>A Simple Story</td></tr>
<tr><td>SAMUEL JOHNSON</td><td>The History of Rasselas
The Major Works</td></tr>
<tr><td>CHARLOTTE LENNOX</td><td>The Female Quixote</td></tr>
<tr><td>MATTHEW LEWIS</td><td>Journal of a West India Proprietor
The Monk</td></tr>
<tr><td>HENRY MACKENZIE</td><td>The Man of Feeling</td></tr>
<tr><td>ALEXANDER POPE</td><td>Selected Poetry</td></tr>
</table>

The Oxford World's Classics Website

www.worldsclassics.co.uk

- Information about new titles
- Explore the full range of Oxford World's Classics
- Links to other literary sites and the main OUP webpage
- Imaginative competitions, with bookish prizes
- Peruse the Oxford World's Classics Magazine
- Articles by editors
- Extracts from Introductions
- A forum for discussion and feedback on the series
- Special information for teachers and lecturers

www.worldsclassics.co.uk

American Literature

British and Irish Literature

Children's Literature

Classics and Ancient Literature

Colonial Literature

Eastern Literature

European Literature

History

Medieval Literature

Oxford English Drama

Poetry

Philosophy

Politics

Religion

The Oxford Shakespeare

A complete list of Oxford Paperbacks, including Oxford World's Classics, Oxford Shakespeare, Oxford Drama, and Oxford Paperback Reference, is available in the UK from the Academic Division Publicity Department, Oxford University Press, Great Clarendon Street, Oxford OX2 6DP.

In the USA, complete lists are available from the Paperbacks Marketing Manager, Oxford University Press, 198 Madison Avenue, New York, NY 10016.

Oxford Paperbacks are available from all good bookshops. In case of difficulty, customers in the UK can order direct from Oxford University Press Bookshop, Freepost, 116 High Street, Oxford OX1 4BR, enclosing full payment. Please add 10 per cent of published price for postage and packing.